PLACE IN RETURN BOX to remove this checkout from your record.
TO AVOID FINES return on or before date due.

T5-ANY-200

DATE DUE	DATE DUE	DATE DUE
108	FEB 3 7 2003	MICHIGAN STATE UNIVERSITY LIBRARY
AUG 0 0 1999	AUG 0 9 2006	AUG 14 2025 WITHDRAWN
OCT 2 5 199?	NOV 1 1 2007 DEC 0 7 2009	
MAY 1 0 1975	011010 MAY 02 11	
MAGIC 2 JAN 0 9 1999		

MSU Is An Affirmative Action/Equal Opportunity Institution

Comparative education
Contemporary issues and trends

In the series 'Educational sciences':

Landsheere, G. De. *Empirical research in education.* 1982. 113p
Zverev, I. D.. *Teaching methods in the Soviet school.* 1983. 116p.
Kraevskij, V. V.; Lerner, I. Y. *The theory of curriculum content in the USSR.* 1984. 113p
Léon, Antoine. *The history of education today.* 1985. 117p.
Bronckart, Jean-Paul. *The language sciences: an educational challenge?* 1985. 105p.
Mialaret, G. et al. *Introduction to the educational sciences.* 1985. 106p.
Camilleri, C. *Cultural anthropology and education.* 1986. 171p.
Siguán, M.; Mackey, W. F. *Education and bilingualism.* 1987. 147p.
Kabalevsky, D. B. *Music and education.* 1988. 150p.
Bhola, H. S. *World trends and issues in adult education.* 1989. 177p.
Duric, Ladislav. *Essentials of educational psychology.* 1989. 163p.

Educational sciences

Comparative Education:
Contemporary Issues and Trends

Edited by W. D. Halls

Jessica Kingsley Publishers/Unesco

© Unesco 1990

First published in 1990 in Great Britain by
Jessica Kingsley Publishers
118 Pentonville Road
London N1 9JN

and the United Nations
Educational, Scientific and Cultural Organization,
7 place de Fontenoy, 75700 Paris, France

ISBN 92-3-102564-3

British Library Cataloguing in Publication Data
Comparative education : contemporary issues
    and trends. - (Educational science series).
    1. Comparative education
    I. Halls, W.D. (Wilfred Douglas, *1918*-)
    II. Unesco III. Series
    370.19'5

ISBN 1-85302-010-9

Printed and bound in Great Britain by
Biddles Ltd, Guildford and King's Lynn

'Und wenn du ganz dich zu verlieren scheinst,
Vergleiche dich. Erkenne, was du bist.'
('And if thou appearest to be entirely lost,
Compare thyself. Know what thou art.')
- Goethe, *Torquato Tasso*, v.5

Contents

Overview	9
Introduction	11

PART I
Trends and issues in comparative education *W. D. Halls* — 21

PART II - COMPARATIVE EDUCATION AROUND THE WORLD

Western Europe *Brian Holmes*	69
The Socialist countries *H. G. Hofmann and Zia Malkova*	109
North America *Robert F. Lawson*	145
Latin America *A. Oliveros*	175
Asia and the Pacific	198
China, India, Japan and Korea *Tetsuya Kobayashi*	200
Australia and New Zealand *Robin Burns*	227
Africa *Alin Babs Fafunwa*	257
The Arab states *Khemais Benhamida*	291

PART III
The national and international impact of comparative education infrastructures *Robert Cowen* — 321

Overview

Comparative educationists whose main work was done in the 1960s saw its main thrust as improving education, so as to stimulate a better life for society and the individual. Meliorism was hardly called into question as one of the basic justifications for comparative studies. The 1970s were a decade of reappraisal. Surveying the world scene, comparative educationists observed that education had not proved to be the total social panacea for all ills: it palpably had not wrought more effective economic progress, as the experience of the developing countries proved; it did not appear perceptibly to have reduced social inequalities, as Jencks' study of inequality in the United States, in which British data is also freely drawn upon for the purposes of comparison, also made clear. It had not turned out to be a beneficent instrument for political socialization: on the contrary, in the West it had helped to produce the student unrest of the late 1960s and early 1970s; in the emergent countries, campaigns for universal primary education and literacy had given rise to expectations impossible of fulfilment. Whilst these pessimistic, over-hasty judgements are in process of revision, the comparative educationist now views the world scene more cautiously. Whereas past research had often revolved round topics such as political literacy, national development and social class, such themes now appear less rewarding. Since education was no longer the preeminent national concern (although in the Third World it retained a higher priority than in the First World), some turned to international research projects of a less ambitious kind: the processes of instruction; the virtues (or otherwise) of non-formal or informal education as opposed to formal education, population education, health education, the place of women in education, vocational education at a lower, more practical level. For the comparative educationist such a more modest research agenda might indeed be more rewarding, in the sense that his findings could more readily influence the policymaker than the macro-studies that had characterized earlier research.

The dispute about micro- or macro-levels of research is a long-standing one. However, as early as 1966 Rokkan thought he perceived a way of uniting the macro- and the micro-levels:

> 'The essential aims of cross-national analysis are 'micro' replications and the testing of 'macro' hypotheses. In replicative research the aim is to test out in other national and cultural settings a proposition already validated in one setting.'

He held to this view despite the fact that he thought the crucial tasks of cross-national analysis lay at the macro-level.

Introduction

This book has an ambitious aim. It seeks to depict globally the status of a very amorphous field of pure and applied studies, comparative education. It has the advantage of being produced under the auspices of the oldest international agency in the field, one that from its inception has been concerned with comparative studies, the International Bureau of Education. The present volume, Janus-like, looks back over the past decade of comparative education, identifying past trends and tendencies, and projecting prospects by the end of the century. In one respect it can be seen as a record of the achievements of the 'generation of 1960', the date when some maintain that comparative education came of age. Many scholars of that vintage are now of retirement age. At the same time, it assesses the work of those still fully committed in the field, as well as those just beginning their career. No doubt the 'generation of the year 2000' will have very different concerns from those voiced in this volume. What will they think of what has been done in the exciting 1960s in the despondent 1970s and in the 1980s, the decade of renewal?

In some respects the status of the field still resembles the emerging social sciences at the end of the nineteenth century. At that time new academic areas within the 'science of society' - the psychology of peoples, political geography, cultural anthropology, to name only three - were struggling each to delimit its territory, to establish a distinctive 'field' academically, and to seek practical applications for their labours. Sociology, long held to be the catalyst for this explosion of the social sciences, was struggling to shake off the fetters of normative social philosophy, fighting for its own scholarly validity. Theories and approaches borrowed from other, more 'respectable', established academic disciplines were being experimented with, and varying degrees of success achieved.

If the social sciences sought to know more about the way society functions they also sought how it could be improved - and, as the examples already cited amply demonstrate, the comparative approach was an important instrument in their investigations. Much the same holds good for comparative studies today: a striving to enhance our knowledge of education, and an ambition to improve its institutions, content, processes and methods. Within its own broad field comparative education, like the social sciences, has already spawned a number of sub-areas of interest, as will be amply demonstrated.

The year 1960 has been cited as one crucial, albeit approximate date. By then pioneers in the field - Sadler, Kandel, Rosselló, Schneider, Hans, to name only a few - had already carried out their seminal studies. Comparative educationists still often wrote in terms of 'driving forces' (*Triebkräfte*), 'national factors' and the like, although others such as Lauwerys were already advocating a more 'scientific' approach. By 1960 the first association of comparative scholars had been established, the North American Comparative Education Society, and a European society was already mooted. A new take-off in comparative studies, with new methods and a new content, was possible. The world had recovered from the cataclysm of war, academics had reforged contacts broken for decades, faith in education as a social and economic regenerator was beginning its brief - but then unchallenged - reign. International and academic institutions reacted accordingly, providing (by present standards) lavish provision for study of other education systems. The Third World was on the point of achieving political autonomy, and it was surmised that educational autonomy would quickly follow. The barometer looked set fair for great expansion and significant advances in comparative studies.

Indeed, the 1960s was the decade of optimism. It was one that saw the publication of works, still basic to the comparative educationist today, by Bereday, King, Holmes, and Noah and Eckstein. It was an era of travel and observation. Americans visited the USSR to study what they termed the 'changing Soviet school' - change was in fact the slogan of an era. Educators from Eastern Europe came to look at British boarding schools. UNESCO was beginning to send its educational missions all over the world. Comparative educationists, as they circled the globe, enjoyed goodwill everywhere. 'Bliss was it in that dawn to be alive, but to be young was very Heaven.' Some twenty years later, Harold Noah stated that '... the fundamental assertion of comparative study is that we can truly comprehend ourselves only in the context of a secure knowledge of other societies', and went on to condemn 'parochial knowledge' as 'partial'. After all, a science of medicine that was narrowly nationally conceived would be derisory; the same holds good for education.

The 1960s were followed by a decade and a half of uncertainty. By the first oil crisis (1973) belief that education would prove to be the universal social and economic panacea was discredited. It was evident that educational expansion alone brought neither greater equality of opportunity nor greater economic prosperity. Governments reacted accordingly. Education ceased to be the 'priority of priorities'. Negative factors hit comparative education particularly hard. Research, always expensive because of its international dimension, was drastically curtailed. Institutions of higher education channeled greatly reduced funds to education departments, and comparative education, for long considered by academic colleagues both in and outside education departments to be over-expensive, suffered disproportionately. What has been termed the 'identity crisis' of comparative educationists became acute. Within the education field the concentration was on activities directly related to *Praxis*, an area in which, at the time, comparative educationists had done relatively little work.

Nevertheless, the post-'60s were not all 'gloom and doom'. Although the growth rate of comparative education slowed, its constituency was greatly enlarged. The reasons for this are many and varied. The achievement of independence meant that new nations were free to decide their own educational destiny. When they looked abroad for models, it was by no means exclusively towards the former colonial powers that they turned. This was specially true of Africa, most of whose fifty-one nation states have been independent for less than a quarter of a century. It was also true of the vast Indian sub-continent. China, particularly since the ending of the 'cultural revolution', has increasingly looked both East and West for relevant educational ideas. During the 1970s the Arab states became ever more conscious of the need for Arabization and of their common religious identity, accelerating educational consultation and co-operation between them. Comparative educationists in the industrialized countries, where they were called in to help, responded, sometimes effectively, sometimes ineptly, to the challenge. Nevertheless, the decade saw a massive upsurge in what became known as international development education. UNESCO's commanding role has already been mentioned, but there was also increasing involvement by other international, as well as regional and supra-national organizations, which provided expertise and finance. Thus, for example, educational planning in South America, under the initial impulsion of UNESCO, developed its own regional organizations under an international umbrella. Public bodies such as the World Bank, and philanthropic agencies such as the Ford Foundation employed comparative educationists on a variety of tasks. Almost overnight, comparative studies, which had largely originated and been sustained in the industrialized countries, found their sphere of activity greatly enlarged.

Such activity entailed vast movements of personnel. In Africa, for instance, this was expressed in the engagement of expatriate staff. Student movement likewise increased: by the end of the decade there were a third of a million foreign students in the USA, and a similar number in the USSR. Smaller countries such as France took in a massive 130,000; Britain some 40,000. Youngsters in organizations such as the Peace Corps or Voluntary Service Overseas - and similar movements - gave what help they could in campaigns for literacy, health and primary education programmes. Professionals, students and auxiliaries alike took back to their own countries, on completion of their contract or their studies, the knowledge of the foreign education system they had acquired - indeed some became comparative educationists in their own right. Such a climate of international exchange has inspired this present volume, to which we must now turn.

There has been no comprehensive review of the status of comparative education since the late 1970s, and none of those published at that time was on a world-wide, systematic basis. The present volume aims at filling this gap. What are sometimes termed 'state of the art' studies are periodically useful, particularly in cases where the field is diffuse. With comparative studies the diffuseness is both geographical and conceptual. The field now embraces the globe: no continent or country does not have at least a number of officials and a few academics who are looking at education beyond their own confines. Depending upon local conditions, the focus of interest will vary enormously; hence the conceptual diffuseness. Although comparative education began with its roots firmly grounded in history and philosophy, since the late 1960s it has broadened its base and established linkages with many other disciplines. It is this extended dimension, both global and academic, that serves as the point of departure for this volume. Since UNESCO is made up of nation-states, it would have been logical, in a work published by the International Bureau of Education, to have used these as the structural framework. However, for reasons of expense and space, if for no other, this is patently impossible. Instead the basic unit has been taken to be the region or sub-region, whereby, it is hoped, world coverage will nevertheless be assured. The problem here is naturally one of making a rational judgment on what, for the present purposes, constitutes a region or sub-region. It has been solved - not altogether satisfactorily, as will become apparent - by using the UNESCO definition of a region, with some exceptions and adjustments, such as the inclusion of a chapter on North America. For one chapter recourse has had to be made to more than one author, and in two other cases - Latin America and Eastern Europe - other writers provided invaluable background papers, which are not published here, but gave additional sources of information.

Part I of the book comprises a general review of the background to the seven regional studies that follow in Part II. It deals with the overall historical development, the modifications in the concept of comparative education that have occurred, the general approaches, methods and theories that have emerged in recent years, the problems and concerns that have arisen, and remarks on content and practice, all in relation to research. The purpose is to synthesize and supplement the information given in the regional reports. The emphasis in the section is thus on contemporary trends and issues. It is hoped that this will serve as an introduction to Part II, which consists of the regional reports. These are given in chapters as follows:

Western Europe: For the purposes of this book this includes all the member or associated countries of the Council of Europe.

The socialist countries: Some reference is made in this chapter also to socialist countries outside Europe, such as Cuba and South Yemen.

North America: the United States and Canada.

Latin America: this also includes the Caribbean area.

Asia and the Pacific: a division of labour was deemed necessary here. The chapter is divided in two so as to ensure adequate coverage not only of mainland Asia and Japan, but also of South and South-East Asia, and the Pacific countries.

Africa: this excludes the Arab States of North Africa.

The Arab states.

The writers of these 'regional' chapters have all been drawn from the areas concerned, or have had long experience of them. Strictly speaking, they were invited to contribute 'essays' rather than comprehensive reports. Allowing for some inevitable subjectivity, it is nevertheless hoped that papers will reflect the main trends and tendencies.

Although each chapter may be organized slightly differently, a certain uniformity has been observed. A brief summary of the history of comparative studies within a region emphasizes in the main recent history. Most writers have nevertheless tended to go back to the late 1960s and early 1970s, which is rightly seen as the 'hinge' on which a new era of comparative studies turns. A few have deemed it necessary to go back even earlier, for history is a 'seamless web'. Some description is given of the major research centres and research training before an appraisal is made of the major research projects undertaken during the period, and the publications that have emerged from them. An indication is given of the lines of enquiry on which contemporary research is proceeding. On the premise that different areas will use different approaches and methods, depending upon local conditions, the topics to be investigated, and researchers' preferences, writers were invited to describe generally the major schools of methodology and the methodological trends, as well as how research has impacted upon their own educational systems, where this is appropriate. The place of comparative education as a 'discipline' or course at institutions of higher education, particularly in teacher-training institutions, is also mapped out. Indications are likewise given of the existing support structure for comparative studies in any given area, such as journals and meetings of comparativists.

Part III, in fact, deals with what might be termed the national and international infrastructures of comparative education in more detail: societies, associations, centres, journals, etc. and the impact these have on theory and practice. The work is supplemented by a selective bibliography, which it is hoped will be of use to scholars and administrators alike. One of the most encouraging features of the 1970s - a decade that was generally not propitious for comparative studies - has been the development of the activities of the national and regional comparative and international societies, now numbering eighteen in all, most of which are members of the World Congress. The same holds good for the World Congress itself, the initial impetus for which came in 1971, and which has always had an invaluable ally in the International Bureau of Education.

Any collective work sometimes encounters difficulties, particularly when harmonization is required. Gratitude must be expressed for the tolerance of the contributors in that their reaction to comment has always been favourable and helpful. Clearly a world community of scholars in comparative education exists, to which the writers of the regional essays belong, (although some also double as academic administrators). It says much for the goodwill that prevails between IBE and its constituency of comparative educationists that strong cooperation and mutual understanding have marked the preparation of this volume.

Thanks indeed are due to all who have contributed to it - not only to contributors but also to those who have criticized their work. Last - but by no means least - the world of comparative education owes a debt to IBE for making the work possible. Our particular gratitude goes to Dr Yuri Alferov, until recently its Programmes Officer, upon whom the main burden of day-to-day administration and preparation has fallen. And there are others, working behind the scenes, to whom our thanks are also due.

'All comparisons are odorous', said Shakespeare. But for once we hope we have proved the Bard to be wrong.

- W. D. Halls.

PART I

Trends and issues in comparative education

W. D. Halls

This paper makes no claim to completeness. It is based upon an analysis and synthesis of the regional essays that follow, supplemented by information and comment derived from elsewhere. It therefore also makes no pretension to objectivity, which in any case, in the social sciences, is not of this world.

For convenience, the essay is divided into four sections. The first looks generally at the field, considering briefly definitions and characterizations, typologies, historical development and some of the problems and concerns that comparative educationists encounter in their day-to-day work. A second section deals with approaches, theories and methods. It is recognized that the treatment in these two sections cannot be encyclopedic, and that the selection of topics will not please everybody: the regional contributions, if nothing else, already demonstrate the wide diversity of views held by scholars. A third section treats the content of comparative studies, research themes and trends in research. A final section looks at trends and tendencies in what are loosely termed the infrastructures of comparative education, its teaching, training and research centres, its teachers and where they operate, and the communications network that is so vital a component of a field that is by definition international.

The field

In search of a definition and a typology

Because 'comparative education' has always been conceptually awkward to define, a survey of its present status cannot shirk the preliminary task of examining how far our understanding of it has changed since about 1970.

It is, of course, conceived of both as a method and an object of study. Re-reading earlier literature, it is therefore legitimate to speculate on the road comparative educationists have travelled since earlier definitions of their studies. Those scholars that continued to be the arbiters until the mid-1960s showed remarkable agreement as to the theoretical ambit of their field. Kandel claimed that the purpose of comparative education was to discover the differences in the forces and causes that produce differences in educational systems. Hans asserted that the objective was to discover the underlying principles governing the development of all national systems of education. Schneider would not have dissented from either view. In the event, however, most other studies remained largely descriptive, amplified 'travellers' tales'.

Over the past decade and a half, however, as the regional surveys set out below reveal, comparative studies have indeed moved in practice increasingly away from a descriptive, historical, even philosophical function to one that is interpretative, aetiological and lays claim even to be predictive. In this they have followed one important trend in the social sciences. Thus today a definition derived from one characterization of comparative sociology might be more appropriate. The following might then be postulated as aims:

1. to provide an educational morphology, i.e. a global description and classification of the various forms of education. (This has been one function of UNESCO and particularly of the IBE).
2. to determine the relations and interactions between the different aspects or factors in education, and between education and society. (This may be the stage that 'comparative education' has now reached).
3. to distinguish the fundamental conditions of educational change and persistence and relate these to more ultimate philosophical laws. (This millenarian task is one that some comparative educationists, like most historians, believe is beyond accomplishment).

All three goals require the establishment of correlations, and the identification of links that bind customs, formal laws and social practices with educational institutions - elements of analysis that were not made so explicit, and certainly not followed, in what might be termed the pre-Darwinian phase of comparative studies.

Such an academic definition assumes that in this case an increase in knowledge and the establishment of truth regarding education is arrived at, not by some *logical* process, but by an *analogical* one. On the other hand, as we are constantly reminded in the area reports below, many, if not most, comparative studies in education, like those in similar fields such as comparative law or criminology, are undertaken for *meliorist* purposes. We study the phenomena of foreign education with the intention of improving our own education system.

Nevertheless, as the regional reports amply show, an attempt to place comparative studies in the overall context of the study of education encounters difficulties of acceptability. Attempting to generalize from the reports, the following typology is offered as a working model:

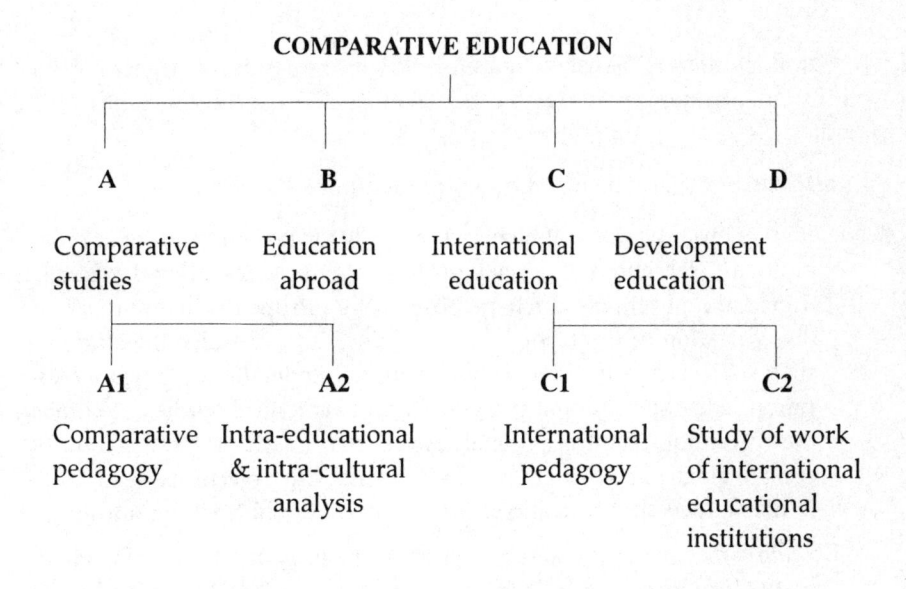

COMPARATIVE EDUCATION

A	B	C	D
Comparative studies	Education abroad	International education	Development education

A1	A2	C1	C2
Comparative pedagogy	Intra-educational & intra-cultural analysis	International pedagogy	Study of work of international educational institutions

Such a model suffers from many defects, but is the best that can be gleaned as to what is actually subsumed under 'comparative education' today. It is of course flawed because the categories are not mutually exclusive - there is patent overlap. Moreover, there is clearly no agreement among comparative educationists as to the use of terms, as is borne out by the confusion that often arises between 'international education' and 'development education', both of which are value-laden terms. However, as used in the above classification, each of the terms may be amplified as follows:

A. *Comparative studies* may be sub-divided into:

  i. *Comparative pedagogy*, defined as the study of teaching and the classroom process in different countries, e.g. the development of science teaching through transatlantic borrowings such as occurred in the 1960s.

  ii. *Intra-educational and intra-cultural analysis*, which investigates education by its various levels, and also systematically researches the historical, social, cultural, political, religious, economic and philosophical forces that partly determine and are partly determined by the character of education systems, and compares the resultant outcomes in two or more systems, areas or even globally. The approach may also be thematic.

B. *Education abroad* ('Auslandspädagogik') is the study of aspects of an educational system or systems other than one's own; this includes area studies.

C. *International education* may be sub-divided into:

  i. *International pedagogy*, which is the study of teaching multinational, multicultural and multiracial groups, e.g. in international schools, transnational schools (such as those of the European Community), or the education of linguistic or ethnic minorities; it is also the study of such subjects as education for international understanding, peace education, and international population and ecological studies. It entails the resolution of intra-national differences regarding the teaching of controversial subject-matter, and efforts made to 'objectivize' textbooks, to harmonize curricula and establish international teaching norms.

  ii. *Study of the work of international education institutions*. This overlaps with (i), but is more concerned with policy matters, such as the establishment of international acceptability of qualifications, the promotion of educational exchanges and the initiation of cultural agreements.

D. *Development education* is the production of information and plans to assist policymakers, particularly in 'new nations', the development of appropriate educational methods and techniques, and the training of personnel to implement programmes.

Such a classification of the work carried out by comparative educationists can only be provisional, but would seem to indicate the direction that they have taken since about the mid-1970s, and in some cases even earlier.

A note on recent history

Interest in education in other countries, as evinced by the journeyings of nineteenth century travellers from Britain, France, Germany and the United States, has been well documented, as have the practical outcomes of their travels. Those of travellers from elsewhere, such as Russia, Spain, the Arab world, Japan and China, have been less thoroughly recorded. Yet reports of all these wandering educationists - comparativists *avant la lettre* - influenced, directly or indirectly, their burgeoning education systems. So do today the 'field studies' of latter-day travellers.

However, although from the literature it can be seen there is no dearth of modern 'travel reports', since the world has largely opened up to the comparative educationist, a variety of other reasons account for the development of comparative studies, as the regional reports reveal. In recent times a prime cause would appear to be *political circumstances*. The various 'caesuras' in contemporary history have been the starting-points for a renewed interest in education beyond the bounds of one's own country: the 1917 Revolution (USSR); the immediate post-War years since 1945 (Asia and European countries, both East and West); the 1960s (African and Arab countries after independence) - to cite only three such historical 'cut-offs'. For individual countries specific recent events can even be cited: thus since 1976 Chinese comparativists have turned to look with fresh eyes at both East and West. Since education is one of the paramount concerns of governments it is unsurprising that international and national political events should have acted as a spur to comparative education.

However, *ideology* has also played a part. Thus, following a tradition initiated by Lenin, socialist countries after World War II have collaborated in the construction of a Marxist school system. Likewise cooperation between capitalist countries has been strong: one recalls the interest that Swedish reforms generated throughout Western Europe, or the fruitful exchange of ideas that has occurred between the United States and English-speaking countries, and between France and Quebec. And many other examples could be cited.

Common *cultural links* have also profoundly stimulated comparative and international studies. An outstanding example is Latin America, where inter-ministerial conferences on education have been a feature from 1955 onwards. Here not only a common or mutually comprehensible language, but also the initial similarity between administrative structures and school systems have facilitated comparisons. Another instance where official intervention has been beneficial to comparative studies is the increasing cooperation between the Arab States on educational affairs, within the overall framework of the Arab League. To these must be added - since the two often seem to go together - the catalyst effect of *international organizations*, particularly in Latin America but also in the Third World, where educational planning has been closely linked to social and economic development. After independence countries relaxed their ties with former colonial powers (although these have still played a not inconsiderable role in educational assistance to some African nations, for example), and have relied on help from UNESCO and other international agencies, in addition to that provided by world powers such as the USA and the USSR. This impetus to comparative education has been particularly strong.

On occasion, moreover, *pedagogical problems* - often with societal overtones - can give rise to comparison. Thus, for instance, within the socialist countries a common concern for the appropriate relationship between school and working life has produced collaborative research. Beyond Europe, countries such as Canada and Australia, faced with the task of educating massive numbers of migrants, have broadened their educational horizons to cope with this new phenomenon. The 'old' countries of Western Europe, likewise confronted with a new migration of peoples, have also sought the aid of comparative studies.

Yet another causal factor in the increasing growth in comparative studies has been the *academic* constituency itself. There can be little doubt that the input in the early 1970s of the social sciences was a revivifying force in comparative studies generally. It may well be that other intellectual developments, such as the advances in information technology, will provide a fresh fillip in future years.

However, it would be wrong, despite the examples cited, to ascribe the contemporary development of comparative studies in any one country to a single cause. In every nation political, ideological, international, pedagogical and academic factors have all been strong mobilizing forces. And there are doubtless others.

Problems and concerns

The *lack of a precise definition* of the field of 'comparative education' has continued to block its development. However, attempts by scholars to assert that they alone are qualified to define it have been refuted. The typology above proposed only one classification: many others have been propounded. One difficulty arises from the appellation itself: 'comparative education' connotes above all comparison. Yet findings by Koehl in 1977 demonstrated that between 1957 and 1977, of the papers published in one of the leading journals, the *Comparative education review*, only some 39 per cent, out of 386 papers, dealt with two or more countries, and only five per cent dealt with a dozen countries or more. The present writer has updated these findings, using a different journal, the *International review of education*, scanning numbers that appeared between 1975 and 1985. Using the conventional analysis of classification by countries, an opportunity sample of sixty published papers revealed that:

- 10 (17 per cent), mainly dealing with the Third World, were not classifiable according to country;
- 24 (40 per cent) dealt principally with one country; 18 (30 per cent) dealt with two to six countries; and only
- 8 (13 per cent) with seven or more countries.

The last group comprised a wide range of topics. However, all statistics must be treated with reserve, since judgments were made as to whether the odd reference to other countries justified inclusion in one category rather than another. Interestingly, however, relatively few papers concentrated on levels of education; rather the approach was thematic. A recent impressionistic review of all three main journals, to bring the position up to date, reveals the situation as virtually unchanged, as does data given in the regional reports: straight comparisons are few. It is nevertheless true that papers written by non-nationals about other countries often give rise to implicit comparisons. Moreover, the same situation appertains in other disciplines using the comparative method, such as comparative law or comparative literature.

Indeed, it can be argued that a foreigner writing about systems other than his own sheds new light on them for the indigenous educationist. Nevertheless, the foreigner brings to the study of another system his own cultural prejudices, which may tend to cloud the judgment and invalidate conclusions. This other question, of unconscious bias, has exercised researchers in comparative education greatly in recent years. As always, the balance of advantage and disadvantage is finely drawn.

Another concern has been whether one can describe *comparative education as a discipline*. This is a controversy that dates back at least to 1964, when C. Arnold Anderson argued that it was not. It is a problem that has concerned also East German comparativists. Kienitz in 1973 insisted that it was a discipline, and was backed by Ilse Gerth, who affirmed its independent existence. On the other hand Herzig and his associates believe that comparative education research can only 'be seen as a cooperative activity of the various branches of science' and reject 'the need for a special division of educational science for researching into the development of education internationally.'

The sheer *extent and nature of the field* gives rise to difficulty. A pointer as to how it has grown and the direction that it has taken is given in some statistics published by Huebner et al. Between 1971 and 1980 the following figures give the number of publications appearing, the bodies that published them, and the division between the various geographical areas:

- First or Second World: 13,500 - 15,000, of which 10 per cent were published by UNESCO and similar bodies, and 90 per cent by universities and similar institutions.
- Third World: 10,000 - 11,000, of which 55 per cent were published by UNESCO, et al., and 45 per cent by universities, et al.

The massive intervention by UNESCO and similar bodies in relation to the Third World is evident.

Other figures, moreover, demonstrate that the balance of interest, as measured by publications, is steadily moving away from industrialized to developing societies: whereas in the 1970s only some 39 per cent of publications related to the Third World, by the 1980s this had risen to some 43 per cent. Another relevant fact is that by the 1980s the number of all published items had increased by just over half, as compared with the 1970s. Such comparative statistics illustrate graphically the extent to which the world is becoming educationally a global village, despite the fact that comparative studies in academic institutions plummeted steeply in the 1970s.

The dangers of *ethnocentricity* are still very apparent. From developing countries it is reported that too often comparative educationists from the industrialized world descend upon them, carry out research, propound solutions and disappear, producing later a published report but having made little contact with local comparative educationists, and without even bothering to forward a copy of their findings to the countries concerned. If the host country is too little consulted at the planning, evaluatory or report stages the value of the work is nullified.

Ethnocentricity is also apparent in the seeming lack of much contact between industrialized regions. For example, with a few exceptions, South Americans come little into contact with West Europeans. Between the Asian nations and Europe in general contacts are too infrequent: for Westerners the language barrier is the biggest obstacle - as indeed it is for studies within Europe itself. Although shortage of physical facilities is often the cause, Westerners require to make an effort to study not only Asian languages, but also Asian culture, if they are to understand the Far East. The same applies elsewhere. Translations are no substitute for direct communication.

A particular form of educational 'narcissism' is *political* ethnocentricity. Despite the ideological divide that seems to separate the capitalist and the socialist worlds, the convergence theory reminds us that the two camps have much in common. The theme, for example, of the proper relationship of education to working life is one of vital concern to all, as indeed are many of the other themes that the International Bureau of Education has discussed at recent biennial conferences. On the technical plane, and in the spirit of the Helsinki Agreement, it is surely possible for greater collaboration to occur.

Although complete objectivity is not of this world, the comparative educationist, above all other scholars, should surely avoid ethnocentricity for the plague that it is.

In recent years the question has been much debated as to what should be the *dimension of comparison*. Whereas in the 1960s and, to a slightly lesser extent, in the 1970s, the comparison was virtually always made as between nation-states - and this is largely the case today, even with a large research enterprise such as the IEA Study - this style, derived from Kandel and Hans, is now called into question. In its place other alternatives have been used. World systems analysis has been attempted. This is of course nothing new, as the study of Harbison and Myers (1964) on the educational correlates of wealth reminds us. Today, however, the emphasis is different, with divisions being made between ideological systems. Another view - the one on which the present volume is based - takes the regional dimension as the basis for comparison. It is argued that the world can be divided roughly into six or seven regions with the educational systems within them possessing sufficient common features to justify inter-regional comparison. The 'Three Worlds' concept and the 'North-South' divide, both ultimately relating to degrees of prosperity, are variants of this approach. Whether this view of the field, in which there are as many contrasts as comparisons, will prove rewarding is difficult as yet to say. Moreover, local or 'intra-national' - 'regional' in miniature - comparisons are common in Latin America and beginning to be attempted elsewhere. The field here is comparatively unploughed: juxtapositions of the state of education within the various American states, the Canadian provinces, or the constituent Republics of the USSR might prove rewarding. Thus in England measurements have increasingly been made of the correlation between the sum per pupil spent in the various local authorities and the level of achievement as gauged by the number of examination passes. (Incidentally, it has been found that the authority that spends most does not always achieve the best examination results, a finding of practical interest to policymakers). Perhaps, however, the most ambitious comparisons are those that are *thematic*: the position of women in education; the relationship of education to employment; educational budgets - the list is endless. The questions that arise from such differing taxonomies are also endless. Will world, or thematic comparisons, be so 'stratospheric' as to be almost meaningless? Are local comparisons basically flawed because the fundaments of comparison are too narrow? Do regions exhibit sufficient commonality for effective, detailed comparisons? Shall we not eventually be thrown back upon the tried and tested method of national comparisons? The next decade may yield answers to these all-important questions. The fact remains that other entities for comparison are at present being tried, and this is an important new development.

One final key concern remains to be discussed: what is the role of the social sciences generally in comparative education? Sparked off by the predominance of sociology in educational studies as a whole between 1965 - 1975, and by the publication of Noah and Eckstein's work, which advocated the methods of the social sciences and acted within the comparative field as a catalyst, societal factors have played a large part. Specialists in other fields such as psychology, economics, political science and history have also used comparisons more readily in their research, and included in them an educational component. Comparative educationists, it would seem, have no monopoly in making comparisons. Indeed, their numbers have not increased proportionately to the general growth of Academe, because they have often deserted to the ranks of their social science colleagues. In many cases this has merely represented a reversion to their original discipline. But the reason is often because they have experienced a certain frustration at the lack of consensus on the content, theories, methods and techniques in comparative education proper. However, this collaboration and participation in educational comparisons by different social scientists has greatly enriched the field, particularly in the domain of theory.

Harold Noah himself has since disclaimed any intention of staking an exclusive claim for the social sciences. He did not wish, he said, to eliminate entirely the historical and philosophical mode of comparative analysis, but merely to increase the options and range of interest. Too narrow a use of social science methods would, for example, diminish the role of judgment and interpretation. Nevertheless, this certainly occurred for a while, particularly in the realm of approaches and theory, to which we must now turn.

Approaches, theories, methods

At least half a dozen different 'approaches' to comparative education can be identified. Since most of these are either of recent origin or recent extensions of older ones, it is useful to review them here.

The oldest approach may be described as *historico-philosophical*. Pioneers in the field made use of it. The aim was largely descriptive and explanatory. It made little attempt to extrapolate the future development of educational phenomena. Kandel sought, for example - and not only through history - to identify 'the intangible, impalpable spiritual and cultural forces which underline an education system.' In Eastern Europe even today the emphasis is on discovering 'driving forces' and 'laws' that underpin educational policy and practice. Although the historical element in comparative studies is not very prominent, there have been some distinguished recent examples of it in the work, for instance, of Fritz Ringer. Moreover, in the socialist countries there is an insistence upon respect for 'historical conditions'.

Closely linked to it is what has been described as the *national character* approach, which views education as the typical phenomenon of the nation state. Already in 1907 Sadler had written: 'A national system of education is the outcome of national history and a sure index of national character.' Moehlman even postulated a 'national style', which he defined as 'the pattern of performance which a civilization shows in coping with the paramount issues of its times'. In Europe the leading exponent of it in recent years has been Mallinson. Critics of the approach have attacked it because it is too amorphous, but that it is not dead is demonstrated by the recent (1986) onslaught upon it by Lé Thành Khôi, a leading French comparative educationist. He attacks those who explain French education through the allegedly characteristic feature of French intellectualism, asserting that this trait is common to a number of the Latin countries, and derives from Antiquity and Catholic theology.

Having affinities with Hans' 'structural sociologisms' and 'determining factors', a *culturalist* approach (Halls, Klafki) has also been advocated. Using a definition of culture given by Bourdieu and Passeron as 'standardized patterns of activity and belief that are learned and manifested by people in their collective life', it can be argued that a cultural typology must give rise to a similar educational typology. Cultural and educational features are linked, and act reciprocally upon each other. The learning process is in part the result of the educational process. Thus legitimate research studies would include the interaction between the dominant political ideology in a society and its educational system; or cultural attitudes towards concepts such as scientific progress or religious belief as they affect, and are affected by, the educational system. Bourdieu's work on educational 'reproduction' has since overshadowed the culturalist approach proper, since his own theories have become identified with a particular ideology.

There are indeed a number of approaches that insist upon the *contextual* element. With this are associated the important studies on education in the industrialized countries carried out by Edmund King in the 1970s, which can best be described as *eclectic and pragmatic*. King rejects the view that comparative education can lead to the formulation of laws or that *per se* it can have predictive value. What it *can* do, he argues, is to provide the grounds for informed decision-making. The possibility of forming hypotheses is not rejected - the policymaker does this almost subconsciously, in any case. The task of the comparative educationist is to analyze and recommend, but the insights he alone can provide are always subject to the new context, or the 'ecology' in which they have to be applied. Renate Nestvogel has recently developed further the 'total social context' approach (*Gesamtgesellschafts-Kontext-Ansatz*). Comparative analysis must always be undertaken within the specific social, economic and political context, drawing a distinction between the rhetoric of intentions - what the education system purports to do - and its actual achievements. Since such an analysis cannot be carried out by the educationist alone, the plea is for interdisciplinarity - cooperation between all the academic disciplines involved. Comparative research that fails to take the whole social context into account lays itself open to a charge of superficiality.

If the approaches outlined above represent a more 'literary' view of comparative studies those that follow can best be categorized as 'scientific'.

One of the most well-known is the *problem-solving* approach associated with Brian Holmes. In recent years Holmes has refined and expanded his original views, which date from the 1960s. The approach is based on a theory of social change: 'Problem analysis can usefully start from identified change in any of the three patterns in (a) taxonomy, namely the normative, the institutional and the natural environmental'. The aim is predictive, to anticipate the outcomes of policy: 'Hypotheses and generalizations may be stated as policies, normative laws, sociological laws or functional propositions, and take the general form of 'If...when'. The main constituents of the problem-solving approach are: problem analysis (or intellectualization) - hypothesis (or policy solution formulation) - specification of initial conditions (or context) - the logical prediction from adopted hypotheses of likely outcomes - the comparison of logically predicted outcomes with observable events. Comparative education thus becomes a pure and an applied science. Holmes goes on to recommend the use of ideal-type, normative models, examines induction and ethnomethodology but finds them wanting. He continues to advocate a combination of Dewey's problem-solving approaches and Popper's hypothetico-deductive method of enquiry.

The *quantitative* approach is perhaps more a method than an approach, but is dealt with here because it has been so hotly debated in recent years. The IEA Study, which is discussed in detail elsewhere, began in the late 1960s, continued throughout the 1970s and early 1980s, and has plans that will carry through to the 1990s. It was the first full-scale enterprise that brought quantification to any large extent into comparative studies, and is linked to the names of Torsten Husén and Neville Postlethwaite, as well as a host of internationally known scholars, not all of whom would wish to be identified with comparative education. Recently the approach has been joined to the process-product research paradigm: 'presage' and 'context' variables, separate but interacting, react with 'process' variables, generating 'product' variables, which can be measured. This contrasts with the qualitative approach, which is considered over-descriptive, lacking the neutrality of hard figures, and based on overt or unconscious biases that falsify conclusions. The non-quantifiers have counter-attacked the quantitative paradigm on the grounds that research cannot possibly take into account all variables, some of which are in any case unmeasurable.

The *economic approach* represents a particular kind of quantification, with its focus on education and economic growth. This approach faltered at the beginning of the 1970s when there was a certain defeatism as regards the economic returns to educational investment, and ambiguities arose as to whether economic growth caused education or *vice versa*. However, there is now a resurgence of confidence in comparative economic studies, associated with names such as George Psacharopoulos and Maureen Woodhall. The World Bank has become the principal sponsoring agency, with interest centred on Third World countries. Active in the field since 1972, recently it has concentrated on the external efficiency of educational investment, its equity implications, and the links between educational investment and other sectors of the economy. Psachoropoulos' most recent verdict (1985) is that the level of investment in education must be 'country-specific', but there are 'broad criteria' that must be followed. This plainly allows for meaningful comparisons between countries to be made.

The most general approach, however, that continues to find favour ever since Noah and Eckstein formulated it in 1969, is undoubtedly that of the _social sciences_, which represented a breakaway not only from the historico-philosophical view, but also from the inductive ideas of George Bereday. Noah has most recently (1985) set it out as a four-stage process: to identify, validate and measure variables; show the connection between the variables in each country; compare cross-nationally these relationships; explain and generalize, using other concepts (e.g. national character) as necessary. No exclusiveness is claimed for this approach. Indeed, the fact that no one approach necessarily excludes others is increasingly recognized. Each has its uses: its application will depend upon circumstances.

Perhaps the greatest advance in the field over the past fifteen years has been in the development and use of relevant *theories*, regardless of their provenance. This has come about through the patient observation and collection of data, which have enabled a picture to be built up of the structures of reality, in this case educational facts (which Durkheim would have insisted must be regarded as 'things'). The classification process led to the discovery of regularities in a phenomenon. To cite an example, the structural-functionalist paradigm, which long dominated comparative studies, demonstrated that the correlation between level of education and social class was observable in many countries. Causal explanations followed, and the stage of generalizability was reached. Thus Coleman's conclusions were shown by Jencks to be valid for both British and American societies. Upon this generalization could be postulated a 'law', i.e. a prognosis that when certain social and educational conditions were fulfilled educational inequality, followed by social inequality, would arise. The example spelled out here demonstrates what was only dimly perceived by a previous generation of comparative educationists, i.e. that the comparative method, being analogical, is a surrogate for the experimental method of the exact sciences. This marks perhaps the greatest step forward in comparative education over the past decade.

However, the legitimacy of the analogical method needs no further advocacy. Suffice to say that among the industrialized countries it is one that is being increasingly applied, as education authorities look over one another's shoulder in respect of such problems as the relationship of education to employment. Countries are busy imitating training courses, youth employment schemes, and vocational initiatives introduced elsewhere (Britain and France are a case in point). It is, incidentally, a pity that comparative educationists are not more actively involved in such enterprises, if only to indicate the pitfalls of too slavish 'borrowings'. (One recalls the misconceptions of the 1960s, when Admiral Rickover compared American education unfavourably with provision elsewhere, or when the Robbins Committee for the reform of British higher education, after a few cursory visits abroad, produced an appendix to its main report that, as regards foreign educational systems, was replete with errors). There is manifest proof that the comparative method can only be successful if analogies (or lack of them) are precisely formulated. The fact remains, however, that the utility of the method has now been tacitly acknowledged by decision-makers, and it behoves those who believe in a *macro*-role for comparative studies, i.e. in the formulation of policy, to make their voice more clearly heard.

Perhaps the premise that has held sway longest in comparative education was based on the *convergence* theory. It was argued, at least up to a few years ago, that cultural and technological imperatives were forcing educational systems into the same mould (Glowka, Halls, Grubb). This was held to be particularly true of industrialized societies. There are many instances of this. Even the United States and West Germany, where federal systems are long established, like many other educational systems, are moving towards greater centralization. Another example is that of curricula, where a remarkable convergence has taken place. A more utilitarian approach to mathematics teaching, in history the emphasis on the contemporary world, in science the massive introduction of teaching about technology, the return of civics education in one form or another to school programmes, the quantification of geography - the instances of curriculum 'congruence' or 'concomitance' are many and convincing. Likewise there has been everywhere in the First World the introduction of 'new' subjects, such as sociology, economics, information technology, design, even psychology, although they may differ in name from one country to another.

A further example of such convergence in industrialized countries is in the field of qualifications. Western European countries in the EEC came together to create, for the children of their civil servants gathered together in certain places, a unified secondary leaving examination, the European baccalaureate. This is perhaps a special case of the *transactional* theory in international relations, which states that the more contacts there are transnationally the greater the prospects are that countries will cooperate and consent to surrender their cultural autonomy. Bilateral cultural agreements, with strong educational spin-offs, as well as international accords on the mutual recognition of qualifications (in which field UNESCO and regional organizations such as the Council of Europe have been especially active), have reflected this convergence of interests.

In all three areas - the moves towards a 'harmonization' of curricula, the creation of common examinations, and the 'equivalence' of qualifications - comparative educationists, particularly in Europe, have played a useful role. Much work remains to be done within the convergence-divergence paradigm. One example dates from the early days of UNESCO when it took the lead in bilateral and multilateral tasks on the elimination of bias from textbooks. Such work urgently needs updating, in the light of the present ethnocentricity apparent in some education programmes. Sweden, by contrast, has embarked on a deliberate policy for the total 'internationalization' of its education, a move that has aroused much interest among comparative educationists in Japan. In specific fields, such as comparative sports education and adult education, belief in convergence theory is strong. It is perhaps significant that the World Council on Adult Education publishes (from Toronto) a journal entitled *Convergence*.

If convergence theory is, by its nature, specific to comparative education, *structural functionalism* has been the dominant social theory for at least three decades. It has been one that lent itself well to the purposes of comparative educationists and of social theorists such as Margaret Archer who engaged in educational comparisons. The particular comparative question raised is: how does the structure of a society, and in particular that of its schools, which can be conceptualized as systems, contribute to the viability of that society, its survival and efficiency: in other words, what link is there between structure and function? Some researchers have found that the structuring of the education system was appropriate in performing the function of 'slotting' young people into employment; in other societies malfunctioning existed. In Third World societies education was held to perform a function of integration. Elsewhere Neo-Marxists studied the conflicts of value and interest in schools: was the education system one more means of the coercion of the weak by the strong?

To this some added a theory of *cultural capital*, derived from *reproduction theory* (Bourdieu, Passeron, Bourdan), which stated that intellectual advantages were unequally distributed, and that the holders of power in society determined the content of education to their own advantage. In other words, they not only defined who was to inherit a society's cultural capital, but of what knowledge it was to consist. According to this, an educational oligopoly existed that frustrated the smooth running of a society in structural functional terms. These concerns are reflected in recent work by comparative educationists to test whether such a theory holds validity cross-nationally. It is clearly related to *social control* theory, which seeks to show that education has been, and is, a weapon of constraint or even repression, a means of maintaining an oppressive status quo. On the other hand, others argue that the schools have a duty to turn out patriotic citizens, imbued with ideals of community service, and that such a purpose is a legitimate use of State power, and legitimate form of social control. This whole cluster of theories has been a fruitful basis for a number of studies by comparative educationists in recent years.

Before dealing with theories that appear more relevant to the Third World, it is appropriate to summarize how *Marxist theory* has been applied to comparative education. For Marxists, 'comparative education works according to the method of dialectical and historical materialism'. The emphasis is on the use of a scientific method based on Marxism-Leninism. There is a belief that 'general laws' relating to educational theory and practice may be deduced, particularly when comparing socialist countries, despite national differences arising from separate histories and different national traditions. Practically, great reliance must be put on the social and physical sciences, as well as general pedagogics. Techniques do not differ greatly from those already mentioned: description should be followed by interpretation, leading to analysis and, finally, a comparison of educational systems *as a whole*, viewed in the prevailing social and economic context.

As regards the developing countries, the view has been held that *modernization theory* is a useful tool. There is 'the need for the developing countries to achieve economic, political and social modernization'. If this is so, the question then arises: what kind of schooling will bring about this state of affairs? The idealists held education to be the chosen instrument for assisting these countries to 'join their century'. It would help Africa, the 'dark continent', which is a prey to what the head of the UN Economic Commission has characterized as its seven ills: drought, demography, dependency (a correlate of modernization), disequilibrium, destabilization, debt and desertification. Through a vast programme of education, the fifty African members of UNESCO, independent for the most part for only a quarter of a century, and representing half a billion of the world's population, it is argued, have achieved a more adaptable labour force, with trained professional and managerial cadres, and agronomical and technological specialists. However, the pace with which the continent has developed its own natural resources has not been consistent with this development of human capital.

Thus there is a certain disillusionment with 'modernization theory', with the power of education to banish what Arab writers have called 'the sinister trio of poverty, illiteracy and sickness'. Comparative educationists who have charted the role in Africa of education, not only in economic specialization, but also in social differentiation and political development, have also perceived a revulsion from what had been essentially a process of Westernization. 'Disbenefits', arising from too ready an adoption of the educational precepts and practices of industrially advanced societies are now more apparent. Traditional education, whether tribal or religious in nature, has valuable elements that are threatened. Hence the Arab states are equally concerned with carrying out a policy of Arabization and Moslemization, which represent neglected elements of a rich past culture and value system. Comparative educationists have begun to question whether the move from tradition to modernity should follow in the path of European societies, for example, by providing technical institutions (Foster, Noah). In Third World societies informal education, even simple information on how to repair a bicycle or to purify water may be more important.

Modernization theory has been closely linked to *dependency theory*, a term first used in South America to characterize the economic dependence of the sub-continent upon industrialized countries. In the late 1970s it began to be applied to all Third World countries. In North America its exponents have been Carnoy, Arnove, and Altbach and Kelly. In one particular form it was postulated that the former colonial powers, whose influence in the countries they once ruled is still great, would allow indigenous educational systems to develop only insofar as they believe it to be to their economic or strategic advantage. Thus education dispensed in the form of aid to these systems has merely brought about a mismatch with the real needs of the Third World economies, and may lead to *under*-development. A 'client' relationship has emerged that is deleterious, and is paralleled financially by massive Third World indebtedness. Linguistic dependency - principally the predominance of English and French - has made matters worse (although, to be fair, it has been argued by some Third World educators themselves that the vernacular in their countries is not yet viable as an educational medium at higher levels). In any case, the knowledge that has been dispensed has been determined by the First World, in the northern hemisphere, and has flowed south to the Third World, a form of 'cultural imperialism'. These and other ramifications of this theory have been well researched by comparative educationists.

Among general theories of interest to comparative educationists is *legitimacy theory*, based on Habermas' premise that as the role of the State increases the need for legitimation increases. Levin asserts that educational reforms spawn needs and expectations that the State, with insufficient resources, cannot meet. Thus the State loses legitimacy. Hans Weiler speaks of 'compensatory legitimation' as the process whereby the State compensates for the loss of legitimacy by greater application of legal norms, the appeal to expertise and the device of participation. The educational corollaries to this theory have not yet been fully worked out, although it has interested comparative educationists.

Economic theory, already touched upon, has given rise to a number of comparative studies, based upon sub-theories. *Human capital* theory, which postulated that education is the catalyst for the progressive appreciation in value of human capital, demonstrated that physical capital must be used in conjunction with a trained labour force. Although in the 1970s the crude assertion that there was a direct correlation between education and economic growth was questioned in the light of experience, there has recently also been a revival of comparative studies relating to *cost-benefit* theory. However, comparative rates of return are now only recognized as approximate indicators of the effectiveness of educational systems. Higher attainment, in a cycle of unemployment, does not necessarily lead the individual to a correspondingly higher placing in the work hierarchy. There has also been a recrudescence, in the context of comparative educational planning, in *manpower forecasting* studies. Longitudinal studies, whereby a less developed country measures itself against a more developed one, and predicts how much more education - couched in rather crude terms - is needed for it to 'catch up', have also been undertaken. It is perhaps in South America that educational planning in relation to economic conditions has been most practiced.

Of the various theories that have been expounded here it might be said that only one, convergence theory, is, so to speak, exclusive - by its very nature - to comparative education. The rest have been largely borrowed from the social, economic and political sciences, sometimes blended with a tincture of philosophy and history. In the 1970s the influx of social scientists of every kind into the field meant that they brought the theories of their disciplines with them and tried, almost experimentally, to apply them in a comparative context, redefining and refining them, so to speak, as they went along. By and large, however, with one or two notable exceptions, as the regional reports show, theory has not been a main preoccupation of comparative educationists, who have preferred to be busy in the field rather than in the study.

The British sociologist Andrewski has somewhat harshly observed:

'...those who can, discover, and those who cannot, take up methodology.'

He also notes that in the past:

'The history of the natural sciences (and, thus, by implication, that of comparative education) shows that no advances were made by people who tried to *apply* conceptual frameworks: the great discoverers were interested in how and why things happen, and in order to find out they had recourse to any helpful ideas or techniques which they knew... [To do otherwise] amounts to putting the cart before the horse - it is a sterile logomachy.'

To which the theorist might perhaps retort: what cart, what horse?

However, this is not the place to enter into a long and detailed discussion of methods, which occupy little attention as such in the regional reports. Here it would appear that eclecticism is the rule: any method - indeed, any approach or theory - that seems appropriate in a given context is used. Perhaps, however, one more recent method, the *ethnographic*, may be mentioned, since it is increasingly being mooted by comparativists such as Altbach and Kelly, and applied in the field of comparative pedagogy. The ethnographic-sociolinguistic paradigm, consisting of systematic, qualitative descriptions of classroom or school processes has up to now been little used in comparative research, save between certain English-speaking countries, where there is a certain cultural and linguistic commonality of discourse. Outside such cultural limits the barriers to effective studies are, of course, enormous, since they require the direct participation of the researchers in minute, expensive and time-consuming tasks. Yet, as Husén has written with great perception, we should be educationally the poorer 'if we were to think that there was no common denominator of concepts and methods across cultures and nations. If we accept such a pessimistic view we might just as well abandon all our attempts to conduct cooperative and comparative studies.'

From a review of the regional reports it is difficult to see any unity of approaches, theories and methods emerging among comparative educationists. Thus as yet there can be no ordered classification of these to indicate which are appropriate for each kind of study. The most that can be done is to summarize and comment for particular regions, noting, in passing, that in the *Arab states* there is little interest in theory-building, and much emphasis on practicalities.

Although a 'theoretical and methodological' approach is specifically referred to in the report on *Africa*, this is not amplified further. The insistence is upon the *historical and descriptive*, the necessity for which is patent in a part of the world where information is still scarce and communications difficult.

In the *Asian and Pacific* regional report a great variety of methods are mentioned. In Japan there seems little attempt to persuade comparative educationists to consider collectively questions of method. The *historical and descriptive* is again well to the fore, particularly with a view to establishing causation. The methods of *sociological survey* are employed, but there is little correlation analysis. The impression given is that common sense and a knowledge of general 'scientific' method (which should surely characterize all academic studies) are the two most widespread bases for investigations. Australia likewise ascribes a 'low priority to methodological considerations', and this is allegedly explicable by the fact that most comparative educationists are *not* drawn from the social sciences field, whereas curriculum specialists are well represented. However, they may well apply methods drawn from their own original disciplines. Nevertheless, a whole gamut of methods, ranging from those based on *structural functionalism*, neo-Marxism (*dependency theory*), *modernization theory* (for studying developing countries), to *ethnomethodology*, to name only a few, are mentioned. Studies may be *quantitative, analytical*, or *hermeneutic* (the present vogue term for interpretative analysis). Some studies, such as graduate theses, are *literature-based*, for reasons of feasibility.

Latin America, where severely practical studies relating above all to educational planning as a component of total planning have been the order of the day, has been much influenced by Pedro Rosselló, a former director of IBE, with his concept of *currents and trends*, which gives rise to treatment by themes. The possibilities of *quantification*, even in comparative curriculum studies, have been successfully explored. *Hermeneutics* are also employed and 'causal explanations' are sought. North American methods, although known, have not had much impact on research.

However, it is in *North America*, where the massive invasion by the social sciences of the comparative field originated, that methods derived from them have proliferated. To a certain extent, this holds good also for *Western Europe*. *Structural functionalism* theories are still used, but are less in vogue, but *Marxist and neo-Marxist theory, modernization, conflict*, and *legitimation* theories, *quantification* and *psychometric* methods, all find a place alongside the beginnings of applications of *ethnomethodology*. Some methods are clearly used concurrently, justifying the view that comparative education should be *interdisciplinary*.

In the *socialist countries*, as might be expected, theories derived from *Marxism-Leninism* predominate, in which the concepts of *dialectical* and *historical materialism* play a large part. Some *quantitative analysis* occurs, but great stress is laid upon *literature studies*, the careful scrutiny and evaluation of documents being held superior to *observation*, which cannot attain total objectivity. The *analytical* and *structural-functional* also find a place. Moreover, emphasis is laid upon *systems analysis*, where the object of study is examined in its component parts in order to discover the relation of each element to the whole, as well as the relationships existing between elements; the relation of the object of study to the external environment must also be investigated. One hesitates to use the term 'structuralist', but such an approach is at least not far removed from Cartesianism, and also relates felicitously to the general principles of scientific method, although of course the gloss put upon outcomes may differ.

Reading the sections of the regional reports devoted to research and theories and methods, one cannot fail to be struck by the gulf that at present divides the former from the latter.

Over the last decade and a half, however, comparative education has been enriched by a host of theories that practitioners all over the world are beginning to try out. This is welcome, because the more such studies are made, the more applications of approaches, theories and methods are experimented with, the greater the possibility that a corpus of techniques specific to comparative education will arise, at which point it will be more plausible to speak of it as a discipline.

Content, research and research trends

The content of comparative studies

The regional studies clearly highlight the fact that potentially the content of comparative studies is as broad as studies of education itself. The upshot of this is that specialization has quickly occurred: one group of scholars may carve themselves out a niche in concentrating on a particular country or region, another may treat the macro-functions of education, or yet another concern itself with a special level of schooling. The danger here is of fragmentation, with failure to achieve a broad conspectus. It is valuable therefore to consider what kind of studies have tended in fact to be undertaken, what ideal lists of subjects have been drawn up by comparativists, and what views have been expressed regarding the themes of the present research agenda.

One basic distinction has been the division between studies of industrialized and non-industrialized countries. This has already been touched on elsewhere. In connection with the review of articles published in the *International review of education* between 1975 and 1985 previously mentioned (see p.27) further analysis was carried out. It was found that out of 55 papers published that were classifiable according to whether they dealt with developing or industrial countries, 223 (42 per cent) fell into the first category, 22 (40 per cent) into the second. It is also noteworthy that ten papers brought together comparisons from both the Third and the First World, on topics, for example, as diverse as moral values in education and guidance and counselling. The figures reflect favourably on the balance achieved by the editors, and may not only indicate editorial preference but also mirror the kind of work carried out over the decade.

However, how have others viewed what might be termed 'ideal' lists of content?

One Soviet source has stated that comparative studies ideally should include:

> legislation - finance - administration - pre-school education - access and 'openness' of the school system - educational standards - extra-mural institutions - quality of general education - differentiation - preparation for work - preparation for higher education - vocational training facilities - opportunities for individual interests - moral education - teachers and teacher training - research.

Such a list contrasts in some respects with that given in the report for Africa:

> curriculum - planning - finance - examining - indigenous educational systems - mother tongue education - non-formal, vocation and technical education - education and employment - literacy - the education of women.

However, the compilers of both lists agree that topics studied must be of immediate utility, and it is apparent that their choices prove to be only loosely connected to the theory-building approach that has dictated the selection of topics elsewhere, particularly in North America.

Interestingly, the *Vienna Centre*, which acts as the European coordination centre for research and documentation in the social sciences evaluated eighty studies relating to comparative education that it had received between 1975 and 1980 and classified the themes summarily as follows:

> schools and school systems - higher education - the state of education - educational goals.

Moreover, its conclusion, after evaluating these materials, was likewise brief and succinct: it was, not everything is wholly comparable. ... A word to the wise.

Another well-known comparativist, Professor Postlethwaite, until recently associated with the influential IEA Study, cites the following themes as actually comprising the research agenda for comparativists in the early 1980s:

> economics of education - educational planning and policy - pre-school education - teaching and teacher education - curriculum - educational statistics - higher education - non-formal education - adult education - human development.

However, for him this list is not exhaustive, because it subsumes many sub-categories. Moreover, he confirms that 'there seems hardly to be a domain of education where "comparative educators" have not dared to tread'.

Earlier discussion has already given some indication of how varied is the content of what actually has been studied. The lists given of the interests of Japanese, Indian and Korean comparativists (see p.199 et seq) exemplify that interests will vary enormously from region to region. It is indeed obvious that the specialisms that have arisen have been stimulated by geographical, cultural or ideological considerations. Thus in South America the stress on educational planning is very apparent, inspired by the various inter-governmental and regional meetings of all kinds that have taken place. In Eastern Europe a common political ideology has been the basis for the mutual study of the various educational systems, and it is clear that a large measure of harmonization has been achieved between them in this way. East Germany also maintains a strong interest in West German education, one that is reciprocated by the West Germans, who have also concentrated on Africa. In the United States comparative educationists have been active in Latin American studies, as well as in 'anglophone' Africa. The British have also been concerned with the same group of African countries, and other

Commonwealth countries, and have undertaken many area studies, particularly in Western Europe. The main thrust in France has been, naturally enough, concerned with 'l'Afrique francophone'. Indeed, African countries have tended to crystallize into two groups that represented the old colonial divisions of now independent nations, although recently cross-fertilization has begun between them. Australia is developing its contacts with Asia, and in particular with Japan and China. The Japanese interests have already been mentioned, but their particular work in moral education is also noteworthy. China has now developed great interest in the more industrialized countries, both to the East and West of it. Australia is strengthening contacts with Asia, especially Japan and China, as well as with the USA and maintaining its continuing links with the Commonwealth. As can be seen, the motives for these orientations in comparative studies are very mixed.

The near-hegemony of the social sciences approach at one stage all but squeezed out historical studies in comparative education, whether on a world scale and in the Ulich tradition, or relating to smaller entities. However, Fritz Ringer's historical work on education in Europe already mentioned, and Michalina Vaughan and Margaret Archer's historical comparison of early nineteenth century education in France and England, as well as the massive historical content in Margaret Archer's work on social systems and education - to cite but three examples - demonstrate that the tradition is by no means dead. Indeed, the indispensability of the historical dimension is particularly insisted upon by Soviet comparativists such as Professor Malkova.

The 'unfinished agenda' for comparativists is thus practically limitless, and constantly expanding. Apart from the regional reports - analyzed separately - other sources, however, mention in particular more recent developments such as ethnographical studies of pedagogy, intra-national variations in the provision of education, sexual differences in education, ethnicity, the role of international agencies, exchanges and student placements, financing expedients such as voucher systems, and a closer examination as to whether increasing educational provision is linked to political *unrest* rather than economic growth. There is increasing concern that studies should be policy-oriented - writers in the German Democratic Republic, for example, explicitly state that, as well as dealing with the teaching and upbringing of the young, research should above all treat basic policy questions.

The study of the content of schooling has not been so intense as might have been expected, due perhaps to the expense involved in such research and the various practical difficulties. The joint authors of the Asia and Pacific regional report both state that literature- or library-based studies have often to serve as a surrogate for on-the-spot investigation. Such 'paper' studies can obviously be of great use when they are historical, but critics argue they may tend to be over-descriptive and analytical, providing little opportunity for the generation of theory or too fragile a basis for policymaking. This may be particularly true of research into curriculum content, including the processes of schooling. Yet the utility of in-depth comparisons founded on both documents and empirical methods for a diversity of subjects that might range from the teaching of languages to the inculcation of moral and civic values is self-evident. In North America the lack of interest in recent years in such studies has been apparent, although there are signs that this is now changing. In Europe, in any case, this interest in the pedagogical aspect of comparative studies has always been present. Keith Simkin, an Australian, has perceptively summarized the position:

> 'European comparative education is still firmly focused on philosophy, pedagogy and system organization and has resisted the positivist methodology and structural-functional bias that has dominated North America.'

It is therefore not surprising that the few large-scale international studies, to which we must now turn, that have been attempted have nearly all originated in Europe, as the following examples will demonstrate.

Perhaps the most important study is the ongoing International Educational Achievement Study (IEA), which started in Sweden, and with which are associated Torsten Husén, a Swede, and Neville Postlethwaite, an Englishman. Its origins go back to a UNESCO (Hamburg) pilot study of 1959-61 that compared mathematical achievement in a dozen countries in early secondary education. It was followed in swift succession by a series of major studies in the early 1970s of comparative achievement in mathematics (at other stages of secondary education), science, reading, literature, French, English as a foreign language and civics. Up to nineteen countries, including four developing countries, participated in these studies, which tested attainment at various levels. A second round of subject-based studies in mathematics and science, new studies of the classroom environment, attainment in written composition, the transition from school to work, and pre-primary schooling, involving up to thirty-eight countries, has already been embarked upon or is envisaged over the next few years. Almost a half a million pupils world-wide will have been tested. The enterprise, which between

1967-76 alone generated eleven substantial volumes of reports, has been carried out with the cooperation of many comparative educationists with other specialists.

Although the IEA disclaims any intention of running an international 'horse-race', there is no doubt that a number of ministries of education have been interested in its findings. In 1977 in Rome, Signor Malfatti, the then Italian minister of education, spoke of the 'electric shock' of the results, although these have sometimes been distorted by the media. Commenting on the findings of the mathematics study, the Swedish press ran headlines such as 'Sweden at the level of developing countries'. What is primarily of interest here, however, is the fact that the IEA is the first genuinely worldwide comparative study where an impact on policy is clearly demonstrable. Thus it is claimed that the virtual abandonment of 'new' mathematics in the United States was one outcome. Similar findings brought decision-makers up with a jolt: for example, pupils in selective schools did not perform better overall by the end of their course than did those in a comprehensive system; whereas levels of attainment in industrial countries are roughly comparable, levels in developing countries fall short of these standards; a longer period of schooling does not necessarily go with higher achievement. The complete list of applicable findings is long. If countries were at first interested because they wished to compare the outcomes of their school system with those achieved elsewhere, it is now the 'fine print' - the detailed conclusions - that attracts attention.

Comparative educationists everywhere took note of the IEA Study. But an attack upon its methodology was not long in coming. It centred round the fact that the approach was psychometric and over-quantitative. A quantitative positivist methodology not only favoured the status quo but also, according to dependency theorists, smacked of neo-colonialism. We were reminded that Kandel, speaking of educational measurement procedures, had declared that whilst they could measure outcomes, they could not identify goals and causes. However, an attempt is being made to meet such criticisms in the new studies being undertaken in the 1980s. The great merit of the enterprise nevertheless remains: almost for the first time in the comparative field it attempted to *measure*, in an era when comparative qualitative evaluations were the rule.

Four other less ambitious, international or supra-national studies that are practice-oriented, deserve brief mention here. One was privately sponsored, three were under the aegis of three regional official bodies. All deal with the qualification awarded at the end of secondary education. The first study, privately initiated, and termed the International Baccalaureate, is among the most significant attempts at practical international educational cooperation in recent years. Its aim was to create a secondary school leaving qualification based upon an international curriculum. In it many comparativists, particularly in Western Europe, were involved either as curriculum developers or examiners. Today some 250 international schools and institutions all over the globe, as well as State institutions in some countries follow a common two-year terminal course leading to this entrance qualification to higher education, which most countries will accept in lieu of their own entrance qualification. By 1983 some 29,000 students of 130 different nationalities had followed the programme and those successful had entered 700 universities in fifty-one different countries.

The bases for the curricula that were followed emerged as a result of action research. The aim was to 'internationalize' the course, and use it as a modest implement to promote international understanding. The new programmes were negotiated after meetings in which comparative educationists, teachers from international schools, and State school inspectors and officials drawn from many nations all participated. After extensive trials in pilot schools the programmes and qualification now seem firmly established. The result of such operational research was inevitably a compromise, but it represents at least a common denominator against ethnocentricity.

Among official action-oriented projects with a comparative dimension must be mentioned the European Baccalaureate. This is a programme leading to a leaving qualification that is taken in the dozen or so schools of the European Economic Community (EEC), which are designed for the children of EEC officials scattered over Western Europe, although other, local children are also admitted to them. This is another example of curriculum cooperation, this time between twelve member states, although, so far as is known, few comparative educationists were involved in the elaboration of programmes.

Another, more fact-finding venture was conducted under the auspices of the Council of Europe, which comprises twenty-one Western nations. The Oxford/Council of Europe Study for the Evaluation of the Curriculum and Examinations (OCESCE Study) set out, *inter alia*, to compare in detail the content of the syllabuses of academic secondary leaving examinations in member states to see how far harmonization was possible. The concept of a European secondary leaving examination had already been much discussed in the 1950s, and the German comparativist, Wilhelm Flitner, had written an appraisal of possibilities for the Council of Europe. As a result of the

OCESCE Study 11 qualitative monographs on various curriculum subjects were published. The comparativists involved were mainly British, but presented the results of their enquiries, which included a little actual classroom observation, to international meetings of education officials. What was demonstrated was the somewhat negative result that there was not a great overlap between programmes.

Another interesting official study is that carried out by Dr Angel Oliveros Alonso (the author of the regional chapter on Latin America) under the auspices of the Oficina de Educación Iberoamericana. Primary (1975) and secondary (1981) programmes were evaluated in Spain and Latin American countries. The results provide a description and analysis of overall patterns and relevant factors. In secondary education one of the purposes has been to collect together documents useful for the eventual creation of a secondary leaving examination common to all the countries concerned, a suggestion that was mooted at the fourth Iberoamerican Educational Congress held in Madrid in 1979.

Large-scale studies of higher education, in contrast to the preceding studies, which concern school, have been few. Such investigations as have been undertaken tend to point up salient facts, such as the increasing control of universities and other institutions by central government, and the use of higher education for economic ends. The rise (and decline) of 'participation' in the administration of universities, the growth of new institutions to meet fresh industrial and commercial needs, and similar topics have also been charted. Clearly the field here is still wide open for comparative educationists.

This section has selected examples of the content of comparative studies, both theoretically- and practically-oriented, from the field. It has also provided a number of lists of subjects that might legitimately be included within that field. No one would claim that what has been cited is exhaustive. What appears to emerge, when this section is compared to that devoted to theories, is the wide gulf that divides the two. Some comparativists would argue that this 'credibility gap' is one that has to be bridged. If one aim of comparative education is to influence policies then it has to be demonstrated that practitioners in the field have available the tools to investigate what has constituted policy in the past, to collect data that is relevant for the decision-makers of the present and, some would say, to be able to predict the outcomes of policy. It would seem that there is still a long road to travel.

Research themes

From the regional reports the variety of research being undertaken in all parts of the world is apparent. More than 160 topics, themes, area studies and other kinds of investigation are mentioned. Taking into account the two categories of research projects, both those conducted by groups and those by individuals (which predominate), as well as the subjects treated at congresses, workshops and seminars, all occasions for presenting the results of research, the various topics and themes from which research results have emerged can be grouped under no less than nineteen different headings. Such a classification, however must be arbitrary, as considerable overlap exists between each group. Whilst it is clearly impossible to treat each category in detail (if only because essential data is missing), some outline of the content of this wide spectrum of research is essential in order to assess the present-day ramifications of comparative studies. The largest category naturally concerns the various *levels* of education. Interestingly, only Africa and Latin America specifically mention *pre-school* education, although it is known that, with the renewed insistence on the benefits accruing later from nursery school attendance and the increasing proportion of working mothers in the labour force, this has also been a current theme in Western Europe. Studies of *primary* education and education for *basic needs* seem to predominate in Latin America and Africa, for obvious reasons - Kenya, for example, has looked at the situation in Tanzania. Practically every region has produced studies on *secondary general and vocational* education: China has looked generally at secondary structures; the socialist countries have been concerned with the provision of 'all-round' education, and everywhere there has been a resurgence of interest in the relevance of vocational education to work.

It would seem to be the Japanese that have most concentrated on research into *higher education*: structures, selection procedures, student aid programmes and 'internationalization' have all been investigated. China has also examined college entrance, and Korea the prospects for higher education reform. In general, as might be expected, the developing countries have tended to concentrate on the lower levels of education, whereas the industrialized countries have looked more at the higher levels.

Closely linked with, and indeed inseparable from, the study of levels of education, has been research on *reforms and innovation*, with their evaluation being particularly stressed in North America. Korea has looked at world trends in reform. Japan has considered the reform process in the light of tradition, a problem too often ignored by over-zealous reformers, as experience in Africa at Western hands also demonstrates. The latter continent, doubtless as part of its ideal of Africanization, has devoted its energies to the field of curriculum development. Japan has also considered such minor - but often important - topics as corporal punishment and school violence, an alarming phenomenon of the 1980s in many parts of the industrialized world. Research on schooling and *school processes* is becoming more widespread. Thus Poland has looked at problems of pedagogical differentiation. It has also carried out analyses of textbooks used in capitalist countries. In the United States ethnographic studies of other school systems are under way, and what might be termed 'school cultures' have been compared, as well as the degree and effectiveness of schooling. Latin America has studied comparatively the factors that determine educational achievement - not all, of course, directly school-related. Africa has examined functional education in relation to discipline, but curiously, little mention is made of research into individual school subjects, although art has been investigated comparatively. The vexed question of language has continued to preoccupy African comparativists, where the debate on whether, and for how long, primary education should be given in the vernacular continues unabated. (Incidentally, for at least a generation UNESCO has recommended that initially all schooling should be in the mother tongue). It is also one that has been examined by comparativists in the socialist countries in relation to the developing countries.

Indeed, it may well be that African nations, confronted with a Babel of tongues, could learn from the solutions adopted, for example, in the Soviet Union, where Russian and the indigenous languages flourish side by side.

Evaluation techniques, psychometrics and psychology do not appear to have greatly attracted the attention of comparativists, although within the socialist countries learning processes have been examined, in which some evaluation of 'school experiments' has been undertaken. In Africa there is interest in assessment procedures generally, and child psychology theories have been compared. Such a relative dearth of research into what underpins the processes of instruction might indeed merit more attention, although few comparativists have psychological qualifications.

It is on the underdeveloped countries, and particularly in the African and Latin American regions, that the focus of research on *adult, non-formal and rural* education has been centred. North American studies of Latin America appear to be particularly numerous. The impetus that was given to comparative adult education in the early 1970s seems, however, to have temporarily slackened, although in Western Europe some interest has been restimulated by the need for industrialized countries to update and retain its adult work force in the light of the advance of technology, and particularly information technology.

Indeed, the dominant feature of education in the early 1980s has been the linking of it to *technology and working life*. Research carried out in vocational education has already been touched upon. In Eastern Europe the impact upon schooling of scientific and technological progress, as also the aspiration to improve the quality of polytechnical education, have sparked off a number of comparisons between socialist countries. Some of these have focused on the construction of new curricula and the introduction of new subjects in this connection. Australia has studied the problem in China, which itself has been concerned with the right 'mix' of education and work. In Latin America education for employment has also been investigated comparatively. Likewise the *application of technology to education* has been the subject of comparisons, ranging from (in Western Europe) computer-assisted learning, to learning by television and radio in Latin America and Africa.

Thus far the research described has been directly related to education, in a sense, 'intra-educational'. Such a catalogue would not be complete without *teacher education*. It is a question that has greatly preoccupied at least three regions: Africa, Asia, and Latin America.

At one degree removed from schooling proper are themes such as *statistics and abstracting, planning and administration*, and *economic and financial* matters. Thus in Latin America comparative studies have not only contributed to, but have been greatly aided by, the building up of a comprehensive statistical network and the creation of abstracting of information services. Such valuable tools for the comparativist might well be supplemented by work that has gone on in Poland in the field of definitions. It is perhaps in North America that the politics and institutional context of educational planning have been most researched, whilst South Korea has examined the problems of long-term planning. In Latin America the twin themes of management and decentralization have given rise to studies. Educational planning is considered as a component of *total* planning, research as particularly relevant to economic growth. Economic and financial comparisons are also mentioned in connection with West Africa and Australasia.

Reflecting the strong social sciences orientation of comparative studies since about 1970, research that may be subsumed under the headings of education and *modernization* and education and *society* has been well to the fore. In Africa the congruence of educational systems and society, and its relationship to 'social dynamics', have been examined. On a more practical plane, how education relates to agriculture and a rural economy has been investigated. On a greater level of abstraction, North America has produced studies linking societal, political and educational institutions, and also on the role played by education in effecting modernity and social change. India has also reviewed education in the light of development, equality and social change. How far educational policy and thought impacts upon social policy has been a related topic.

It would appear that in Asia and Australasia research in *international* education has been most carried on. India's interest in education and a new international order is well-known. Japan, as previously mentioned, has investigated the 'internationalization' of education, seeking international consensus and understanding. Australia has considered the reverse of the medal: international crises - perhaps the modest part that education may play in eliminating them? - and peace studies. On a more immediate note, Japan has undertaken a review of the role of educational exchanges, and cooperation within Asia.

Mirroring even more profound interests, there have been studies of *religious and moral* education, and the development of *personality*. Africa refers to Koranic education, which is widespread in many countries of that continent. Japan displays continuing interest in the inculcation of moral principles and practice. In the socialist countries personality development has been studied in relation to schooling.

Educational *thought and culture* have been researched in a variety of ways. Thus in Ghana a notable comparison has been made between the Meiji era in Japan and Ghanaian nationalism. Korea has examined ideal human 'images' in East and West. China has studied the thought of early Soviet educators. Bulgaria has undertaken an analysis of 'bourgeois' educational thought. This is clearly a field of some significance that is as yet relatively unexplored, bridging, as it does, education, intellectual history and the history of ideas.

What might loosely be termed *philosophical* ideas have also been a subject of study. The socialist countries report research in an attempt to discover ultimate general laws governing educational development, and the particular laws governing such development in emergent states (Cuba). Since the debate on ultimate 'laws' allegedly discoverable through comparative studies has also been a perennial preoccupation of one school of Western comparativists, such research assumes a high profile.

Certain *overarching themes*, which defy even the approximate classification used here, can be identified. Thus the socialist countries have studied the promotion of talent, whereas Australia has looked at quality and inequality, where there are patent contradictions to be resolved. Equality and parity of educational provision in relation to several dichotomies - urban/rural, boys/girls and vocational/general education - have been of general concern in Eastern Europe, as has also how to implement fully a putative policy of 11-13 years of free education for all. If North America has examined comparatively the role of the international agencies, Australia has studied generally the impact that development aid makes upon education. One topical subject that has arisen in North America is the problems that arise regarding the production, dissemination and use of knowledge itself.

A question also of great topicality has been the position of *women and girls* in education - what is often referred to, somewhat ambiguously as 'gender studies'. This is usually taken to mean the unequal schooling received by females. Such studies have proliferated, particularly in North America, in the last few years. In Australia, for example, Papua New Guinea, and in particular Bali, have been examined in this context.

A number of other *special problems* have been identified as suitable for comparative research. In Africa it has been the question of wastage and school drop-out. In Japan such diverse questions as the relationship of education to national identity, sex education, anti-drug instruction, educational legal cases, and 'cultural polarity' have all been researched. A highly important problem has been the question of multicultural and ethnic education, researches in which are particularly reported from Western Europe, Japan, Australasia and Zimbabwe. There can be no doubt that in an age of transmigration of peoples on a scale not seen since the early medieval period this is a key topic to which the comparativist has an important contribution to make.

Certain *area-specific* subjects of research must also be noted. General or policy studies on South-East Asia as a whole are reported by Japan, Vietnam, India and Australasia. Cuba has also sought an overview of education in the Caribbean and Latin America. The United States, as one of the principal 'host' nations for education, as well as one which sends a large number of its own students abroad, has looked at the part played by foreign study. Japan has examined the problems experienced by Japanese youngsters returning home after education abroad.

Few *area studies* are mentioned in the regional reports, but this may be because they are considered too routine to be singled out for particular attention. From other sources we know that they are very common. Ghana and Australia refer to them, without specifying the foreign countries involved; Hungary alludes to studies it has made of education in Austria and Italy. *Research* itself has been the subject of investigation. For example, reviews of it have been made in Africa. There can be no doubt that such 'state of the art' reports, if they are analytical and critical, serve a useful purpose. Research, last but not least, is mentioned relating to *comparative studies* themselves. China and Australia have looked at the teaching of comparative education in colleges and universities. Australia has also considered the theories that underpin the field. Japan, on the other hand, records that, although some work has been done on theory-building and use, it has not been a major preoccupation of researchers, who have refrained from utilizing much theory in their work. It is perhaps noteworthy that countries as diverse as Nigeria, South Korea and Bulgaria, which are not habitual participants in the ongoing debate over the nature, theories and methods of the field, have also considered the topic.

The above review, whilst trying to encapsulate the essence of the various regional reports, has also essayed a tentative classification. The salient fact that emerges is the wide-ranging field of research. Is it possible to complete the matrix by examining each region or sub-region to see what other areas of the world it concentrates on? The regional reports give some indications, which are set out below:

Africa: On Africa itself, but with some reference to the United States and a few other countries.

Japan: Mainly on the industrialized nations, and in particular on the Federal Republic of Germany and the German Democratic Republic, France, the United Kingdom, USA and USSR. The report specifically mentions that little attention is paid to the rest of Asia, parts of Europe other than those mentioned, Latin America, the Middle East, Canada and Africa.

Australasia: Asia, particularly Papua New Guinea and Fiji; the United Kingdom and USA.

Latin America: On the countries of Latin America.

North America: Latin America, parts of Africa, India and Nigeria: little interest in Europe.

Eastern Europe: the socialist countries themselves; developing countries, particularly the socialist ones; the Federal Republic of Germany and the German Democratic Republic; capitalist countries, particularly the USA.

Research trends

It is difficult to distinguish any emerging trends in comparative research. Perhaps two general tendencies are discernible. The one, most characterized by North America, is concerned with themes that are in keeping with world-analysis theory, attempting at least to play down the nation-state as the unit of comparison. Such a school might be described as perhaps more academic, less oriented to *Praxis*. The other, more typical of the socialist countries and the Third World generally, retains the nation-state as the object of analysis, but seeks out what certain countries, possibly sharing the same *Weltanschauung*, have in common. Here studies need not be narrowly scholarly - although they often are - but are more meliorist, more deliberately aimed at the improvement of practice. Admittedly some countries, such as Japan, or even Western Europe as a whole, fit uneasily into such a rough classification.

As already noted, the regional reports, insofar as they deal with research, do not appear over-concerned with 'theories' and 'approaches'. Indeed Japan, it would appear, is notable for its methodological eclecticism and general atheoretical stance. The report on Japan cites a survey (not otherwise identified) which shows that the American *Comparative education review*, out of 287 papers it had published, published 110 related to theory, whereas the *Japanese Comparative Education Society bulletins* published only 11 (out of 88) relating to theory. To some extent the general tolerance of a non-theoretical basis - with the notable exception of North America - may be conditioned by the fact that the financers of comparative research, whether national or international, are forced to adopt a pragmatic, very down-to-earth approach. The bodies to which they are responsible may well put pressure on them to achieve short-term results. One of the great merits of the IEA studies, by contrast, is that they were able to combine theory and practice in a long-term perspective.

Another trend has been the move away from the historical method, although this has certainly not occurred everywhere. This lack of historicism may reflect the fundamental rift between many historians and social scientists. Whereas the former regard their work as dealing largely with causality and explanation, and, at the margin, to have premonitory value, the latter may go further, claiming to be not only diagnostic but also prognostic and predictive. To this degree the arguments between comparative educationists reflect divergences in the wider world of scholarship.

A compromise may, however, be beginning to emerge, in the form of a revival of what C. Arnold Anderson long ago termed the 'interdisciplinary' approach. Team research, cooperative investigations, particularly when focused on field work, are becoming more frequent. Specialists from all disciplines, including pedagogy proper, are obliged then to compose their theoretical differences. What are sometimes called 'literature' or 'library' researches - 'views from the study' - will become more the concern of individuals, and here theory can be indulged more easily.

It may be significant that studies relating to educational thought or philosophy, which are more characteristic of the pre-1960s school of comparativists, are now enjoying a slightly higher profile, particularly in the Far East.

Disappointingly, there is little in the summaries of research to indicate which findings, particularly in academically-based research, have had a direct impact upon the policymakers, although this is one of the directions in which comparative education has tried to move. But this lack of a demonstrable link between research and policy, it has been argued, characterizes the whole of educational studies. The most that can be said is that the outcomes of comparative research often tend to legitimate the proposals of the decision-makers. They act, as the report on Latin America indicates, as a stimulus and spur to governments. And the oblique effect is nevertheless perceptible. There can be no doubt, for example, that the wave of 'comprehensivization' of secondary education that swept over Western Europe, or similarly the 'polytechnization' that occurred in the socialist countries at the same period, owed much to studies of schooling in the United States and Sweden in the one case, and to the Soviet Union in the other. Likewise the advances made in non-formal education in Africa, or the struggle for literacy in South America, are indebted to comparisons, if only through the exchange of information and methods, between the groups of countries concerned, often through the intermediary of such organisms as UNESCO and IBE. Perhaps this indirect 'spin-off' from research in relation to policymaking is as much as the comparative educationist can hope for.

A further, more 'technical' trend must also be mentioned. This is the reinstatement of the value of qualitative analysis of data. The 'little renaissance' of comparative education in the late 1960s coincided with the belief in the social sciences, almost held as an article of faith, that everything was 'measurable'. Quantification was the order of the day. Now, without entirely abandoning quantification, which would be a retrograde step, there is a realization that no matter how many 'variables' are 'manipulated', thousands more variables, perhaps equally relevant, cannot be included in a study, and in any case inter-country variables are sometimes nominal rather than real. Qualitative analysis must always accompany the quantitative approach.

Trends, therefore, are uncertain. New lines of research are emerging as education is changing to accommodate the next century. We may be on the verge of another 'great leap forward' in comparative studies, such as was seen at the end of the 1960s, but this time without the frustration of an economic crisis that inhibited its full flowering.

Infrastructures

From the regional reports and the very detailed chapter on infrastructures a few general points emerge. Any field of study requires centres where it may be taught and researched, and personnel to man those centres. This is particularly true for comparative education, which is by definition a global field, and therefore must also possess a sound communications network. It may be seriously questioned, from a study of the regional surveys, whether the infrastructure is adequate in these respects.

At the international level, however, comparative education is well served. This is largely because of an historical accident: the International Bureau of Education existed before UNESCO and its hand was considerably strengthened when it was taken over by the larger international organization. Today it forms the indispensable hub of an information network, as well as a prime initiator of comparative studies. Moreover, it links the official world with the academic world in a unique fashion. At the national level, however, the position is by no means so clear-cut, as a few examples will demonstrate.

The locus of comparative education

In North America, Japan, Asia and the Pacific the physical basis of comparative studies has been, and continues mainly to be the universities and other institutions of higher education. This is not necessarily true for the socialist countries, where specialized institutes working in collaboration with the national academies of pedagogical sciences, or within such bodies, as in the Soviet Union and GDR, have played perhaps the main role. Nor is it entirely true for Western Europe. Thus in the Federal Republic of Germany institutions such as the Max Planck Institute in West Berlin or the International Institute for Educational Research in Frankfurt, although closely linked to neighbouring universities, are nominally autonomous. However, university centres such as Hamburg, Bochum, Marburg, Heidelberg, and Giessen, have also flourished over the last decade. In Britain, where many years ago such pioneers of comparative studies as Arnold and Sadler worked for the national education authority, it is the universities that are now predominant.

France presents an interesting case. Despite Durkheim, in whose debt all comparative educationists are in respect of method, universities up to recently have played a minor role. This may be because departments of educational sciences in universities were only established after 1968, and have been threatened with extinction more than once. Except for some of the Paris universities - in particular Paris V (René Descartes), Caen and Grenoble - comparative studies are not represented in universities in strength. On the other hand there are a large number of official organizations that have either concentrated on comparative studies, or who regard the study of educational developments overseas as an important part of their work. The prominent role of the CIEP at Sevres, which many of the world's comparative educationists have visited at least once, deserves particular notice. It was from there that the French comparative education society, AFEC, was launched in the late 1960s. The Institut National de la Recherche Pedagogique (INRP), the national educational research organization, has a comparative education section. The overall situation has meant that methods and theory have been much less debated. The stress has been above all on the practical, with the aim of solving real life problems, particularly in the Third World. The location on French soil of UNESCO, IIEP, and a number of supra-national organizations such as OECD and the research institute of the European Cultural Foundation, has of course also stimulated such studies.

In Africa, the Arab states, and Latin America links with the academic world are not so strong as elsewhere, although they are developing rapidly. Half a dozen countries in South America, for example, have established chairs of comparative education in their universities. On the other hand official organizations, such as in the Arab world, have continued to represent the major strength in comparative studies. It would appear, from some of the regional reports, that the way forward is for the academic and the official worlds at the national level to seek closer cooperation.

Although the role of official national organizations in comparative studies is crucial, it would be a pity if this meant that higher education institutions - and many other establishments not of university rank are becoming increasingly interested - lacked the means to maintain their interest. If practice is to advance, then methods and theories also must continue to be discussed, and the appropriate forum for this may well be higher education.

Teaching, research and training institutions

Although teaching and training in comparative studies are largely carried out in institutions of higher education, principally at university level, some independent agencies concerned with development aid also accept trainees for practical work in the field. Of 37 countries specifically cited in the regional reports, the overwhelming majority also carry out research and research training in universities. As regards teaching, it is notable that in some African countries introductory courses in comparative education are given to undergraduates. In Latin America one source reports that most teacher training institutions offer courses in comparative education. In the industrialized countries both these practices have become much rarer. Japan reports what is more usual in them: graduate rather than undergraduate programmes are offered - indeed doctoral thesis preparation is one of the main means of training potential comparative educationists.

In recent years, however, the numbers following comparative education courses have declined. The low priority given to them by the authorities is partly responsible for this fall-off. The report on Australasia draws particular attention to this phenomenon - yet a decade ago Australia looked set to make a spectacular take-off in the field. This contrasts markedly with the exceptional vigour of comparative studies still displayed in Japanese universities. However, practically everywhere in the lean years of the 1970s comparative studies comprised a programme that could conveniently be omitted as being a 'luxury offering' for those that had constituted its main clientele: intending teachers. In any case the decline in their numbers, because of an alleged 'surplus' of teachers, at least in Western Europe and North America, reduced the number of potential takers considerably. In Britain, for example whereas there were some 136,000 future teachers in training in 1972, by 1981 this had dropped to 44,000. Although the in-service training of teachers increased, this brought little growth in the numbers studying comparative education. Moreover, as posts with international and national educational organizations became scarce, a knowledge of international educational developments was less readily marketable.

This decline in clientele affected the realization that the constituency for comparative studies included many that did not style themselves specialists in the field. Not only did it comprise academics working in related fields, but also numerous national official and semi-official educational organizations whose work concerned the international sphere, from student and academic exchange organizations to those dealing with voluntary service overseas or the assessment of foreign qualifications for further training, education or employment. Some comparative educationists acted as consultants for such bodies. The crisis - for it was nothing less - also caused many comparative specialists to consider how, like their colleagues in other areas of educational studies, they might make a contribution to applied studies for the improvement of education. Thus fashionable themes such as sexual differentiation, multiculturalism and classroom practices began to be tackled. Philip Altbach (CER 27:2, June 1983, Chicago, p.165) has even spoken of the 'outreach' of comparative educationists. It is a term with missionary overtones, but none the less apt.

Specialist teachers of comparative education - always thin on the ground - thus declined in numbers. Moreover, there was less interchange between countries. The Australasia report, however, does refer to the fact that teachers of comparative courses are not usually native-born Australians. This, of course, is nothing new. Kandel, an immigrant to America, taught for a while in Britain; Hans left Czarist Russia for England in 1917; Lauwerys was born in Belgium. The late (and much-loved) George Bereday was even successively Polish, British and American by nationality. Indeed, this cosmopolitan feature has always been a source of enrichment for comparative education.

The communications network

Cosmopolitanism is above all a matter of ability to *communicate*. This has not been easy in a period when travel facilities have been greatly curtailed. An IBE questionnaire addressed to African academic institutions revealed a very serious position. Not only are the possibilities of convening meetings very slight, but, even worse, communication by means of publication was very difficult. Several institutions reported that many typescripts were seeking publishers in vain. Indeed the question of dissemination is a vicious circle: publishers in First World countries are reluctant to accept manuscripts from Third World scholars who are not sufficiently known to them. But the would-be authors continue to be 'unknown' precisely because they have not achieved publication. It is true that comparativists from the industrialized countries have likewise found the situation more difficult than ever before. Perhaps group authorship might prove to be a solution, as a temporary expedient. Altbach and Kelly (*Education and colonialism*, 1978), speaking of the distribution of knowledge in the Third World, have gone so far as to call the problem of publication one of neo-colonialism, a latter-day manifestation of 'cultural imperialism'.

In one respect, however, the circulation of information has gone from strength to strength. In the matter of the publication of statistics UNESCO has served the comparative educationist well. Continuing a tradition that goes back to its foundation in 1925, IBE has been active in the provision of specialist bibliographies upon topical themes and of regular appraisals of current developments. Moreover, UNESCO has produced a valuable series of publications in a variety of areas, ranging from the international comparability of qualifications to the education of teachers. Other UNESCO agencies such as IIEEP (Paris) and the UNESCO Institute for Education (Hamburg) have in recent years supplied invaluable literature dealing respectively with educational planning and lifelong education. Regional organizations of all kinds, such as the comparatively recently established UNESCO Institute for Higher Education (Bucharest), and UNESCO's regional offices have likewise been a catalyst for the flow of information. Whereas even as late as 1970 there was a general dearth of printed information available to the comparative educationist in a language he was able to read, as regards official publications the problem today is almost one of embarrassment of choice.

Language itself of course remains a formidable hindrance to communication. Thus contacts in Africa between 'anglophone' and 'francophone' comparativists, although improving, are still inhibited by language difficulties. In his regional report Professor Kobayashi refers to the huge efforts that have had to be expended by Japanese scholars in making translations of Western books. One suspects, moreover, that the traffic is almost one-way. If English-speaking comparativists have interested themselves so little in continental Europe one may surmise that it is because of the language hurdle. There is, in fact, only one American journal, *Western European education*, that specializes in translations of important documents from its chosen area, although the Council of Europe, in its *News bulletin*, does reproduce documents in English and French emanating from all its member countries. Moreover, there can be no guarantee that in the next millennium English and French, as the *linguae francae* of the industrialized world, will retain their present virtual monopoly: Chinese, Russian and Spanish are obvious challengers to their hegemony. Some journals, such as those published in Japan - but only one of the three main internationally known journals - publish abstracts of papers in two or three languages alongside the original; in Eastern Europe, *Vergleichende Pädagogik* commendably does this in Russian, English and French. The practice is surely worthy of imitation. For comparative studies to thrive the linguistic barrier remains the greatest to be overcome.

Bibliography

Altbach P., Kelly G., *Education and colonialism*, New York, London, 1978.

Altbach P., Arnove R., Kelly G. (eds.) *Comparative education*, New York, London, 1982.

Anderson C. A., 'Methodology of comparative education', *International review of education*, Hamburg, 7:1, 1961.

Andrewski S., *Elements of comparative sociology*, London, 1965.

Arbeitstelle für Auslandspädagogik, Akademie der pädagogischen Wissenschaften der DDR, *Beitrage zur schulpolitik und pädagogik des auslands*, 1982, Heft 1: *Bildungsysteme kapitalistischer länder Europas in den achtzigen jahren*, (East) Berlin, 1982.

Bennett C., Kidd J. R., Kulich J. (eds.), *Comparative studies in adult education: an anthology*, Syracuse, N.Y., 1975.

Carnoy M., *Education as cultural imperialism*, New York, 1974. *Comparative education review*, (USA) Special number on the 'state of the art' of comparative education, No. 21:3/4, June/October 1977.

Gerth I., 'Hat die vergleichende pädagogik als teildisziplin der pädagogischer wissenschaft eine berechtigung, oder gibt es nur interdisziplinäre forschung zur schulpolitik und pädagogik im ausland?' *Vergleichende pädagogik*, 3:1973 (East) Berlin.

Glowka D., 'Konvergenztheorie und vergleichende bildungsforschung', *Bildung und erziehung*, 24: 6, November-December 1971, Bonn.

Grubb W. N., 'The convergence of educational systems and the role of vocationalism', *Comparative education review*, (USA) 29:4, November 1985.

Habermas J., *Legitimation crisis*, Boston, Mass., 1975.

Halls W. D., 'Towards a European education system?' *Comparative education*, (Oxford), 10:3, October 1974.

Halls W. D., 'Kultur und erziehung: der kulturalistische ansatz in vergleichenden studien,' *Bildung und erziehung* 24:6, November-December 1971, Bonn.

Herzig T., Kling W., Mahr H., 'Zur marxistich-leninistichen Theorie und methodologie vergleichend-pädagogischer untersuchungen aus weltanschaulich-philosophischer sicht', *Vergleichende pädagogik*, (East) Berlin, 4:1973.

Holmes B., *Comparative education: some considerations of method*, London, 1981.

Kienitz W., 'Fortschritte des bildungswesens in der etappe des entwickelten sozialismus - I', *Vergleichende pädagogik*, (East) Berlin, 2:1984; - II, ibid., 3:1984.

King E. J., *Comparative studies and educational decision*, London, 1968.

Kobayashi T., 'Internationalisation of Japanese education', *Comparative education* (Oxford), 22:1, 1986 (Special issue on education in Japan).

Kurze H., Mantzke U., 'Zu neuen anforderungen an die marxistisch-leninistische vergleichende pädagogik unter dem aspekt der entwicklung der sozialistischen staatengemeinschaft', *Vergleichende pädagogik*, (East) Berlin, 4:1973.

Lé Thành Khôi, 'Towards a general theory of education', *Comparative education review* (USA), 30:1, February 1986.

Malkova Z. A., *School and pedagogy abroad*, Moscow, 1983.

Marklund S., *The IEA Project: an unfinished audit*, Stockholm, 1983.

Milec A., 'Die vergleichende pädagogik im system der pädagogischen wissenschaften -ein tschechoslowakischer standpunkt', *Vergleichende pädagogik*, (East) Berlin, 10:2, 1974.

Moehlmann A. H., *Comparative education systems*, New York, 1963.

National Board of Education, Utbildningsdepartmentet, *Samverkanmitwirkung*, Stockholm, 1973.

Nestvogel R., 'Education and society in Algeria: Disparities between intentions and achievements' in: Mitter W., Swift J. (eds,) *Education and the diversity of cultures*, Cologne, Vienna, 1985.

Niessen M., Peschar J., *Comparative research on education, overview, strategy and applications in Eastern and Western Europe*, Pergamon Press, Oxford, and Akademiai Kiado, Budapest, 1982.

Noah H. J., *The use and abuse of comparative education*, inaugural lecture, November 1, 1983, Teachers College, Colombia, New York, 1983.

Noah H. J., 'Comparative education: methods', in: *International encyclopaedia of education*, ed. by T. N. Postlethwaite, Oxford, 1984.

Noah H. J., Eckstein M. A., *Towards a science of comparative education*, London, 1969.

Peterson, A. D. C., *Schools across frontiers*, New York, 1986.

Poggeler F., 'Erziehungswissenschaft als vergleichende erziehungswissenschaft', in: U. Baumann (ed.), *Vergleichende erziehungswissenschaft*, Wiesbaden, 1981.

Postlethwaite, T. N., 'Comparative education research: can it be improved?', Keynote address to EVO Conference, October 4, 1985, Ede (Netherlands), 1985.

Postlethwaite T., Lewy A., *Annotated bibliography of IEA publications (1962-1968)*, IEA, University of Stockholm, Stockholm, 1979.

Psacharapoulos G., Woodhall M., *Education for development. an analysis of investment choices*, Oxford, 1985.

Ringer F., *Education and society in modern europe*, Bloomington, Indiana, 1979.

Röhrs H., 'Aufgaben und methoden der vergleichenden erziehungswissenschaft' in: Rohrs H. (ed.), *Schule und bildung im internationalen gesprach*, Frankfurt, 1966.

Spaulding S., Singleton J., Watson P., 'The context of international development education', *Review of educational research*, 36:3 (1971), Washington D.C.

Stenhouse A., 'Case study in comparative education: particularity and generalization', *Comparative education* (Oxford), 15:1, 1979.

Thomas M., *Comparing theories of child development*, Belmont, Cal., 1979.

Vaughan M., Archer M. S., *Social conflict and educational change in England and France, 1789-1848*, Cambridge, 1971.

PART II

Comparative education around the world

Western Europe

Brian Holmes

Nineteenth-century scholar-administrators, entrusted with the task of guiding policy in order to build up new national education systems, began a modern tradition of studying schools outside their own country, thus reviving a practice that goes back in Western Europe at least to Erasmus, and even to Plato himself. Initially the risks intrinsic in such cross-national borrowings were not sufficiently perceived. Some, however, of the new breed of 'comparative educationists' did recognize the fact that each national system possessed an ethos, or 'living spirit', that might militate against its adoption elsewhere.

Nevertheless a precedent was established (which has recently come under critical examination) that made *national* systems the units of comparison. One important outcome of this was the scrutiny of policy by comparativists through a study of national educational legislation. Furthermore, it was recognized that often policy problems are common to many national governments - and today this is true in both industrialized and Third World societies.

Since education as a field of study hardly existed in universities, initially comparative studies flourished outside academic institutions. Thus they were undertaken by men such as Cousin, a philosopher turned politician and Arnold, a poet and literary critic (although he was also a school inspector), to cite but two examples. Such observers were uniquely placed to influence, through their comparisons, the development of their respective education systems.

Moreover, they worked in a climate of opinion that was increasingly scientific. It was realized early on that, following the earlier taxonomical approach in other fields by Buffon and Montesquieu, the data that were collected regarding foreign education systems could be systematically classified. Even today, this principle of classification remains an important feature of the comparativists' work. Indeed, the detailed collection and arrangement of data regarding foreign education systems, in particular, can be traced back to Jullien de Paris, who is thus often viewed as the founding father of comparative education.

Another important principle that has been adopted by modern comparativists has been that of causation: events are explicable through their antecedent causes, a viewpoint that derives from historiography no less than science. However, it is important to note that, at a time when new doctrines such as Positivism and Marxism were finding favour, few comparative educationists in Western Europe shared the belief of some social philosophers that the purpose of their enquiry was to discover general laws of development relating to economics, political science and psychology, which could be related to education. Early twentieth century comparativists developed further many of the methodological principles of their predecessors: the induction of educational principles and policies from: the collection and classification of data on foreign educational systems; the study of relevant legislation; the search for an ethos that marked off each national education system; the evaluation of national traditions and social factors. There was a recognition that each system was unique, although features shared in common were indeed held to be comparable. Moreover, at least until 1945, the inductive method was widely accepted.

That method was first challenged by the publication of Karl Popper's *The open society and its enemies*.[1] Even before this, moreover, Einstein's theories, in the scientific field, the rise of logical positivism, applied in the field of social philosophy, and the beginnings (in Germany) of ethnomethodology, had seemed to run counter to classical inductivism. Nonetheless, it was within the earlier framework that the major centres of comparative education took up their research again after the Second World War.

As in the inter-war years, it was in fact European scholars who still predominated. This is not to deny the merits of men such as Sandiford, Monroe[2] and then Kandel[3] himself, who had initiated comparative studies at Teachers College, Columbia. But in Germany academics such as Schneider[4] and Hilker, in England others such as Hans and Lauwerys (neither of whom, incidentally, was born in England), in Switzerland, Rosselló - a Spaniard residing in Geneva - were pre-eminent in the field. By then comparative education had taken firm root in some universities. They were served by two main publications: the *International review of education*, founded by Schneider in Germany, and still published in the Federal Republic of Germany today, under UNESCO auspices; and the *Yearbook of education*,[5] the very influential publication founded by Lord Eustace Percy, a former English education minister, initially for the discussion of education problems within the then British Empire, and based at the London University Institute of Education.

Pioneers though they were, these early comparative scholars were also touched by idealism. They believed that through the study of foreign education systems international understanding might grow. Although hopes had been shattered by the war, even during it a Committee of Allied Ministers of Education had met in London to plan jointly a renaissance of their education systems. Lauwerys, at the London Institute, played no small part in these and other plans to promote educational cooperation after peace was restored. Indeed, he was involved in the creation of UNESCO itself - no small achievement for a comparative educationist. (This first international organization was followed of course by others, such as the Council of Europe, OECD, and the EEC, which have played a part in the development of comparative studies in Western Europe by the promotion of research).

Political developments, indeed, impinged directly upon the work of comparative educationists at the time, as two examples may make plain. In the Federal Republic of Germany scholars such as Merck (UNESCO Institute, Hamburg) and Schultze (Hochschule für Internationale Pädagogische Forschung, Frankfurt), built bridges back into the international community. In France and Britain, as the two countries dissolved their empires, interest in education in the former colonial territories grew, and was sustained, among comparative educationists. Politics caused the field to broaden. One topic that preoccupied practitioners in the field was the adoption in many Western European countries of the principle of universal secondary education. The interest was not only in comparative structures, but also, because of the knowledge explosion and its repercussions upon industry and commerce, in a complete renovation of the curriculum, both themes to which comparative educationists had much to contribute.

Nor must the informative role of the international organizations themselves be omitted. UNESCO and IBE played a major role in the refinement of classificatory systems and the dissemination of educational data. Rosselló, as deputy director of IBE was not only influential in such developments, but also in the methodology of comparative education itself. The *International yearbook of education*,[6] no less than the various *Recommendations to the ministers of education* emanating from the education conferences convened by IBE, demonstrated that consensus on educational matters was internationally possible, and common trends discernible. UNESCO's *World surveys of education*[7] and data collected by various regional organizations were also invaluable. In having so many international and supra-national organizations physically located on their territory, Western European comparative educationists found themselves in a privileged position.

However, since inter-governmental bodies are not the main theme of this report, we must turn in detail to the centres where comparative studies thrived.

The 1961 comparative education conference in London

1961 marks a turning point for comparative education in Western Europe when Lauwerys, then professor of Comparative Education at London University and Robinsohn, Director of UNESCO Institute for Education in Hamburg, called a meeting in London. Out of this conference the Comparative Education Society in Europe was born.

The organizers deliberately refrained from restricting the membership of invited participants to Western Europeans, and a few academics from elsewhere attended: Bogdan Suchodolski from Poland and Hans Espe[8] from East Berlin - founder members of the CESE - were quickly followed by members from Czechoslovakia and Yugoslavia; a Canadian (Joseph Katz), two Americans (one of whom was George Male) and two Japanese professors attended the conference and became members of the Society. Nevertheless the majority of participants were Western European scholars or members of one or other of the international organizations located in Europe. The latter were, however, invited to attend as individuals who had made a contribution to comparative education in their own right.

The Conference showed that, while in practically every Western European country there were scholars interested in comparative education, the major centres of research and teaching could be identified. Britain was strongly represented with 25 participants, reflecting not only the fact that Hans and Lauwerys were very active but that the conference was held in London. Next came the Federal Republic of Germany with representatives from Bonn, Frankfurt, Hamburg, Heidelberg, Marburg, Munich and Saarbrücken. It is not surprising that most of these cities remain important centres of research and teaching. The smaller number of participants from other countries does not diminish the status of the scholars who came from Belgium (three, from Brussels, Liège and Ghent), the Netherlands (two, of whom Ph. J. Idenburg[9] later became President of the Society), France (three, including E. Hatinguais, Directrice of the Centre International d'Etudes Pédagogiques at Sèvres, and R. Thabault,[10] an Inspector Général). L. Borghi came from Italy, K. Grue Sørensen from Denmark, V. G. Hoz[11] from Spain and E. Edlund from Sweden. Leo Fernig's position as Assistant Director of the Division for the Study and Advancement of Education in UNESCO ensured that its position as an international organization contributing to comparative education was recognized. Pedro Rosselló was the sole representative of the many scholars in Switzerland interested in the New Education movement and comparative education. Both men were joined in CESE by members of the secretariats of UNESCO in Paris and the IBE in Geneva. Additional members were quickly recruited from Britain, Austria, France, the Federal Republic of Germany, the Netherlands, Belgium, Italy, Spain, Yugoslavia, Scandinavia (Denmark, Norway and Sweden), Canada and the United States. New members joined from international agencies such as the World Bank, and from Australia, China, Iran, Ireland and Portugal.

The importance of the meeting lies in the fact that as a result of it not only was a European society established and that subsequently national sections (in the United Kingdom and the Federal Republic of Germany) were set up but that eventually societies were established in Spain, France (for French-speaking comparativists), the Low Countries (for Dutch speakers) and Italy. The societies have enabled Western Europeans to cooperate with scholars world-wide, and at the same time have provided forums for the discussion in comparative perspective of European educational problems.

In spite of the broadly-based international character of the inaugural meeting of the Comparative Education Society in Europe, there was considerable agreement on research methods. Two generations of scholars were there, and Kandel, who was not able to attend, gave the meeting his blessing; Schneider, Hilker, Hans and Rosselló were all leaders in the field and had either written standard works[12] or were soon to do so. All shared to a greater or lesser extent the same nineteenth century positivist assumptions, although the emphasis in their work was somewhat different.

Schneider and Hans were very much alike. They were both interested in methodology designed to explain difference between school systems. They both identified the same 'factors', 'forces' or 'causes' in the light of which such differences could be explained. Both had established centres of research and teaching - modest though these were. Hans in London attempted to establish a statistical data base for comparative educationists.

The books written by Schneider and Hans after 1945 stand out, with Kandel's classic, as the most influential methodological treatises at the time of the 1961 conference. They became texts through which students were introduced to the study of comparative education. The methodological assumptions on which they were based persuaded subsequent authors to accept the implicit determinism and to classify educational data and the societal forces influencing them in accordance with the forces or factors of religion, race, language and geopolitical space and ideology. This tradition lives on in Western Europe. In the 1960s it took on a new lease of life, when empirical and statistical studies[13] were conducted within the same nineteenth century deterministic paradigm.

Hilker's starting point was somewhat different. Indeed, he did not always agree with Schneider on the constituents of comparative education but, as a former Director of the Documentation Centre in Bonn, his chief intellectual interest was in the development of classificatory systems in the light of which educational data, rather than information about their infrastructure could be collected and classified. Influenced no doubt by such precursors as Jullien, and notably by the 1963 conference held at the UNESCO Institute for Education in Hamburg on *Relevant data in comparative education*,[14] Hilker helped to establish a taxonomy based upon the stages of education which was further developed by Holmes for the IBE.[15] It allows educational data to be systematically collected from education ministries and avoids some of the ambiguities associated with earlier terminologies. Hilker's approach, described in his book published in 1964, admirably states a method of research drawn from J. S. Mill's *System of logic*. Like that of Bereday, it is a classic statement of induction as the scientific method of enquiry applied to comparative education.

Rosselló, being dependent on information provided for him by the governments of member states, was much less systematic in his search for and classification of data. He has been criticized for accepting too readily data which might be regarded as neither valid nor reliable. Legislation always, however, had an important part to play in the information he regarded as important. Undoubtedly his major contribution to methodology was his ability to discern trends of development in the evolution of education systems and in his insistence that intra-national research studies were viable and useful.

A second generation of scholars were very much in the mould of Schneider, Hans, Hilker and Rosselló. Lauwerys continued to speak of the determinants of education. Husén,[16] using empirical data, was influential in setting up a major cross-national study of school achievement (IEA). On the other hand a new generation of comparative educationists, such as

Robinsohn, Holmes[17] and King[18] were soon to reject the determinism and positivism so much in evidence in discussion of methodology in 1961. In many ways the 1961 conference can be seen as a watershed in the evolution of research methods, in the sense that the consensus which existed at that time was disturbed. Since then the assumption of the pioneers have been increasingly called into question and new approaches developed. In recent publications the earlier traditions linger on.

Post-1961 developments

The London conference marks a turning point in Western European comparative education in several respects. The problems facing educationists in general and policymakers in particular were changing. The post-war baby boom was working its way through the education systems of Europe. By the early sixties, the debate about secondary education for all having been won, the pressure on the elitist universities of Western Europe to admit more students had become great. A study prepared for the International Association of Universities[19] showed that for every university place available there was an average of 2.5 candidates. Such was the euphoria during the 1960s that policymakers attempted in a variety of ways to meet the demand. Existing universities expanded massively; new universities were set up, and after about 1965, short-cycle higher education institutions were established to accommodate the growing numbers of young people who sought access to higher education as an undeniable right. Considerable attention was given to promoting education on a lifelong basis.[20]

At the same time large numbers of adolescents were passing through reorganized secondary schools. Slowly it became apparent to educators that the content of second-level education which had suited the needs and abilities of those few destined to go on to university was not necessarily appropriate to all those entering second-level schools, particularly those converted to common schools for all pupils. Several comparative educationists alerted the authorities to the need for research on curricula - not least Robinsohn[21] in the Federal Republic of Germany. Hence interest in the comparative study of curricula developed during the 1960s.

At the same time interest in education as a form of economic investment increased. National governments, having expanded educational provision as a human right, were anxious to justify the considerable expenditure on it. The economists of education persuaded them that investment in education would bring its own economic rewards. Attention was consequently directed to research into recurrent education and to the relationships between the education system and the world of work. Until well into the 1970s, full employment was not only accepted as a matter of policy by Western European governments, but was still capable of being realized in practice. The oil crisis changed the situation dramatically: since then European governments have had to cope with high levels of unemployment and even greater levels of youth unemployment. The situation was complicated in many countries by the presence of so called 'guest workers' who had been encouraged to leave their home countries to meet the employment needs of the highly industrialized Western European countries, such as France, the Federal Republic of Germany, Sweden and the United Kingdom. The children of these workers had to be educated. Frequently, neither their home language nor their religion was that of the host country, and difficulties arose which have been examined in several comparative education conferences.[22] Associated with the movement of foreign workers has been the growth of urban centres in Europe, leading to the identification by comparative educationists of educational problems peculiar to urban areas.[23] By the late 1970s the euphoria which had earlier informed research had given way to pessimism. The kind of research carried out reflected this changed climate of opinion. Moreover, confidence in some of the research methods developed in the 1950s and early 1960s was shaken by events. This was in part the result of disillusionment. Policies advocated on the basis of social science research had clearly failed to realize policy aims in practice. Furthermore, debates among the philosophers of the natural sciences were attracting the attention of social scientists.[24] Some comparative educationists played a leading part in questioning some of the assumptions on which economists, sociologists and educational planners had conducted their work.

Since debates among philosophers of science influenced opinion among comparative educationists, the consensus that had reigned at the time of the 1961 conference began to break down when a new generation of authors expressed views incorporating those of the pioneers but nevertheless theoretically very different. Positivism and induction as the method of science came under criticism. While few, if any, Western European comparative educationists believed that the careful collection and classification of 'facts' would lead to the discovery of general laws of development in the light of which the future destiny of man and society could be prophesied, there was general agreement that some general principles of policy could be induced from either the collection of educational data or careful analysis of the factors which were the causes of educational events. A distinction should be made between the positivism of Schneider, Hans and Kandel and the inductionism of Hilker. Both positions have continued to inform the work of European comparative educationists, but alternative paradigms have been put forward recently in books written by a number of authors whose epistemological theories can in no way be regarded as ethnocentric. The acceptance of theoretical paradigm cuts across national boundaries and it would be unwise to regard the authors as representing in their general books uniquely European points of view. Since 1975 a number of discussions of method serve to illustrate this.

For example, the position outlined by Hilker in *Vergleichende pädagogik* is shared by Bereday, whose *Comparative method in education*[25] was published two years later. Both accept, though not explicitly, induction as the method of science applicable to the study of comparative education. Both claim that researchers in comparative education should start from the objective observation and recording of facts. These facts or events should then be interpreted from a number of perspectives. In the case of Hilker the factors are identified as tradition and change, economics and technology, economic development and technology, political tendencies and cultural endeavours, and the state and society; in other words, from economic, historical, political, sociological and technological perspectives. The next stage, juxtaposition, Hilker relates to Rosselló's approach by identifying the participation of nations in educational trends. For Hilker, comparison can be made in the light of hypotheses induced from the facts and how they have been interpreted. He makes specific reference to the book by J. F. Cramer and G. S. Browne, *Contemporary education: a comparative study of national systems*,[26] and to Bereday's comparison of school reforms in France and Turkey. A lengthy description of the stages identified by Hilker and Bereday is necessary because many subsequent authors accept that their work was influenced by them.

This is true of Jean Tusquets,[27] who exerted a profound influence on the revival of comparative studies in Spain. More recently Jose Luis García Garrido acknowledges in the introduction to *Educación comparada: fundamentos y problemas*[28] his debt to his colleagues in Barcelona, where Tusquets is, and in Madrid, but also makes special mention of Bereday, whose charm, he states, sometimes obscured his valuable ideas. Certainly the many references to Bereday and the approach made in a more recent book when Garrido provides a number of carefully structured area studies of national systems of education confirm the influence of Bereday and Hilker on his approach to comparative education.

In *Educación comparada*, however, Garrido surveys the field by discussing the fundamentals of the subject, its characteristics and limitations, its methodology, and comparative education and the sciences of education, before looking at some major educational issues, such as the centralization of education and employment, and the future of national systems of education. However, Garrido's methodology is eclectic, rather than distinctive.

The other wing of the positivistic approach to comparative education is represented by Margaret Scotford Archer in *The social origins of educational systems*[29] and Torsten Husén in *The school in question*.[30]

Archer's book is clearly in the tradition of Kandel's *Comparative education*. She uses case studies of Denmark, England, France and the Soviet Union, to demonstrate general principles about the influence (historical) of centralized and decentralized systems of control on stability and change in education. Widely esteemed as one written by a sociologist, the book merely adds interesting details and historical insights to the work undertaken by Kandel.

Husén, on the other hand, shows how far he has moved from the empirical positivism of his earlier work in comparative education, when he inspired research on comprehensive schools in Sweden and played a central role in the IEA studies of achievement in the 1960s. Then Husén was committed to the kind of correlationship studies advocated by C. A. Anderson, Harold Noah and Max Eckstein. All these studies were undertaken within the framework provided by Mill's *System of logic*. In view of Husén's reforming zeal it must be assumed that the correlation studies were designed to show that there was a causal relation between achievement in mathematics and economic productivity and that high achievement was caused by in-school and out-of-school factors. In *The school in question*, Husén is less optimistic about the power of schools to encompass social revolution. He writes as a humanist scholar with extremely wide experience of education systems throughout the world. There is no dogmatic attachment to any particular methodology - just a certain sadness that things did not work out quite as he anticipated in the high days when confidence in psychometric inductivist techniques was at its height. Nevertheless, he shows the value in comparative education studies of empirical and statistical data.

Of the many books by Germans, that of Hermann Röhrs stands out as an expression of a personal commitment not only to the place comparative education has within a general theory of education but to a different approach to comparative studies. In *Forschungsstrategien in der vergleichenden erziehungswissenschaft*,[31] Röhrs claims that educational thought should not be constrained by national boundaries and that from an anthropological perspective any understanding of mankind is impossible without comparison. He takes up the long-standing debate between Schneider and Hilker about the differences between *Auslandpädagogik* and *vergleichende erziehungswissenschaft* and comes down firmly against the view that the starting point of comparative research should be the careful classification of data. Rather, the starting point or *tertium comparationis* should be when the research worker formulates a precise question to an unclear problem. Contrary to the Bereday-Hilker position, he argues that research objectivity is the result of a self-critical approach to experience, and not that the observer's position is free from subjectivity and bias. He implies, along with ethnomethodologists, that a researcher should become a participant in the events he is observing. In summary, Röhrs' position is neither that of Hilker nor of Schneider. The origins of his method go back to W. Dilthey and it is described as a hermeneutic-empirical process. Within a framework of general educational theory he sees comparative education as playing a parallel role to that of the history of education. Educational anthropology, psychology, sociology, economics and technology make interpretations possible on a number of issues such as school pedagogy, vocational education, methods of teaching, social health and welfare education, and sport education.

Röhrs' position is radically different from the positivism of earlier German pioneers. He comes nearer than most comparative educationists, apart from Edmund King, to an ethnomethodological and phenomenological view of research. The context is all important and in some senses unique. There are however, references[33] to this approach in recent research in the Federal Republic of Germany. Lé Thành Khôi's position also represents an alternative to positivism and classical interpretations of Marx. He acknowledges Popper's criticism of Marx but insists that neither Marx nor Engels expected to discover universal laws of societal development. His position is interesting in that he seems to have been much more influenced either directly or vicariously by Popper's views of scientific method than he cares to admit. In *L'éducation comparée*,[33] a title chosen deliberately to show that education has a wider connotation than pedagogy, he identified the stages in a complete research programme as (1) the identification of a problem, (2) the formulation of hypotheses or questions, (3) the collection, analysis and treatment of given facts, (4) the verification of the hypotheses and (5) generalization. Elsewhere in the book he discusses description, classification and the relationship between knowledge and action. He warns that description is not simply a collection of facts; classification is a process which permits abstractions and generalizations to be made. Apart from the final stage, linked with the formulation of generalizations, which according to Lé have not yet in the social sciences reached the status of laws in the natural sciences, the stages in scientific method as outlined by him are almost identical with those laid down by Dewey, who wished to verify hypothetical solutions to problems in order to solve them, and Popper who held that the responsibility of the theoretical scientist should be to refute generalizations or hypothetical statements. Indeed there is some suggestion that for Lé the outcome of research is the discovery of trends of development as the ultimate stage in scientific research. In this respect he differs considerably from Popper and Dewey but does not go as far as the positivists and inductionists in claiming for researchers the possibility of discovering universal irrefutable laws of social development.

In a chapter in *New approaches to comparative education*,[34] edited by Altbach and Kelly, Lé Thành Khôi accepts even more fully a position made explicit in Popper's *The open society and its enemies*, namely that distinctions should be made between normative and sociological theories. The characteristics of the two types of theory bear a close resemblance to the characteristics of normative laws (or hypotheses) and sociological laws, the use of which is advocated by Holmes in *Problems in education* (1965). Normative theories proposed by philosophers and educators are based on conceptions of what constitutes a good education and how it ought to be realized in practice. Sociological theories, on the other hand, make it possible to analyze reality and to assess the changing role of education in society. Links can be made between normative and sociological theories, but neither type of theory is neutral, in the sense that it is there to be discovered. Both are devised and used by persons who hold power, and become in their hands the instruments of social production and reproduction. Lé goes on to discuss the nature of laws, which is not unlike the way in which Holmes has discussed differences between the natural laws of physics, chemistry and even biology, and the laws of sociology, economics and education. Clearly this convergence of views, different as it is from the positivism of the pioneers, is reached from somewhat different ideological perspectives. Lé is unwilling to abandon Marx. Holmes, while accepting the value of many aspects of Marxian analyses accepts, more readily than Lé, Popper's critique of Marx and the method of scientific investigation identified by Dewey as 'reflective thinking'.

Indeed, Holmes, as a former physicist interested in the philosophy of science and as an educationist in the pragmatism of Dewey, first made direct reference to Popper in 1958 in an article in the *Comparative education review*.[35] Since then he has attempted to reconcile Dewey's pragmatism with Popper's critical approach. His taxonomy derives from Popper's critical dualism or critical conventionalism. His concept of natural and sociological laws is in line with the views of Dewey and Popper. His classification of educational aspects owes much to the work of Hilker. His views of the relationship between comparative educationists and the practical reform of education systems is that either of a theoretical scientist or of an applied scientist. The theoretical scientist attempts to differentiate between alternative solutions to an identified problem, usually by discovering under stated conditions which of the solutions will not work, i.e. by refuting the hypotheses which should be stated as a sociological law. The social engineer has the task of stating what contextual conditions will have to be changed if an adopted solution is to work in a given country. In order to operationalize what in the literature has been referred to as national character, Holmes advocates the establishment of Weberian ideal typical models, not to stereotype the behaviour of individuals, but to help in the analysis of problems and in attempts to predict how adopted policy solutions will be received in a particular country in practice.

Within each of these general positions a number of general textbooks have been published. Some of them are well structured on the basis of a clearly identifiable taxonomy, others are more idiosyncratic. Among those in which an attempt is made to compare similar features of national systems of education, Garrido's *Sistemas educativos de hoy*[36] compares, within socio-natural, socio-political and socio-cultural contexts, aspects of education systems from pre-school to professional education in Germany, England, France, the USA, the USSR and Spain. He then investigates problems and perspectives which are specific to the particular countries. Equally systematic, but with comments on the general structure of education systems, national character and methodology, is the book *Pàedagogia comparativa*[37] by Battista Orizio, professor of educational philosophy and psychology at the Institute of Education in Brescia, who has translated the books of A. Vexliard[38] (a very good review of comparative education in French) and George Bereday. Orizio's book offers a review of the field by discussing the growth in comparative education literature, definitions, methods, and comparative education as a science. The author goes on to review Bereday's method, while at the same time referring to many of the theoretical issues debated by comparative educationists. If a judgment were to be made, Bereday's influence on Orizio has been greater than that of any other author. In his chapter on methodology, for example he describes only Bereday's approach in any detail and places Noah, Husén and Edding along with Hans, Kandel, and Schneider as authors who analyze the factors of educational development.

Maria Grazia Carbonne Pighetti's *La scuola in Europa*[39] is on the other hand an example of straightforward comparisons based on a fairly clear but somewhat idiosyncratic taxonomy. She deals with education and work, the democratization of the school, recurrent education, primary, secondary and higher education, languages of instruction and foreign languages. An interesting feature is an opening chapter in which the author presents three ideal typical national education system models: the USA, Sweden and the USSR. Some may quibble about the choice of Sweden, but the notion that against such models comparisons can be usefully made is an interesting and useful idea for comparative educationists. Interesting, too, is the wide range of literature the author refers to when making her points, and particularly useful is her choice of countries - they are all members of the EEC (or at the time had applied to join the community).

Die vergleichende erziehungswissenschaft[40] by Walter Berger and Karl H. Gruber of Austria follows a well-known pattern. The authors start by recording that in 1973 comparative education officially found a place in the Austrian universities. They cover the debate on terminology, after which they review the background to the development of the subject, making frequent reference to Robinsohn and Dilthey. The stages of the method described owe something to Hilker and Bereday and something to Robinsohn, who was considerably influenced by the work of Popper. Issues such as centralization and decentralization, with historical and present-day illustrative cases, are mentioned, as are individual differences, and setting and streaming based on English practices. There are also studies of education systems involving two-nation comparisons of aspects of education in the USA-USSR and middle comprehensive schools in England and France; the reforms and development of teacher education in Sweden, England and the Federal Republic of Germany and examinations in German-speaking lands and the USA. The book reflects a problem-centred approach but is based on a systematically identified taxonomy.

The *Histoire mondiale de l'éducation*[41] prepared by Gaston Mialaret and Jean Vial (Volume 4), provides a series of case studies; some of them regional, such as Europe since 1945.[42] These are followed by a section on methods, the changes in the programmes and teaching of separate school subjects such as mathematics, the mother tongue and science. The third section includes articles on contemporary problems: the democratization of education, women's education and the stages of education, family education and agricultural education. Part five deals with the evolution of research in the educational sciences, and the last part consists of an article by Amadou Mahtar M'bow on international organizations.

Of considerable interest in terms of comparative education in Western Europe is the carefully researched and documented book by Guy Neave on *The EEC and education*.[43] This book deals essentially with the way the European community has approached issues of educational policy in member countries and, in so far as the Treaty of Rome allows, how the Commission has attempted to harmonize and influence policies. A list of topics makes interesting reading: the education of migrants and their families, the transition from school to work, education and training, cooperation in higher education, equality of educational opportunity, the European dimension in education, education and training for disabled children and young people, the micro-electronic revolution, information and policy development in the European community, EURYDICE, and, finally, international relations. This provides a taxonomy of the issues, with some exceptions, in European education which comparative educationists have addressed in recent years. Some, such as equality of educational opportunity, are perennial problems; others, such as the transition from school to work, have a contemporary ring. Of particular interest to many comparative educationists are the problems of policy which have arisen as the result of the free movement of labour within Europe and into Europe from outside the EEC.

Finally, *Equality and freedom in education*,[44] edited by Holmes, is an example of a study in which a dilemma is analyzed on the basis of a carefully worked out and accepted taxonomy of education systems. Since 1945, heightened aspirations to increase equality of opportunity and provision in education have been linked to the persistent desire of parents to provide for their children the best possible education. Though both expectations find expression in the United Nations Declaration of Human Rights, they cannot easily be reconciled. This book, prepared by members of the Comparative Education Department at the University of London Institute of Education, examines the dilemma in terms of the aspects of education adopted by the IBE for the preparation of the reports prepared for the biennial international conferences on education. It blends an analysis based on an identifiable problem with a classification of aspects of education so that the comparisons are clear and systematic.

This sample of the more general books which have been published since 1975 is provided to illustrate not only the different epistemological positions now adopted by comparativists but to indicate the kind of courses on offer throughout Western Europe. Undoubtedly, earlier books, many of which have been mentioned, are used as well. What is significant is that whereas in 1961 a majority of the well-known general introductions to comparative education were in German or English, the range of European languages in which such books are now available is much greater. One of the difficulties associated with the promotion of comparative education, namely facility in a foreign language, has been largely overcome for young students.

Teaching and training centres in Western Europe

The availability of general textbooks in several languages has influenced the growth of teaching comparative education in Western Europe. University traditions allow students, except in the United Kingdom, freely to attend courses of their choice. By the same token academics are free to offer courses in accordance with their changing interests. These traditions find expression in many universities today.

The situation in the Federal Republic of Germany, as described by Mitter,[45] is fairly typical. In the FRG, he writes, there are generally speaking 'no structured programmes at all'. The general study programmes in education, however, contain lectures and seminars which may deal in varying degree with themes that contain elements of comparative education. Attendance at these lectures and seminars is not compulsory and is usually interchangeable with courses in the history, philosophy and sometimes the sociology of education. However, students may choose to participate fairly systematically in seminars in comparative education and are then able to write their 'diploma paper' or their master's or doctor's dissertation on comparative themes. Much depends upon the interpersonal communication built up between lecturers and students.

Lé Thành Khôi[46] reports that the teaching of comparative education in France is no more systematic. Courses are offered in some universities at one or more levels - *licence, maîtrise, doctorat* - but not always under the title comparative education. In Spain, according to Francesc Pedro,[47] comparative education is normally taught as a compulsory subject in the last two years of the *licenciatura en ciencias de la educación*, lasting one year. Almost all universities offer postgraduate courses in comparative education for the doctor's degree. Some primary teacher training colleges provide brief courses. Madrid, Barcelona and Valencia are probably the strongest centres of teaching in Spain. These examples are not atypical of the situation in most Western European universities. Professors in Switzerland (particularly Geneva), Scandinavia (Stockholm especially), the Netherlands, Belgium, Austria and Greece are able to give lectures and seminars either on comparative education or on themes with a comparative component and are able to prepare students to submit the appropriate master's and doctor's dissertation.

The United Kingdom, as in many aspects of university life, is an exception. Courses are provided on a much more systematic basis and students may choose to include comparative education as an option in prescribed undergraduate studies for a B.Ed. degree or for the postgraduate Diploma or Master's degree. Ph.D. research degrees are awarded solely on the basis of a written thesis. In many universities these have either a comparative education component or are written from a comparative perspective.

Centres of teaching in Britain include the universities of Oxford, Cambridge, Glasgow, Reading, Cardiff, Manchester, Leeds and Hull. London University has the only established Chair of Comparative Education in the country. It was established on the retirement of Joseph Lauwerys and has been occupied by George Parkyn and Brian Holmes, who on his retirement in 1985 was replaced by Guy Neave. At the London Institute of Education, specialist courses are run at the undergraduate, postgraduate diploma, and master's levels. Systematic training in research methods was previously provided for students wishing to proceed to a doctorate.

Among the disciplines, education is a relative newcomer and, among the sciences of education comparative education plays a less prominent role than, say, the philosophy, psychology, history and sociology of education in the training of teachers. This is reflected in the position of academic staff. Thus, for example, in Spain, while many professors participate in comparative education teaching and research, there are no tenured positions in the subject. Senior professors hold chairs in other fields, for example, in the history of education (Garcia Garrido) or the foundations of education (Marin Ibañez). Frequently the courses are taught by junior professors who may work on a contract basis.

In other countries scholars teaching courses in comparative education are either philosophers, historians, geographers or linguists. Some are basically psychologists. Their teaching reflects the perspective from which they view comparative education. Michel Debeauvais (Paris VIII) and Lé

Thành Khôi (Paris VI) for example, are both originally economists. M. Debesses, an important French pioneer in the field, was a philosopher-geographer. P. Furter[48] in Geneva has a linguistic background and Torsten Husén in Stockholm a background in psychology. Until comparative education is firmly established and taught systematically as an undergraduate study its practitioners are bound to be scholars whose academic training has been in related fields. The diversity of backgrounds from which professors teaching comparative education come gives rise to a lack of cohesion, which was not apparent in 1961 when the number of university teachers was relatively small.

In summary, therefore, comparative education in Western Europe is only slowly emerging as a discipline in the universities. In most universities courses are available and in some cases they may be offered as an option within teacher training institutions, as for example, in Britain. Comparative education does not enjoy, partly because it has a short history, the prestige and status of the other foundation disciplines of education and in contrast to them is rarely a compulsory part of teacher training programmes.

Nevertheless, in many universities in Western Europe, teaching for doctorates is undertaken and staff carry out research in comparative education. It is not possible to report the precise number of doctoral students in each university or the number of successful dissertations which have been presented. In some countries the tradition that theses at the doctoral level should be published has almost disappeared - in others it remains only to some extent. In these the number of publications is some reflection of the number of theses prepared. Certainly in the Federal Republic of Germany for example, many doctoral theses are published as such. Elsewhere, hardly any are published.

There are indeed many difficulties in attempting to make a comprehensive survey of research theses in comparative education. It is not easy to decide precisely what constitutes a comparative thesis. Some are characterized simply by a method of research. Others deal in depth with an educational issue or problem in one foreign country even though the perspective from which the issue is viewed is comparative. Less often, for reasons of expense, and familiarity of the student with more than one foreign language, the same issue or problem is examined in two or more countries, one of which is frequently the home country of the researcher. The most difficult theses to prepare are those which illustrate a carefully identified problem by drawing data and interpretations from several countries. Heavily statistical theses using original data from many countries are rarely tackled by individual doctoral students.

Consequently no attempt is made here to present a comprehensive survey of university research centres in Western Europe. Only examples, based on a knowledge of the field, can be given. Clearly, the traditional centres of excellence remain strong and prepare many doctoral candidates. New centres have emerged, particularly since 1961, whose contributions can most easily be assessed by the number of publications which have been prepared either by students or members of staff.

For the training of future research workers in comparative education, the Federal Republic of Germany stands out. The main research interest differs from university to university but, in practically all of them, concern centres on education in the USSR, the German Democratic Republic, the People's Republic of China and other socialist countries. Indeed, research reflects the interests of professors. Several leading professors have collected round them scholars with special expertise in particular foreign countries. Centres are found in Marburg under Leonhard Froese, in Bochum, led by Oskar Anweiler, and Kassel, where Ulrich Teichler (who has written extensively on education in Japan) directs a very active group of research workers. Following G. Hausman, Neville Postlethwaite and staff at Hamburg University have retained an interest in the problems of education in Third World countries. Jürgen Schriewer at the Johann Wolfgang Goethe University in Frankfurt is very interested in research methods and Hermann Röhrs attracted a strong group of younger scholars to his centre in Heidelberg. No longer is it possible, as in the days of Schneider and Hilker, to say any one professor dominates the field in Germany, although Philips University at Marburg, and those at Hamburg, Bochum, Frankfurt and Berlin are particularly strong centres.

Information about comparative education in France has been provided in an article by Michele Tournier[49] (an indefatigable bibliographer), in the *Revue Française de pédagogie* (No. 54, Jan-March 1981, pp. 76-90). In several of the bulletins of the French-speaking Comparative Education Association (AFEC), *Education comparée*, a list of courses offered at French universities is given. For example, in the year 1978-9 the following were announced in *Education comparée*:[50]

> Lé Thành Khôi 'Objet et méthodes de l'éducation comparée' at René Descartes (Paris V); A. D. Marquez on the theme 'La coopération internationale et les politiques éducatives nationales' at Vincennes (Paris

VIII); Bertrand Girod de l'Ain offered a research seminar at Dauphine (Paris IX) on the objectives, strategies and types of government associated with different types of higher education institutions; at Nanterre, teaching in comparative education was linked with the economics and sociology of education and taught by H. Laderrière; educational courses in which comparative notions were included were offered in Caen; and Jacques Champion ran *licence* and *maîtrise* courses in comparative education at Grenoble.

A representative list of thesis titles in education gives some flavour of the research done in French universities (*Thèses de sciences de l'éducation*, Université René Descartes (Paris V), No. 11, Oct. 1983). It indicates the range of research topics viewed in comparative perspective. Many are case studies in the sense that the topic is examined exclusively in one foreign country. Algeria ranks very high in the list of countries, followed by Morocco and Lebanon. Regionally, African countries head the list of those on which research had been done. In the year under review no theses were written on the United States and of the nearly 800 theses listed some 28 were classified as based on a comparative analysis, but the vast majority were not cross-national studies. These illustrative figures do not fully represent the interest shown in France in comparative education and particularly in Third World issues. There are many experts in aspects of education in particular foreign countries and the conferences held by AFEC at the CIEP in Sèvres attract participants from many parts of France, the rest of Europe, Africa and Latin America.

The number of successful Ph.Ds in comparative education prepared at the University of London Institute of Education is over 100.[52] The topics vary from case studies of selected issues in a selected overseas country to comparisons between education in two or more countries, in Asia, Africa, North America and Latin America. Most have tackled their subjects from a particular methodological perspective, namely that pioneered by Brian Holmes. This has been adopted by students in other universities: for example, in Cardiff, where two of Holmes' former students teach, and in Durham, where Richard Goodings formerly worked on the *World yearbook of education*. Many successful theses have been prepared at Reading University, particularly when Vernon Mallinson was in charge of the subject. Research theses have been presented in Oxford, where W. D. Halls is an expert on French and European education and has developed his own culturalist approach to comparative studies.[53] Cambridge has entered candidates for Ph.Ds in comparative education and Glasgow has a strong school of postgraduate students.

In the European traditions, teaching of research by individual students in universities has been paralleled by research carried out in special research institutes and by individual scholars throughout Western Europe. Some examples of this research are now given.

Research in comparative education

Before 1961, research in comparative education was minimal. In London (in collaboration with Teachers College, New York) the *(World) yearbook of education* had initiated students on topics such as education and technological development, economics of education (1956), education and philosophy (1957), guidance and counselling (1955), but generally the material available was mostly descriptive in character, or analytical in the Hans-Schneider tradition. The *1956 yearbook of education* on economics and education stimulated research[54] into the role of education as a form of economic investment. By the same token the *1954 yearbook* initiated studies designed to investigate the implications of technological advances on the world's educational systems. The two approaches came together in research into the planning of education and the role of technical aid and assistance in the development of education systems in countries on the point of developing economically. International agencies, such as UNESCO and, later, OECD, were collecting information which showed comparatively how far the goal of providing first and second level education to all regardless of sex, race, language, religion and domestic circumstances was being achieved internationally. Case studies, rather than truly cross-national research, examining the success of reform movements involving the reorganization of second level education had been undertaken.

The 1960s was the decade when educational research took off. As part of the explosion, comparative studies found an important place, at least in some countries. In the Federal Republic of Germany, G. Picht's[55] identification of the German educational catastrophe probably did more than anything else to stimulate research. Another major research project, undertaken after an initial survey by the UNESCO Institute for Education in Hamburg, was centred in Stockholm. The various IEA projects have given rise to an enormous number of publications, commentaries on them, and data about school and family situations in countries throughout the world. The committee chaired by economist Lionel Robbins in England carried out a comparative study, ostensibly to learn something from what was going on elsewhere in relation to the expansion of higher education.

Much comparative research, however, was conducted by international agencies located in Europe. By their terms of reference some of these - like UNESCO and the IBE - could do little more than collect and classify information, thus increasing the database available to individual comparative educationists. The Council of Europe likewise prepared surveys describing aspects of education systems in various European countries. Such research, although having direct bearing on some policy issues, might be classified as area studies. They have the virtue of containing cross-national data on a scale which few non-governmental agencies have the resources to acquire.

OECD was set up to advise governments on how best to improve their economies. By intention, therefore, research was interventionist. Much of it was undertaken to legitimize vast expenditure on educational provision, on the assumption that investment in education would bring its own economic rewards not only to individuals but to society. Expansionist policies were accepted and research was designed to justify economically policies that in Western Europe had been accepted in the belief that education should be provided for all as a human right regardless of circumstances. The Centre for Educational Research and Innovation offered alternative approaches. Those who commissioned research from CERI were much more interested in questions relating to the success of policy initiatives. A major investigation was designed to investigate on a cross-national basis how innovation strategies at national, regional and local levels had been successful.[56] Case studies in different countries and levels of administration were used to illuminate not only what policies were available and had been adopted in a particular country but in what political and economic circumstances they had been successful. CERI initiatives helped to redirect OECD educational research away from simple relationships and econometric studies to policy-related studies. The national case studies undertaken by OECD are a good example of the approach taken.[57] These are based on critical reviews by foreign experts of stated national policies. They began when a Swedish policy document was used as a basis for critical analysis.

Although the Treaty of Rome excluded educational policies from EEC involvement, in 1969 education began to figure significantly in the work of the Commission. Research has since been carried out on aspects of education in member states. In 1975 a review of the literature on the learning difficulties of migrant children was made; then an analysis of bilingual education programmes. Pilot projects are the core of the Community's efforts on the transition from school to work. It has developed intervention instruments in the field of vocational training for youth in areas of high unemployment. Certain research projects concern the difficulties young people with handicaps experience in their transition from education to working life. It must be said, however, that the Commission's role is in the formulation of policies of interest to member states rather than in direct policy-related research.

As a non-governmental organization, the direct contribution of the European Cultural Foundation to comparative education[58] began in 1972 with the launching of the project *Europe 2000*, which investigated likely trends in all aspects of education from primary schooling through to higher education and lifelong education until the new millennium. Partly as an outgrowth of this exercise, the Foundation took the initiative in 1975 of setting up the (now) European Institute of Education and Social Policy. The Institute, located in Paris with an office in Brussels, has mainly been concerned with policy analysis in post-compulsory education. Its work has focused on Western industrialized countries, and more specifically on those in the EEC, though by no means exclusively so. The current (1986) thrust of its research can be grouped under four main headings; higher education, and in particular in the regular review of *New trends in European higher education*, which has appeared biennially since 1978; education and work; European cooperation in education (again in higher education) and more recently education and the new technologies. Previously, in the 1960s the European Cultural Foundation generously supported publications prepared from the biennial conferences of the Comparative Education Society in Europe. It has published a number of research studies and occasional papers; that by Neave interpreting equality of educational opportunity with theological concepts is among the more unusual and interesting.

Reviews of comparative research are few and somewhat disappointing. That edited by Manfred Niessen and Jules Peschar[59] restricts the notion of research almost exclusively to work based on empirical models. In his foreword, Husén claims that international research in education with an empirical orientation seeks to arrive at more generalizations than can be achieved by study within a particular national or cultural setting. Such a view stems from a traditional belief in the efficiency of induction. By empirical research the editors mean all those studies which are systematic investigations into social reality, carried out in a methodical, controlled and documented way.[60] Such a statement could include research based on induction, ethnomethodology and problem-solving, identified as the three main positions earlier in this paper. In the event, much attention is given to the empirical studies and many spin-offs from the IEA research.

By the same token, the admirable review of educational research *La recherche en éducation dans le monde*[61] prepared by Gilbert De Landsheere is heavily empirical in the traditional sense.

The works of Binet, Bloom, Buyse, Claparède, De Landsheere himself, Galton, W. S. Gray, Piaget, Stanley Hall, T. Simon, Thorndike, Tyler and Wundt figure largely in the index but, apart from frequent references to Dewey, research of a more qualitative and interpretative kind is under-represented or receives less attention than it might. Husén and Psacharopoulos are mentioned, both of whom favour psychometric and econometric methods, but many worthwhile pieces of comparative education research find no place in an otherwise excellent review of educational research, principally from a psychological viewpoint.

In the *World yearbook of education*,[62] edited by John Nisbet, Jacquetta Megarry and Stanley Nisbet, on *Research policy and practice* accounts are given of research in the United States, Australia, France, the Federal Republic of Germany, India, Latin America, Sweden, Singapore, New Zealand and the Netherlands, and new directions are identified. There are useful surveys of a general field of research which has grown greatly in the last 25 years and in which comparative and international studies find a place.

In the 1930s, Hans found that, working alone in London, it was difficult to generate statistical data on an international basis. Now, since much of the information has been collected by an international agency, it can be used by individual comparative educationists to provide comparative area studies. An example of such studies is found in the volumes[63] edited by members of the Comparative Education Department of the University of London Institute of Education who mainly used data provided by British Council officers throughout the world to prepare profiles in which the information was strictly comparable. Such studies are more easily undertaken by individual research workers when not more than two or three countries are involved. Many general textbooks are of this kind.

The studies undertaken by Hans and Schneider, in which the 'causes' or 'factors' behind educational development were used to classify data and examine differences between systems, have on the whole been replaced by relationship studies, whether or not these imply problem areas. Connections between the social class background of pupils entering second level schools of their choice and access to high status schools is an example of a relationship which occupied many research workers during the period of reorganizing secondary education in Western Europe along comprehensive lines. Relationships between age cohorts in secondary education and numbers entering higher education have also been the subject of considerable research. More recently the relationships between educational background and entry into the labour force have been the subject of intense comparative research.

In general, relationships between aspects of the educational system have formed one kind of study. A second kind of relationships study has been based on the assumption that there are relationships between the infrastructure of societies and aspects of education. Some of these studies are identified below, although it is impossible here to do justice to all the work that has been done recently.

Research centres

If too fine a distinction is not drawn between funded research and that carried out by individuals as part of their normal university duties, the two major national centres of comparative education research in Western Europe are the Federal Republic of Germany and the United Kingdom, although Spain may well soon seriously compete in terms of the number of studies.

In the Federal Republic of Germany, according to Wolfgang Mitter, 1963 was a turning point in research into education and comparative education in particular. The new Federal Chancellor, Ludwig Erhard, declared that educational issues were as pressing today as they had been in the nineteenth century, and the Standing Conference of Länders Ministers of Education called for an assessment to be made of the financial requirements which would be needed to meet the demand for school places. He also cites the establishment of the Max-Planck Institute for Educational Research as the second federal institution to be set up (1963) to undertake research in education. Both the German Institute for International Research and the Max-Planck Institute have contributed in a significant way to comparative research.

The introduction of empirical methods of research, multidisciplinary and policy oriented research, as against the German tradition of research into the history of pedagogical ideas, typifies this turning point. Mitter points to the debates which arose between the positivist empiricists and the hermeneuticists, but argues that in the 1970s there was evidence that the three approaches had to a certain extent been amalgamated.

In *Mitteilung und nachrichten*, published by the German Institute, there are articles, news and reviews. Frequently given are reports of the activities undertaken by members of the Institute. In December 1980 the Director, Mitter, commented on the international orientation of the Institute in the course of overall development taken by comparative education research in the Federal Republic. Workshops are held and foreign speakers are invited to lecture. Lists of papers published by members of the Institute are given. The classification is in accordance with the organization in which members play a role - field work and visits abroad, international conferences attended and collaboration with foreign scholars. The range of topics investigated in comparative education is impressive.

When the Max-Planck Institute for Educational Research was first set up under Director Helmut Becker three leading scholars, Friedrich Edding, Dietrich Goldschmidt and Saul B. Robinsohn, were appointed to give direction to research respectively in the economics of education, the sociology of education and general education. Robinsohn chose to promote educational research from a comparative perspective, but unfortunately died prematurely in 1972.

Nevertheless he had established a tradition of research which continues. A whole range of contemporary problems have been studied at the Max-Planck Institute. They are available, frequently with an English summary, in *Studies and reports (Studien und berichte)* and in a series of books on educational research published by the Institute *(Veröffentlichungen des Max Planck-Instituts für bildungsforschung)*. Both series contain case studies of educational developments in the Federal Republic of Germany and elsewhere. There are also cross-national comparative studies, e.g., the theory and practice of curriculum development in the United States, Sweden and England, by Klaus Huhse. The publications exemplify how comparative studies throw light on problems and policies directly relevant to the country in which the research is undertaken. Characteristic of the work done is the continuing interest in American educational development and in Japan, in studies undertaken by Ulrich Teichler. Perhaps less emphasis has been given than in other German comparative education centres to education in socialist countries.

Of the many university centres, the Forschungsstelle für Vergleichende Erziehungswissenschaft at Marburg was the first to respond to the research initiatives taken in the early 1960s by undertaking a considerable amount of research in comparative education. The staff, directed by Leonard Froese (whose short introductions to several publications on the boundaries and possibilities of comparison are models of clarity and conciseness), comprises a number of national system experts. Heinz Stubig has written extensively on English educational reforms; Viktor von Blumenthal and Bodo Willmann on Sweden, and Bruno Nieser on France. Frequently publications on education in these countries are prepared by members of the group, under contract from the Ministry of Education and Science. Doctoral dissertations are also published in the same series, *Marburger beiträge zur vergleichenden erziehungswissenschaft und bildungsforschung*. There have been multinational and binational studies of education systems on equality of opportunity and on occupational systems. Earlier studies appeared on the relationships between qualifications and the development of science and technology, as an example of the reform of second level schools in England, Italy, Sweden, the United States and the USSR (Uwe Zanker is an expert on the USSR). The study is not quite in the tradition of comparative education, notice having been taken of the work of Habermas, Schumpeter and Schelsky, Marxist analyses, and within the theoretical framework of discussion exemplified by Habermas and Galbraith among others. Members of the faculty have made detailed studies of the work of A. S. Makarenko, and comparisons between aspects of education in the Federal Republic of Germany and the USSR. Marburg also publishes the periodical *Ost und West*. Froese's comments in fact admirably summarize some of the methodological debates among comparative educationists. In *Grenzen und möglichkeiten des vergleichs*[64] he refers to the work of Schneider, Hilker, Robinsohn, King, Mitter, Kandel and himself, declaring that the methodological problems associated with comparative education are as old as learning itself. He quotes Kandel as saying that 'the methodology of comparative education is determined by the purpose of the study'. The Hilker-King position is stated to be that there is no uniform method of comparison, but the material itself determines the enquiry. Robinsohn is quoted as holding the view, along with Schneider, that comparative method is central to all enquiry. Mitter's view is that comparisons should be undertaken in concrete situations. In intra- and between-system comparisons the contexts define the boundaries and possibilities of comparison. The studies undertaken under the heading *Bildungswesen, chancengleichheit und beschäftigungsystem* explicitly bring together both approaches by enquiring into the same issue in several countries.

From the Institute of Asian Studies in Hamburg well over a hundred studies have been prepared, one of which, by Jurgen Henze, on education and science in the People's Republic of China was prepared in cooperation with the Institute for Education at Bochum University. Neville Postlethwaite, well known for his long involvement with the IEA research, continues to promote research into education in developing countries.

The comprehensive university at Kassel has a centre of research into vocational and higher education (Wissenschaftliches Zentrum für Berufs- und Hochschulforschung). *Bildung und beschäftigung: probleme, konzept, forschungsperspektiven* by Dirk Hartung, Reinhard Nuthmann and Ulrich Teichler is an example of the kind of research undertaken on the relationships between education systems, occupational systems and social structures. A number of issues are analyzed within the framework of admissions to universities and higher education, unemployment and the economic situation. All three authors have written either in cooperation with others or as individuals on the relationships between higher education and the labour market. D. Mertins is also a prolific writer in this field. Ulrich Teichler occupies the chair in Kassel and, as stated, is also an expert on Japanese education as well as an authority on employment and higher education in many countries. A series of *Werkstattberichte* and *Arbeitspapiere* give examples of research carried out. Occasionally a list of publications is given, and in 1981 a retrospect on the first ten years of the comprehensive university at Kassel was published.[65]

A somewhat recent arrival among Germany universities, Bochum quickly built up a strong centre for comparative education research under the leadership of Oskar Anweiler. Again, much attention has been given to research into education in socialist countries, including the People's Republic of China. The Ruhr-Universität Bochum, Institut für Pädagogik Arbeitsstelle für vergleichende Bildungsforschung, publishes regular bibliographical abstracts of studies in comparative education. The classification of material reflects the various interests of the centre. In the first category are summaries of comparative and related publications; these are followed by research studies on the German Democratic Republic, reports on other socialist countries and, finally, by accounts of education in the People's Republic of China. Books, reports and unpublished material of interest from all parts of the world offer extremely useful summaries of material relevant to comparative education.

In each of these national and university centres within each group of research workers are specialists in the education of one or other major countries, such as France, the Federal Republic of Germany, Italy, Sweden, the USSR and the United Kingdom. Researchers are too numerous to survey their work here comprehensively, but it reflects the extremely powerful presence, in the Federal Republic of Germany, of comparative educationists committed to research and until recently, because of generous funding, able to devote much time to it.

The situation in Britain is somewhat different. Funding agencies have not so generously supported comparative research in the established centres. Much work has been done, as mentioned, on education in developing countries which were former British colonies. Much time is spent in English universities teaching on well-structured courses. The many books published by W. D. Halls, Edmund King, Nigel Grant, Brian Holmes, Arthur Hearnden, Vernon Mallinson and Keith Watson testify to the vigour with which comparative education is pursued. Mallinson's[66] major interest is in the European ideal in education, as his recent book confirms. Hearnden[67] is an expert on education in the two Germanies. Halls has written several outstanding studies on French education and Grant's[68] expertise lies in the education systems of Eastern Europe and the USSR. However, the number of research studies published is not as impressive as that of the Federal Republic of Germany, although through the London Association of Comparative Educationists (LACE), until recently closely associated with the University of London Institute of Education Comparative Education Department, a number of Ph.D. theses have been published in summary form in *Occasional papers*.[69]

While undoubtedly the biggest centre of comparative education research in Britain is still London, with its long traditions in the field, many scholars, as mentioned, contribute to research. They tend to be somewhat isolated. Whilst David Philipps[70] edited a volume on the German universities after World War II for the Department of Educational Studies at Oxford, Halls has for many years carried the burden of the work undertaken. In contrast, London has an expert in Soviet and East European education (jointly with the School of Slavonic and East European Studies) in J. J. Tomiak, and one in Western European education: Martin McLean; Robert Cowen is interested in education in Latin America and Ghulam Saqeb has written extensively on education in Islamic countries. Hearnden's[71] book on *The British in Germany after 1945* was written by those who carried out the mandate to ensure that education eliminated Nazi doctrines. Holmes, recently retired as professor in London, is particularly interested in research methodology. His successor, Guy Neave, has written extensively on research into higher educational policies. E. King,[72] who retired in 1979, is well-known for his general textbooks and for the research he undertook on post-compulsory education in five European countries.

Major research publications have been published less frequently in Spain and Italy but mention should be made of Guglielmo Malizia's *Né scuola né fabbrica*, and the work of M. Reguzzoni.[73] In the Netherlands, a major conference on quality in education resulted in publication under the editorship of B. Creemers, W. Hoeben and K. Koops of *De kwaliteit van het onderwijs*.[74]

The involvement in the IEA research and Husén's personal contribution places the University of Stockholm high on the list of universities in which substantial research in comparative education has been carried out. France has suffered, perhaps, as a consequence of the number of international organizations which have their headquarters in Paris. Mention has been made already of the work undertaken by UNESCO and OECD, but in research, particularly into planning and education development in Third World and developing countries, the UNESCO Institute for Educational Planning has played a major role. A succession of directors including Hans Weiler and Michel Debeauvais have given a comparative emphasis to work done frequently from an economics of education standpoint.

A complete survey of research from a comparative perspective in education would undoubtedly include the findings of many scholars who do not claim to be comparative educationists. Indeed the research of a great many, if not most social scientists, has recently included a comparative perspective. Even this review of the research done by those who claim to be comparative educationists is by no means fully comprehensive. What has been attempted is a survey which illustrates by example the kind of work completed since about 1976.

Periodicals

Just as it is difficult to define precisely what research should be classified as 'comparative education research' except by reference to the stated position of the person carrying it out, so it is difficult to state which of the many journals dealing with education can be truly and unambiguously classified as comparative education periodicals. A distinction can, however, be made between those specially intended to meet the needs of comparative educationists and those which from time to time contain articles of value to them. The former are usually published by an international governmental agency or by a national centre committed to teaching, research and the dissemination of information. On the other hand nearly all educational journals, and particularly those in which articles from social scientists appear, include articles with a European, global or international flavour, written from a comparative or international perspective. What follows is a selective list of journals in which articles of interest to comparative educationists in Western Europe appear either regularly or occasionally.

International governmental organizations located in Western Europe publish a great many useful periodicals, and issue catalogues in which the full range of them can be found. Among UNESCO's many publications may be mentioned; *Courier*, *Prospects* (a quarterly review of education), and *International understanding at school* for its Associated Schools Project.

The International Bureau of Education in Geneva, UNESCO's centre for comparative education studies, publishes *Educational innovation and information* as the Newsletter of the International Educational Reporting Service. The *Bulletin of the International Bureau of Education* contains annotated bibliographies of selected issues and aspects of education. Both UNESCO's International Institute of Educational Planning (IIEP) and OECD Development Centre (both 'interventionist' organizations) publish a *Newsletter*. The Council of Europe's documentation centre for education in Europe issues an *Information bulletin and newsletter*. In cooperation with the European Cultural Foundation's Institute of Education and Social Policy, the Council of Europe publishes the *European journal for education* (since 1979). Formerly *Paedagogica Europaea*, the journal includes cross-national studies and case studies of direct relevance to comparative educationists and is one of the leading comparative education journals in Western Europe.

Other journals are associated with well-known organizations in the field of comparative education. The Comparative Education Society in Europe publishes an occasional *Bulletin* to inform members of the society's activities. Several of the national associations which emerged from the CESE keep in touch with their members in a similar way. While in no sense merely a house magazine, *Education comparée* (formerly the Bulletin of AFEC) is used by the French-speaking Comparative Education Association (AFEC) to inform its members and other comparative educationists about activities in the field. It publishes not only substantial articles but reports of conferences and international events. Conferences, and the reports appearing in *Education comparée* are used as vehicles for the initiation of research and the preparation of international conferences like those held by the Comparative Education Society in Europe and the World Council of Comparative Education Societies.

Compare, the journal of the British Comparative and International Education Society, rarely includes information about Society activities. It is a specialized periodical which publishes articles from many parts of the world. The same may be said of *Bildung und erziehung* edited by a member of the Deutsches Institut für Internationale Pädagogische Forschung on its behalf. It has, however, published reports of international comparative conferences.

Among the truly comparative education journals with no institutional affiliation *Comparative education* (Oxford) ranks high. It is edited by Edmund King, and is widely regarded as one of the leading journals in the field. In not quite the same way, reference should be made to *Education in Western Europe*, published by M. E. Sharpe in the United States. This journal brings together abstracts or direct translations of relevant articles on Western European education. Sometimes a theme is used to give coherence to the volume.

Peripheral to the field but relevant, are a number of periodicals dealing with special aspects of education, such as the *European journal of science education*, the *International newsletter on physics education, Journal of European training*, and *Vocational training* of the European Centre for the Development of Vocational Training and Higher Education in Europe. The *European journal of sociology* and *Comparative studies in society and history*, published in The Hague, are in the field of sociology but have relevance to comparative education.

Many national periodicals have a comparative and international flavour - at least occasionally and in some articles. There are too many of them to list exhaustively here. The following are examples of journals which may be of interest to comparative educationists.

FRANCE
Revue française de pédagogie is an official periodical published by the Institut de Recherche et de Documentation Pédagogiques in Paris. *Le monde de l'éducation, Revue tiers-monde, Éducation permanente* (from the University of Paris Dauphine) and *Recherche pédagogique et culture* (formerly *Dossiers pédagogiques*) of the University for the Development of Education in Africa and Madagascar, are examples of some of the interests shown in education by French writers and research workers. *Les amis de Sèvres*, published by the International Centre of Educational Studies (CIEP) is an outstanding periodical in the field of international understanding and comparative international education.

UNITED KINGDOM
Interest has always been shown in educational development in the Commonwealth and developing countries. The following journals are examples of these interests. *IDS Bulletin*, from the Institute of Development Studies,

Sussex; the Council for Education in the Commonwealth has a *Newsletter*; the Hull University *Studies in education*, the Leeds University, *Studies in science education* have included comparative articles. Special mention should, however, be made of the *Oxford review of education* associated with a number of Oxford academics, among them W. D. Halls, its founding editor. The *New era*, the journal of the New Education Fellowship, has for many years actively promoted international understanding and a commitment to progressive teaching methods. *Education today*, the journal of the College of Preceptors, increasingly includes articles about education in foreign countries, where many of its members work. *Trends* is a periodical issued by the Department of Education and Science.

BELGIUM
Paedagogica historica (with which R. L. Plancke has been closely associated) and *Scientia paedagogica experimentalis* are two notable Belgian journals.

DENMARK
Dansk paedagogist tidsskrift publishes from time to time comparative education articles and material of relevance to research workers.

PORTUGAL
Perspectives is the Portuguese edition of the UNESCO *Education Review* and is published in Lisbon.

THE NETHERLANDS
Of the journals published in The Netherlands mention may be made of *Counterpart* (formerly *Higher education and research in the Netherlands*) from the Universities Foundation for International Co-operation in the Hague which gives an international dimension to higher education in the world. *Development and change* is prepared by The Institute of Social Studies also in The Hague.

FINLAND
Mention may be made of *Kasvatus* prepared by the University of Jyvaskyla.

SWEDEN
R and D for Higher Education and *School Research*.

NORWAY
The *Scandinavian journal of educational research* is published by Universitetsförlaget in Oslo, (formerly *Pedagogisk forskning*).

SWITZERLAND
Bulletin of the Centre Suisse de documentation en matière d'enseignement et d'éducation, Geneva.

SPAIN
Perspectivas pedagogicas published in Barcelona and very much influenced by Juan Tusquets, presents substantial articles, news of conferences and conference reports. *Revista española de pedagogica* is published by the Instituto de Pedagogia San Jose de Calasanz in Madrid.

FEDERAL REPUBLIC OF GERMANY
Reference has been previously made to the many periodical publications prepared by national research institutions and university centres. Two other periodicals may be mentioned. *Bildung und wissenschaft* (formerly *Education in Germany*) and *Bildung und wissenschaft: Das hochschulwesen*.

Conclusion

The year 1961 has been taken as a watershed in the teaching and researches in comparative education. Before the conference held in that year at the University of London Institute of Education, there was a large measure of agreement about the epistemological foundations on which research should be carried out. Differences turned on whether comparative studies should start with the collection and careful classification of data about national systems of education from which limited generalizations could be drawn, or from an analysis of the 'forces', 'factors' or 'causes' of educational development. Virtually every practitioner agreed that these causes were to be discovered in the societal infrastructure of individual nation states.

The question was whether the juxtaposition of descriptions of national education systems constituted comparative education or whether it should be regarded merely as a study of foreign education. The dilemma has not been resolved by comparative educationists in Europe, who basically justified their methods of research by an appeal to the inductive method advocated by Aristotle, Francis Bacon and J. S. Mill.

This model informed the research of a new generation of comparative educationists in the 1960s who looked for the causes of educational development, and differences between systems, not in terms of religion, language, race and geopolitical space, but in factors such as social class, economic investment and political ideology. Much of the research undertaken by the economists of education was based on principles adopted by other social scientists. The IEA studies were based on conceptually similar foundations but instead of econometric methods of research psychometric methods were adopted to show the influence of socio-economic factors on the achievement of pupils in various countries.

After 1961, comparative educationists, influenced by the writings of Karl Popper in the history and philosophy of the natural and social sciences, rejected the paradigm (or parts of it) within which most research had been conducted. Two positions were advanced as alternatives to induction as the method of comparative education research. Brian Holmes pioneered the 'problem-solving approach' based on the work of John Dewey and Popper. Edmund King followed him arguing against determinism and in favour of an ecological model which owed much to Popper. A second approach commanded the respect of several German comparative educationists, namely the empirical hermeneutic approach which has its origins in the writing of Wilhelm Dilthey and the Frankfurt school of philosopher-sociologists. This position finds expression in the book prepared by Hermann Röhrs and is acknowledged in some of the research undertaken by German research workers.

Lé Thành Khôi in Paris, without abandoning Marxism, has clearly been influenced by the debates among natural scientists and adopts a somewhat eclectic position which does violence neither to the Neo-Marxists nor to the Popperians. These positions inform the teaching and research in most countries in Western Europe. Since several general textbooks have been added to the standard works which were the foundations of the subject before 1961, it is possible to infer from them the kind of teaching undertaken in centres in various countries. It seems reasonable to suppose that, at least for students being introduced to the subject, a text in their native language will if possible be used. Before 1961 the most influential books were in English and German. Since then books have been published in French, Spanish and Italian. The approach advocated by Hilker (in German) and Bereday (in English) are frequently quoted texts in the Spanish and Italian literature. This is hardly surprising, since the method of induction which informs the methods advocated has its origins in the works of Aristotle.

A major influence on the development of teaching and research in Western Europe has been the Comparative Education Society in Europe and the national societies which have been established, in the first place, as sections of that Society. The reports of conferences and the journals published by the societies have added greatly to the literature and in many cases have initiated further research - such as multiculturalism - from a comparative perspective. The emergence and strength of the national societies reflect the historical position among the Western European nations of comparative education as an academic subject in its own right. As educationists face major problems of policy towards the end of the twentieth century it is likely that comparative education studies will receive fresh and important stimulus.

References

1. Popper, K. R. *The open society and its enemies*. 1st ed. London, Routledge & Kegan Paul, 1946.
2. Peter Sandiford's *Comparative education* was published in 1918. He and Paul Monroe were members of the Institute of International Education at Teachers College, New York, where Dr James Russell gave a course on comparative education in 1898-1899.
3. Kandel, I. L. *Comparative education*, Boston, MA, Houghton Mifflin, 1933, is a classic which merits re-reading.
4. The *Internationale zeitschrift für erziehungswissenschaft* was founded by Schneider in 1931. It became an organ of the Nazis, but reappeared in 1947 under its founding editor.
5. The aim of the first post-War *World yearbook of education, 1948*, London, Evans, 1948, edited by J. A. Lauwerys and N. Hans, was to give an account of the effect of the Second World War on education in Europe and the English-speaking countries. It contained some poignant yet inspiring articles.
6. The *International yearbook of education* was suspended after Volume XXXI in 1969. Publication was resumed in 1980 with Volume XXXII. It is now published annually.
7. UNESCO, *World survey of education; a handbook of educational organization and statistics*, Vols 1-5. Paris, UNESCO, 1955-1971, was published from time to time and did much to systematise the collection of educational data. In each volume a consultant drew together trends of development at different stages and levels of education. See also Goldstone, L. An International Standard Classification of Education (ISCED), *Prospects*, (Paris, UNESCO) Vol III, No. 3, Autumn 1973, p. 390-397.
8. Espe, H., ed. *Der aufgabenbereich der vergleichenden erziehungswissenschaft*. Berlin, ORBIS Verlag, 1956.
9. Idenburg, P. J. *Theorie van het onderwijsbeleid*. Groningen, Netherlands, Wolters-Noordhoff, 1971.
10. Thabault, R. *Education and change in a village community: Mazières-en-Gâtine, 1848-1914*. London, Routledge & Kegan Paul, 1971. (Translated from the French)
11. Hoz, V. G. *Principios de pedagogía sistemática*. Madrid, Rialp, 1968.
12. Schneider, F. *Triebkräfte der pädagogik der völker*. Salzburg, Austria, Otto Müller Verlag, 1947 and *Vergleichende erziehungswissenschaft*. Heidelberg, Germany FR, Quelle & Meyer, 1961.; Hilker, F. *Vergleichende pädagogik: eine einführung in ihre geschichte, theorie und praxis*. München, Germany FR, Hüber, 1962; Hans, N. *Comparative education*. 3rd ed. (rev.) London, Routledge & Kegan Paul, 1958;

Rosselló, P. *La teoría de las corrientes educativas: cursillo de educación comparada dinàmica.* La Habana, Centro Regional de la UNESCO, 1960.
13. Noah, H. J.; Eckstein, M. A. *Toward a science of comparative education.* London, Macmillan, 1969, summarizes the position very well.
14. Holmes, B.; Robinsohn, S. B., eds. *Relevant data in comparative education.* Hamburg, UNESCO Institute for Education, 1963.
15. Holmes, B. *International guide to education systems.* Paris, UNESCO, 1979. See also Holmes, B. *International yearbook of education, Vol. XXXII - 1980.* Paris, UNESCO, 1980.
16. Husén, T., ed. *International study of achievement in mathematics: a comparison of twelve countries.* Stockholm, Almqvist & Wiksell; New York, Wiley, 1967.
17. Holmes, B. *Problems in education: a comparative approach.* London, Routledge & Kegan Paul; New York, Humanities Press, 1965.
18. King, E. J. *Comparative studies and educational decision.* New York, Bobbs-Merrill; London, Methuen Educational, 1968.
19. Bowles, F. *Access to higher education* Paris, UNESCO and the International Association of Universities, 1963.
20. Prominent among the writers on recurrent education was Denis Kallen when he was at OECD. See *The universities and permanent education.* London, London Association of Comparative Educationists, 1980.
21. Robinsohn, S. B. et al. *Schulreform im gesellschaftlichen prozess: ein interkultureller vergleich.* Bd 1: Bundesrepublik Deutschland-Deutsche Demokratische Republik-Sovjetunion; England und Wales, Frankreich, Österreich, Schweden. Stuttgart, Germany FR, Klett-Cotta, 1970, 1975.
22. Holmes, B. ed. *Diversity and unity in education: a comparative analysis.* London, Allen and Unwin, 1980, and Mitter, W.; Swift, J., eds. *Education and the diversity of cultures: the contribution of comparative education.* Köln, Böhlau Verlag, 1985.
23. Holmes, B. ed. *Education in cities. World yearbook of education, 1970.* London, Evans, 1970.
24. Gouldner, W. *The coming crisis of western sociology.* London, Heinemann, 1971.
25. Bereday, G. Z. F. *Comparative method in education.* New York, Holt Rinehart & Winston, 1964.
26. Cramer, J. F.; Browne, G. S. *Contemporary education: a comparative study of national systems,* New York, Harcourt, Brace and World, 1957.
27. Tusquets, J. *Teoría y práctica de la pédagogía comparada.* Madrid, Magisterio Español, 1969. Tusquets also translated Bereday's *Comparative method in education,* which partly explains the popularity of Bereday's approach among Spanish authors.
28. Garcia Garrido, J. L. *Educación comparada: fundamentos y problemas.* Madrid, Dykinson, 1982. See also Benavent, J. A. La metodología comparativa de George

Z. F. Bereday. *Perspectivas pédagogicas* Barcelona, Spain, Instituto de Pedagogía Comparada, Universìdad de Barcelona), vol. V, no. 17, 1966, p. 63-76; vol. V, no. 18, 1966, p. 249-276.

29. Archer, Margaret Scotford. *The social origins of education systems.* London, Sage, 1979.
30. Husén, T. *The school in question: a comparative study of the school and its future in Western society.* Oxford, Oxford University Press, 1979.
31. Röhrs, H. *Forschungsstrategien in der vergleichenden erziehungswissenschaft.* Weinheim, Germany FR, Beltz, 1975.
32. Mitter, W. *Educational research in the Federal Republic of Germany: institutions, approaches, trends. Three studies.* Frankfurt am Main, Germany FR, Deutsches Institut für internationale pädagogische forschung, 1981.
33. Lé Thành Khôi. *L'éducation comparée.* Paris, Armand Colin, 1981.
34. Altbach, P. G.; Kelly, Gail P., eds. *New approaches to comparative education* Chicago, IL, University of Chicago Press, 1986.
35. Holmes, B. The problem approach in comparative education: some methodological considerations. *Comparative education review* (New York), vol. 2, no. 1, June 1958, p. 3-8.
36. Garcia Garrido, J. L. *Sistemas educativos de hoy.* Madrid, Dykinson, 1984.
37. Orizio, Battista. *Pàedagogia comparativa.* Brescia, Italy, Editrice la Scuola, 1977.
38. Vexliard, A. *La pédagogie comparée.* Paris, Presses Universitaires de France, 1967.
39. Carbone Pighetti, M. G. *La scuola in Europa.* Consiglio regionale della Liguria, 1979.
40. Berger, W.; Gruber, K. H., *Die vergleichende Erziehungswissenschaft,* Wien, Jugend und Volk, 1976, and Berger, W. *Schulentwicklungen in vergleichender Sicht: USA, England, Frankreich, BRD, Schweiz, Österreich,* Wien, Jugend und Volk, 1978.
41. Mialaret, G.; Vial, J. *Histoire mondiale de l'éducation, Vol. 4: de 1945 à nos jours.* Paris, Presses Universitaires de France, 1981.
42. Cowen, R. L'évolution des idées et des pratiques pédagogiques en Europe occidentale. In Mialaret, G.; Vial, J. *op cit.,* p. 11-20.
43. Neave, G. *The EEC and education.* Stoke-on-Trent, UK, Trentham Books, 1984.
44. Holmes, B., ed. *Equality and freedom in education: a comparative study.* London, Allen and Unwin, 1985.
45. Wolfgang Mitter in a letter to the author.
46. Lé Thành Khôi in a letter to the author.
47. Francesc Pedro in a letter to the author.
48. see Furter, P. *Les systèmes de formation dans leurs contextes.* Berne, Peter Lang, 1980.
49. Tournier, Michèle. Aperçus sur l'évolution de l'éducation comparée en France et à l'étranger. *Revue Française de pédagogie,* (Paris, Institut national de recherche pédagogique) No. 54, janvier-mars 1981, p. 76-90

50. Programmes en éducation comparée dans les universités françaises (pour l'année universitaire 1978-1979). *Éducation comparée*, No. 18-19, décembre 1978 - février 1979, p. 173-180. (Paris, Association francophone d'Éducation comparée)
51. Champion, J. *Langage et pédagogie en France et en Afrique*. Paris, Anthropos, 1986.
52. University of London Institute of Education. Department of Comparative Education, *Research, 1947-1983*, London, 1983.
53. Halls, W. D. *Education, culture and politics in modern France*. Oxford, UK, Pergamon, 1976.
54. See Edding, F. *Internationale tendenzen in der entwicklung der ausgaben für schulen und hochschulen*. Kiel, Germany FR, Universität Kiel, 1958. and Ökonomie des bildungswesens: Lehren und Lernen als Haushalt und als Investition. Freiburg im Breisgau, Germany FR, Rombach, 1963.
55. Picht, G. *Die Deutsche bildungskatastrophe*, Freiburg im Breisgau, Germany FR, Walter Verlag, 1964.
56. OECD, CERI. *Case studies of educational innovation, Vols. 1-4*. Paris, 1973.
57. OECD. *Reviews of national policies for education*, various country studies including for example Sweden, Italy, Germany, Japan, New Zealand, Australia. (various dates)
58. From a letter to the author from G. Neave.
59. Niessen, M.; Peschar, J., eds. *Comparative research in education: overview, strategy and applications in Eastern and Western Europe*. Oxford, UK, Pergamon; Budapest, Akadémiai Kiadó, 1982.
60. Ibid., p. xiv.
61. Landsheere, G. de. *La recherche en éducation dans le monde*. Paris, Presses universitaires de France, 1986. See also Landsheere, G. de. *Empirical research in education*. Paris, UNESCO, 1982.
62. Nisbet, J.; Megarry, J.; Nisbet, S., eds. *Research, policy and practice. The World yearbook of education, 1985*. London, Kogan Page; New York, Nichols Pub. Co., 1985.
63. Holmes, B. et al. *International handbook of education systems, Vols. 1-3*. Chichester, UK, Wiley, 1983-4.
64. Froese, L. Grenzen und Möglichkeiten des Vergleichs. In: Willman, B. *Bildungswesen, chancengleichheit und beschäftigungssystem: vergleichende daten und analysen zur bildungspolitik in Schweden*. (Marburger Beiträge zur Vergleichenden Erziehungswissenschaft und Bildungsforschung, Bd. 10) München, Minerva Publikation Saur, 1979.
65. Kluge, N. et al. *Gesamthochschule Kassel, 1971-81: rückblick auf das erste jahrzehnt*. Kassel, Germany FR, Stauda, 1981.
66. Mallinson, V. *The Western European idea in education* Oxford, UK, Pergamon, 1980.

67. Hearnden, A. *Education, culture and politics in Western Germany.* Oxford, UK, Pergamon, 1976; and *Education in the two Germanies.* Oxford, UK, Blackwell, 1974.
68. Halls, W. D. *op cit.*, and Grant, N. *Soviet education* (4th ed.) Harmondsworth, UK, Penguin, 1979; and Society, schools and progress in Eastern Europe. Oxford, UK, Pergamon, 1969.
69. *Occasional papers* (London, London Association of Comparative Educationists), nos 1-11.
70. Phillips, D. *German universities after the surrender: British occupation policy and the control of higher education* Oxford, UK, University of Oxford, Department of Educational Studies, 1983.
71. Hearnden, A., ed. *The British in Germany: educational reconstruction after 1945.* London, Hamish Hamilton, 1978.
72. King, E. J. *Other schools than ours.* 5th ed. London, Holt, Rinehart and Winston, 1973, is well known. See also King, E. J., et al. *Post compulsory education: a new analysis in Western Europe.* London, Sage, 1974.
73. Malizia, G., et al. *Né scuola né fabbrica.* L'Aquila, Italy, L. U. Japadre Editore, 198 . Reguzzoni, M. Secondary education and employment within the European Community. *Comparative education* (Dorchester-on-Thames, UK) vol. 12, no. 1, March 1976, p. 67-79.
74. Creemers, B.; Hoeben, W.; Koops, K. eds. *De kwaliteit van het onderwijs.* Groningen, Netherlands, RION; Wolters-Noordhoff, 1983.

The socialist countries*

H. G. Hofmann and Zia Malkova

The role and function of comparative studies in general pedagogics
Comparative education is an integral part of educational sciences in socialist countries, where it came into being with the emergence of Marxist-Leninist pedagogy. It is based in principle on the findings of N. K. Krupskaya.

In 1914 Lenin had already suggested that N. K. Krupskaya, his wife, should devote herself to an examination of the development internationally of educational ideas and politics of education so as to transform any useful and valuable results of earlier educational developments in a dialectical way for the planned socialist revolution and to apply them to the education of young people in a socialist society. The basic principles of comparative education are set out in her well-known study, *Education and democracy*, which constitutes what might be called the birth certificate of Marxist-Leninist comparative education.

The lines of comparative education studies in the first few years after the 1917 Revolution were dictated by the urgent need to build a new school system in the Soviet Union. They largely consisted of applied research projects designed to help solve specific teaching problems. At the same time, research was under way into the fundamental trends in educational developments throughout the world.

Individual countries and regions were studied, the principles underpinning the school systems in societies with different socio-economic structures were compared, and the impact of education on social development was

---

* *This chapter was prepared before the events of 1989 and 1990. It was thought better to publish the chapter as it stands since the field is in a state of flux.*

analyzed. The works of such prominent Soviet educational scholars as P. P. Blonsky, N. N. Ilyin, M. S. Bernstein, I. M. Soloviev, I. F. Svadkovsky, N. A. Konstantinov and others, who analyzed trends in education under the impact of socio-economic factors, are still of considerable interest today. They studied a broad range of countries not only in Europe and North America, but also in Asia and Africa. Soviet comparative studies are distinguished by internationalism and a sincere desire to help all nations overcome their cultural backwardness, and acquire and implement the right to an education conforming to modern requirements. The authors of comparative studies do not confine themselves to inventories of facts. They explore the policies pursued by classes seeking to perpetuate their privilege of knowledge; they describe both the social and the educational obstacles to quality schooling for children of families from humble backgrounds; they analyze the consequences of social inequality in education and its implications for both society and the individual. The main yardstick in assessing the situation in a country or region is the extent to which schools conform in terms of organization, content and teaching methods to the principles of social equality and the objective need for the comprehensive development of all individuals.

With the emergence of a socialist type of school - first in the Soviet Union and after World War II in countries forming the community of socialist states - comparative education also received new impetus. Its fields of research are determined by new international processes in education, in educational and youth policy and children's welfare services, mainly manifested in the formation of certain multilateral or international organizations (UNESCO, Unicef). The growing trend towards internationalization in the educational sphere, above all, in the people's democracies, promoted the development of comparative education and central research facilities in socialist countries.

From the outset, comparative education proved to be effective in exploring international developmental trends favouring a modern educational policy in the interest of all children. In this context, comparative education in socialist countries interpreted international discussions, first of all within the framework of UNESCO, its International Institute of Educational Planning (IIEP) in Paris and its International Bureau of Education (IBE) in Geneva, and supported by special studies the work of these organizations. In due course, comparative education in socialist countries focused on the work of emerging international educational organizations dealing with essential problems of education in today's world.

Whereas Polish comparative educationalists were involved in international activities immediately after World War II, Soviet, Czechoslovak and Hungarian scholars intensified their research work from the middle of the 1950s. By the end of the decade, research in the German Democratic Republic was also paying greater attention to questions of international educational politics and sciences. Thus comparative education at different levels and times succeeded in fixing and analyzing important trends in international educational development. From the 1950s onwards, a special concern of comparative education was to highlight the convergence in organizing school and education within the socialist countries of Europe. From 1960, a new international type of a socialist school has come into being in these countries characterized by a growing common basis for the study of all essential problems. An important role of comparative education is to analyze that new type of school as one offering boys and girls in urban and rural areas equal opportunities for acquiring comprehensive scientifically based knowledge closely linked to life. At the same time, it shows individual national developments of that common type of school in socialist countries. In their collective work *The school in socialist European countries* which was published at the beginning of the sixties, comparative educationalists proved that in all countries of the community of socialist states children are educated on a scientific basis, that in general children in urban and rural areas are offered equal conditions of education, closely linked to life and that polytechnical education was fully introduced by around 1965.

An important purpose of comparative education is to distinguish the driving forces and laws determining educational policies and sciences of socialist countries. It analyzes the development of educational systems, their aims and content, revealing common and similar features as well as differences. By descriptive and explanatory methods it compares and interprets the data collected concerning concrete historical conditions in particular socialist countries.

Research reveals common and specific features of certain national education systems. An insight into problems of national development enables conclusions to be drawn from international experiences. Comparative education is a source of information for central national boards of education.

While in recent years research in comparative education has been aimed at analyzing and comparing achievements of the socialist school, work is at present directed to problems of further development of national school systems and educational provision.

Such work is greatly influenced by the increased pace of scientific, technological and social progress. Today, greater attention is paid by comparative education specialists in all socialist countries to analysis, comparison and evaluation of future developments in schooling in a socialist society. Important aspects of comparative analyses of educational development in socialist countries are:

- the mass formation of all-round development of young socialist personalities;
- ensuring conformity to the constitutional law of the practice of equal education for all;
- extensive inclusion of social forces in the state education of young people;
- harmonizing high-level education, socialist personality development and outlook;
- ensuring equal education of boys and girls from urban and rural areas at all levels of general education and vocational training;
- ensuring 11-13 years of continuous schooling for all;
- extensive allocation of scholarships and allowances as well as other socio-political provisions for students.

For instance, in recent years, a research team in comparative education headed by Prof. Dr. Jarkina of the Academy of Pedagogical Sciences of the USSR analyzed findings in the field of elaborating educational content and teaching methods in European countries of the Council for Mutual Economic Assistance (CMEA). In their study published in 1984 they concluded:

- in all socialist countries educational content underwent modernization in relation to the demands of scientific and technological progress and overall social development;
- educational issues have essential consequences for the guidance of all processes of social development in the countries of socialism as it exists;
- education to a high level of all becomes a typical feature of modern socialist society;
- the social potential of education grows in importance, since only a high level of general education enables all citizens to take an active part in social management.

All provisions for educational modernization are directed to this end. Jarkina et al. prove that a high educational level has become a major condition for the development of socialist democracy and for organizing an up-to-date socialist way of life. According to Jarkina a typical feature of socialist education is the complex approach to the modernization of the whole educational system in all its stages as well as improving educational structures and quality in all CMEA countries.

These are long-term changes based on complex programmes. The new determination of educational aim and content takes into account to a greater extent the ages of pupils and the actual conditions of schooling in particular countries.

Besides common aspects, the study points to differences in modernizing the content of education. For the GDR school, for example, Jarkina indicates the emphasis on polytechnical education in the framework of general socialist education. The special contribution of the school system in Bulgaria to providing unity between instruction and education is stressed in the above mentioned study by showing the new forms of differentiation at secondary level. The Bulgarian school is characterized by the close connection between general education and vocational training.

Furthermore, the significant experiences of Czechoslovak scientists in the field of didactics and their essential findings in formulating educational content as complex systems of knowledge are emphasized by the study. It shows that education is not an end in itself but a means of forming pupils' convictions and character. Thus, education provides decisive prerequisites for the development and moulding of a socialist personality.

According to Jarkina the common position of socialist countries in the CMEA is distinguished by a broad conception of the content of education being understood simultaneously as the totality of knowledge and activity. Stressing certain aspects of that development, Jarkina points to the fact that in the GDR the emphasis of didactics lies in the formulation of educational aims, whereas in the CSSR it is understood as process. There, work on internal differentiation of teaching as well as on extra-curricular differentiation is intense and linked with cooperation with Soviet educationalists to limit the autonomy of particular subjects by the growing integration of teaching units.

In the study great attention is paid to problems of teaching method, for example, subject-centred teaching, special stress on the pupil's role, greater emphasis on pupils' experiences and on extra-curricular information to be used in the process of teaching as well as a focus on self-education, i.e. the relation of special abilities connected with social interests to the point of the teaching as well as to increasing self-education of pupils. Analyses prove the need to reduce the volume of subject content in certain countries, moving from mainly descriptive forms of teaching to the purposive, active and creative acquisition of knowledge applicable to everyday life.

In all socialist countries attention is focused on main issues. Growing significance is given to differentiated teaching, taking into account the abilities and interests of particular pupils. As a result, the traditional schema of 'explanation, exercise, fixing in the mind, control', is changed by such forms of work as research, observation, private study, participation in seminars and discussions, essay-writing and processing of information.

The fundamental and applied methods of comparative studies

The subject-matter of comparative education studies embraces the theory and practice of the education of the young in countries with different socio-economic and political systems. Hence it is marked by great complexity, diversity, mobility and the presence of a considerable number of factors. Comparative studies are productive only if they are based on a solid fundamental methodology and use methods appropriate to the subject under study. Comparative education scholars in the socialist countries rely on the fundamental principles of dialectical and historical materialism.

The study of educational phenomena in close connection with political and economic factors

Education forms an organic part of society, a vital and developing cell of it, as it were. A scholar wishing to understand the mechanism of educational development and change cannot therefore confine the scope of his inquiry only to pedagogical phenomena. It must embrace the fundamental motivating forces that determine educational evolution, i.e. economics and politics. The nature and major direction of change in education must be accompanied by an in-depth study of changes in material production, the levels of workforce skills and training, and state policy; change in these shapes the demands society makes on schools and forms the nucleus of their operations. Indeed, the causes and nature of school reform in industrial countries over the past 25 years can only be appreciated through a careful scrutiny of the major directions of the scientific and technological revolution and its implications, resulting in the creation of new materials, technologies and sources of energy, as well as in a demand for non-manual labour and thus for higher standards of general and occupational training.

The content, major directions and course of school reforms can only be explained through an understanding of the policies pursued by the main sectors social sectors; analysis of policies enables one to understand the inconsistencies and limitations of school reforms wherever conservative forces seek to preserve their educational privilege.

Objectivity and specificity in the study of social phenomena

According to dialectical materialism, an inquiry into social phenomena should be based on a study of concrete facts of real life, rather than on the building of abstract schemes. True science, Marx wrote, begins where speculation ends and the scholar embarks on a study of practical activity, the practical process of life. The principle of objectivity calls for reliance on a solid foundation of facts, i.e. the sum total of facts relevant to the subject under study.

A scholar dealing with such a complex and varied subject as education in different countries, abounding in different facts, is compelled to rely on representativity, whereby from a multitude of facts those that reflect the typical and the essential are selected.

The technique of selecting representative facts is particularly necessary with decentralized school systems, when a researcher comes up against a veritable ocean of conflicting facts, phenomena and events. In such cases, it is essential to compare evidence from different regions so as to extrapolate, for instance, a fairly accurate and typical school curriculum and ascertain its typical content.

The historical approach to the subject of study

No social phenomenon can be understood without a study of their genesis and the major stages of their development. The historical principle is essential to any study. In fact, the historical and the logical constitute a unity. Social patterns or trends can only be ascertained from an analysis of the history of their evolution, i.e. how a phenomenon originated, what stages it passed through in its evolution, and what its current state is.

The historical principle is intrinsic to comparative education research. Only such an approach makes it possible to identify trends in education and assess the status of an education system or its various components worldwide, in a given region or a country. Thus contemporary Soviet schooling should be studied with due regard for what the Soviet state inherited from the tsars (almost total illiteracy, particularly among non-Russians, absence of compulsory education laws, low enrollment rates hardly reaching 20 per cent, etc.); the fascist period of 1941-45, which destroyed the school system in the country's western regions and greatly reduced the number of teachers; the major stages in the development of Soviet society, each with its own priorities in educational goals and educational research.

A scientifically correct evaluation of trends in education in the newly independent states of Africa and Asia also involves excursions into the past to identify the principal stages the countries and their school systems have passed through and to assess the changes brought about by each stage. Such a historical approach allows stable phenomena and the links between them to be identified, thus ensuring reliable generalizations and conclusions.

The systems approach in comparative studies

A study of phenomena in isolation and without consideration of their connections and interdependencies produces a distorted idea of the object under examination; it cannot reveal its nature, dynamics and lines of development. The systemic nature of evolution is an essential element of the dialectics of world development, while the systems approach is central to a scientific study of the world. The systems approach views the subject under study as a certain community of elements that interact closely and function according to the laws inherent in the object and its components. It calls for consideration of the object's structure and network of connections and relationships among the elements within the whole. It demands determination of the object's properties on the basis of the new quality resulting from the integrity of the object, rather than from a mere summation of the interacting elements. It also calls for the object's connections with its environment and hierarchically higher systems to be identified.

The systems approach should be one of the principal methods in comparative education studies, which are concerned with systems with complex internal structures and which concurrently maintain multifarious connections with other systems. Science, technology and schooling, production, politics and schooling, the social environment and schooling, the school and the family, the school *vis-à-vis* other stages of education, historical and cultural traditions and schooling - these are but some of the most important interconnections that must be described to understand the state and trends in school developments.

These connections inevitably direct the scholar's attention to economics, politics, ideology, history and national culture. In comparative studies an interdisciplinary approach involving specialists in various fields is essential. For example, the study of the economic effectiveness of education in the United States, the Federal Republic of Germany and Japan, carried out by Soviet economists A. I. Martsinkevich, M. B. Kolchugina and A. I. Sokolov furnishes an abundance of data that supplement and clarify the findings of comparative education scholars of the systems in those countries.

In addition to its diverse external connections, the school system is distinguished by a complex internal organization with a multiplicity of structural elements and their interdependencies. No objective evaluation of primary schooling in a given country can be made without a close scrutiny of the other components of the school system, such as the overall goals of education, major directions in educational policies, teacher training, the nature of the links between pre-school, primary and extra-mural institutions, as well as between primary and secondary schooling.

Yet an assessment of the current state of an education system as a systemic entity requires a scientifically grounded criterion and a set of indicators for researchers. The choice of such a criterion lies in the realm of fundamental philosophical methodology and the problem of making a suitable choice has been tackled in different ways. Some scholars have suggested enrollment ratios of government spending on education as the major criteria. The state of education in various countries would be compared on the basis of a comparison of these quantitative data.

Numerical indicators are, of course, important in evaluating education. Yet the major criterion for evaluating a school system is the extent to which it attains the goal of ensuring the comprehensive development of all young people, in keeping with ideas of democracy and social progress and the objective needs of the scientific and technological revolution.

The following set of indicators might be formulated, making it possible to evaluate, with a sufficient degree of objectivity, the quality of a school system and compare it with those in other countries:

1. Legislation on schooling: how far it reflects the goals of all-round development, social equality in education, its free provision and accessibility;

2. Financing of education: sources, dynamics of the share in the GNP or national income, expenditure per student, the structure of educational spending, instances of inequality in education, shortages of financing in education and how they manifest themselves;

3. Educational administration: structure, specifics (centralized or decentralized), public participation;

4. Pre-school public education: access, organization, links with formal schooling, trends;

5. Access to schooling: duration of compulsory studies, guarantees of access (free tuition, material assistance to pupils, instruction in the mother tongue, organization of school-systems in urban and rural communities), enrollment ratios of various population groups, dropout rate, its causes, the social breakdown of school dropouts;
6. The 'openness' of a school system: absence of 'blind alley' schools and of overt or covert selection resulting in social inequality, continuity between levels of education, opportunities for gainfully employed young men and women to study further, facilities for lifelong education;
7. Educational standards of the population: illiteracy rate, percentage of secondary school-leavers and university graduates in the workforce, standards of education for women, the educational attainments of national and ethnic minorities;
8. Extra-mural (out-of-school) institutions: their network, financing, spheres of activity, links with schools;
9. The quality of the general education available to all young people: the balance between different courses in the curriculum from the point of view of the all-round development of the individual, the academic standards of the curriculum, i.e. correspondence between syllabuses and relevant fields of knowledge, the balance between the theoretical and practical aspects in the content of education and its relevance to life, polytechnical standards in the curriculum, the level of ecological training;
10. The nature of differentiation in instruction: the criteria underlying differentiation, degree of differentiation, level at which it starts and the standard of general education on which it is based;
11. Preparation of school students for work: share of work-related subjects in the curriculum, nature of preparation for work, organization of careers guidance;
12. Preparation of school students for higher education: availability of university-oriented streams, percentage of pupils following university preparation courses and their social composition, percentage of school-leavers enrolled in institutions of university standing;
13. Facilities for vocational training: the system of vocational institutions, their connections with general schools standards of training (general and skill-related), employment opportunities provided;

14. Opportunities for pursuing individual interests and developing aptitudes and creative talents;
15. The goals and content of moral education;
16. The teaching profession: educational standards, the social and material status of teachers, activities of teacher organizations;
17. Teacher training: its structure, content and methods;
18. Educational research: its organization, the main directions and most important accomplishments (the theoretical standard of major projects, their impact on school practice).

Such is the basic framework followed by comparative education scholars in the socialist countries in their joint project *Comparative analysis of educational development in the contemporary world*. The various components of the programme are, naturally, complemented and clarified, and some may overlap, yet the objective of the study remains to ascertain how far existing school systems meet mankind's prime goal, i.e. to ensure the all-round development of each member of society. In this context, comparative education reveals international trends of development and change in both world systems.

Investigations into general developments in schooling and the educational sciences are carried out in order to analyze and evaluate special development in both capitalist and Marxist world systems and to prove that different social factors and laws determine developments in educational policy and sciences. For this purpose, comparative education examines the development of school and society in both world systems and the emergent states and evaluates all educational changes and reforms with regard to social, scientific and technological progress and its influence on adolescents. Basic material is gained from national, regional and problem studies. Of great importance are interpretations of generalized studies elaborated by UNESCO and its institutions, above all IBE and IIEP.

Another field of research in comparative education of socialist countries is that of *educational developments in developing countries*. The more countries of Africa, Asia and Latin America build up an educational system serving their own aims, the greater the efforts of Marxist-Leninist comparative education to reveal trends and laws underlying those processes, in accordance with statements of UNESCO demonstrating that educational developments in Asia, Africa and Latin America are closely connected with political and social changes in the emergent states. Marxist-Leninist comparative education has concluded that the educational problems of those countries reflect essential issues of social progress. Thus, in countries with a socialist orientation democratic educational systems are organized with the aim of a gradual granting of equal rights to education for all children. After national independence great success was attained in the field of alphabetization, in organizing the elementary level and a differentiated secondary level with special attention to vocational training and technological orientation. The determination of the objects and content of education is closely linked with the emerging social strategies of national democratic movements in those countries. A growing differentiated use of national languages during alphabetization, as well as in primary education, and a full use of languages of former colonial powers for the benefit of social progress may be observed. Educational politics have increasingly become concerned with economic requirements, taking into account the necessity of vocational training for the majority of pupils and their preparation for working life. The extension and improvement of teaching mathematics and natural sciences became a central target, along with an intensified socio-political education. In African countries, the youth is educated by an ideological concept of African authenticity and identity with the state - for instance, one is educated to become a Zambian.

In their investigation of 'educational development in emergent states of Asia and Africa' experts in comparative education of the GDR show that in those countries special attention is paid to eliminating illiteracy and to providing elementary education. Their analyses of the UNESCO conference in Harare in 1982 and other regional conferences of educational ministers and organizations in the framework of OAU confirmed the growing interest in this problem.

Research work is also being undertaken for analyzing and summarizing experiences of solidarity and support for emergent states in the field of education by socialist countries.

Research in comparative education also explores the efforts of international organizations, above all UNESCO, to support educational progress in emergent states. At the same time, new educational concepts of former influential colonial powers and other countries are examined.

Research also deals with the activities of regional, international and non-state educational organizations, primarily in African countries, where the African Organization for Socio-Political Teaching, the African Organization for Curricular Designing and the African Bureau of Educational Sciences came into being in the early sixties. It also studies the organization of the Swedish International Development Service, the World Bank and the Educational Research Namibia/Swapo, founded by the University of Bremen (FRG), etc.

Cooperation of socialist countries in the field of comparative education gathered momentum as a result of the work of the Multilateral Expert Council for Investigating Educational Politics and Sciences in Non-Socialist Countries. At present, the Council focuses on multilateral scientific research, primarily with regard to the historic competition between different socio-economic systems in the field of education. As a result of analysis of current educational developments the Council gathered various new findings concerning the improvement of general education and schooling. The experiences of non-socialist countries have been explored and evaluated. Based on analyses of educational systems in the eighties, the Expert Council prepared general papers on the main trends of educational development in both Marxist and capitalist systems under the conditions of scientific and technological progress and new socio-political developments. A third field of research concerns the development of educational studies in selected capitalist countries. Analyses are aimed at revealing general trends of development in educational studies in advanced capitalist countries, the impact of education in them as well as national features of particular educational systems and problems and reforms concerning them.

These investigations into the educational developments of capitalist countries helped to reveal new trends in the development of schooling and educational sciences. The school and educational sciences respond more quickly than before to new requirements of scientific and technological progress and, connected with it, social changes. It was shown that, under the influence of these factors, the gap between mass and elite education had widened and that schooling in advanced capitalist countries responds to the various demands of scientific and technological progress by changing general education.

Comparative education also examines the contribution of trade unions, workers' parties and many humanist and liberal educationalists to educational progress. In accordance with educational principles aimed at peace and mutual understanding on an international level, laid down in UNESCO documents, research also reveals the reactionary doctrines of anticommunism typical of certain capitalist educational systems.

A relatively new field of research in comparative education analyzes and evaluates schooling experiments and comprehensive organizational measures in both world systems. It investigates the reasons for experiments, describes their aims and the application of their results in practice in order to find out whether they increase the efficiency of educational processes or change the organization of schooling. At the same time, the social effects of experiments over a longer period are examined, showing the different aims of similar experiments - for example, assessing the value of information technology in general education in both world systems within general social factors.

Research techniques in comparative studies

The subject of inquiry of comparative education - the theory and practice of educating the young in countries with different socio-economic and political systems - is complicated owing to the complexity of its components and their relationships, the dynamics of the processes involved and the multiplicity of factors affecting it. Productive investigations are feasible only if a combination of techniques is used. The following techniques or methods would be essential:

The study of primary sources encompasses normative documents and material determining the activities of educational institutions. These are fundamental laws (constitutions), school education acts, directives, decisions, reports by central education authorities, accounts of debates on educational matters in parliaments, documents of teacher congresses and conferences, documents resulting from conferences or conventions held by political parties, including education programmes, etc.

Education's close links with economics and politics necessitates expansion of the data base to embrace documents concerned with the socio-economic and political strategies of the given country, training and retraining of the workforce, and long-term development programmes. The sum total of relevant socio-economic and political documents makes it possible to understand society's demands on schooling under specific conditions.

Essential for comparative education scholars are curricula, syllabuses and textbooks, a close analysis of which helps in gaining an insight into the substantive content of the school operation. Various other school documents, such as pupils' note-books, school newspapers, teacher-prepared assignments for pupils, pupil records, etc., supplement norm-setting documents and provide an insight into the actual atmosphere of a school environment.

In many countries, including the UK, the USA and Japan, educational institutions use testing. A study of the content of tests and their application in the instructional process is important for understanding the system of schooling in those countries.

The statistical method, one of the central techniques in comparative studies, helps produce important indications of the current state and trends in education, such as the evolution of the network of educational institutions, student enrollments, their distribution among various types of institution, teachers and their qualifications, educational spending, etc.

Analysis of publications is used widely in comparative studies, since it helps understand the theoretical thinking behind school activities and reveals the difficulties and problems facing schools, the ways to solve them and prospects for education within society. In many countries, the volume of education literature is enormous - monographs on pedagogics and educational psychology, education journals, encyclopaedia, dictionaries and glossaries, and information publications. A scholar has to tackle the difficult task of selecting literature that deals with fundamental issues, provides accurate data and influences educational thinking in the country concerned. Educational encyclopaedias, directories and dictionaries help researchers clarify terminology, identify personalities and obtain basic information on various matters. Journals, magazines and newspapers furnish data on topical education issues, since they cover problem areas, debatable questions, experiments and the most important events. A continuous study of periodicals, in comparison with monographs and other sources, enables the scholar to perceive the emergence of new phenomena and follow their evolution.

Observation, although of less importance than the study of written sources, is psychologically significant, since it provides researchers with first-hand personal impressions of the object of inquiry and complements impersonal figures and generalized facts with visual and emotional perceptions. There are two types of observation: extensive and intensive. Extensive observation involves short-term, single visits to a large number of educational institutions following a pre-determined observation pattern, which gives the scholar a chance to compare and identify stable phenomena and make generalizations. Intensive observation aims to make an in-depth inquiry into school life and study its specific climate. This entails a lengthy observation period in one school, including attendance at classes and after-school activities, compilation of projects in classrooms and hobby groups, recording of interviews, filming and photographing. Intensive observation makes it possible to appreciate the school's internal life.

Observation techniques require good communicative skills from the researcher, as well as considerable educational experience and professionalism. If good relations develop between the researcher and teachers, sociological techniques, such as questionnaires, interviews and conversations can be used, which add considerably to personal observation.

Organizations and centres of comparative education in socialist countries

The value of comparative education to socialist countries is manifested by the fact that within the last 20 years educational research centres as well as universities and colleges of education have established special facilities for comparative education.

The Soviet Union has an extensive system of educational research institutions. Educational research is conducted by such national centres as the Academy of Pedagogical Sciences of the USSR, comprising 15 research institutes, the Scientific Research Institute on Problems of Higher Education, the All-Union Scientific Research Institute of Vocational Education, as well as the scientific research institutes of education in 15 national republics and more than 200 chairs of education at the universities and pedagogical and other institutes.

There are several departments and sections conducting research in the sphere of school and pedagogy in foreign countries:

- the department of contemporary school and pedagogy abroad of the Scientific Research Institute of General Pedagogics of the Academy of Pedagogical Sciences of the USSR (Moscow). The department consists of three sections: the school and pedagogy in the socialist countries; the school and pedagogy in the developing countries; the school and pedagogy in the capitalist countries;
- the department of higher education in foreign countries of the Scientific Research Institute on Problems of Higher Education of the Ministry of higher and secondary specialized education of the USSR (Moscow);
- the section on problems of vocational education and training in foreign countries of the All-Union Scientific Research Institute of Vocational Education (Leningrad);
- the division concerned with problems of education in foreign countries of the Scientific Research Institute of Pedagogy of Ukraine;
- the section on problems of adult education in foreign countries affiliated with the all-Union society 'Znanie' ('Knowledge');

- the section of comparative pedagogy in the Moscow V. I. Lenin State Pedagogical Institute;
- the section of comparative study of textbooks of the publishing house 'Prosveschenie'.

Studies in comparative pedagogy are also being conducted by specialists in departments and occupying chairs of education (pedagogics) at Tashkent, Moscow and Piatigorsk pedagogical institutes. A number of institutes affiliated with the Academy of Sciences of the USSR (Institute of USA and Canada Studies, Institute of Asian and African Studies, Institute of World Economics and International Relations and others) have specialists studying culture and education in foreign countries.

The department of modern school and pedagogy in foreign countries of the Scientific Research Institute of General Pedagogics of the Academy of pedagogical sciences of the USSR coordinates the entire activity in the sphere of comparative pedagogy within the whole country. Meetings and discussions are regularly held on topical problems of comparative education research, its methodology and results. Particular importance is attached to the quality and efficiency of research. One way of improving the quality of studies in comparative pedagogy lies in using an interdisciplinary approach. Sociologists and economists participate with educators in studying education in foreign countries. For example, the economists M. B. Kolchugina and I. B. Martsinkevich (whose works *School and economics in the FRG* (1976) and *Economic efficiency of education in the USA* (1975) are widely known in the country) participated in preparing the book *School and school policy in the capitalist countries* (1975).

There is no periodical in the USSR devoted solely to problems of comparative pedagogy. Considering it as an integral part of general pedagogy, the leading theoretical journal of the Academy of Pedagogical Sciences, *Soviet pedagogy*, contains regular items on school and pedagogy abroad. Three to four articles on comparative pedagogy are published every month. Articles are also published in *Narodnoe obrazovanie*, the journal of the Ministry of Education of the USSR, and in other pedagogical journals and newspapers, the total number of which throughout the country exceeds 100.

To provide Soviet teachers with fresh information on foreign schooling and pedagogy collected reviews of books and articles by foreign authors entitled *School and pedagogy abroad* was published in the fifties and sixties. At present the Centre of Pedagogical Information of the Research Institute of General Pedagogics regularly publishes three types of materials about school and pedagogy in foreign countries: the bulletin *Education abroad*; analytical reviews of actual problems of comparative pedagogy; and abstracts of books and articles by foreign authors. These publications are extremely popular with teachers and are distributed not only in the Soviet Union, but in many foreign countries through *Mezhdunarodnaya kniga*.

Information bulletins are also published by these departments and centres covering problems of higher education in foreign countries, and vocational training in foreign countries.

Reviews, reports and essays are prepared by specialists in comparative pedagogy studying the current situation and main trends in the development of education systems, school and pedagogical thought in foreign countries. Important works on public education in various countries of the world have been published over the years:

A. Nusenbaum, *Public education in India*, 1956;

V. Aranskij, V. Lapchinskaya, *The system of education in Great Britain*, 1967;

B. Vulfson, *School in modern France*, 1970; *Pedagogical thought in France*, 1983;

Z. Malkova, *The modern school in the USA*, 1971;

V. Gomonnaij, *Public education in Hungary*, 1972;

N. Vorobjev, *Higher education in the GDR*, 1976;

R. Sanzhaasuren, I. Zhernose, *Education in Mongolia*, 1978;

L. Filipova, *University education in the USA*, 1981;

Stecjak, J. P., Mansfeld, P. P., *School in socialist Yugoslavia*, 1976;

Goncarov, L. N., Leontyeva, O. S., *Modern educational policy in the USA*, 1984;

Marcinkovski, I. B., *Current problems of higher education in capitalist countries*, 1981;

Rodionov, M. L., *Japanese school at the cross roads*, 1981;

Leontyava, O. S., Pisareva, L. J., *Bourgeois opinion-polls on youth problems*, 1984;

Pilipovski, V., *The growth of conservative-technocratic trends in modern bourgeois pedagogics*, 1983;

Yu. Durasevich, *Education and pedagogy in Cuba*, 1981

D. Mansfeld, *Public education in Yugoslavia*, 1982.

The volume of studies on trends in the development of education and pedagogical thought in a number of countries with different socio-economic systems has increased during the last ten years. The following works have been published:

Z. Malkova, B. Vulfson, *School and pedagogy in the capitalist countries*, 1976;

A. Shirinskij, *Problems of education in the developing countries*, 1977;

T. Yarkina, (ed.), *Upbringing in schools of the socialist countries*, 1984;

Z. Malkova, B. Vulfson, (eds), *Bourgeois pedagogy at present stage of development*, 1984;

V. Pilipovskij, *Theories of forming a personality in bourgeois pedagogy*, 1985.

The analysis of history and geography textbooks with the view to removing facts and other materials contrary to the socialist ethic is an important trend in comparative studies. Soviet-Finnish and Soviet-French sections of specialists in comparative analysis of school textbooks on history and geography have been working for several years. Soviet-American groups of similar specialists co-operated during the period of 1978-1980.

The accumulated scientific material allowed us to include extensive material on school and pedagogy abroad in the four-volume work, *Pedagogical encyclopaedia* (1964-1968) and to publish an encyclopaedia, *School and pedagogy in foreign countries* (1973). A new edition of the latter is now being prepared.

Efficiency of comparative studies is a major problem. The results of these studies are used by educational researchers, administrators of public education, teachers and students of pedagogical institutions, school teachers, etc. A compulsory course of lectures under the general title *School and pedagogy in foreign countries* is given in the majority of pedagogical institutes. Curricula of many institutes include optional courses which can be chosen by students in accordance with their interests, such as: *Pedagogical thought in the capitalist countries, Formation and development of national systems of education in newly independent countries, School and pedagogy in the socialist countries* and so on. In the seventies a general course on *Comparative pedagogy* developed by the section of comparative pedagogy headed by Dr. M. A. Sokolova was in use at some faculties of the Moscow V. I. Lenin State Pedagogical Institute.

Special textbooks containing generalized characteristics of the development of school and pedagogy in foreign countries (e.g. Z. Malkova, *School and pedagogy abroad*, 1984; A. Shirinskij, *Education in developing countries*,

1982) have been written for use by teachers, students, and participants in advanced training courses. Results of comparative studies help us to develop teachers' and future teachers' pedagogical awareness in the spirit of internationalism, and their perception of general and particular issues in educational development.

The Central Institute of Educational Research of the Ministry of Education of the People's Republic of Poland as well as Polish universities and colleges of education may look back to certain traditions in comparative education. Comparative education is highly regarded at the University of Warsaw. For several decades the department of comparative education of the Central Institute of Education has contributed to the exposition of international trends in educational politics and sciences. It examines national features of educational developments and their efficiency as well as issues of educational politics and studies of special interest for their own country. It recently compiled surveys on educational politics in capitalist countries based on current bourgeois educational concepts and explored problems of educational differentiation in advanced and backward capitalist countries. Research deals with analysis of didactic differences and their importance for intensified learning, with analyses and interpretations of curricula and their targets as well as findings of bourgeois educationalists concerning effective forms of educational differentiation.

Great attention is given to textbook analyses - especially of textbooks for history lessons - of particular countries, above all, of the Federal Republic of Germany, France, Spain, Greece and Finland. They are of special interest to the People's Republic of Poland with regard to the aftermath of German fascism.

Immense experience was gained through comparison of international textbooks. The Institute exchanges textbooks with more than 44 countries. Important results followed from comparing them. The GDR and the People's Republic of Poland, for instance, carefully compared their textbooks, especially those for history, geography and civics. Thus, recently, a historically true and concrete picture of the neighbouring country was gained. Polish scientists strive to compare textbooks of all European countries so as to revise contents that do not correspond to historic truth. In the last five years intensified investigations have been made into general educational developments at the secondary level in socialist countries. Findings in this context have been summarized in a comprehensive study *Secondary education in European countries and educational innovation in the world*. Of great value are documents and data compiled on current international educational reforms and experiments as well as monographs and information on the educational theory and practice of both world systems and new developmental trends. In the seventies, research work dealt with educational developments in emergent states, primarily in Africa.

Apart from research work done at the University of Sofia, comparative education was established at the Bulgarian Institute of Education *Samodumov*. Bulgarian scholars presented essential findings concerning the theory and methodology of comparative education. The department of comparative education of the *Samodumov* Institute wants to support further steps and measures of general innovation and improvement of the Bulgarian educational system by findings based mainly on comparative analyses of socialist educational systems. Of great relevance are analyses of general issues of bourgeois educational thought completed by the Institute in close co-operation with the Institute of modern social theories at the Academy of Sciences of the People's Republic of Bulgaria. For socialist countries the results of those analyses are an important addition to our knowledge of the educational development of bourgeois systems.

Comparative education has received a strong impetus in such young socialist countries as the Democratic Republic of Vietnam and Cuba. In both countries special departments have been established at centres for educational research. At the Institute of Education in Hanoi a large department of comparative education came into being in the last decade. It gathered data on the educational development in South-East Asia in connection with investigations of the regional institutes of UNESCO. At the same time, analyses of educational thought in the USA with regard to cultural politics in South-East Asia were completed.

Comparative education in Cuba also made noteworthy contributions towards common analyses of the development in educational politics and sciences carried through by Marxist-Leninist comparative education. Of great importance are enquiries into the driving forces, trends and changes in education of the Caribbean region, Central and South America. Research is aimed at realizing national requirements to build a Cuban educational system which provides at the same time a comprehensive analysis of the laws and driving forces of educational development in emergent states. These findings should be widely used by comparative education of socialist countries.

Great attention is paid to comparative education by the Central Institute of Education of the Ministry of Education of the Czechoslovak Socialist Republic and the *Komanski* Institute of Education at the Academy of Sciences of the CSSR. Recently, a special working group was formed to examine developments of educational politics in socialist countries and special issues of educational politics and sciences in capitalist countries. The result consists of studies on the interrelation of school and society in socialist countries compared to capitalist ones. Of great importance are analyses of new trends in the educational development of advanced capitalist countries.

Headed by A. M. Effenbergerova, research workers in the field of comparative education at the Educational Research Institute of Prague, at the Ministry of Education of the Czech Republic, explored the main problems of educational developments in general schools of socialist countries with regard to educational politics and its consequences for educational sciences. They revealed that basic educational problems in all socialist countries play an important role in government policy. Growing importance is attached to the education of youth and their preparation for work and life. To a growing extent in the CSSR educational problems are solved from a system-theoretical position. Under new conditions structures of school are changed and greater demand is made for the further education of all members of socialist society. The following trends may be stressed:

- prolongation of education
- re-designing of secondary education as general polytechnical education with the aim of preparing young people for permanent learning and self-realization
- consistent modernization of educational content
- the strengthening of the pedagogical and psychological fundamentals of education
- stressing the importance of communist education
- intensification of relations between school and society, school and family, school and youth organization
- deepening of the internal differentiation of secondary education.

At the same time, the importance of forming a scientifically founded ideology for pupils and of reforming the content of socialist general education is stressed with regard to determining the necessary optimum of education for all and promoting the abilities of each child. Czech educationalists point to practical difficulties for teachers as a result of changes in educational content and timetables. They arise from time limitations for education and the demands of science and technology, of society and culture. It is necessary to improve interdisciplinary relations between single subjects and to determine exactly the required level of education. A. M. Effenbergerova points to the clash between traditional knowledge and modern elements of education, and between growing scientific information and time limitations. She thinks it indispensable to educate the all-round developed personality with regard to given processes of production, given conditions of division of labour and requirements for qualified cadres. Great attention is paid to problems of educating youth according to humanist traditions of socialism and peace.

A significant impetus has been given to comparative education in the Hungarian People's Republic. A centre was established at the National Institute of Education, the central research institute of the Ministry of Education and Culture. A special working group brings together all national research workers. In this context, the work of the National Educational Library and the Hungarian Educational Society has had a significant impact.

Under the guidance of the National Institute of Education, comparative education was also established at universities and colleges. Essential educational problems of international relevance are explored in close co-operation with institutes of UNESCO. Great emphasis is laid on the impact of the scientific and technological progress on school education in both world systems. Detailed analyses reveal problems of educational development in both world systems and their mutual influence, as well as educational activities of the World Bank and the International Monetary Fund in emergent states.

A comparative study on main problems of educational development in both social systems has been carried out by the Hungarian educationalist, Eva Szechy. It highlights the fact that major educational reforms are realized simultaneously in both world systems for contrary reasons. In socialist countries those processes aim at providing a high educational level for all children, whereas in advanced bourgeois states the gap between elite and mass education is widened. Changes in schooling of both world systems are connected with similar demands of the scientific and technological revolution but following contrary targets. In this context, Hungarian scientists stress that in socialist countries the aim of educational reform is to improve social conditions and to offer to each child the greatest opportunity for personality development based on a high level of practical education. Bourgeois schooling, on the other hand, serves the aims of bourgeois society, with limited possibilities as compared to socialism. The study points to educational issues to be followed up to the year 2000 by both world systems and to forces of bourgeois countries being in the position to realize a democratic educational conception offering chances to all children.

Enquiries into the educational development of particular capitalist countries, e.g. Austria and Italy, are examples of Hungarian research in comparative education.

Immediately after World War II comparative education was established at the National Institute of Education of the Socialist Republic of Romania. It is closely linked to the Centre for information and documentation of the Institute. Of great value for educationalists of socialist countries are trend reports of international educational developments, documentation of current politics of education in both world systems, as well as problem-centred studies on general education and vocational training, effective organization of secondary education and analyses of timetables for school lessons.

Comparative education in the German Democratic Republic came into being with the foundation of the German Central Educational Institute in 1949 and was intensified following the establishment of the Academy of Pedagogical Sciences of the GDR. A special laboratory of comparative education provides necessary data for national educational sciences and leading educational authorities. Results of research work and relevant informations are used by lecturers in colleges of education, educational authorities and teachers. The research objectives of comparative education are fixed in five-year plans. Its work consists of complex and problem-centred analyses of general developments in school and education of both world systems and emergent states. It promotes the discovery and application of generally accepted laws for the organization of school and education in socialist countries. Research carried out by the department of *Studies of socialist educational politics and sciences* within the laboratory of comparative education of the Academy of Pedagogical Sciences of the GDR, covers general problems of unity and differentiation of education in socialist countries with regard to their special developmental and historical conditions.

New issues in different educational fields are initially approved on national level and later gain the importance of general trends and requirements for other socialist countries. Thus, according to analyses of Soviet scientists concerning the educational reform of 1984, special findings in the field of polytechnical education in the GDR were carefully explored and used for decision-making. Equally, findings of the Soviet educationalists Krayevski and Lerner concerning the organization of academic teaching were applied and adapted in didactics by GDR experts.

The department provides suggestions for the development of a new type of school under socialism. Research is closely linked to analyses of common general processes for the formation of an educationally well-rounded personality, above all, in relation to providing all children a scientifically-based education, close to life. Its findings on the development of school and education in socialist countries point to the impact of educational politics and thought on social policy of socialist countries. They help to reveal a growing similarity and commonality of socialist countries in the field of education and show the objective universality of certain findings, pointing to the way that countries of the community of socialist states make use of them within their national conditions.

A new target of comparative education at the Academy of Pedagogical Sciences of the GDR is to examine principal problems of education in developing countries under the conditions of the historic competition of both socio-political systems - socialism and capitalism.

With the research project *Main trends of educational developments in the national and social liberation movement of particular emergent states*, started in 1981, 33 investigations were focused on:

- analyses of educational developments in particular countries in accordance with research planning;
- preliminary surveys of the regional and international educational organization of the Organization of African States (OAU), of regional educational associations and particular national and international organizations and their role in emergent states;
- problem-centred analyses of the function of school and aims and contents of schooling, of the relation between school and society, above all, the economy and education;
- exposure of activities and content of neo-colonial educational assistance;
- imparting experiences of socialist educational policy and sciences to interested emergent states.

The general findings on politics of education in emergent states were:

- that the main targets of activity in educational politics of countries with socialist orientation are the organization of a national and democratic educational system, the alphabetization and the shaping of an effective primary education for all, providing a close connection between general education and productive labour of pupils;

- that educational progress is to be reached by imparting to all children equal, systematic, scientifically-based education, close to life;
- the accelerated access of youth and grown-ups to forms of education necessary for their personal existence;
- that targets and the content of education are increasingly determined by the social strategy of forces inducing progress in developing countries;
- the timely training and further education of teachers regarding new educational demands at all levels;
- that to a growing extent national languages are used in a differentiated way both for eliminating illiteracy and for promoting a national language (e.g. in Ethiopia the Amharic language) in primary education, while, on the other hand, the languages of former colonial powers are used for official aims (administrative language);
- the systematic orientation of education to the requirements of economic development together with growing realization of the first steps in mass vocational training of pupils.

In this context, recent results of assistance to emergent states were summarized and analyzed to find out how progressive educational experience was used by emergent states in a creative way.

Recent changes in the relation between society, the economy, educational policy and sciences in capitalist countries under the conditions of the historic competition of both world systems are explored by the department *School and education of capitalist countries* of the laboratory of comparative education at the Academy of Pedagogical Sciences of the GDR.

The following main findings were reached:

- that developments of educational policy in the eighties reflect the growing influence of conservative, neo-liberal educational strategies (USA, England, FRG) and changes in socio-reformist educational targets (France, Sweden, Austria);
- that educational systems respond immediately to the demands and opportunities of scientific and technological progress with regard to changes of educational content, the relation between general education and vocational training and the promotion of pupil's abilities and skills to perform new production processes (information technology and computer processing);

- that there is growing application of microelectronics and information technologies in school, above all, at secondary level and in spare time activities;
- that education responds to the challenge of extended reproduction by deepening the external division and internal differentiation of mass and elite education;
- that changes in educational concepts are closely connected with norms and values of the current political forces.

The image of and demands on teachers, their political and social role and mission range from growing depreciation to partial reassessment for the upbringing of a future generation with different educational and vocational levels. National and international shaping of education are essential features of modern educational policy. National and international organizations (OECD, EC, European Council, the Nordic Council and the Club of Rome) intensify their educational activities. Problems of future relations between school and society in the form of regional, global and 'alternative' models are the main issues of educational concepts of various political movements. In different concepts of the workers' movement models of a 'democratic' school play a key role.

Led by Prof. Dr. Becker, research workers of the department of comparative education at the Academy of Pedagogical Sciences of the GDR published a study on *The Character, features and trends of bourgeois educational research and practice in the 1980s*, revealing that due to new social conditions questions of the principle regarding relation between school and society again became a central issue of educational thought and policy. These questions are solved at present in accordance with the regional attachment of each country.

It was clear that this central question is the starting point and aim of all strategical concepts of education of various political forces in the bourgeois world striving for solutions of a quite different kind and sometimes very contrary character.

Bibliography

Akademie der Pädagogischen Wissenschaften der DDR, Arbeitsstelle für Auslandspädagogik, *Probleme der bildung und erziehung der jugend in national befreiten staaten Afrikas und Asiens* [Problems of educating youth in emergent countries of Africa and Asia]. Berlin, German DR, 1978 (Beiträge zur schulpolitik und pädagogik des auslands, 1978, 2)

Akademie der Pädagogischen Wissenschaften der DDR, Arbeitsstelle für Auslandspädagogik, *Bildungssysteme kapitalistischer Länder Europas in den 80er jahren* [Educational systems in European capitalist countries in the 80s], Berlin, German DR, 1982. (Beiträge zur schulpolitik und pädagogik des auslands, 1982, 1).

Akademie der Pädagogischen Wissenschaften der DDR, Arbeitsstelle für Auslandspädagogik, *Bilanz der forschungen des multilateralen expertenrates: studium der schulpolitik und pädagogik kapitalistischer länder von 1974-1983 zur unterstützung der lehreraus-und-weiterbildung* [Findings of the Multilateral Council of Experts: investigations into educational politics and sciences of capitalist countries from 1974-1983 to be used for teacher training and further education]. Berlin, 1984.

Akademie der Pädagogischen Wissenschaften der DDR, Arbeitsstelle für Auslandspädagogik, *Schule im kapitalismus: analyse der bildungsentwicklung in den USA und kapitalistischen Ländern Europas* [School in capitalism: analysis of educational development in the USA and in European capitalist countries], Berlin, German DR, 1984. (Beiträge zur schulpolitik und pädagogik des auslands, 1984, 2).

Akademie der Pädagogischen Wissenschaften der DDR, Zentralstelle für pädagogische Information und Dokumentation, *Charakter, merkmale und tendenzen der imperialistischen bildungsstrategie und praxis in den 80er jahren* [Character, features and trends of imperialist educational strategy and practice in the 80s]. Berlin, German DR.

Akademie der Pädagogischen Wissenschaften der DDR, Arbeitsstelle für Auslandspädagogik, *Elementare volksbildung in entwicklungsländern* [Primary education in emergent countries], Berlin, German DR, 1985. (Beiträge zur schulpolitik und pädagogik des auslands, 1985, 3)

Balogh, L.; Zrinsky, L., Gegenwärtige situation und entwicklungstendenzen des bildungswesens in Italien [Present day state and trends in educational development in Italy]. In: Akademie der Pädagogischen Wissenschaften der DDR, Arbeitsstelle für Auslandspädagogik, *Schule in kapitalismus: analyse der bildungsentwicklung in den usa und kapitalischen Ländern Europas*, Berlin, German DR, 1984, p. 60-91, (Beiträge zur schulpolitik und pädagogik des auslands, 1984, 2).

Bartel, H., *Bildungspolitik und pädagogik ausgewählter national befreiter staaten*, Bd. II [Educational politics and sciences in selected emergent states, vol. II]. Akademie der Pädagogischen Wissenschaften der DDR, Arbeitsstelle für Auslandspädagogik, Berlin, German DR, 1984.

Bartel, H., *Zur funktion der schule in rahmen der demokratisierung des bildungswesens in national befreiten staaten mit sozialistischer alternative des entwicklungsweges (als beitrag zur ausprägang einer revolutionär-demokratischen bildungspolitik im sozialistischen äthiopien, in der VR Angola, in der VR Mocambique und in der VDR Jemen)* [Functions of school during democratization of education in emergent states with socialist orientation (contribution to the implementation of a revolutionary democratic policy of education in Socialist Ethiopia, in the People's Republics of Angola, Yemen and Mozambique)]. Akademie der Pädagogischen Wissenschaften der DDR, Berlin, German DR, 1985 [Diss. B]

Becker, H.; Levelt, D., Analyse der lage der schulbildung in der BRD [Analysis of the educational situation in the FRG]. In: Akademie der Pädagogischen Wissenschaften der DDR, Arbeitsstelle für Auslandspädagogik, *Schule im kapitalismus: analyse der bildungsentwicklung in den usa und kapitalistischen ländern Europas*, Berlin, German DR, 1984, p. 167-197 (Beiträge zur schulpolitik und pädagogik des auslands, 1984, 2).

Benedek, A., Osszehasonlító pedagógia a Szovjetunióban [Comparative education in the Soviet Union]. *Pedagógiai szemle* (Budapest), XXXI. évf., 7-8. SZ., 1981 július-augusztus, p. 692-697.

Benedek, A., *Az összehasonlító pegagógia az oktatáspolitikai döntések kialakításában és a fejlesztési folyamatok orientálásában* [The place of comparative educational policy and in the orientation of the developmental processes] Országos Pedagógiai Könyvtár és Múzeum, Budapest, 1985.

Benedek, A., Zusammenhänge der technologischen entwicklung mit der modernisierung der fachausbildung [Connections between technological development and modernization of special education]. In: Akademie der Pädagogischen Wissenschaften der DDR, Arbeitsstelle für Auslandspädagogik, *Weltbedeutung und internationaler charakter von theorie und praxis der sozialistischen schule*, Berlin, German DR, 1985, p. 256-260 (Beiträge zur schulpolitik und pädagogik des auslands, 1985, 1).

Bielas, L., Zu methodologischen grundlagen der ausarbeitung eines begriffskatalogs auf dem gebiet der auseinandersetzung (thesen) [On methodological questions in compiling a catalogue of terms for counter-propaganda (theses)]. In: Akademie der Pädagogischen Wissenschaften der DDR, Arbeitsstelle für Auslandspädagogik, *Die aufgaben der marxistisch-leninistischen pädagogik in der ideologischen klasseneinandersetzung zwischen sozialmus und imperialismus: kritik moderner bürgerlicher persönlichkeitsauffassungen und erziehungskonzeptionen*, Berlin, German DR, 1979, p. 29-44. (Beiträge zur schulpolitik und pädagogik des auslands, 1979, 2).

Bielas, L., UNESCO-Konferenz 'Umweltschule auf dem lande' [UNESCO conference 'Environmental school in the countryside']. *Vergleichende pädagogik* (Berlin, German DR), 16. Jahrg., heft 1, 1980, p. 76-77.

Billerbeck, W., Positionen und entwicklungstendezen der bürgerlichen sozialkritischen pädagogik [State and trends in the development of bourgeois socio-critical pedagogics]. *Vergleichende pädagogik* (Berlin, German DR), 16. Jahrg., Heft 1, 1980, p. 24-34.

Cakarov, N., Soziale ungleichheit im bildungswesen: konzeption der 'Neuen Rechten' in Frankreich [Social inequality in education: concepts of the 'New Right' in France]. *Vergleichende pädagogik* (Berlin, German DR), 17. Jahrg., Heft 2, 1981, p. 171-176.

Cakarov, N.; Bizkov, G. *Sravnitelna pedagogika* [Comparative education], Sofija, Sofijski universitet 'Kl. ohridski', Filosofski fakultet, Katedra 'Teoria i istorija na pedagogikata', 1986.

Cepicka, K.; Vlaciková, M., Das neue schulgesetz der CSSR [The new educational law of the CSSR]. *Vergleichende pädagogik* (Berlin, German DR), 21. Jahrg., Heft 4, 1985, p. 364-368.

Copilu, D., Vergleichende pädagogik im institut für pädagogische und psychologische forschung in Bukarest [Comparative education at the Institute of Educational and Psychological Research in Bucharest]. *Vergleichende pädagogik* (Berlin, German DR), 15. Jahrg., Heft 1, 1979, p. 44-46.

Dorzok, M., Die neue schule in der volksrepublik Benin [The new school in the People's Republic of Benin]. *Vergleichende pädagogik* (Berlin, German DR), 16. Jahrg., Heft 4, 1980, p. 384-391.

Effenbergerová, A. M., Analystische ubersicht über das bildungssystem in Spanien [Analytical survey of the Spanish educational system]. In: Akademie der Pädagogischen Wissenschaften der DDR, Arbeitsstelle für Auslandspädagogik, *Schule in kapitalismus: analyse der bildungsentwicklung in den USA und kapitalistischen ländern Europas*, Berlin, German DR, 1984, p. 215-230 (Beiträge zur schulpolitik und pädagogik des auslands, 1984, 2).

Effenbergerová, A. M., Grundrichtungen der entwicklung von bildung und erziehung in der allgemeinbildenden schule sozialistischer länder [Main trends in educational development of the compulsory general school in socialist countries]. In: Akademie der Pädagogischen Wissenschaften der DDR, Arbeitsstelle für Auslandspädagogik, *Bildungsentwicklung im kampf der entgesetzten weltsysteme*, Berlin, German DR, 1984, p. 19-51 (Beiträge zur schulpolitik und pädagogik des auslands, 1984, 1).

Effenbergerová, A. M., Zum kommunistischen charakter und zur humanistischen mission der sozialistischen schule [On the communist character and humanist mission of the socialist school]. Akademie der Pädagogischen Wissenschaften der DDR, Arbeitsstelle für Auslandspädagogik, *Weltbedeutung und internationaler charakter von theorie und praxis der sozialistischen Schule*, Berlin, German DR, 1985, p. 271-278 (Beiträge zur schulpolitik und pädagogik des auslands, 1985, 1).

Gahler, H.; Huck, G., Revolutionaire umwälzungen im bildungswesen der VDR Jemen [Revolutionary changes in education in the People's Republic of Yemen]. *Vergleichende pädagogik* (Berlin, German DR), 16. Jahrg., Heft 4., 1980, p. 373-383.

Gerth, I., 50 jahre Internationales Büro für Erziehung in Genf [50th anniversary of the International Bureau of Education in Geneva]. *Vergleichende Pädagogik* (Berlin, German DR), 15. Jahrg., Heft 2, 1979, p. 209-211.

Gräfe, G., *Gruntendenzen der Vervollkommnung der erziehungsfunktion der sowjetischen mittelschule der gegenwart* [General trends of perfecting the educational function of Soviet secondary schools today]. Akademie der Pädagogischen Wissenschaften der DDR, Berlin, German DDR, 1981.

Gräfe, G.; Saro, G.-J., Das sowjetische bildungswesen in einer neuen entwicklungsetappe [Developments of the Soviet education system]. *Vergleichende pädagogik* (Berlin, German DR), 21. Jahrg., Heft 1, 1985, p. 4-22.

Gräfe, G. et al, *Gemeinsame entwicklungstendenzen der schule bei der erziehung der jungen generation in den ländern der sozialistischen gemeinschaft in den 80er jahren* [Common trends of educational development in bringing up the young generation in countries of the community of socialist states in the 80s] Berlin, German DR, Akademie der Pädagogischen Wissenschaften der DDR, Arbeitsstelle für Auslandspädagogik, 1986.

Grigorova, S., *Osnovni tendencii v razvitieto na obrazovanieto* [Major trends in educational development]. Sofija, Narodna prosveta, 1984.

Grigorova, S., Die Vorzäge des realen sozialismus auf dem gebiet des volksbildungswesens [The advantages of socialism as it exists in the field of education]. In Akademie der Pädagogischen Wissenschaften der DDR. Arbeitsstelle für Auslandspädagogik, *Kriterien für eine tiefere begründung der überlegenheit des realen sozialismus gegenüber dem kapitalismus bei der lösung der bildungsfrage in unserer zeit*, 1980, 9-26 (Beiträge zur schulpolitik und pädagogik des auslands, 1980, 1).

Gyaraki, F., Analyse und kritik der konzeption des 'globalen lernens' des Club of Rome [Analysis and critique of concepts of 'global learning' designed by the Club of Rome]. In: Akademie der Pädagogischen Wissenschaften der DDR, Arbeitsstelle für Auslandspädagogik, *Bildungsentwicklung im Kampf der entgegengesetzten Weltsysteme*, Berlin, German DR, 1984, p. 164-180 (Beiträge zur schulpolitik und pädagogik des auslands, 1984, 1).

Hofmann, H.-G., Die reform der schwedischen schule in der gegenwart, *Vergleichende Pädagogik* (Berlin, German DR), 15. Jahrg., Heft 2, 1979, p. 157-172.

Hofmann, H.-G., Die schule des sozialismus in der gegenwart [The socialist school today], *Vergleichende pädagogik* (Berlin, German DR), 20. Jahrg., Heft 1984, p. 121-139.

Hofmann, H.-G.; Gräfe, G., eds, *Erkenntnisse und erfahrungen der sowjetischen schule und pädagogik und ihre internationale bedeutung in der gegenwart* [Achievements and experiences of Soviet school and educational sciences and their present international relevance]. Akademie der Pädagogischen Wissenschaften der DDR, Arbeitsstelle für Auslandspädagogik, Berlin, German DR, 1985.

Horvàth, M., Az összehasonlító pegagógia kutatások és a közoktatás mai szükségletei [The needs of comparative educational research and public education] Országos Pedagógiai Könyvtár és Múzeum, Budapest, 1984.

Illés, M., Der kampf der Französischen Kommunistischen Partei um die demokratisierung der schule [The struggle of the French Communist Party for the democratization of education]. *Vergleichende pädagogik* (Berlin, German DR), 19. Jahrg., Heft 3, 1983, p. 280-288.

Illés, M., Az oktatásüy a nyolcvanas években és fejlesztési tendenciái nemzetközi összehasonlításban [Education in the eighties and the international comparison of developmental trends]. Budapest, Tudományos Ismeretterjesztö Társulat, 1984.

Iniewski, F., Die internationale bedeutung der internationalistischen ideen bei der sozialistischen erziehung der Polnischen jugend [The impact of internationalist ideas in socialist education of Polish youth]. In: Akademie der Pädagogischen Wissenschaften der DDR, Arbeitsstelle für Auslandspädagogik, *Weltbedeutung und internationaler charakter von theorie und praxis der sozialistischen Schule*, Berlin, German DR, 1985, p. 158-166 (Beiträge zur schulpolitik und pädagogik des auslands, 1985, 1).

Jarkina, T. F., ed., *Vospitatel'naja rabota v skolah stran socializma: voprosy teorii i praktiki* [Educational work in schools of socialist countries: theoretical and practical issues]. Moskva Pedagogika, 1982.

Jarkina, T. F., et al, Soversenstvovanie soderzanija obrazovanija i metodov obucenija v stranah socializma [Perfecting educational contents and teaching methods in socialist countries]. In Obzory po informacionnomu obespecenija celevyh kompleksnyh naucno-pedagogiceskih programm i programm po reseni vaznejsih naucno-pedagogiceskih problem. *Obzornaja informacia* (Moskva), 4-jg., no 4, 1983, p. 1-45.

Juva, V.; Liskar, C., *Uvod do srovnávací pedagogiky* [Introduction to comparative education]. Pragha, Státní pedagogické nakladatelstí, 1982.

Kienitz, W., *Der übergang zur mittleren bildung für alle und die schulentwicklung der sechziger und siebziger jahre in der sowjetunion: länderstudie im rahmen der vergleichenden untersuchung von entwicklungstendenzen im bildungswesen der RGW-länder Europas in der etappe des entwickelten sozialismus (unter den aspekten der veränderungen im inhalt der allgemeinbildung und in den systemen des bildungswesens)* [Transition to secondary education for all and educational development in the '60s and '70s in the Soviet Union: comparative study on trends in educational development of advanced socialist CMEA countries in Europe (with regard to changes of contents in general education and of educational systems)]. Akademie der Pädagogischen Wissenschaften der DDR, Arbeitsstelle für Auslandspädagogik, 1979 (Beiträge zur schulpolitik und pädagogik des auslands, 1979, 1).

Kienitz, W., Fortschritte des bildungswesens in der etappe des entwickelten sozialismus: ein überblick über internationale tendenzen [Educational progress in advanced socialism: a survey of international trends]. *Vergleichende pädagogik* (Berlin, German DR), 20. Jahrg., Hejt 1984, p. 140-163.

Klarin, M. V., Razrabotka imitacionno-modelirujuscih ucebnyh igr v sovremennoj burzuaznoj pedagogike [Imitating teaching playus in modern bourgeois pedagogics]. *Sovetskaja pedagogikaN, (Moskva), no. 3, 1982, p. 109-112.*

Kodytková, D., Gegenwärtiger entwickungsstand der theorie der weltanschaulichen erziehung in der CSSR [Present state of development in the theory of ideological education in the CSSR]. *Vergleichende pädagogik* (Berlin, German DR), 20. Jahrg., Heft 1, 1984, p. 24-33.

Kolar, Z., Die beziehung von erziehung und bildung in einigen konzeptionen der bürgerlichen pädagogik [Relations between upbringing and education in some bourgeois educational concepts]. In: Akademie der Pädagogischen Wissenschaften der DDR, Arbeitsstelle für Auslandspädagogik, *Die Rolle der bildung und erziehung im ideologischen kampf*, Berlin, German DR, 1981, p. 6-17. (Beiträge zur schulpolitik und pädagogik des auslands, 1981, 2.

Kovalenko, J. I., Die erziehung der Sowjetischen schüler zu frieden und völkerverständigung [The education of Soviet pupils for peace and mutual understanding of peoples]. *Vergleichende Pädagogik* (Berlin, German DR), 17. Jahrg., Heft 3, 1981, p. 243-253.

Krupskaya, N. K. Volksbildung und demokratie [Education and democracy] in Krupskaya, N. K. *Sozialistiche pädagogik* Bd. 1., Berlin, German DR, Volk und wissen, 1972, p. 239-338

Kuzmina, M. N., ed., *Skola evrepejskih stran socializma: poslevohnoe razvitie i sovremennie problemy* [School in European socialist countries: post-war development and current problems]. Moskva, Pedagogika, 1976.

Le, Kan, Aktuelle aufgaben der bildungspolitik und pädagogik in der sozialistischen republik Vietnam [Present tasks of educational politics and sciences in the Socialist Republic of Vietnam]. In: Akademie der Pädagogischen Wissenschaften der DDR, Arbeitsstelle für Auslandspädagogik, *Weltbedeutung und internationaler charakter von theorie und praxis der sozialistischen schule*, (Berlin, German DR), 1985, p. 99-100 (Beiträge zur schulpolitik und pädagogik des auslands, 1985, 1)

Mammo, G., Die Äthiopische nationale alphabetisierungskampagne ist nicht nur lippenbekenntnis [The Ethiopian national campaign of alphabetization is not only mere words]. *Vergleichende pädagogik* (Berlin, German DR), 16. Jahrg., Heft 4, 1980, p. 414-417.

Mehnert, W.; Baumann, R., *Entwicklung des schulwesens in national befreiten staaten Asiens und Afrikas: einige aktuelle tendenzen und probleme* [Educational development in emergent states of Asia and Africa: some current trends and problems]. Akademie der Pädagogischen Wissenschaften der DDR, Arbeitsstelle für

Auslandspädagogik, Berlin, German DR, 1981. (Beiträge zur schulpolitik und pädagogik des auslands)

Mirtschewa, V., Die sozialistische bildung: eine triebkraft des wissenschaftlich-technischen fortschritts [Socialist education: a driving force of scientific and technological progress]. In: Akademie der Pädagogischen Wissenschaften der DDR, Arbeitsstelle für auslandspädagogik, *Weltbedeutung und internationaler charakter von theorie und praxis der sozialistischen schule*, (Berlin, German DR), 1985, p. 80-88 (Beiträge zur schulpolitik und pädagogik des auslands, 1985, 1).

Malkowa, S. A., An der grenze der gefahr: zum bildungsbericht der USA [At the border-line of danger: on education in the USA]. Akademie der Pädagogischen Wissenschaften der DDR, Arbeitsstelle für Auslandspädagogik, *Bildungsentwicklung im kampf der entgegengesetaten weltsysteme*. Berlin, German DR, 1984, p. 105-112 (Beiträge zur Schulpolitik und Pädagogik des Auslands, German DR, 1984, 1).

Nemzetközi Oktatásügy [Current problems of education all over the world] (Budapest, Országos Pedagógiai Könyvtar és Múzeum), 1967- (2 a year).

Ngakeni, P., Entwicklung und probleme im bildungswesen der Volksrepublik Kongo [Educational development and problems in the People's Republic of Congo]. In: *Weltbedeutung und internationaler charakter von theorie und praxis der sozialistischen Schule* Akademie der Pädagogischen Wissenschaften der DDR, Arbeitsstelle für auslandspädagogik, Berlin, German DR, 1985, p. 118-125 (Beiträge zur schulpolitik und pädagogik des auslands, 1985, 1).

Nagy, S., Methodologische probleme in der bürgerlichen didaktik-forschung [Methodological problems in bourgeois research work on didactics]. *Vergleichende pädagogik* (Berlin, German DR), 20. Jahrg., Heft 1, 1984, p. 68-73.

Neumann, P., Das bildungswesen der volksrepublik Polen [The educational system of Poland]. *Vergleichende pädagogik* (Berlin, German DR), 21. Jahrg., Heft 3, 1985, p. 236-249.

Opato, R., Der XV. parteitag der kommunistischen partei der Tschechoslowakei und die aufgaben der pädagogik [The XV Congress of the Communist Party of Czechoslovakia and targets of pedagogical sciences]. *Vergleichende pädagogik* (Berlin, German DR), 13. Jahrg., Heft 3, 1977, p. 241-252.

Osszehasonlító pedagógiai füzetek [Comparative educational studies] (Budapest, Országos Pedagógiai Kónyvtár és Múzeum), 1984- (3-4 a year).

Pancesnikova, L. M., K voprosu ob izucenii zarubeznoj metodiki [On comparative research concerning methods of teaching abroad]. *Sovetskaja pedagogika*, (Moskva), no. 3, 1977, p. 68-75.

Pomykalo, W., Einige probleme bei der erarbeitung des begriffskatalogs für den kampf gegen bürgerliche ideologie [Some problems of compiling a catalogue of terms for counter-propaganda to bourgeois ideology]. In: Akademie der Pädagogischen Wissenschaften der DDR, Arbeitsstelle für auslandspädagogik, *Die rolle der bildung und erziehung im ideologischen kampf.* Berlin, German DR, 1981, p. 178-180 (Beiträge zur schulpolitik und pädagogik des auslands, 1981, 2).

Pomykalo, W., Einige aspekte der entwicklung im bildungswesen der volksrepublik Polen [Some aspects of educational development in the People's Republic of Poland]. *Vergleichende pädagogik* (Berlin, German DR), 20. Jahrg., Heft 2, 1984, p. 195-202.

Rosenzweig, M., Persönlichkeits und erziehungsauffassungen der neothomistisch orientierten pädagogik [Concepts of personality and education in neothomistically orientated pedagogics]. In: Akademie der Pädagogischen Wissenschaften der DDR, Arbeitsstelle für Auslandspädagogik, *Die rolle der bildung und erziehung im ideologischen kampf,* Berlin, German DR, 1981, p. 18-36. (Beiträge zur schulpolitik und pädagogik des auslands, 1981, 2).

Rosenzweig, M., Philosophische grundlagen und dominanten der persönlichkeitsformung in der bürgerlichen pädagogik der gegenwart [Philosophical fundamentals and dominants of personality formation in modern bourgeois pedagogics]. *Vergleichende pädagogik* (Berlin, German DR), 17. Jahrg., Heft 2, 1981, p. 122-137.

Sirinskij, A. E., *Obrazovanie v razvivajuscihsja stranah* [Education in developing countries]. Moskva, Prosvescenie, 1977.

Sokolova, M. A: Kuz'mia, E. N.; Rodionov, M. L, *Sravnitel'naja pedagogika* [Comparative education], Moskva, Prosvescenie, 1978.

Szczesniak, A. L., Die zusammenarbeit sozialistischer länder zur vervollkommnung von geschichtsbüchern [Cooperation among socialist countries in perfecting history textbooks]. *Vergleichende pädagogik* (Berlin, German DR), 17. Jahrg., Heft 1, 1981, p. 64-69.

Széchy, E., Hauptprobleme der bildungsentwicklung in den entgegengesetzten gesellschaftssystemen [Main problems of educational development in antagonistic social systems]. In: Akademie der Pädagogischen Wissenschaften der DDR, Arbeitsstelle für Auslandspädagogik, *Bildungsentwicklung im kampf der entgegengesetzten weltsysteme,* Berlin, German DR, p. 7-17. (Beiträge zur schulpolitik und pädagogik des auslands, 1984, 1).

Tanguiane, S., Education and the problem of democratization. *Prospects* (Paris, UNESCO), vol. VII, no. 1, 1977, p. 14-31.

Thielemann, G., Die nordische zusammenarbeit auf dem gebiet des bildungswesens [Nordic co-operation in education]. *Vergleichende pädagogik* (Berlin, German DR), 15. Jahrg., Heft 2, 1979, p. 198-200.

Thomas, R., Staatsmonopolistische regulierung als mittel zur internationalen ausformung spätbürgerlicher bildung und erziehung [State-monopolist regulation - as means of international organization of late bourgeois education]. *Vergleichende pädagogik* (Berlin, German DR), 22. Jahrg., Heft 2., 1986, p. 126-137.

Tmej, K., Erziehung zum sozialistischen patriotismus und internationalismus [Education for socialist patriotism and internationalism]. *Vergleichende pädagogik* (Berlin, German DR), 20. Jahrg., heft 2, 1984, p. 189-194.

Tschakarov, N., Die bürgerliche erziehungsphilosophie als wichtiger gegenstand kritischer analyse [Bourgeois educational philosophy as a significant subject of analysis]. In: Akademie der Pädagogischen Wissenschaften der DDR, Arbeitsstelle für Auslandspädagogik, *Die rolle der bildung und erziehung im ideologischen kampf*, Berlin, German DR, 1981, p. 90-100 (Beiträge zur schulpolitik und pädagogik des auslands, 1981, 2).

Tschakarov, N., *Gegenwärtige bürgerliche pädagogik* [Modern bourgeois educational sciences]. Sofia, Volksbildung, 1986.

Weiser, E., 'Open education' wirkt in jungen staaten Asiens und Afrikas ['Open education' - its effects in emergent states of Asia and Africa]. *Vergleichende pädagogik* (Berlin, German DR), 16. Jahrg., Heft 4, 1980, p. 392-403.

Weiser, E., *Ausgwählte nationale, regionale und internationale organizationen im Afrikanischen raum: entwicklung, charakter und wirkung auf dem gebiet der bildung und erziehung* [Selected national, regional and international organizations in Africa: development, character and effects on education]. Akademie der Pädagogischen Wissenschaften der DDR, Arbeitsstelle für auslandspädagogik, Berlin, German DR, 1985.

Wulfson, B. L., Die beziehung von allgemeinem und besonderem in der gegenwärtigen bürgerlichen pädagogik als methodologisches problem [Relations between general and special issues in modern bourgeois pedagogics as a methodological problem] in: Akademie der Pädagogischen Wissenschaften der DDR, Arbeitsstelle für Auslandspädagogik, *Die aufgaben der marxistisch-leninistischen pädagogik in der ideologischen klasseneinandersetzung zwischen sozialmus und imperialismus: kritik moderner bürgerlicher persönlichkeitsauffassungen und erziehungskonzeptionen*, Berlin, German DR, 1979, p. 9-15. (Beiträge zur schulpolitik und pädagogik des auslands, 1979, 2).

Wulfson, B. L., Gedanken zum wechselverhältnis von allgemeinen und unterschiedlichen zügen in der bürgerlichen pädagogik als forschungsproblem [On interrelations between general and different features in bourgeois pedagogics as a problem of research]. *Vergleichende pädagogik* (Berlin, German DR), 15. Jahrg., Heft 4, 1979, p. 410-423.

North America[1]

Robert F. Lawson

Comparative education as an organized field began in North America with the establishment of the Comparative Education Society in the United States in 1956. The growth of other national Comparative Education Societies, including the Comparative-International Education Society of Canada, which plays an interesting role in the North American region, has not changed the primary status of the United States Comparative Education Society (whose name changed to Comparative and International Education Society in 1969, hereafter referred to as CIES) and of its organ the *Comparative education review*. The major thrust toward the formation of the World Council of Comparative Education Societies in 1970 came from 'internationalist' Canada, but was viewed initially with suspicion by the CIES, partly because of the prospect of bearing a proportional share of support costs (which would have been unbearable). The doubtful benefit of a body with no feasible goals other than meeting and creating goodwill loomed large, and still does, regardless of the slow momentum of triennial meetings.

Establishment of the comparative education organization was, of course, preceded by the work of the so-called elder statesmen of the field: in North America, I. L. Kandel and Robert Ulich; elsewhere, Nicholas Hans, Friedrich Schneider, Franz Hilker, Erich Hylla, and J. A. Lauwerys, of whom Kandel was most generally revered. Before them in North America the forerunners were primarily government officials seeking information on education practices abroad.[2] The early leaders in the field, once it had been defined in North America, included George Z. F. Bereday, William W. Brickman, Gerald Read, C. Arnold Anderson, and Claude A. Eggertsen. Bereday and Brickman were both in New York at the time, and New York has remained a centre of comparative education activity. Teachers College, Columbia University, emerges as the intellectual centre and produced graduates of significance to the field. Bereday edited the *Comparative education review* for ten years, and was succeeded by Harold Noah, also at Teachers College. Brickman was first president through 1958, and again in 1967, and has been the chronicler of the field. His presentation of the initial objectives of the Comparative Education Society has been referred to regularly, and remains the basic statement.[3] Differences of opinion are reflected within this statement, that is, on interpretation or priority, but not about its general acceptability. Read, who appears to have been instrumental in organizing the Society, devoted his major effort to making comparative education visible and informative to the many teachers and school administrators who followed him abroad. In doing this, he also opened up Eastern Europe and other inaccessible areas for comparative education study.

The impact over the next twenty five years of the work of Anderson and his colleagues at Chicago and of Eggertsen at Michigan was critical. These two professors were honoured as the first honorary fellows of the CIES at the Society's 1986 conference in Toronto.

The Chicago program, because of its emphasis on sociology and economics, contributed strongly to development research and linked itself to international or national organizations needing that expertise. The Center's frame of reference was, however, never narrowed to one geographical or research concern. The 1957 memo (reprinted in *Comparative education review* Kent, OH, vol.17, no.2, June 1973, p.154-159) outlining projects of the proposed Comparative Education Center includes in its main topics those which would still be designated general or mainstream concerns of comparative education in North America, such as: international (and intra-national) comparisons of the extent, distribution or incidence, and selectivity of schooling; comparative studies of value attitudes, content of education, and the role of schools in education; inter- and intra-national comparisons of effectiveness of education (and problems of its measurement), as well as topics of more limited but continual concern such as provincialism in school curricula and evaluation of education as investment in human capital.

The program at the University of Michigan traced the interests of its staff in comparative/international education back to 1879 (William H. Payne and Burke Aaron Hinsdale) and of its doctoral students to dissertations from 1904, but its contributions to the organized field began with a series of actions between 1958 and 1964, supported by National Defense Education Act funds, to stimulate graduate study and research in the area. Probably the strongest discipline emphasis has been social history, and the geographical emphasis, with the exception of a concentration on India, and the work of notable individuals, has been on industrialized countries: England, Ireland and Wales, Canada, Germany, the Union of Soviet Socialist Republics and Japan. Although no program in this period could be primarily an 'applied' program, a purposive orientation led to readiness for broader international involvement, and was undoubtedly, with similar individual orientations of others and changes in the conception of what was necessary to make comparative education effective in the real world, the basis for arguments for changing the name and broadening the scope of CIES after 1968.

Columbia, Chicago and Michigan, vibrant over the history of the field in North America, have diminished as clearly dominant centres. Successors and students from these and other early programs have taken a leading role in the field, dispersing the teaching and research in comparative education.

Although the Canadian Society functions independently, there is necessarily an overlap in the work and affiliation of active members of CIES and CIESC (Comparative and International Education Society of Canada). Presidents of CIES from Canadian Universities include Joseph Katz, University of British Columbia, and Reginald Edwards, McGill University, in the early group; Robert Lawson and Mathew Zachariah from the University of Calgary, and Joseph Farrell from The Ontario Institute for Studies in Education.[4] Their colleagues Ratna Ghosh, Roger Magnusson, Thomas Eiseman, and Margaret Gillett at McGill, Roger Woock, Jeffrey Jacob, Richard Heyman and Ralph Miller at Calgary, David Wilson at OISE; in addition to Douglas Ray and David Radcliffe at University of Western Ontario, Werner Stephan and Dan Dorotich at University of Saskatchewan, Jacques Gagné and Joseph Kattackal at University of Ottawa, Jacques LaMontagne and Avigdor Farine at Université de Montréal, and Kazim Bacchus, Glen Eyford, Raj Pannu and colleagues at the University of Alberta map out the centres of activity in Canada.

The support structure for the field in North America encompasses now a number of universities (estimated at around 25) with substantial commitments, two journals specifically covering comparative and international education, major research collaboration, and links to book publishers, international and regional agencies, national and state or provincial governments,[5] and the organization of regular national and regional conferences, which now undertake academic recognition of certain kinds.

The *Comparative education review* has been edited, for the ten years to 1966 by George Bereday, by Harold Noah at Teachers College, Columbia, to 1970, by Andreas Kazamias at the University of Wisconsin, to 1978, and by Philip Altbach from then to the present. Since 1978, it has been published by the University of Chicago Press. The policies of the *Review* have been at issue from time to time, but usually as part of more general methodological differences to be discussed later. Its independence of special interests over the long run and its academic standard have been beyond question, and therefore allows its use in this chapter as a primary source of literature. However, its particular selection casts some doubt on a stated editorial policy of serving the field and its practitioners, considering the mainstream of research and teaching in comparative education.[6]

From 1967 to 1970, the Comparative and International Education Society of Canada issued a series of 'Papers,' the first containing the 'Founding Papers,' the second covering the theme of 'Foreign influences in Canadian education,' the third on the 'Unique characteristics of Canadian education,' and the fourth on 'Comparative studies in higher education.'[7]

Canadian and international education was founded in 1972, and has depended on external grant and university support for its continuation. Its editors have been Shiu Kong, David Radcliffe, Jacques LaMontagne, Richard Heyman, and currently Ralph Miller. The character of the journal is not easily definable, but it does represent what its title purports, and is therefore somewhat closer, where a distinction is made, to international education.

Since the business of the Canadian Society has been less formal, and the meetings of CIESC have taken place, in the Canadian tradition along with other learned societies once a year, rotating regionally among universities, elaboration is not of major significance to the comparative education organization as such. It might be noted that there is less of an academic infrastructure to the field in Canada, but relatively more organizational involvement in the Society, and more direct affiliations with international bodies and other comparative education societies.

The CIES Newsletters have carried communications of importance to the members professionally, have disseminated news and policies of the Society's Board, and have included reference information, notably for years the column of 'Recent and Noteworthy Publications' put together by Franklin Parker. Some issues (e.g., May, September 1974) have sought to broaden the coverage, including personnel updates, teaching information, position papers, and news of other societies. From the books and papers advertised, from mention of other Associations, of travel programs and study opportunities, from jobs listed in recent *Newsletters*, it is apparent that voices in favour of broader CIES activity have been heard, but also that nothing systematic or comprehensive could be done, probably because of economic pressures in the universities, and a reward system that tends to give most recognition to international scholarship but local service. Similarly with CIES committees, other than those necessary for nominating officers and planning conferences, the valiant attempts of a few presidents and committed members, to use action committees such as the International Education Committee, the Professional Affairs Committee, the Career Analysis Commission, and the *ad hoc* Impact Committee, or working groups such as the Conference on Teaching, Research and Service in comparative and international education at Kent State in 1981, have not led to any concerted action or change in collective behaviour, although important policy statements have been issued. An exception, but one in line with the continuing thread of intellectual interest in CIES were the Committees to determine criteria, and then to recommend awards for honorary fellows and for the best article of the year published in the *Comparative education review*, both of which have provided well-deserved recognition for Society scholars.[8] Another form of recognition has been provided by the Claude Eggertsen lecture series, given at annual conferences since 1980, respectively by Brian Holmes, William Brickman, Wolfgang Mitter, Hans Weiler, Judith Torney-Purta, W. H. G. Armytage, and Philip H. Coombs.

CIES conferences have been held at widespread locations including, recently Washington, DC, San Francisco, Toronto, New Orleans, Ann Arbor, Michigan, Vancouver, Tallahassee, New York City, Atlanta, Houston, Stanford University, and once outside North America, in Mexico City. Although some conferences have had 'themes,' the content has always diverged from any single idea or approach. Some of the themes which have run through conferences, special issues of the *Review*, and Newsletters recently include evaluating educational reform, international educational achievement, foreign students, women and education in the third world, minority education, human rights, policy issues, educational planning, relation to international organizations (especially for Canada, and especially the theme of the United States and UNESCO), comparative education in teacher education and in undergraduate programs, development theory, planning and ideology, community development and non-formal education, approaches to comparative education, politics of education, and higher education.

Problems with the organization and content of comparative education in North America over the last twelve years have been partly methodological, but they are also related to differences of opinion on participation and role. There is no doubt that outside pressures on academics, and particularly educationists, and the internal tension of a field trying to do too much, have exacerbated these differences. Nevertheless they have been around in some form for a long time, and should be noted in regard to the organization. In 1975, I identified three 'singular' positions which were counter-productive in comparative education communication:

> 'The first would close the field boundaries by subjecting standards of comparative study to criteria of general knowledge and critical ability. The field would be logically defined by those with wisdom to comprehend, to judge, to prescribe. (...) Not only is this position ideologically dangerous, but *in its exclusiveness* it conflicts with a necessarily relative and cautious attitude on the part of the researcher in comparative techniques for managing research, stipulation of end-points and restrictions on findings - in short, scientifically and publicly accountable means of proceeding toward results which may contribute to what we know about, hence what we can do about, effective education in societal contexts.
>
> This argument is liable to lead, however, to a second singular position from the empirical tradition in natural science, adopted in certain versions of objective research in social science, in behaviouristic psychology, and lately in competency-based program policy. The rules of research here are rigid: findings must be narrow, authority shifts to the technical means, and policy implications are likely to be either over-specific or necessarily inconclusive. In its exclusiveness, this position only discriminates measurable from non-measurable data and legitimate scientific methods from those not accepted as having research capability; it can exclude more open-ended, synthetic, or thematic studies but cannot govern the quality of manipulations or the coherence of concomitant research efforts. Interpretive judgment, theoretical soundness, and significance may be as easily overlooked here as are constructs of validity or tools of research in the previous instance.
>
> Finally, there is the ideological singularity of a given political position, which may or may not be acknowledged, but which frequently lies behind an attempt to unify comparative study or international education in a particular direction. This is not to ignore the social and ideological constructions of knowledge and reality, but to recognize a forced conformity of research and social action to narrowly defined political objectives prescribed by certain doctrines. In this case, we pretend to be talking

about educational studies or related activities, when we are actually assuming irreconcilable political positions. It is not the masking of real differences which is at issue here, however; it is the exclusiveness of the application of *political religion* to social science, which denies legitimate opposition and encloses all scholarly activity within political parameters.'
Comparative education review, vol. 19, no. 3, October 1975, p. 345-346)

At that time also the need was identified for an associative model of comparative education organization, which would go beyond an occasional meeting such as the World Congress, and would forge operational connections with other groups engaged in international studies, with others teaching in similar disciplines or in related areas of education, systematically with government and international organizations, and finally, among ourselves. Letters to the *ad hoc* Impact Committee supported and elaborated the connections and objectives necessary for the present and future of comparative education, and such dialogue has continued regularly since.[9]

The four directions emerging from change in communication and in the conduct of comparative education research have been: 1) to take a wider view of the scope and associations of the field; 2) to emphasize the practical and purposive outcomes of comparative education; 3) to relate comparative education and teaching, or teacher training more closely; and 4) to accept methodological variations as natural at this stage of field development. These points will be threads through the pages of this chapter. Their effect on research and teaching of comparative education has been felt.

For the formal organization, however, it appears to have been beyond the capability of the Society to act on these directions for the formal organization, but not its will to give them up.[10]

Not to overdraw the 'singularities' noted above, there has been some continuing tension around those aspects which separate us, particularly where there appears to be elitism or exclusiveness.[11]

The perception that the organization of comparative education may be closed, a more serious concern because the organs purport to be open, has surely had some effect on the strength of the field as such in North America. Some serious comparative educationists appear to find a more satisfying professional and intellectual environment in other comparative education journals and in other academic organizations. It would be instructive to editors and the publishers to find out what is read most from the several English-language journals in the field, and what is used most in teaching and research by practicing comparative educationists. With regard to the organization itself, although CIES can still claim to be the largest and oldest comparative education society, its relative position in terms of growth and research output is questionable, as is the tendency to subsume even international studies within the framework of American issues. The Canadian-American organizational split should also raise the question of why it has seemed necessary to create a multitude of unconnected *national* Societies in an international field.

The name change signified a formal recognition by the Society that purpose was necessary and the primary purpose was international activity. Disagreement about the decision was formally reflected in retention of the journal title as *Comparative education review*, but the basic difference ran deep, and was reflected as late as 1985 in an informal debate between panel members promoting the use of comparative education data and challenges from the floor bewailing the subordination of scholarly purpose. The rift is more complicated than it first seems. The term 'international education,' having been defined by Bereday,[12] has meant, in terms of Society policy and academic endeavour, at least the following: activity in international organizations, international studies, studies of international causes, or phenomena, and internationalizing the schools, especially curricula. Even within these topics, the acceptability to strict comparative educationists of work with UNESCO or the World Bank or on educational achievement, is, for example, very different from work with state or provincial agencies or work on world peace or the physical environment. The point of accepting a broader umbrella, from source to purpose, was accepted, but the limits and character of that umbrella remained unclear. For many, 'development' became a clarifying concept[13] in that it specified inherently an application of research, social sensitivity, and practical means to real social educational problems, especially as the concept became separated from narrow geographical and ideological limits and referred not only to an institutional process but also to a set of human interactions, with historical as well as contemporary sources and with two-way information targets. But the disputes about the proper scope and application of development research grew at the same time, and the claim of some - which has regularly plagued comparative education - that only their approach, methodologically or ideologically, their content, even their colleagues, are entitled to define the work, threatens to impede the chance of resolving this long-standing division. Some of this conflict arises out of or leads to interpersonal conflicts, which are real in higher education, but cannot be discussed here. The methodological differences are however critical to the status of the field.

The published work in comparative education seems to have reached a second level, where the concern is with particular research problems and environments, and with methodology in specific reference to the assessment or verification of findings. There are virtually no surveys of national systems in the current North American literature. In fact there is little writing that could be characterized comparative education as represented by the forerunners and by the national survey work.[14] Out of the respective program emphases of university departments have come a continuation of solid area studies, and socio-economic studies, and work focused on the immediate concerns of education (e.g., pedagogy, training, curriculum, school management). There appear to have been three main statements on the proper nature of work in comparative education: 1) one reflected in the early debate on the discipline bases of comparative education and represented most clearly in the past and present writing of historical- philosophical scholars who, though 'softer' methodologically, nevertheless defined the field as strictly as their alternative; 2) probably represented collectively by the 'Chicago school' but having its clearest methodological statement in Noah and Eckstein's attempt to harden the lines of research through strictly scientific methods of empirical investigation[15]; and 3) that taking as an advantage the flexible boundaries and interactive content bodies of the field, now generally accepted as a conclusion to endless verbal differences over academic identification.[16]

There is basic agreement on the range of methodologies which communicate widely in the field, and Kazamias' listing of a) structural-functionalism, b) history as social science, c) theories of development and modernization, and d) methodological empiricism is still generally applicable.[17] Furthermore, the research problems and the content and objectives of comparative education, are circumscribed by intellectual communication in the field. For example, identifying the significant questions for increasingly larger results, building one step at a time toward explanatory models, and relating socio-educational change to predictive conclusions on system - specific effects are strategic to comparative education. The inclusions of behaviours and attitudes affecting the process of education, and, underneath, the analysis of cultural effect are understood to be as relevant to comparative study as functional relationships and outcomes. The value and knowledge prescriptions built into the institutions of a society have to be used as prior assumptions to specific educational analysis - in fact, that relationship is probably *only* visible through comparative methods. It is possible then to describe some of the assumptions and operational agreements, at the same time avoiding any attempt at narrow methodological closure.[18]

It is in fact usual for many researchers to work across disciplines and methodologies, for example, to relate institutional development to collective behaviour, and both to political processes and structures, using comparison in order to address an educational question. This reflects the complexity and overlap of variables in the real world, although we may start with 'laboratory' environments and our own methodological restrictions.[19] Comparison in other fields is a method used by a disciplinary sub-group, who do not seek to define themselves outside the parent discipline. The conclusion that comparative education is what comparative educationists do has allowed comparison to be defined in relation to the object of study and methodology to become refined through its operational use.

But there is turbulence beneath that surface. Although 'new research concerns' may correspond to concerns traditional in the field, and the attempt to elucidate the *process* of education through qualitative methods may not surprise anyone, for some writers these suggestions take on a new meaning.[20] Partly from changes toward relativism in the sciences, partly from the position of the 'vaguely left,' partly from schools such as 'world systems analysis,' and partly from differences between development theorists, the real openness of research, and particularly qualitative research, is not what it seems.

Development research and practice have exposed a number of legitimate methodological or content problems, such as how the economic value of education relates between individuals and societies or between high and low-income countries; whether 'culture' is a key variable or a 'residual category' in development strategies; whether analysis needs to be structured, and whether the structure of analysis relates to the structure of content or environment; what utility there is to dependency models, and what contradictions reside in presumed first-world to third-world effects; and what differential socio-political messages may be carried by educational strategies in developing countries.

At the same time, some have used these differences as a springboard to advance their own ideological opposition to western models or to promote a prior political position. Probably most destructive is the patronizing pretense of cultural relativity combined with a preconceived notion of what the 'revolutionized' society should look like, without either comparative perspective or social responsibility for potential outcomes. The North American circle here is identifiable by its language, its repetitive slogans, and its tightness of association. It is, as Anderson once put it, composed mainly of 'sophists who are riding on a few clichés and on much superficial information about how education functions in a society.'[21]

Those blanket challenges to western models (and presumed motives of domination) and quantitative or structural-functional methodologies suffer from three serious faults other than the use of untested theory and variations on theory. First, the judgment rendered of social issues and structures as well as that allowed or indeed required in preferred qualitative methodologies lays claim to a moral position to which no one has exclusive right and which undermines scientific inquiry in any form.

Second, in terms of method itself, the term 'qualitative' needs elaboration. The 'qualitative' literature extends from earlier important works in comparative education and related histories of education and political studies.[22] In fact, most of the work in comparative education has been qualitative, and although the *Comparative education review* now approaches a balance, qualitative articles still slightly outnumber quantitative. The once faint quantitative challenge to the qualitative mainstream has helped to build the knowledge base and taxonomic structure of the field without which research cannot be accumulated and theory cannot be formulated. To restrict the definition of qualitative, in terms of approach or content is to distort a rubric recognized generally in the field to prefer a particular research convention (e.g., ethnography, critical ethnography, ethnomethodology, etc.), without necessarily referring to the technical or philosophical variations within that convention.[23] It is not unusual to exaggerate academic fashions in North America;[24] it is problematic only when the definition of field or research becomes confused by it.

Where 'qualitative' refers to philosophically demanding phenomenological modes, it is apparently overlooked, in the excitement of the terminology, that the requirements of such high abstraction not only limit those able to pursue research effectively, but also prevent their communication in those intellectual idioms.[25] Where 'qualitative' is a shorthand for opposition to structural-functionalism it should be recognized that 'clean' social research requires some aspects at least of this approach. Even for most Marxists, it is the purposes and outcomes of structural-functional analysis rather than the method itself which need to be questioned.[26]

The third fault of the 'new critics' is, paradoxically, their preoccupation with American issues, if not ethnocentricality with America itself. Where the claim to moral right and the emphasis on academic 'hotspots' apply more or less to Canada and the United States (the first perhaps relatively more to Canada, the second relatively less), this is essentially a phenomenon of American thinking - paradoxically, because it is set in a context of anti-western polemic. The paradox can be accommodated because of the selective use of traditional American beliefs in right, benevolence, and assimilation. Although no longer acceptable in their original crude forms, these concepts may be adapted to support 'righter than Right,' better than benevolent, intellectually assimilationist ideas. The expressions may sound radical, but the ideas are close to the current centre of academic discourse. The problem, again, is the attempt to universalize particular positions, even ethnocentric ones, and the dismissal of legitimate challenges as 'old' (traditional) or examples of co-option.

Just as the saner voices have concluded on open methodology at this stage of the field's development, so have they concluded on the relevance of purpose and connection to practice. Possibly from the deep-down sense that 'societies are not going to support schools at higher levels of financing unless the products *seem* to acquire certain capabilities which the society thinks it can judge and which the society regards as important,'[27] with the implication of this for the targets of research, there has been increasing discussion of practical objectives. One result has been greater interest in joint and large-scale research on topics such as educational achievement, effectiveness of schools, and financing, using methods which appear to give concrete answers. Another result is the re-organization of university programs in education to direct the humanistic and scientific studies toward practical ends, often in combination with other education specializations. Some of this re-direction is forced and artificial, but it leads also to natural applications of comparative education, such as policy analyses, internationalization of the school curriculum, and in reference to domestic comparisons, political and cultural. Particularly in regard to minority or ethnic studies, to issues of multiculturalism and bilingualism, the tools of comparative education are well suited to distinguishing traditions, to identifying socio-political environments, to making economic analyses, and otherwise to explaining and drawing research conclusions in these areas. They are less suited to the applied side, of translating into specific policy recommendations, or of contributing to program development in schools or for minority groups. In spite of the obvious need for comparative education expertise by governments, by groups such as Native Americans or Canadians, and in teacher training, it is unfortunately the case that comparative educationists have offered too little that others want, and have been too long indifferent to this. Major organizations use comparative educationists (IEA,

OECD), and many individuals contribute tirelessly to local, national, and international efforts to apply comparative knowledge to educational improvement, but only now is the necessity clear for the *field* to be oriented to the *use* of data, and only now is the opportunity present for a breakthrough in policy impact.

In the past four years North American governments have engaged in extensive reviews of schooling in their jurisdictions. In at least two instances comparative education specialists were called on to provide documentation to review bodies.[28] Many more have contributed in various ways. From this experience we have learned some important lessons about the relationship of researchers to policy makers. Both the presentation of data and its use may be inappropriate or misleading.

On the part of the policy makers mistakes may include: making international comparison only to raise an alarm about the alleged poor performance of students in one's own jurisdiction as compared to other students in very different educational systems, while ignoring promising but different educational practices in other countries; failing to distinguish between adequate comparative studies and rough-shod comparative observations, and not making the effort to follow up with questions to elicit the specific information they need; neglecting the procedural importance of providing for several stages of public discussion and for interaction between government leaders and researchers on intention, findings, and recommendations.[29]

On the part of comparative educationists, it is necessary to assert the cautions we take as read. One country's definition of a problem should not be adopted as another country's definition without attention to major differences in educational systems and contexts. Assuming quality of information, the *kind* of information is crucial. To be effective, or even used, the information should be determined by what others want rather than what we prefer to give. This does not deny the importance of expert judgment or the conscience of our scientific practice and critical role.[30] It is simply to say that use is at least partly a function of fit of information to the question at hand. It is also a function of communication and political tactics.

Researchers presenting comparative research generalizations must attempt to understand the cognitive styles, interests, values and situational constraints of policy makers requesting data. They should use language that facilitates rather than hinders public communication, and should take as given the political motivations of governments or political actors. To what extent the researcher must himself move into the political sphere to ensure that the information is heard is an old and vexing question not approachable here. Even the extent to which the conclusions of research should move into policy recommendations is problematic, but there is a middle ground here. Without departing from the data base, the research may point to policy decisions through the interpretation of summary points that are, through the explication of points arising out of public and professional choices made in one or more other systems. Such interpretation represents the meeting of research and responsible expert judgment.

Whatever else is happening in comparative education in North America, the journals, primarily the *Comparative education review*, must be taken as indicative of the predominant lines of research. I have, therefore, used the *Comparative education review*, from 1975 to 1986 as the source of the following report on emphases and trends.[31] *Canadian and international education*, for the same period, will be used to comment on Canadian differences, although the overlap of academic communication and the complexity of the Canadian-American relationship advise wariness in such comment. Of the 303 items examined, 51 were categorized as method articles.[32] Although such articles including presidential addresses, appeared throughout the period, they were concentrated in three issues, one of these relating comparative education to teacher education and one being a 'state of the art' issue. In *Canadian and international education* there was virtually no emphasis on methodological issues.

In line with increasing North American interest in the third world and with the conceptual utility of 'development' as a process of change under environmental conditions, the *Comparative education review* showed strongest geographical interest in third-world countries.[33] *Canadian and international education* shows a similar emphasis on the third world, but a much stronger representation of articles dealing with North America. The area representation was in order of major blocks: Asia, Europe, Africa, North America, and Latin America, but that in Asia and Africa has increased. The Middle East has been relatively neglected. Australia had one surge of emphasis.

Development articles predominate in most journal issues over the period, and the increase of development-international articles is matched by a marked decline in comparative pieces of a traditional kind. At the risk of categorizing where the boundary lines blur regularly, the current period shows development issues and methods superseding traditional comparative ones, and 'international education' to be scarcely represented in the *Comparative education review*. There continues to be little cross-over between studies covering industrialized and those covering developing societies. *Canadian and international education* appears to show a relative preference for international education, for North American issues, and for traditional comparative education forms.

Boundary lines between categories used in methodological discussions also blurred regularly when the actual articles were considered. It is clear however that qualitative analytic studies have the edge. Quantitative work, especially if the inclusion of numerical data is considered, makes a strong showing. Except for the gradually continuing increase of quantitative studies, the proportions have not changed much over this ten-year period, suggesting that the range and dominant mode of methodologies have stabilized for the moment. Highly technical studies are present, but not frequent. Although they appear to represent one of the best opportunities for the field to progress in large-scale comparisons, they are not a widely understood medium of research communication in the field. Descriptive pieces as such have almost disappeared, and purely interpretive pieces are rare. Periods of generalizing about world or third-world issues seem to alternate with longer periods of increasing specificity of concern. The only significant difference from this summary in the *Canadian and international education* articles is a relatively greater representation of descriptive and organizational pieces, and of education (school and administration) concerns as such.

In general, although criticism is infused into many of the studies, there is, as Koehl discovered in 1977, little systematic criticism of the intellectual rather than ideological kind.[34]

The multidisciplinary nature of the field is apparent in the range of disciplines represented in articles. Sociology and history are clearly predominant, with economics and political studies the only important runners-up. Probably the only long- range change is the negligible representation of philosophical studies, and the only departure from emphasis in the social sciences generally is the minimal influence of psychology. Again, the pattern is similar in *Canadian and international education*, but the latter has a much greater representation of undefined 'education' references and education fields as such (including a relatively strong influence of higher education). If there is any trend in the *Comparative education review*, it is toward an increase in definable disciplinary mix.

In 1977, Koehl listed the following topics highest in frequency of appearance in the *Comparative education review*: educational reform, methodology, educational theory, educational research, educational achievement, education for development, teaching comparative education, higher education, educational planning, history of comparative education, and colonial education.[35] For the current period, the greatest interest has consistently been in the topic of educational opportunity and inequality, including Marxist analyses and some reference to domestic American problems. Methodological differences, politically inspired and between hard technical methods and subjective reflections of 'social reality' are clearest in the exposition of this topic.

Policy/administration topics have been increasing through the early 1980s. Theory and methodology; financing (cost effectiveness, human capital investment, resource allocation); cultural reproduction and transmission; higher education; labour market and occupational status studies; and studies of women are also all high-frequency topics on the increase in the 1980s. Interest in higher education has been marked. Studies concentrating on women - cultural differences and the relation of culture to their situation, family influences, the effect of education on roles, the effect of access to higher educational opportunities, market outcomes, and level disparities, have been evident only in this period.

Planning and reform including much of the traditional emphasis on comparative education - structural models, systems, conditions of change, evaluation - were high in topic frequency, but seem to have peaked between 1978 and 1983. Given their importance to work in the field however, interest is likely to remain high. Pieces on adult and nonformal education, including vocational education, have been prominent in the period, but less in evidence recently. The same holds true for articles on achievement, though they show increasing refinement of analysis, discrimination, and criteria of assessment. Attention to minority questions, unless embedded in a broader social context or inferred from another analytic angle, has not been apparent in the 1980s. All in all, the topic trends suggest a theoretical shift to the left, but a regression from the momentary gains of the 1970s in practical concerns.

Other than what has been identified in the *Canadian and international education* pattern, for example the emphasis on Canadian national and international issues and organizations, little can be said of Canadian directions. Not exclusively but especially in Canada, the field is eclectic, the scholars are unusually dispersed, the organization is highly personalistic, and there is 'a certain lack of vision, of excitement, in the field as a whole.'[36]

Complementary to the literature are the actual programs and perceptions of those working every day in comparative education. From consultation with some colleagues throughout North America, the following picture of their view emerges.

At the undergraduate level, although comparative education (including development education) may be offered, it is rarely required and is usually present only as a component of a more general social foundations course, if at all. It does not seem to have gained a permanent foothold in degree programs, despite the possibilities for comparative education to relate to internationalizing curricula, the introduction of 'global education' in schools, and multicultural education. It is quite possible that comparative education has penetrated the programs directed to these purposes and comparative educationists have taken a role in their planning and in-service teacher training.

At the graduate, or post-graduate level, comparative education courses are usually available (the sample includes only schools with comparative education specialists), but even where there is a recognized centre of comparative education activity, comparative education programs are uncommon. Programs are normally in 'foundations' with comparative education components or *ad hoc* opportunities for specialization. There are of course, notable exceptions. Possibly because of the dearth of university vacancies in recent years, there appears to be much more activity at the Masters' level and more likelihood that students will study comparative education to enhance their qualifications, rather than to gain them, and to return to or seek jobs in the private or governmental organization sector unless they are already securely placed in education.

Responses about the purpose of offerings seem to bear out the broader and more practical inclinations of the field in recent years. Some schools are still able to proclaim theoretical purposes and provide specialist training, which is 'the way it's supposed to be' in the university. More frequent however are purposes pertaining to the general education of all students and to the general information of educators. Comparative educationists may well be involved with peripheral activities such as exchanges, helping foreign students, and promoting human rights. Where comparative or development education programs are offered they are now likely to be decidedly practice-oriented, geared toward international activity in the real world.

Unless there were to be an expansion of university teaching posts in comparative education, this profile represents as much as can be done. It is unusual to find more than two full-time comparative education specialists in a department, and though they may rely somewhat on colleagues with related interests, they are not likely to have the research or teaching support that their European counterparts enjoy. With the research and consultation demands, program development has probably reached its limit with present resource levels.

Throughout this chapter I have referred to universities and scholars taking a lead in comparative education in North America, either in organization or research, or both. Out of this, and verified by others, the following list of dominant university comparative education centres emerges: University of Pittsburgh, The State University of New York (SUNY) (Albany), The State University of New York (SUNY) (Buffalo), The University of California Los Angeles (UCLA), Stanford, and Florida State University.[37] The two Canadian universities listed (by both American and Canadian respondents) were the Ontario Institute for Studies in Education and The University of Calgary. There is a strong sentiment that centres can no longer be identified in general however, because of differential specializations and emphases, and because both scholarship and service in the field are now widely dispersed, possibly stronger in some other organizations than in any single university (e.g., the World Bank, and the International Development Research Centre in Canada).

With regard to methodology and focus, it is clear that developing countries, particularly in Asia and Africa but differentially according to department specializations and funding, now figure prominently in the field. Although 'area studies' are not universally respected, partly because so many have been uninformed and the good ones have spoken only to those with the same interest, most comparative educationists still communicate their interests in geographical terms. Sociology is probably the strongest discipline base, with economics and history often combining with it in the conduct of studies. Anthropology has always been of functional relevance to comparative education, and is being 'rediscovered' with some currently popular methods. The split, or balance, between qualitative and quantitative emphases remains unchanged. There is some feeling that quantitative studies have more visibility. Proponents of both see the necessity of systematic investigation and theory building.

Shifts in the field show what is in store for the immediate if not long-range future. Comparative education remains the umbrella field. The openness of recent years has only reinforced the status of comparative education as 'more than a discipline,' as 'an interdisciplinary partnership on unstated terms,' as a pursuit of the metaphors and idioms which may reveal if not explain the unknown.[38]

The practice of teaching and research shows a shift to development education, to international development education, or to a fusion of comparative and development education. Subjects deriving from that research context have come to the fore. System effectiveness, the effects of schooling - socially and in educational quality as indicated by concrete measures, the relationship of productivity and investment in education, and how this varies, the importance of technology in education, and also cognitive effects and attitudinal components of educational strategies, and the unique role of women in development are intrusive questions.

There is probably less theoretical pre-occupation, more disciplinary rigour but also more determination, at least among students, to seek the specific knowledge which will relate directly to practical requirements of schools in societies, both domestically and in international efforts. This brings the field much closer to some other education specializations, such as curriculum, evaluation, planning and management, than has been the case. Although the search for suitable methodologies allows for mystery, the practice of the work has increasingly specified a return from the 'romantic '60s'[39] to the institutional and individual realities of given environments.

The funding picture is unclear, but it is safe to say that major efforts depend now and will continue to depend on government and private sources outside universities. Since these sources are more interested in international aspects of teaching at home and on development issues abroad, they are probably responsible to some extent for the visible shifts in field concerns. There is substantial support available for directed research, and some comparative educationists have oriented their programs and research to the funding targets, especially in the USA. They compete, however, and not exceptionally well, with others promoting international teaching or research programs. Otherwise, comparative education does not appear to be better or worse off than most specializations in education, perhaps better off than other fields in 'educational foundations.'

The concern with *policy*, as a particular approach and focus for comparative work, may be the most wide-reaching change in field orientation. The policy framework requires that comparativists refer their work to practical institutional questions, that they deliver accurate and often prescriptive information as well as their ideas to policy makers, but also, and perhaps most importantly in terms of the norms and ideals of the field, that they caution against 'quick fixes,'[40] that they challenge policy decisions not proving effective in practice, and that they bring honest and, if necessary, aggressive criticism to the misuse of international data in the public disinterest.

If the methodological discussion in the field over the past ten years has concluded anything, it is that singular positions are incompatible with the reality of research and that black-white views distort social reality and hinder the progress of research. This understanding should diminish the methodological and ideological differences, and lead comparative educationists in North America to concentrate on cumulative work, on dialogue about the direction and purpose of the work, and on the theoretical integration which will unify the vast knowledge gains of the past thirty years.

Notes

1. I am indebted for advice and judgments on selections of this paper to Ratna Ghosh, Werner Stephan, Don Adams, Victor Kobayashi, George Urch, Stephen Heyneman, Claude Eggertsen, Kal Gezi, Val Rust, Kim Sebaly, and Erwin Epstein. For assistance with the preparation of the manuscript I wish to thank Corrie Marles at The University of Calgary.
2. The background has been repeated in many publications. For this particular distillation, I am indebted to W. Brickman and A. Kazamias in *Comparative education review*, vol.21, No.2/3, June/October 1977. More generally, the summary of S. Fraser and W. Brickman, *A history of international and comparative education*, Glenview, IL, Scott, Foresman, 1968 and by H. J. Noah and M. Eckstein, in *Toward a science of comparative education*, London, Macmillan, 1969 and the literature review done by Robert Koehl in *Comparative education review*, Vol.21, No.2/3, p.177-194, are to be recommended.
3. Brickman, W. W. Ten years of the Comparative Education Society. *Comparative education review.* (Kent, OH), vol.10, no. 1, February 1966, p.7-8: '1. to promote and improve the teaching of comparative education in colleges and universities; 2. to encourage scholarly research in comparative and international studies in education; 3. to interest professors of all disciplines in the comparative and international dimensions of their specialties; 4. to promote intervisitation of educators and on-the-spot studies of school systems throughout the world; 5. to co-operate with specialists in other disciplines in interpreting educational developments in a wider cultural context; 6. to facilitate the publication of studies and up-to-date information on comparative education; 7. to encourage co-operation among specialists in comparative education throughout the world in joint studies, exchange of documents, and first-hand descriptions of education; 8. to co-operate whenever possible with such organizations as UNESCO, International Institute (i.e., Bureau) of Education, Organization of American States, etc.'

4. Presidents of the CIES, from 1957 to 1987 are, in order: William W. Brickman, University of Pennsylvania; W. H. E. Johnson, University of Pittsburgh, Joseph Katz, University of British Columbia; C. Arnold Anderson, University of Chicago; Claude A. Eggertsen, University of Michigan, R. Freman Butts, Teachers College, Columbia; Donald K. Adams, University of Pittsburgh; David G. Scanlon, Teachers College, Columbia; William W. Brickman, University of Pennsylvania; Stewart E. Fraser, George Peabody College for Teachers; Reginald Edwards, McGill University; Philip J. Foster, University of Chicago; Andreas Kazamias, University of Wisconsin; Cole S. Brembeck, Michigan State University; Harold J. Noah, Teachers College, Columbia, Robert F. Lawson, University of Calgary; Rolland G. Paulston, University of Pittsburgh; Susanne M. Shafer, Arizona State University; Joseph P. Farrell, Ontario Institute for Studies in Education; Mathew Zachariah, University of Calgary; George A. Male, University of Maryland; Thomas J. LaBelle, UCLA; Erwin Epstein, University of Missouri - Rolla; Max A. Eckstein, Queens College, CUNY; Barbara A. Yates, University of Illinois; John N. Hawkins, UCLA; R. Murray Thomas, University of California, Santa Barbara; Gail P. Kelly, SUNY, Buffalo; Peter Hackett, University of Michigan.

   Presidents of the CIESC, from 1967 to 1986 are: Joseph Katz, University of British Columbia; Andrew F. Skinner, University of Toronto; Lionel Desjarlais, University of Ottawa; Roger Magnusson, University of Ottawa; Avigdor Farine, University of Montreal; Douglas Ray, University of Western Ontario; John Mallea, Queens University; Margaret Gillett, McGill University; Shiu Kong, University of Toronto; Dan Dorotich, University of Saskatchewan; Jacques La Montagne, University of Montreal; Vandra Masemann, Masemann & Mock Consultants, Toronto.

5. For elaboration of these in the USA see Altbach, P. G. Editorial: 'The *Review* at thirty.' *Comparative education review*. (Chicago, IL), vol.330, no.1, February 1986, p.1-3.

6. Editorial policy stated in the *Comparative education review*, vol.15, no.3, October 1971, p.264 and never refuted was that the journal would impose 'no limits on any kind of inquiry,' and would 'seek to serve all students of comparative education [...] by facilitating communication among the various specialists and practitioners.'

7. These were supported by the Donner Canadian Foundation, and contained main contributions by: 1967) E. E. Stewart, Margaret Gillett, Robert Lawson, and Colin Smith; 1968) Andrew Skinner, Louis-Philippe Audet, Willard Brehaut, and Rodolph Schnell; 1969) W. G. Devitt, M. P. Lupul, J. D. Wilson and J. Dahlie, C. J. Jaenen, A. Tremblay, R. J. Love, and Margaret Gillett; 1970) Robin Harris, J. Roby Kidd, Leonard Marsh, Lucien Michaud, Harold Entwhistle, David Smith, and Roger Magnusson.

8. The first honorary fellows have been mentioned. The award articles in the *Comparative education review* were: Catalina H. Wainerman. The impact of education on the female labor force in Argentina and Paraguay. vol. 24, no. 2, part 2, June 1980 p. S180-S195; Alan Sica and Harland Prechel. National political-economic dependency in the global economy and educational development. vol. 25, no. 3,

October 1981 p.384-402; George Psacharopolous. The economics of higher education in developing countries. vol. 26, no. 2, June 1982 p.139-159; Gary L. Theisen, Paul P. W. Achola and Francis Musa Boakari. The underachievement of cross-national studies of achievement. vol. 27, no. 1, February 1983 p.46-68; Catherine C. Lewis. Co-operation and control in Japanese nursery schools. vol. 28, no. 1, February 1984 p.69-84; and Joseph P. Farrell and Ernesto Schiefelbein. Education and status attainment in Chile: a comparative challenge to the Wisconsin model of status attainment. vol. 29, no. 4, November 1985, p.490-506.

9. Memorandum to CIES Board of Directors, February 23, 1977. For example: 'CIES should extend its interests to bring in the interests of social scientists;' 'Assistance should be extended to sociologists, political scientists, etc. to include material on educational development abroad in their regular courses.' (Barbara Burn); 'CIES should play a strong role in international studies at the pre-collegiate level.' (Thomas LaBelle); 'CIES should collaborate with U. S. and foreign associations in the development of school materials aimed at global or international understanding.' (Michael Chiapetta); 'A larger hearing should be given by CIES to those of our members whose interests lie outside schools of education - development projects, defense schools, etc.' (Joseph DiBona); 'Meetings with other associations can be an effective strategy for strengthening CIES -ISA, AERA, AACTE, American Anthropological Association, American Sociological Association, etc.' (John Singleton); 'We should build linkages with other associations involved in teacher education - social studies, curriculum development, educational administration, counselling and guidance.' (Cole Brembeck).

10. Among others, see An interview with C. Arnold Anderson. *Comparative education review.* (Kent, OH), vol. 17, no. 2, June 1973, p. 153; Altbach, P. G. Editorial: Comparative and international education'. *Comparative education review.* (Chicago, IL), vol. 27, no. 2, June 1983, p. 165-166; Harman, G. Handling educational policy at the State level in Australia and America. *Comparative education review.* (Chicago, IL), vol. 29, no. 1, February 1985, p. 22-46. In a letter to the author, W. K. Medlin elaborated an idea originally proposed by C. A. Anderson to compile a set of findings from the field applicable to problem areas in education; panels drawn from CIES members might be used for this.

11. An example of suggestions to extend participation, stemming from perceived lack of co-operative effort, is John Lipkins' report of a CIES discussion group (1974) which concluded the following suggestions, some of which were tried:

  1. A directory of all members, including major areas of interest, could be prepared and maintained on a systematic basis.

  2. Interest groups could be identified through the *Newsletter* and time could be allotted for their meetings at the Conference.

3. Panels might restrict their numbers or do away completely with respondents in order to allow for more discussion from the floor.

4. The business meeting should provide a more open forum for the discussion of members' concerns.

5. Graduate students should be given greater encouragement to join and actively participate in the Society.

6. Graduate students should have the opportunity to hear the Presidential Address without paying the banquet fee.

7. Efforts should be made to facilitate job placement of members - particularly graduate students - at the Annual Conference and throughout the year.

8. Members of the Society should be informed of special issues of the *Review* in time to submit contributions.

9. The Society should consider seeking alternative methods of financing its operations and research from both governmental and non-governmental sources.

10. All issues of the *Review* and activities of the Society should give first consideration to members' interests.

12. Bereday, George Z. F. Reflections on comparative methodology in education, 1964-1966. *Comparative education.* (Oxford, UK), vol. 3, no. 3, June 1967, p. 169-187. 'The second specialization [...] has been international education. Long-standing concerns of comparative education in "international understanding" have emerged under this heading as sustained studies of the crosscultural flow of ideas, movement of men across national frontiers, and of the organizations created to co-ordinate them.' (p.182)

13. See Adams, D. Development education. *Comparative education review.* (Chicago, IL), vol. 21, nos. 2/3, June/October 1977, p. 296-310; also Zachariah, M., ed. Development education in Canada in the eighties. *Canadian and international education*, vol. 12, no. 3, 1983, Special issue.

14. Hans, N. *Comparative education.* 3rd ed. London, Routledge and Kegan Paul, 1958. Moehlman, A. H.; Roucek, J. S., eds, *Comparative education.* New York, Dryden, 1952. Cramer, J. F.; Browne, G. S., *Contemporary education: a comparative study of national systems.* 1st ed. New York, Harcourt, Brace & World, 1956. Kandel, I. L. *Comparative education.* Boston, MA, Houghton Mifflin, 1933, and *The new era in education: a comparative study.* Cambridge, MA, Houghton Mifflin, 1955. Mallinson, V. *An introduction to the study of comparative education.* London, Heinemann, 1957. King, E. J. *Other schools and ours.* New York, Rinehart, 1958. Ulich, R. *The education of nations.* Cambridge, MA, Harvard University Press, 1961.

15. Noah, H. J.; Eckstein, M. A. *Toward a science of comparative education.* New York, Macmillan, 1969. See also, the description in Kazamias, A. M.; Schwartz, K. Intellectual and ideological perspectives in comparative education: an

interpretation. *Comparative education review*. (Chicago, IL), vol. 21, nos. 2/3, June/October, 1977, p. 173.

16. Expressed earlier at various points (Anderson, 1973: 'you want openness, looseness;' Lawson, 1975: 'free-form;' Brembeck, 1975: 'divergence and diversity'). The consensus appears to have been reached in 1983, when a preponderant view of 'open' methodology emerged from Epstein's presidential address in *Comparative education review*, vol. 27, no. 1, followed, in that issue by methodological discussions by Carnoy, Foster, Masemann, Noah, and Holmes, after airing substantial differences. Altbach's editorial in June 1983 and Eckstein's address in October carried the same message.

17. Kazamias, A. M.; Schwartz, K. Op cit., p. 159.

18. See Lawson, R. F. Free-form comparative education. *Comparative education review*. (Los Angeles, CA), vol. 19, no. 3, October 1975, p. 350: 'the most we can say generally is that sound micro-studies, thematic or contextual, should be thought of as initiatory to a cyclic development on two planes: on the one, immediately to policy directions, to practical trial, and evaluation; on the other, to abstraction of theoretical conclusions, and thence to the construction of paradigms with interchangeable situational and thematic variables.'

19. For example, I have treated the political and educational relationships in the closed environment of Berlin as a social laboratory for research purposes. See Lawson, R. F. The ring and the book: educational change in Berlin. In: Heyman, R. D.; Lawson, R. F.; Stamp, R. M. *Studies in educational change*. Toronto, Ont., Holt, Rinehart & Winston of Canada, 1972, p. 155-246.

20. Kelly, G. P.; Altbach, P. G. Comparative education: challenge and response. *Comparative education review*. (Chicago, IL), vol. 30, no. 1, February 1986, p. 89/107. The authors list new research concerns as a) women, or gender studies - new but not classifiable with the others; b) ways in which knowledge is disseminated, produced, used, c) ways of looking at educational institutions and their relationship to society, d) trend away from individual outcomes and achievements toward institutions and their relationships, e) charting of institutional content (p. 96). They suggest that reliance on school outcome data has failed to relate outcomes to the process of schooling and suggest qualitative methods pointed to student and teacher interaction, the structure of institutions, and the 'lived culture' of the school (p. 93).

21. Anderson, C. A. Op. cit., p. 154.

22. For example, classically: Kandel, I. L. Op. cit.; Moore, B. *The social original of dictatorship and democracy*. Boston, MA, Beacon Press, 1966. Coleman, J. S., ed. *Education and political development*. Princeton, NJ, Princeton University Press, 1965.

23. In that reference, for example, studies done by Klinzing, Gerhardt and Klinzing-Eurich, Gisela, at Tübingen University.

24. At various times, the literature in the field is almost totally eclipsed by the philosophy, content emphasis or approach of such works as Almond, G. A.; Verba, S. *The civic culture: political attitudes and democracy in five nations.* Princeton, NJ, Princeton University Press, 1963; Kuhn, T. S. *The structure of scientific revolutions.* 2nd ed. Chicago, IL, University of Chicago Press, 1970; Freire, P. *Pedagogy of the oppressed.* New York, Seabury Press, 1970; Young, M. F. D., ed. *Knowledge and control: new directions for the sociology of education.* London, Collier-MacMillan, 1971; Bowles, S.; Gintis, H. *Schooling in capitalist America.* New York, Basic Books, 1976.

This is not to question the importance to the field of these works, but to suggest that exclusive attention is extreme in a prolific research era. Some of the most significant works to the field are given relatively little attention: e.g., Archer, M. S. *Social origins of educational systems.* London, Sage Publications, 1979; Robinsohn, S. B., et al. *Schulreform im gesellschaftlichen Prozess,* Bd. I, Stuttgart, Germany FR, Klett, 1970.

25. See Anderson, C. A. op. cit., p. 151.

While I am not following Bereday's criticisms of 'doctoral dissertations (in comparative education) written by "mules",' it is obvious from even casual observation of communication in education that there is a wide gap between the use of terminology in these modes and the understanding of their meaning in research. See Bereday, G. Z. F. Reflections on comparative methodology in education, 1964-1966. *Comparative education.* (Oxford, U. K.), vol. 3, no. 3, June 1967, p. 180.

26. See Carnoy, M.; Levin, H. M. *Schooling and work in the democratic state.* Stanford, CA, Stanford University Press, 1985.

27. Anderson, C. A. op. cit., p. 151.

28. Eckstein, M. A.; Travers, K. J.; Shafter, S. M. A comparative review of curriculum: mathematics and international studies in the secondary schools of five countries. Submitted to the National Commission on Excellence in Education, April 28, 1982.

   Lawson, R. F. Comparative Studies Project: report from selected countries and American States. Submitted to the Minister of Education in support of the Review of Secondary Education, Province of Alberta, June 15, 1984.

29. Torney-Purta, J.; Lawson, R. F. Background paper to American Educational Research Association Roundtable, 1985.

30. See Adams, D. K. Editorial. *Comparative education review.* (Kent OH), vol. 13, no. 2, June 1969, p. 148 for an early pointed expression of this question.

31. For assistance in this survey, I am indebted to Barbara Juschka, The University of Calgary.

32. The categories used here, though traditional in the field and therefore applicable for communication, are large and not entirely adequate. The difficulty of assigning actual work to categories used in field discussion underlines some definitional problems, and requires some questionable assignments and some duplication in assigning.

33. This differs from the pattern in other comparative and international education journals, if the bibliographies compiled by Y. G-M. Lulat in the *Comparative education review*. are indicative. These show a much stronger interest in Europe, particularly the USSR, and a relative neglect of Africa. Koehl's survey implied a relatively stronger interest in Europe before 1977, though he labels the *Comparative education review*. even then as 'somewhat more Third-World centered than the European journals.' Koehl, R. The comparative study of education: prescriptions and practice. *Comparative education review*. (Chicago, IL), vol. 21, nos. 2/3, June/October 1977, p. 190.

34. Koehl, R. op. cit., p. 192.

35. Ibid, p. 187.

36. Radcliffe, D. J. Editorial. *Canadian and international education*, vol. 5, no. 1, June 1976.

37. Following these, mention is frequently made of University of Wisconsin, University of Chicago, University of Massachusetts, University of Michigan, Michigan State University, Columbia, Harvard and the University of Hawaii.

38. See Koehl, R. Op. cit., p. 193; Lé Thành Khôi. Toward a general theory of education. *Comparative education review*. (Chicago, IL), vol. 30, no. 1, February 1986, p. 15; Eckstein, M. A. The comparative mind. *Comparative education review*. (Chicago, IL), vol. 27, no. 3, October 1983, p. 311-322.

39. Adams, D. K. op. cit., p. 298.

40. Noah, H. J. The use and abuse of comparative education. *Comparative education review*. (Chicago, IL), vol. 28, no. 4, November 1984, p. 550.

Bibliography

Adams, D. 'Development education'. *Comparative education review*. (Chicago, IL), vol. 21, nos. 2/3, June/October 1977, p. 296-310.

Altbach, P. G.; Arnove, R. F.; Kelly, G. P., eds. *Comparative education*. New York, Macmillan, 1982.

Anderson, C. A. Comparative education over a quarter century: maturity and challenges. *Comparative education review*. (Chicago, IL), vol. 21, nos. 2/3, June/October 1977, p. 405-416.

Anderson, C. A. The program of the Comparative Education Center, University of Chicago. In Fraser, S., ed. *Governmental policy and international education*. New York, Wiley, 1965, p. 73-88.

Anderson, C. A., Sociology in the service of comparative education. *International review of education*. Vol. V, no. 3, 1959, 310-318.

Anderson, C. A.; Bowman, M. J., eds. *Education and economic development*. Chicago, Aldine Press, 1965.

Arnove, R. F. Comparative education and world-systems analysis. *Comparative education review*. (Chicago, IL), vol. 24, no. 1, February 1980, p. 48-62.

Barber, B. R. Science, salience and comparative education: some reflections on social scientific inquiry. *Comparative education review*. (Kent, OH), vol. 16, no. 3, October 1972, p. 424-436.

Benjamin, H. R. W. Growth in comparative education. *Phi delta kappan*. (Fulton, MS), vol. XXXVII, no. 4, January 1956, p. 141-144, 165.

Bereday, G. Z. F. Comparative education and ethnocentrism. *International review of education*. Vol. VII, no. 2, 1961, p. 24-33.

Bereday, G. Z. F. *Comparative method in education*. New York, Holt, Rinehart, and Winston, Inc., 1964.

Bereday, G. Z. F. Social stratification and education in industrial countries. *Comparative education review*. (Chicago, IL), vol. 21, nos. 2/3, June/October 1977, p. 195-210.

Berstecher, D.; Dieckmann, B. On the role of comparisons in educational research. *Comparative education review*. (Kent, OH), vol. 13, no. 1, February 1969, p. 96-103.

Borrowman, M. L. Comparative education in teacher education programs. *Comparative education review*. (Los Angeles, CA), vol. 19, no. 3, October 1975, p. 354-362.

Brembeck, C. S. The future of comparative and international education. *Comparative education review*. (Los Angeles, CA), vol. 19, no. 3, October 1975, p. 369-374.

Brickman, W. W., ed. *Comparative education: concept, research, and application*. Norwood, PA, Norwood Editions, 1973.

Brickman, W. W. Comparative and International Education Society: an historical analysis. *Comparative education review*. (Chicago, IL), vol. 21, nos. 2/3, June/October 1977, p. 396-404.

Brickman, W. W. A historical introduction to comparative education. *Comparative education review*. (Kent, OH), vol. 3, no. 3, February 1960, p. 6-13.

Carnoy, M. Education for alternative development. *Comparative education review*. (Chicago, IL), vol. 26, no. 2, June 1982, p. 160-177.

Eckstein, M. A. The comparative mind. *Comparative education review*. (Chicago, IL), vol. 27, no. 3, October 1983, p. 311-322.

Eckstein, M. A. Comparative study of educational achievement. *Comparative education review*. (Chicago, IL), vol. 21, nos. 2/3, June/October 1977, p. 345-357.

Eckstein, M. A.; Noah, H. J. Dependency theory in comparative education: the new simplicitude. *Prospects*. (Paris, UNESCO), vol. XV, no. 2, 1985, p. 213-225.

Edwards, R. Presidential address: the dimensions of comparison, and of comparative education. *Comparative education review*. (Kent, OH), vol. 14, no. 3, October 1970, p. 239-254.

Edwards, R.; Holmes, B.; van de Graaff, J., eds. *Relevant methods in comparative education: report of a meeting of international experts*. Hamburg, UNESCO Institute for Education, 1973.

Eggertsen, C. A. *University of Michigan comparative education dissertation series*. Ann Arbor, MI, School of Education, 1963 - 19726 v.

Epperson, D. C.; Schmuck, R. A. The uses of social psychology in comparative education. *Comparative education review*. (Kent, OH), vol. 6, no. 3, February 1963, p. 182-190.

Epstein, E. H. Currents left and right: ideology in comparative education. Presidential address. *Comparative education review*. (Chicago, IL), vol. 27, no. 1, February 1983, p. 3-29.

Farrell, J. P. The necessity of comparisons in the study of education: the salience of science and the problem of comparability. *Comparative education review*. (Chicago, IL), vol. 23, no. 1, February 19791 p. 3-16.

Fernig, L. The global approach to comparative education. *International review of education*. Vol. V, no. 3, 1959, p. 343-353.

Fischer, J., ed. *The social sciences and the comparative study of educational systems*. Scranton, PA, International Textbook Co., 197

Foley, D. E. Anthropological studies of schooling in developing countries: some recent findings and trends. *Comparative education review*. (Chicago, IL), vol. 21, nos. 2/3, June/October 1977, p. 311-328.

Foster, P. Comparative methodology and the study of African education. *Comparative education review*. (Kent, OH), vol. 4, no. 2, October 1960, p. 110-117.

Foster, P. Dilemmas of education development: what we might learn from the past. *Comparative education review*. (Los Angeles, CA), vol. 19, no. 3, October 1975, p. 375-392.

Foster, P. Education and social differentiation in less developed countries. *Comparative education review*. (Chicago, IL), vol. 21, nos. 2/3, June/October 1977, p. 211-229.

Hansen, W. Economics and comparative education: will they ever meet? And if so, when? *Comparative education review*. (Chicago, IL), vol. 21, nos. 2/3, June/October 1977, p. 230-246.

Henry, M. M. Methodology in comparative education: an annotated bibliography. *Comparative education review*. (Kent, OH), vol. 17, no. 2, June 1973, p. 231-244.

Heyman, R. Comparative education from an ethnomethodological perspective. *Comparative education*. (Dorchester-on-Thames, U. K.), vol. 15, no. 3, October 1979, p. 241-249.

Higson, J. M. The methodology of cross-national comparative analysis of education: a review of the literature. *Comparative education review*. (Kent, OH), vol. 12, no. 3, October 1968, p. 338-349.

Holmes, B. Comparative education and the administrator. *Journal of higher education.* (Columbus, OH), vol. 29, May 1958, p. 249-250.

Holmes, B. Paradigm shifts in comparative education. *Comparative education review.* (Chicago, IL), vol. 28, no. 4, November 1984, p. 584-604Kazamias, A. M. Comparative pedagogy: an assignment for the 70's. *Comparative education review.* (Kent, OH), vol. 16, no. 3, October 1972, p. 406-411.

Kazamias, A. M.; Schwartz, K. Intellectual and ideological perspectives in comparative education: an interpretation. *Comparative education review.* (Chicago, IL), vol. 21, nos. 2/3, June/October 1977, p. 153-176.

Kazamias, A. M.; Schwartz, K. Woozles and wizzles in the methodology of comparative education. *Comparative education review.* (Kent, OH), vol. 14, no. 3, October 1970, p. 255-261.

Kelly, G. P.; Altbach, P. G. Comparative education: challenge and response. *Comparative education review.* (Chicago, IL), vol. 30, no. 1, February 1986, p. 89-107.

Koehl, R. The comparative study of education: prescription and practice. *Comparative education review.* (Chicago, IL), vol. 21, nos. 2/3, June/October 1977, p. 177-194.

Laska, J. A. The stages of educational development. *Comparative education review.* (Kent, OH), vol. 8, no. 3, December 1964, p. 251-263.

Lawson, R. F. Free-form comparative education. *Comparative education review.* (Los Angeles, CA), vol. 19, no. 3, October 1975, p. 345-353.

Lé Thành Khôi. Toward a general theory of education. *Comparative education review.* (Chicago, IL), vol. 30, no. 1, February 1986, p. 12-29.

Masemann, V. Anthropological approaches to comparative education. *Comparative education review.* (University Park, PA), vol. 20, no. 3, October 1976, p. 368-380.

Masemann, V. L. Critical ethnography in the study of comparative education. *Comparative education review.* (Chicago, IL), vol. 26, no. 1, February 1982, p. 1-15.

Massialas, B. G. Education and political development. *Comparative education review.* (Chicago, IL), vol. 21, nos. 2/3, June/October 1977, p. 274-295.

Merritt, R. L.; Coombs, F. S. Politics and educational reform. *Comparative education review.* (Chicago, IL), vol. 21, nos. 2/3, June/October 1977, p. 247-273.

Noah, H. J. The use and abuse of comparative education. *Comparative education review.* (Chicago, IL), vol. 28, no. 4, November 1984, p. 550-562.

Noah, H. J.; Eckstein, M. A. *Toward a science of comparative education.* London, Macmillan, 1969.

Passow, A. H., et al. *The national case study: an empirical comparative study of twenty-one educational systems.* Stockholm, Almqist & Wiksell; New York, Wiley, 1976.

Paulston, R. G. Social and educational change: conceptual frameworks. *Comparative education review.* (Chicago, IL), vol. 21, nos. 2/3, June/October 1977, p. 370-395.

Power, C.; Wood, R. National assessment: a review of programs in Australia, the United Kingdom, and the United States. *Comparative education review.* (Chicago, IL), vol. 18, no. 3, August 1984, p. 355-377.

Przeworksi, A.; Teune, H. *The logic of comparative social inquiry.* New York, Wiley-Interscience, 1970.

Raivola, R. What is comparison? Methodological and philosophical considerations. *Comparative education review.* (Chicago, IL), vol. 29, no. 3, August 1985, p. 362-374.

Rosselló, P. Comparative education as an instrument of planning. *Comparative education review.* (Kent, OH), vol. 4, no. 1, June 1960, p. 3-12.

Ruscoe, G. C.; Nelson, T. W. Prolegomena to a definition of comparative education. *International review of education.* ('s-Gravenhage, Netherlands), vol. X, no. 4, 1964, p. 385-390.

Singleton, J. Education and ethnicity. *Comparative education review.* (Chicago, IL), vol. 21, nos. 2/3, June/October 1977, p. 329-344.

Springer, U. Education, curriculum and pedagogy. *Comparative education review.* (Chicago, IL), vol. 21, nos. 2/3, June/October 1977, p. 358-369.

Templeton, R. G. The study of comparative education in the United States. *Harvard educational review.* (Cambridge, MA), vol. 24, Summer 1958, p. 141-158.

Weiler, H. N. Legalization, expertise and participation: strategies of compensatory legitimation in educational policy. *Comparative education review.* (Chicago, IL), vol. 27, no. 1, June 1983, p. 259-277.

Woock, R. R. Sociological analysis and comparative education. *International review of education.* (The Hague), vol. 27, no. 4, 1981, p. 411-425.

Yates, B. A. Comparative education and the Third World: the nineteenth century revisited. *Comparative education review.* (Chicago, IL), vol. 28, no. 4, November 1984, p. 533-549.

Zachariah, M. Lumps of clay and growing plants: dominant metaphors of the role of education in the Third World, 1950-198. *Comparative education review.* (Chicago, IL), vol. 29, no. 1, February 1985, p. 1-21.

Latin America

A. Oliveros

Latin America is a major area of the world that has produced a great many studies on comparative education in the second half of the twentieth century. These studies are rigorous, precise and soundly based. Despite their virtues, they have not been accompanied by systematic research in the field of comparative education, nor has much thought been given to assessing the various theories and methods of comparative education which, as a subject, does not yet enjoy full academic status in universities and teacher training centres.

More will be said about this aspect later but, in a nutshell, the situation may be described as one in which there is a wealth of material (statistical, social, economic, legislative and organizational data) awaiting comparative analysis of one kind or another.

The reason for this is that studies which involve compiling and arranging data are conducted primarily by international bodies concerned with the economic, social and cultural development of the region. Only after several years, and on a narrower and far less intensive scale, will educational comparative studies be launched by academic centres and specialist associations.

The fact that comparative educational research is initiated and advanced by international organizations gives the process the following special features: (a) high standards, due to the involvement of experts and specialists using reliable, well-proven methods of compiling, arranging and processing

---

The author has used material published by E. Schiefelbein, to whom he owes thanks. He is also grateful to J. Blat, S. Ferrer and José L. García Garrido for their comments and suggestions.

data; (b) impartiality in comparative assessments between countries; (c) broad dissemination, not only in the countries of the region which are obviously the most closely concerned, but also throughout the world, to such an extent that Latin America may be said to have taught the world much about comparative education; (d) the task of interpreting and arranging the data for purposes of comparison has been approached from the important but narrow standpoint of the contribution which education can make to economic and social development. Hence the adoption of a dual, *development-oriented* and *economics-oriented* approach. In other words, the points at issue are, first, how to secure the quantitative increases which will bring education to a greater number of individuals and second, how to ensure that investment in education leads to higher productivity and hence increased national prosperity.

It follows from the above that: (1) a vast body of data is available to researchers; (2) the channels for collecting and regularly updating these data are now established and will continue to produce the necessary raw material; (3) all this material has been subjected to comparative analysis from specific standpoints (social, political and economic), producing findings which may be described as comprehensive (although it is a basic principle of comparative education that studies should be updated every few years); (4) there are many other comparative approaches, particularly those with a bearing on qualitative or technical and teaching aspects, which have been touched upon either not at all or only superficially.

This survey will, it is to be hoped, provide sufficient incentive for the research which is needed in the above fields. The forthcoming celebration in 1992 of the quincentenary of the discovery of America may act as a further stimulus.

History of comparative education in the region

The nineteenth century and the first half of the twentieth century witnessed attempts on the part of well-travelled and versatile scholars to assess national characteristics, governments and educational systems in qualitative terms. These writings tend to be hasty, more closely resembling the fleeting impressions of a news reporter than the sober product of critical investigation.

Studies covering the region as a whole began to appear in the second half of the twentieth century. At the outset they had no direct bearing on education but, rather, related to the social, political and economic phenomena which had a direct impact on development and the structure of educational systems. Later on, studies directly relating to education started to appear.

The historical account given below is intended to throw some light on the way in which these studies have evolved, both qualitatively and quantitatively.

Preliminary remarks

There is a close affinity between the countries compared. First of all, they share a common language (even in the case of Brazil, the linguistic similarities are so great that understanding between Spanish- and Portuguese-speakers is immediate). Over and above this linguistic affinity, administrative and scholastic structures are very similar, which considerably facilitates both comparison and the interpretation of one country's data by researchers in another. Similarly, a common historical background and shared traditions unconsciously but effectively enhance comparison and mutual understanding.

One feature of the last few decades has been the establishment of a number of supranational organizations, at the worldwide, regional or subregional level. They may not all be closely involved in education, but none of them underestimates it as an investment, a basis for a skilled workforce, a factor of development, or a means of easing social tensions. The overall approach which most of these organizations adopt to the region or subregions with which they are concerned inevitably produces comparative studies in which educational factors play a direct or indirect role. Furthermore, in order to assemble the data required for such analytical studies, the organizations concerned must set up and maintain efficient channels for receiving information, and the resulting structures will benefit researchers in all fields, including comparative education. Finally, attention should be drawn to the contribution made by international organizations to the training of specialists in comparative research in all areas, particularly those involving education. In fact, the Latin American countries are so absorbed by their internal problems that, without the international organizations, the trend towards comparative studies in fields such as education would not exist at all.

The following organizations existed in 1950: the International Bureau of Education, which was established in 1929 and has produced comparative studies which form the backdrop for comparative research into education; the Pan American Union, which was established in 1910 and, in 1948, became the Organization of American States (OAS); and UNESCO, which was established in 1945 and launched its Principal Project for the extension and improvement of primary education in Latin America in 1956. The latter two organizations have been extremely active in the region, and the positive impact they have had on comparative education is described below. Mention should also be made of the Economic Commission for Latin America (ECLA), the Inter-American Development Bank (IDB), the Ibero-American Bureau of Education (IABE), as well as the other organizations listed in the Table referred to above.

For the past thirty years, the conferences, seminars and other meetings held under the aegis of these organizations have been an essential catalyst for the development of comparative educational research in Latin America.

Keen interest in the social, economic, cultural and political problems encountered by the countries of the region resulted in the publication between 1955 and 1965 of a number of individual studies of the Latin American situation which laid the foundations for a comparative approach to questions of social significance, including education. The most significant works are listed in the final bibliography.

Lines of development

As far as education is concerned, the overall studies referred to above followed three threads which, although intertwined in practice, should be distinguished in terms of both objectives and results: (a) the educational aspect proper, the emphasis being placed on technical matters relating to curricula, teacher training and further training, school inspection and updating of material and methodology; (b) the political and administrative aspects, focusing on educational planning and, as a consequence, on co-ordination of the educational and other national sectors, the improvement of educational administrative services and the technical enhancement of data collection and processing centres; (c) the economic aspect with its two main components, namely, the cost of buildings, teachers and administrative services on the one hand and the relationship between education and employment, with its repercussions on the growth of national income, on the other.

Sequence of events

Each of the above-mentioned processes followed a similar time sequence: (a) in the initial stage, the studies were simply descriptive and the main objective was to obtain reliable data; (b) these were followed by interpretive comparative educational studies reaching conclusions and predicting trends within the theoretical framework established in 1960 by Rosselló (see page 188 below); (c) the interpretive and explanatory comparative function was then applied both spatially, to specific countries in relation to one another, and in time, to certain quantitative phenomena recorded at intervals of several years.

These stages, which are described in detail below and were characterized by intensive activity in the field of comparative education, were followed in the late 1970s, and until today, by a period devoted to reflection on the work of the past and to the development of comparative educational theory in individual works, academic circles and specialized associations.

To sum up, the comparative studies of the early 1960s which focused on social and economic issues were superseded in the late 1960s and early 1970s by technically-oriented comparative research based on reliable data, which in turn gave way in the mid-1970s to the in-depth study of comparative education and related methods of investigation.

Significant studies and comparative education training centres

This section will review the major comparative studies from which it has been possible to draw conclusions and make predictions of great value for the development of educational policies in the region. These studies have also added to the volume of data which, as suggested above, have not yet been analyzed from all possible comparative standpoints and are available to researchers.

Bearing in mind what has already been said, the studies fall into two main categories:

a) studies by international organization secretariats or working groups; since they are generally collective endeavours, they are anonymous, containing a wealth of data and characterized by their extremely cautious approach to interpretation and the identification of variables;

b) studies by individual researchers, academics or scholars concerned with the problem; even though most of the authors have been connected in some way with international organizations and make use of the latter's data, they tend to formulate hypotheses more freely. Furthermore, since the authors are specialists in different fields of education, the studies in this category have a stronger technical and pedagogical slant than those in the first category, in which the political and administrative component predominates.

Conferences

With regard to conferences and meetings held under the aegis of international organizations, three main stages may be distinguished in the sequence of events.

a) Inter-American meetings, generally convened by OAS and held between 1948 and 1956. They focused on education as a purely scholastic phenomenon, disregarding its links with other social phenomena. The emphasis was placed on standards, prospects and aspirations. They were poorly backed up by statistics and practical studies.

b) Meetings characterized by a concern with planning and the financial bases for education. They helped to launch the notion of technical assistance by supranational bodies and cooperation between states. Cooperation was built up between UNESCO and OAS and a balance struck between them as regards the convening of meetings. These developments took place between 1956 and 1962.

c) Between 1962 and 1979 a number of meetings were held, generally convened by UNESCO in cooperation with OAS, ECLA and, on a less regular basis, other international bodies. These conferences were characterized by their approach to education as a factor, in terms of both cause and effect, of economic development, and they were intended for Ministers of Education and Development.

d) From 1979 onwards, UNESCO's new Principal Project generated meetings that were characterized by very active participation on the part of the Caribbean states and the gradual replacement of international assistance by the idea of co-operation between states.

Following the same chronological order, the contribution made by each of these meetings to comparative education is outlined below.

a) The Conference on Education and Economic and Social Development in Latin America (CEDES), held in Santiago (Chile) from 5 to 19 March 1962 under the patronage of UNESCO, ECLA, OAS, FAO, the ILO and a number of private foundations, was an important milestone - something of a coming-of-age - in the series of meetings on education in the countries of the region.

The conference was important for several reasons. It was the first to be based on serious comparative studies of the actual situation. In other words, it was not confined to aspirations and desires but confronted stark reality in order to 'see what could be done'. Emphasis was placed on data concerning not only education but also concomitant social phenomena such as demography, economic development and social structures. Cooperation among various international organizations was stressed. Specific action targets were set.

The main conference document, and also the most interesting comparative study, bore the title 'The demographic, economic, social and educational situation in Latin America'. Prepared jointly by UNESCO, ECLA, the United Nations Office of Social Affairs and the Latin American Demographic Centre, it reviewed the demographic situation and discussed basic economic factors (with particular reference to those inhibiting economic development), social aspects and, finally, the status of education.

These fundamental aspects were supplemented by contributions from some individual specialists and other international organizations such as the Latin American Demographic Centre, the International Labour Office, FAO and ECLA.

From the comparative standpoint, the 'Compendium of statistics on the demographic, economic and social aspects of education in Latin America' prepared by ECLA and two UNESCO studies on the primary and secondary grades of the school system are worth particular mention.

With regard to the primary level, valuable additional information is provided in the 'Report on the development of the Principal Project for the extension and improvement of primary education in Latin America 1960-62', submitted to the IVth Meeting of the Intergovernmental Consultative Committee for the Principal Project held immediately after the CEDES in Santiago (Chile) on 22 and 23 March 1962.

The studies of the working group on the social aspects of economic development in Latin America which met in Mexico from 12 to 21 December 1960 were also published in 1962. The fourth section of the first volume is devoted to education and the four studies published are extremely useful from the comparative standpoint.

b) The Conference of Ministers of Education and Ministers in charge of Economic Planning in the Latin American and Caribbean countries (MINEDECAL), convened jointly by UNESCO and ECLA, met in Buenos Aires from 20 to 30 June 1966 to study several documents containing valuable contributions to comparative education.

Two of these, drawn up by the UNESCO secretariat, provide an overall picture of education seen from various standpoints. One of them, 'Development of the educational situation in Latin America, 1956-1965' looks back into the past while another, 'Education and development in Latin America: bases for an educational policy' is oriented towards the future.

ECLA prepared a document entitled 'The training of human resources in the economic and social development of Latin America'.

c) The Conference of Ministers of Education and Ministers Responsible for Promoting Science and Technology in Relation to development in Latin America and the Caribbean (MINESLA), convened by UNESCO, met in Caraballeda (Venezuela) from 6 to 15 December 1971. It had before it two basic documents of considerable significance for comparative education, namely, 'Development of education and science policy in Latin America and the Caribbean' and 'Development and growth trends of education in Latin America and the Caribbean. Statistical data'. Mention should also be made of a document confined to medium-level education submitted by ECLA.

Other sources of data

Over and above the major ministerial conferences, a number of more modest projects, publications and activities have helped to stimulate comparative education.

Firstly, one of the first comprehensive comparative studies, carried out at a time when the Principal Project for Latin America had been under way for barely two years, was that coordinated by José Blat from the UNESCO Regional Centre for the Western Hemisphere in Havana. This work, which is similar in style and format to the volumes published by UNESCO in the series 'L'Éducation dans le monde', triggered a series of activities embodied in UNESCO's Principal Project for Latin America.

Secondly, the progress reports on the Principal Project submitted to successive meetings of the Intergovernmental Consultative Committee are another valuable source of data and constitute in their own right comparative studies of the region. These were published from the IIIrd Meeting (Mexico, 14-19 March 1960) onwards, covering the IVth (Santiago, 20-22 March 1962), Vth (Brasilia, 3-6 March 1964), and VIth (Buenos Aires, 20-22 June 1966) Meetings and culminating in the full 'Report of the Assessment Committee of the Principal Project for the extension and improvement of primary education in Latin America' which contains a wealth of statistical data and may be regarded as the best comparative study prior to 1966. The layout of the report corresponds to the objectives of the Principal Project: (1) To stimulate systematic educational planning in the Latin American countries. (2) To promote the expansion of primary educational services by every possible means during the period in question, with the objective of providing the school-age population with appropriate educational services by 1968. (3) To encourage the review of primary school curricula and syllabuses in order to provide equal educational opportunities for all children in terms of number of years' enrollment and levels of study, meet the specific needs of the population in the various areas or regions of each country and adjust to society's changing demands and aspirations in the educational field. (4) To improve teacher-training, encourage continual further post-experience training and enhance the economic and social status of the teaching profession. (5) To build up, for each Latin American country, a nucleus of highly trained educational leaders and specialists capable of promoting the required reforms and advances in Latin American primary education. These five chapters are followed by annexes containing a series of comprehensive statistical tables.

Other more recent projects are discussed below.

Other international bodies

Emphasis should also be placed on the cooperative efforts of other regional organizations which have contributed, each in its specific area of activity, to building up a comparative picture of the region which, directly or indirectly, has exerted an influence on comparative educational research. For the most part, these centres are still in operation and they constitute a network for the exchange of information, publications and operational projects which are often shared among several bodies at the same time. Many of these operational projects have a comparative basis in which education almost always plays a part.

Particular mention should be made of two centres which did not outlive the Principal Project for Latin America (1956-1966) but during that period helped to train more than 600 educational leaders and specialists from all countries of the region, by means of one-year multinational and plurilingual courses in which the comparative method was used as the basis for training. They are the Course for Educational Specialists in Latin America (CEEAL) which was part of the São Paulo University in Brazil, and the Latin American Training Centre for Educational Specialists (CLAFEE) at the University of Chile.

Finally, a research centre in each country coordinated comparative educational studies (as well as other aspects of educational research).

Comparative education training centres

Reference has already been made to CEEAL and CLAFEE, which acted as genuine hubs for the entire continent. It should be pointed out that the fellowship holders attending courses were lecturers in teacher-training colleges, inspectors, and officials from Ministry of Education planning offices and policy units. Some have already held ministerial office and almost all are holding or have held highly responsible posts. From their desks they have helped to promote comparative educational research.

Many Latin American universities run lectures in comparative education, generally as part of educational administration or history of education courses.

A chair of comparative education has been created in some universities, for example San Luis in Argentina, Rio de Janeiro, São Paulo and Rio Grande do Sul in Brazil, the Javeriana University of Bogotá in Columbia, the Autonomous and Monterrey Universities in Mexico, the University of Uruguay and one in Venezuela.

With the exception of Bolivia, comparative education is not taught in teacher-training colleges but, as in the case of the universities, it is often included as part of a broader subject.

Principal research projects and publications over the last ten years

This aspect is discussed in the order adopted for the previous section: (a) studies produced for international meetings and conferences; (b) collective projects; (c) individual studies and publications.

Conferences

Thirteen years after the completion of UNESCO's Principal Project for Latin America, which played a major role in laying the foundations for comparative research in the region, UNESCO, OAS and ECLA, with the support of other regional bodies, put forward the idea of launching a new Principal Project for education in the Latin American and Caribbean region. As in the case of the earlier project, the meetings held in connection with the new one (they are listed below) generated comparative studies which are reflected in the main working documents submitted to each of them. It should be noted that the Caribbean countries, which had by that time become independent, took part in these meetings and provided fresh comparative material for the studies.

The following conferences were held in connection with the new Principal Project:

a) The Regional Conference of Ministers of Education and Ministers in charge of Economic Planning in the Member States of Latin America and the Caribbean, organized by UNESCO with the cooperation of ECLA and OAS and held in Mexico DF in December 1979, had before it two documents which were a sequel to the reports and comparative studies produced at previous conferences. One was a statistical analysis entitled 'Quantitative developments and enrollment forecasts for educational systems in Latin America and the Caribbean' and prepared by the UNESCO secretariat, while the other, prepared by ECLA and entitled 'structure and dynamics of development in Latin America and the Caribbean and the repercussions for education', focused on the economic and social aspects.

b) In the same order of ideas, an Intergovernmental Meeting on objectives, strategies and methods of action for a principal project in the field of education in the Latin American and Caribbean region was held in Quito in April 1981. This meeting produced a document containing ideas and suggestions in respect of the proposed principal project.

c) One year later the Provisional Intergovernmental Regional Committee of the Principal Project, meeting on the island of Saint Lucia (12-17 June 1982), made use of several comparative documents.

d) Finally, the first meeting of the Intergovernmental Regional Committee held in Mexico DF from 5 to 9 November 1984 had before it documents of significance for comparative education in the region, namely: 'Progress and priorities for future action' and 'A regional system and information for the Principal Project for Education in Latin America and the Caribbean'.

Institutional research projects

a) The project 'Development and Education in Latin America and the Caribbean', supported by UNESCO, ECLA and UNDP and managed by Germán Rama, produced a volume of literature - including country studies and comparative studies - which added to the body of knowledge accumulated on the region. Particular mention should be made of a study called 'Development and education in Latin America' which consolidated the work of several years, summing up the findings of a number of more limited studies under six main headings: (1) Changing trends in demographic, economic, labour, cultural and political structures. (2) Education in relation to social stratification and mobility. (3) Relationship between education and employment. (4) Trends in the educational system between 1970 and 1980 with regard to illiteracy and meeting the needs of different age groups. (5) The structure of educational systems. (6) The status of education in rural society.

b) In 1982 the Ibero-American Bureau of Education (IABE) published lists of research centres, Ibero-American educational documentation and information services and study centres dealing with Latin American questions both in the region itself and elsewhere in the world, all of which are a valuable aid to comparative studies. At about the same time it also published a series of files using a system of social, economic and educational indicators for each of the Latin American countries.

c) In 1982 the Ibero-American Bureau of Education also convened a meeting on the harmonization and reform of medium-level education in the Ibero-American countries which, in the preparatory stage, generated a series of comparative studies (see bibliography) on that particular part of the education system. In particular, the comparative analysis of syllabuses for each subject with reference to the Oliveros method is a significant new feature of comparative research.

Individual studies

a) Primary-level teacher training is the subject of two books by Oliveros published in 1975 and based on the methodology referred to on page 188.

b) The same methodology was applied by the same author to secondary education (1981, 1982) and still underpins the work referred to above.

c) Blat Gimeno (1981) is responsible for a comparative study on major educational trends.

d) Laura Oliveros (1982) has made a comparative study of the structures of central administrative bodies of educational systems in the Ibero-American countries.

e) Brunner (1985) has developed a reliable system for drawing up comparisons between Latin American universities and societies.

Main trends in contemporary research

In the countries of the region, educational research in general, and its comparative aspect in particular, have been governed by the political need to ensure that educational systems adjust rapidly to changes in the modern world.

Thus the main trends have been those laid down in the two major projects, namely:

1. The eradication of illiteracy. Changes have been made in rural education, indigenous education, popular education, women's education and other processes in an attempt to ensure that they are geared to the needs of the individuals to be educated. A number of comparative studies have been conducted in the Andean subregion and various Brazilian states.

2. The extension of educational facilities to a larger number of children and young people, together with an increase in the number of years of compulsory enrollment. Many of the studies referred to meet this criterion.

3. The improvement of educational administration at all levels, in all stages of the administrative process (planning, coordination, management, evaluation) and in all sectors of administrative activity (finance, staff, resources, buildings). Here too a number of comparative studies exist, either as separate works or as part of broader undertakings (see bibliography).

4. The enhancement of the status of teachers and, above all, the improvement of pre-service and in-service training have also been investigated (see bibliography).

5. Today, in the mid-1980s, medium-level education is a matter of concern to policy-makers and educators alike. This subject too has been, and will continue to be, researched (see bibliography).

6. University administration is another area in which some comparative work has already been done, and there is every indication that it will continue to receive attention from researchers (see bibliography).

7. The development of research and of information and documentation networks (see bibliography).

Main developments in methodology

Guidelines to the comparative approach to education in Latin American countries were for many years drawn from those provided by the International Yearbook of Education and the volumes dealing with specific subjects from the comparative standpoint published annually by the International Bureau of Education in Geneva. However, since these publications were distributed only through official channels, they were difficult to obtain.

The first systematic contribution to a theory of comparative education and the practical organization of research in that area was made by Pedro Rosselló, formerly Assistant Director of the International Bureau of Education and an official of UNESCO. In 1960, he visited the training centres for educational leaders and specialists at the Universities of São Paulo (Brazil) and Chile, both of which were involved in UNESCO's Principal Project for Latin America, giving a series of lectures which were subsequently published together (see bibliography). The choice of venue was particularly appropriate, since there was a large group of fellowship-holders from different Latin American countries (and, in the case of São Paulo, from the various Brazilian states) at each of the two universities, making it almost essential to adopt a comparative approach to the issues discussed. The courses taught in these centres from 1958 to 1966 also generated a fair number of comparative studies.

Rosselló's theory is one of general trends which emerge clearly when educational phenomena are viewed in a broad context and compared with one another. The study of these trends enables educational policy to be geared more closely to changing requirements. Rosselló bases his theory on his wide experience with the Yearbooks and annual studies published by the International Bureau of Education, and he proposes a list of trends, some of which have proved to be lasting, while others have already disappeared.

The books on comparative education published in Brazil by Riveiro (1956) and Lourenco Filho (1964) are general manuals designed for a course on the subject taught at the university. Nevertheless, their appearance was welcomed in a period when very little was published in this area.

Carmen Lorenzo's work as a comparativist started with a significant contribution to the first two volumes published by the Ibero-American Bureau of Education on 'Education on the International Plane' (1960, 1962, and 1972), in which the results of international and regional conferences and meetings are broken down by subject matter and compared. Her major work, 'The status of teaching staff in Latin America' (1969), was produced by applying the same comparative methodology to legislation.

Oliveros followed Carmen Lorenzo's methodology in drawing up the first comprehensive inventory in Spanish of the recommendations, conventions and declarations of UNESCO; however, his main contribution to methodology relates to the comparison of curricula. Faced with the difficulties inherent in basing comparisons on objectives or dealing with variables such as the methods used by teachers, he developed a comparative technique based on curricula, which have the following advantages: a) they are standard throughout all or at least most of each country, given the centralized structure of Latin American educational systems; b) they are quantifiable since they are expressed in terms of a number of hours per week; c) they enable a description to be drawn up of contents and activities; d) they establish an implicit hierarchy of value and content (compulsory subjects are more important than optional ones, those to which a full course is devoted are more important than those taking up only one term; those repeated in several courses are more important than those taught only once); e) they lend themselves to further study under programmes such as those carried out for various secondary education subjects (see bibliography). (It should be borne in mind that almost all the Latin American countries use the system of courses or academic levels comprising a number of set subjects, rather than the credit or assignment system.)

This methodology may be extended to the comparative study of syllabuses and subjects,[1] an area which started to be explored in 1982 in respect of mathematics, scientific subjects, geography and history.

With regard to comparative research into higher education, Silvio (1985) has put forward novel suggestions concerning methodology.

There are of course other theories of comparative education, such as those developed by Kandel, King, Bereday, Eckstein and others, which are known and used in Latin American academic or university circles, but have not yet been applied to practical comparative research into education. Márquez's book (1972) containing texts compiled from various works has helped to circulate the views propounded by a number of different authors.

It is difficult to say what impact comparative educational research has had on what can be described as the spectacular development of educational systems in the region. To give some indication of the quantitative improvements which have taken place, it may be noted that between 1960 and 1977, primary education increased by 223 per cent, medium-level education by 497 per cent and higher education by 782 per cent. In any event, there seems to be little doubt that the comparative analysis of situations has acted as a spur to many governments for the improvement of education in their countries.

Main specialized periodicals

The periodicals which have most consistently and systematically devoted space to comparative education in Latin America are:

Bulletin of the UNESCO Principal Project for Education in Latin America. Published quarterly by the UNESCO Regional Office, first in Havana and then in Santiago. Thirty numbers were published between 1957 and December 1966.

Education bulletin. (To some extent a continuation of the above publication). Published every six months by the UNESCO Regional Office for Education in Latin America and the Caribbean. First appeared in 1967.

Education. Published quarterly by the Education Division, Department of Cultural Affairs, Pan American Union. First appeared in 1956.

Plana. First published fortnightly, then monthly, then quarterly, by the Ibero-American Bureau of Education (IABE).

Higher Education. Bulletin of the Regional Centre for Higher Education in Latin America and the Caribbean (CRESALC). Published every four months. First appeared in 1979.

Note

1. In order to ensure that the terms used are correctly understood, the following definitions are provided:

    Curriculum: List of subjects to be taught in each grade or year, together with the time (generally expressed in hours per week) to be devoted to each of them.

    Syllabus: Description of the content of each subject in the general curriculum, for each year or grade.

Bibliography

Albornoz, Orlando (1985). *El acceso a la educación superior en América Latina y el Caribe.* Caracas, CRESALC, 38 págs.

Beltran, Martha E. (1979). *La integración de la educación y el trabajo productivo: tres experiencias en América Latina.* (Argentina, Cuba, Panamá) Paris, UNESCO. 57 págs. mimeografiado, holandesa.

Blasco, J. C. (1979). *Indicadores sobre la situación de la infancia en América Latina y el Caribe/Indicators on the situation of children in Latin America and the Caribbean*. Comisión Ecónomica para América Latina: Fondo de las Naciones Unidas para la Infancia.

Blat Gimeno, J. (1983) *Education in Latin America and the Caribbean: trends and prospects, 1970-2000*. Paris, UNESCO.

Brunner, J. (1985) *Universidad y sociedad en América Latina: un esquema de interpretación*. Caracas, UNESCO CRESALC.

Castillo, Alfonso; LATAPI, Pablo. (1983). *Educación no formal de adultos en América Latina: situación actual y perspectivas*. Santiago de Chile, Oficina Regional de Educación de la UNESCO para América Latina y el Caribe, 59 págs.

Centro de investigación y desarollo de la educación (1983). *La red de oferta y demanda de servicios de información sobre educación en America Latina*. Santiago de Chile.

Centro Latinoamericano de Demografia (1962), *Análisis demográfico de la situación educativa en América Latina*. Paris, UNESCO. [Document presented to the Conference on Education and Economic and Social Development in Latin America, Santiago de Chile].

Epstein, Erwin R. (1984) Corrientes ideológicas en la educación comparada. *Rev. Colombiana de Educación*. Bogotá, Univ. Pedagógica Nacional n°. 14, 2° semestre 1984 pp 9 - 38.

FAO (1962). *Estructura agraria y educación en América Latina*. Paris, UNESCO. [Document presented to the Conference on Education and Economic and Social Development in Latin America, Santiago de Chile].

FAO (1962). *El problema de la educación en materia de nutrición y alimentación en América Latina*. Paris, UNESCO. [Document presented to the Conference on Education and Economic and Social Development in Latin America, Santiago de Chile].

Higher education (Caracas, UNESCO Regional Centre for Higher Education in Latin America and the Caribbean), 1979- 3yr.

Ibero-American Bureau of Education (1960). *La educación en el plano internacional: educación primaria*. Madrid.

Ibero-American Bureau of Education (1962). *La educación en el plano internacional: educación media*. Madrid.

Ibero-American Bureau of Education (1972). *La educación en el plano internacional: educación superior, educación especial*. Madrid.

Ibero-American Bureau of Education (1982). *La educación en Iberoaméerica: sistema de indicadores socioeconómicos y educativos*. Madrid, 1980-82. 24 portfolios. [A collection of statistical tables, one portfolio per Member State.]

Ibero-American Bureau of Education (1984). *Guía de centros de estudios iberoaméricanos*. Madrid.

Ibero-American Bureau of Education (1984). *Guía de centros de investigación educativa.* Madrid.

Ibero-American Bureau of Education (1986). *Repertorio de servicios de documentación e información educativa iberoaméricanps.* Madrid.

Ibero-American Bureau of Education (1982). *Estadísticas de la educación media en los países iberoaméricanos.* Oficina de Educación Iberoaméricano, Madrid (AIEMIA/DT/3). [Document presented to the Reunión de trabajo acerca de la Armonización e Innovación de los estudios medios en los Países Iberoaméricanos, Santillana del Mar, Spain.]

Ibero-American Bureau of Education (1982). *Informe sobre la situación de la administración educativa en Iberoamérica.* Madrid, Oficina de Educación Iberoamérica.

Ibero-American Bureau of Education (1982). *Los programas de ciencias de la ensenanza media en nueve países iberoaméricanos.* Madrid, Oficina de Educación Iberoamérica. [Document presented to the Reunión de trabajo acerca de la Armonización e Innovación de los estudios medios en los Países Iberoaméricanos, Santillana del Mar, Spain.]

Ibero-American Bureau of Education (1982). *Primer informe del grupo de trabajo de la OEI sobre los programas de matematicas de la ensenanza media general en los países iberoaméricanos.* Madrid, Oficina de Educación Iberoaméricana. [Document presented to the Reunión de trabajo acerca de la Armonización e Innovación de los estudios medios en los países Iberoaméricanos, Santillana del Mar, Spain.]

International Labour Office (1962). *Evaluación cuantitativa y cualitativa de la mano de obra en relación con las necesidades educativas y de formación profesional concomitantes con el desarrollo económico.* Paris, UNESCO (UNESCO/ed/cedes/13). [Document presented to the Conference on Education and Economic and Social Development in Latin America, Santiago de Chile].

Lauerhass, Ludwig, Jr; Haugse, Vera Lucia Oliveira de Araujo (1980). *Education in Latin America: a bibliography.* Los Angeles, California UCLA, Latin American Center Publications, 431 pags.

Lemke, D. (1975). *La investigación educacíonal en Latinoamerica y el Caribe: una visión histórica.* Santiago de Chile, Oficina Regional de Educación de la UNESCO para América Latina y el Caribe. (SERIE/SEH/INVEST/1). [Document presented to the Seminario Experimental sobre Investigación Educacional.]

Lorenzo, C. (1969). *Situación del personal docente en América Latina.* Santiago de Chile, Editorial Universitaria; Paris, UNESCO.

Lourenço Fillro, M. B. (1961). *Educaçao comparada.* São Paulo, Ed. Meehoramentos.

Márquez, A. D. (1972). *Educación comparada: teoría y metodología.* Buenos Aires, El Ateneo.

Morales-Gómez, D. A. (1979) (ed). *La educación y desarrello dependiente en América Latina,* México, Ediciones Gernika.

Moreira, J. R. (1962). La educación y el desarrollo económico y social de América Latina. *La Educación,* Washington DC, Unión Panamericana, ano VII, n° 25-26, enero-junio 1962, 29-52.

Nassif, Ricardo (1978). *Problemas, métodos y tendencias del desarrollo del curriculo en tres países de América Central.* (El Salvador, Honduras y Nicaragua). Santiago de Chile, Oficina Regional de Educación de la UNESCO para América Latina y el Caribe, 136 págs, mimeografiado, holandesa.

OAS (1963). *Reunión Interamericana de Ministros de Educación.* 3a., Bogotà. *Acta Final.* Washington DC, Organización de los Estados Americanos.

OAS (1963). *Perspectivas de desarrollo de la educación en América Latina.* Informe de la Comisión Especial de la OEA a la III Conferencia Interamericana de Ministros de Educación. Bogotà, 4-10 de agosto, 1963. Washington DC, 1963.

OAS (1979). General Secretariat. *The first decade of the PREDE-OAS Regional Educational Development Programme: prospects and future plans.* Paris, UNESCO. [Document presented to the Regional Conference of Ministers of Education and Those Responsible for Economic Planning of Member States in Latin America, and the Caribbean, Mexico City.]

Oliveros, A. (1981). *La educación secundaria en Iberoaméricana: estudio comparativo.* Madrid, Oficina de Educación Iberoaméricana.

Oliveros, A. (1982). La educación secundaria en Iberoaméricana. *Revista de educación* (Madrid), ano XXX, n° 271, septiembre-diciembre, 183-204.

Oliveros, A. (1975). Change and the Latin American teacher: potentialities and limitations. *Prospects* (Paris, UNESCO), vol. V, n° 2, 230-238.

Oliveros, A. (1975). *Los profesores iberoaméricanos de educación primaria: planes de estudio de su formación.* Madrid, Oficina de Educación Iberoaméricana; Barcelona, Spain, Promoción Cultural.

Oliveros Alonso, A. (1975). *La formación de los profesores en América Latina.* Barcelona, Spain, Promoción Cultural; Paris, Editorial de la UNESCO.

Oliveros Alonso, A. (1977). *La formación de los profesores en Iberoamérica.* Madrid, Oficina de Educación Iberoaméricana (Documento III CIMED/2). [Document presented to the III Conferencia Iberoaméricana de Ministros de Educación, San Juan de Puerto Rico].

Oliveros Martin-Vares, L. (1981). *La administración educativa central en Iberoamérica.* Madrid, Oficina de Educación Iberoaméricana.

Persaud, Ganga (1982). *Educación moral y el curriculo de la escuela primaria: un repaso comparativo de estudios de casos en países escogidos de la America Latina y el Caribe.* Santiago de Chile, Oficina Regional de Educación de la UNESCO para América Latina y el Caribe, 66 págs. mimeografiado, holandesa.

Picon Espinoza, Cesar (1980). *La educación de adultos en América Latina: el reto de los 80*. Patzcuaro, Michoacán, Mexico, Centro Regional de Educación de Adultos y Alfabetización Funcional para América Latina. 175 págs.

Rama, G. W. (1981). Regionalización y disparidades socioculturales en América Latina. *Revista de educación* (Madrid), ano XXIX, n° 267, mayo-agosto, 219-334.

Reunión Iberoaméricana sobre educación para el Desarrollo, I, Madrid (1982). *Acta final*. Madrid, Sociedad Espanola de Sistemas Generales; Fundación para el Desarrollo de la Función Social de las Comunicaciones; Oficina de Educación Iberoaméricana.

Reunión de trabajo de las Universidades de Chile y de São Paulo, asociadas a la UNESCO, São Paulo, Brasil, 22-27 de julio de 1963. *Proyecto principal de educación. boletín trimestral* (Santiago de Chile), n° 19, julio-septiembre 1963, 73-113.

Ribeiro, J. Querino, (1958). *Pequena introduçao ao estudo de educaçao comparada*. São Paulo, Faculdade de filosofia, ciéncias e letras, Universidad de São Paulo.

Rodriguez Fuenzalida, E. (1981), *Alternativas metodológicas para el desarrollo de la educación de adultos en Iberoamérica*. Madrid, Oficina de Educación Iberoaméricana.

Rossello, P. (1960). *La teoría de las corrientes educativas*. La Habana, Centro Regional de la UNESCO.

Santiago Rocca, M. (1957). *Una pedagogía de inspiración lationoamericana*. Mexico, Harrero.

Schiefelbein, E. (1982). *Educational networks in Latin America: their role in the production, diffusion and use of educational knowledge*. Ottawa, International Development Research Centre.

Schkolnik, S. (1981). *Selective bibliography on higher education in Latin America and the Caribbean*. Caracas, Regional Centre for Higher Education in Latin America and the Caribbean, UNESCO.

SECAB (Secretaría Ejecutiva del Convenio 'Andrés Bello'). Educación a distancia en Chile, Perú y Venezuela. *Revista del convenio 'Andrés Bello'*. Bogotá, año VII, n° 17, enero-abril 1983, pp. 95 - 129.

Silvio, J. F. (1984). *Problemas metodólogicos en la investigación comparativa sobre la educación superior en América Latina y el Caribe*. Caracas, CRESALC-UNESCO.

Sociology of development in Latin America (1963). *International social science journal*, vol. XV, n° 4.

UNESCO (1960). *La situación educativa en América Latina*, Paris.

UNESCO (1962). *La educación media en América Latina*. Paris. [Document presented to the Conference on Education and Economic and Social Development in Latin America, Santiago de Chile.]

UNESCO (1962). *La educación primaria en América Latina: problemas y perspectivas.* Paris. [Document presented to the Conference on Education and Economic and Social Development in Latin America, Santiago de Chile.]

UNESCO (1962). *Situación demográfica, económica, social y educativa de América Latina.* Paris. [Document presented to the Conference on Education and Economic and Social Development in Latin America, Santiago de Chile.]

UNESCO (1962). *Informe sobre el desarrollo del proyecto principal para la extensión y el majoramiento de la educación primaria en América Latina.* Paris. [Document presented to the Fourth Session of the Intergovernmental Advisory Committee of the Major Project on the Extension and Improvement of Primary Education in Latin America, Paris, 1962.]

UNESCO (1963). Problemas y perspectivas de la educación latinoamericana: note preparada por la Secretaría de la UNESCO para la Tercera Conferencia Interamericana de Ministros de Educación, Paris, julio de 1963. *Boletín trimestral*, n° 19, julio-septiembre 1963, 23-39.

UNESCO (1964). *Report on a survey of teaching and research in comparative education, 1962-1963.* Paris.

UNESCO (1966). *Education and development in Latin America: bases for an educational policy.* Paris. [Document presented to the Conference of ministers of education and ministers responsible for economic planning in countries of latin america and the Caribbean, Buenos Aires.]

UNESCO (1966). *Educational developments in Latin America 1956-1965.* Paris. [Document presented to the Conference of ministers of education and ministers responsible for economic planning in countries of Latin America and the Caribbean, Buenos Aires.]

UNESCO (1966). Comisión para la evaluación del proyecto príncipal para la extensión y el mejoramiento de la educación primaria en América Latina. Santiago de Chile.

UNESCO (1971). *Development of education and science policies in Latin America and the Caribbean.* Paris. [Document presented to the Conference of ministers of education and those responsible for the promotion of science and technology in relation to development in Latin America and the Caribbean, Caraballeda, Venezuela.]

UNESCO (1979). *Evolución cuantitativa y proyecciones de matrícula de los sistemas educativos de América Latina y el Caribe.* Paris (ED-79/MINEDLAC/REF. 2). [Document presented to the Regional Conference of Ministers of Education and Those Responsible for Economic Planning of Member States in Latin America and the Caribbean, Mexico City.]

UNESCO (1979). *Preliminary study on the need for and the potential of a regional cooperative network for educational innovation for development in Latin America and the Caribbean* (ED-79/MINEDLAC/REF.4). [Document presented to the Regional Conference of

Ministers of Education and Those Responsible for Economic Planning of Member States in Latin America and the Caribbean, Mexico City.]

UNESCO (1981). *Reflections and suggestions concerning the major project on education in Latin America and the Caribbean*. Paris. [Document presented to the Intergovernmental Regional Meeting on the Objectives, Strategies and Methods of Action for a Major Project in the Field of Education in the Latin American and Caribbean Region, Quito.]

UNESCO (1982). *Priorities, targets and strategies for the first implementation phase of the Major Project*, Paris. [Document presented to the Meeting of the interim intergovernmental regional committee for the major project in the field of education in Latin America and the Caribbean, Saint Lucia.]

UNESCO (1982). *Synthesis of national plans of action submitted by the member states of the region*, Paris. [Document presented to the Meeting of the Interim Intergovernmental Regional Committee for the Major Project in the Field of Education in Latin America and the Caribbean, Saint Lucia.]

UNESCO (1984). *UNESCO activities under the major project in the field of education in Latin America and the Caribbean*. Paris. [Document presented to the First Meeting of the Intergovernmental Regional Committee for the Major Project in the Field of Education in Latin America and the Caribbean, Mexico City.]

UNESCO (1984). *The major project in the field of education in Latin America and the Caribbean: progress made and priorities for the future*. Paris. [Document presented to the First Meeting of the Intergovernmental Regional Committee for the Major Project in the Field of Education in Latin America and the Caribbean, Mexico City.]

UNESCO (1984). *A regional information system for the major project in the field of education in Latin America and the Caribbean*. Paris. [Document presented to the First Meeting of the Intergovernmental Regional Committee for the Major Project in the Field of Education in Latin America and the Caribbean, Mexico City.]

UNESCO/CEPAL/PNCD (1981). Proyecto desarrollo y educación en América Latina y el Caribe. *Desarrollo y educación en América Latina: síntesis general*. Buenos Aires, Comisión Económica para América Latina.

UNESCO Regional Office of Education for Latin America and the Caribbean (1977). *Problemas y tendencias de la administración educaional de América Latina y el Caribe*. Santiago de Chile, Oficina regional de educación de la UNESCO para América Latina y el Caribe.

UNESCO (1984). Regional Centre for Higher Education in Latin America and the Caribbean. *Directorio de centros de investigación y unidades de información sobre educación superior en América Latina y el Caribe*. Caracas.

UNESCO (1984). Regional Centre for Higher Education in Latin America and the Caribbean. *Estudios de postgrado en América Latina y el Caribe*. Caracas.

UNESCO (1984). Regional Centre for Higher Education in Latin America and the Caribbean. *Universidad y desarrollo en América Latina y el Caribe*. Caracas.

UNESCO (1985). Regional Centre for Higher Education in Latin America and the Caribbean. *Pedagogía y formación de docentes en la educación superior*. Caracas.

United Nations Economic Commission for Latin America (1962). *Compendio de estadísticas relativas a aspectos demográficos, económicos y socialses de la educación en América Latina*, Paris, UNESCO. [Document presented to the Conference on Education and Economic and Social Development in Latin America, Santiago de Chile].

United Nations Economic Commission for Latin America (1962). *Desarollo económico y educación en América Latina*. Paris, UNESCO. [Document presented to the Conference on Education and Economic and Social Development in Latin America, Santiago de Chile].

United Nations Economic Commission for Latin America (1966). *Human resource training in the economic and social development of Latin America*. Paris, UNESCO. [Document presented to the Conference of Ministers of Education and Ministers Responsible for Economic Planning in Countries of Latin America and the Caribbean, Buenos Aires].

United Nations Economic Commission for Latin America (1979). *Structure and dynamics of development in Latin America and the Caribbean and their implications for education*. Paris, UNESCO. [Document presented to the Regional Conference of Ministers of Education and those Responsible for Economic Planning of Member States in Latin America and the Caribbean, Mexico City.]

United Nations Economic Commission for Latin America; Latin American Institute for Economic Planning (1971). *Secondary education, social structure and development in Latin America*. Paris, UNESCO. (UNESCO/MINESLA/REF/5) [Document presented to the Regional Conference of Ministers of Education and Those Responsible for Economic Planning of Member States in Latin America and the Caribbean, Mexico City.]

Vasconi, T. A.; Reca, I. (1971). *Modernización y crisis de la universidad latinoamericana*. Santiago de Chile, Universidad de Chile.

Vessuri, H.; Diaz, E. (1985). *Universidad y desarrollo científico-técnico en América Latina y el Caribe*. Caracas, CRESALC-UNESCO.

Villarroel, Antonio F. (1985). Proyecto multinacional de desarrollo curricular y capacitación de docentes para la educación básica. Taller sobre comunidades educativas. *Curriculum. Revista especializada para América Latina y el Caribe*. Caracas. Año 9, n° 17, abril. pp. 13 - 91.

Vries, E. de; Medina Echavaria, J.; Higgins, B. (1967). *Social aspects of economic development in Latin America*. Paris, UNESCO.

Asia and the Pacific

Introductory note

This chapter is intentionally presented in two parts. The first, by Professor Kobayashi, relates to China, India, Japan and Korea; the second, by Dr R. Burns, deals with Australia, New Zealand and the Pacific. The reason for this division of labour is one of expediency. Although educational links between the two sub-regions are increasingly being forged, there has up to now been inevitably a lack of commonality as regards problems and policies. Culturally Asia cannot be treated, as yet, as a single educational entity. In this it differs from the other regions considered in this volume, where individual countries within a region share a common tradition or culture: one thinks of the Ibero-Hispanic origins of South America, or Europe, with its cultural roots in Athens, Rome and Jerusalem, for example, where commonality is strong. By contrast, continental and off-shore Asia (with the possible exception of parts of South-East Asia) up to very recently culturally shared very little with those lands lapped on all sides by the Pacific. This is reflected in the lack of comparative studies between their various contingent States and, to a certain extent, a divergence of interests in comparisons made that embrace the rest of the world. Thus, for example, there is no single comparative education society for the whole region, such as exists in Europe and elsewhere.

China, India and Japan represent very ancient civilizations with a long educational tradition. In the 1940s each underwent in turn drastic transformations in their society that impinged upon their education systems: in China, through a revolution; in India, through the achievement of independence from the colonial power; in Japan, through a new beginning after the cataclysm of war. It was from this decade onwards that comparative studies began to take off. Japan, for a while under direct American influence, rebuilt an education system in keeping with its massive industrial expansion. India, as a leading Third World country, looked to see what educational problems and possible solutions it had to face after 1947, and turned to both East and West for tentative educational models.

Along the rim of the Pacific basin a commonality of educational interests is slowly developing between Australasia and the countries with a much longer educational history. Australia, and to a lesser extent New Zealand, has had to face educational problems arising from migrations of peoples from the Mediterranean as well as from Northern Europe. It has therefore become more eclectic in its study of foreign educational systems, which only a generation ago still mainly related to Britain. For example, questions of cultural pluralism and linguistic assimilation have formed a large part of the agenda. The 'old dominions' of the Pacific have also kept a weather-eye on developments in the USA. Nor must the increasing impact of prosperity on education in former 'developing countries' such as Korea be forgotten.

Thus ties between what was once an apparently heteroclite group of countries are only gradually being formed. Nevertheless exchanges between scholars of comparative education in Japan and Australia are now commonplace. There is every indication that such exchanges of ideas and people will increase and be extended to other areas of Asia and the Pacific.

W. D. Halls

China, India, Japan and Korea

Tetsuya Kobayashi

Historical background

In present-day Asia, there is much interest in comparative education in Japan, Korea, India and China, as well as a more diffuse interest in a few other countries. In the first group, this interest has grown to such an extent that comparative educators working at universities and research institutes have formed national associations for comparative education, which have become member societies of the World Council of Comparative Education Societies (WCCES). In the second group, few individual scholars are known to be engaged in teaching and research in this field.[1]

In each of these countries, comparative education has developed along different lines due to differing social conditions, but in most cases it has evolved in a series of roughly similar stages of development. In Asia, of course, the emergence of comparative education as a distinctive field of study is only a recent phenomenon. Before its emergency, however, this region witnessed a long history of rich cross-cultural contacts and exchanges with other parts of the world as well as within its own confines, and it was through these cultural contacts that comparative interest in foreign education began to grow.

In ancient East Asia, for example, the educational system of the Chinese empire was made the model by neighbouring nations, including Japan.[2] Documents show that, as early as 607, Prince Shotoku of the Japanese court sent a diplomatic and academic mission to China, which resulted in the establishment of Japan's first national system of education, modelled on the Chinese. Official missions of this kind for cultural and educational borrowing continued until the middle of the ninth century. The Buddhist priest Kukai, who accompanied one of the missions, wrote a report upon his return home in which he compared popular education in the capital cities of the two nations and suggested the establishment of popular schools in Japan.

Examples of cultural and educational contacts between the Oriental and Western worlds can be also found in the history of Japan. During the sixteenth century, when Jesuit missionaries extended their activities to East Asia, a group of young Japanese converts was sent to Rome, and they reported on the state of affairs in the Western Christian world, including the state of general and higher education there. Although missionary activities were prohibited and personal contacts were restricted in the following centuries, the information about the outside world, including that on education, was made available to a select group through special channels, such as the translation of foreign publications allowed into the country.

It was, however, the efforts to establish modern national systems of education modelled on the Western systems in the late nineteenth and early twentieth century that gave direct impetus to the emergence of comparative education in Japan and other nations in Asia. In the process of searching for a model, foreign systems of education were seriously studied and documented, first by educational practitioners and then by academics, thus stimulating the development of the academic study of comparative education. The process took various forms, as the development of modern national systems of education differed from nation to nation.

By the late nineteenth century not only Japan but also all the other nations in Asia were under both internal and external pressure to modernize. The response to such pressures varied, depending above all on political conditions. Thus it was such countries as Japan and Thailand, maintaining political independence during the period, which first launched, on their own initiative, programmes for modernization of national systems of education based upon Western patterns in the latter part of the nineteenth century. In Thailand, the real modernization efforts began in the reign of King Chulalongkorn, who sent his brother to Europe in 1889 and also a group of officials to Japan during the 1890s and the 1900s, to study educational systems there. It is interesting to note that behind this apparent shift of interest from Europe to Japan lay a comparative judgment of the Thais on which systems would be more suited to their own needs.[3] Such comparative perspectives also existed in Japan, another independent nation, where modelling upon Western educational systems was made on a wide basis of choice.

In Japan, modernization took place after the Meiji Restoration in 1868, but a systematic search for modernization models had already begun during the last period of the preceding Tokugawa era, by sending missions and students abroad, translating foreign legislation and literature and inviting foreign advisers and teachers.[4] Such efforts were continued by the Meiji government even more vigorously. The first code of national education in 1872 was a typical example, drafted after serious studies of Western educational systems had been conducted.

Among the literature on Western education published during this period, Yukichi Fukuzawa's *Seiyo-jijo* (The state of things in the Western world) is worthy of mention.[5] The book was first published in 1866 and ran into several editions. Fukuzawa himself visited Europe and the United States of America, accompanying the Tokugawa missions. In this book he described Western schools, attributing the development of Western civilization to the spread of education among the people. Some dozen statute books dealing with education in Western countries were translated by the government for reference with reference to the formation of its own system. Fujimaro Tanaka, a young official in the Ministry of Education of the Meiji government, after accompanying the Iwakura Mission for a tour through the United States and Europe in 1871-1873, submitted between 1873-1875 a 15-volume report which included a description of educational systems and also a translation of the educational codes and regulations in nine countries.[6] It is interesting to note that in England his group met Matthew Arnold, who through his writings was to become a forerunner of British comparative education; and apparently, on Arnold's suggestion, Tanaka translated Mark Pattison's article on German education for the report.[7]

Such early efforts to study foreign systems of education in a comparative perspective continued in subsequent periods. *Kyouiku-zasshi*, a journal published by the Ministry of Education between 1873-1883, which included articles on foreign education, was reissued under the new title *Mombu-iho* in 1920, and continues to be published even now. Meanwhile, the Bureaux of General Education, Vocational Education and Higher Education within the Ministry each published occasional reports on particular aspects of foreign education. In 1927 such efforts were consolidated into a newly established Research Section, which is still in existence today. This Research Section has published a number of occasional reports, some of which were included in a series of reports of sixteen volumes on systems of education both overseas and at home, between 1831-1942.[8]

The academic study of education in Japan was first given impetus by the translations of Western books on pedagogy, which were widely used in the teacher training institutions established after 1872. In 1887, the Imperial University of Tokyo set up a lectureship in pedagogy, which was occupied first by a German Herbartian scholar who was replaced by a Japanese in

1890. This led later to the establishment of a department of education in 1919. By this time other universities had also set up departments of education both for research and the education of teachers. From the outset, the academic study of education in Japanese universities attached importance to studies of educational thought and practice abroad. Although German pedagogy continued to be the main focus, after 1910 interest was extended to the empirical American studies of education, under whose influence the study of foreign systems of education was conducted systematically and became a part of academic studies of education at universities. A typical example of this is a 46-volume series of studies of educational research published by the Department of Education in the Imperial University of Tokyo between 1927-1948, which includes many articles on foreign educational systems - not only European and American, but also Asian.[9]

Undoubtedly such studies on foreign education were carried out from a comparative perspective, and from this research grew interest in what is now called comparative education. The word 'comparative' was first used in the title of an article in an issue of the Ministry's journal in 1877, which was a translation from an American journal. The first book appeared only in 1916, however, when Hanjiro Nakajima, professor of education at Waseda University, published his *Comparative study of national education - Germany, France, Britain and the USA*.[10] In 1921, *Comparative study of secondary education* was published by the Department of Education at the Imperial University of Tokyo.[11] Shigetaka Abe, one of the co-authors of the work, wrote an article on comparative education in the Educational Encyclopaedia published in 1918, and delivered a series of lectures entitled 'Comparative Study', around this time.[12] In 1935 he published a book on the comparative history of educational systems in Europe and the United States, and in the preface he announced his intention to publish a book on comparative education, although he died before its completion.[13]

The first book entitled *Comparative education*, was published in 1928 by Choichi Higuchi, professor of education at Tokyo Higher Normal School, in which he reported his discovery of the courses and literature in comparative education during his visit to American and European universities in 1919.[14] In 1936 he also published a book on comparative educational systems, in which he referred to works by I. L. Kandel and Nicholas Hans.[15]

Undoubtedly such interest in comparative education stemmed from the educational situation in Japan, in which study of foreign systems of education was needed for its modernization. At the same time, as can be divined from Higuchi's reference, it was also stimulated by the works of contemporary comparative educators in the USA and Europe. In fact, such books as Kandel's *Comparative education* (1933), Hans's *Principles of educational policies* (1926), and two yearbooks of education, published in London and New York respectively, were known to contemporary Japanese at the time. German works such as Friedrich Schneider's *Internationale zeitschrift für erziehungswissenschaft* (1931-1934) and Ernst Krieck's works on comparative education were also known in Japan, although the latter were received as philosophical rather than comparative studies. In spite of such active interest, comparative education in Japan before the Second World War was still in a stage of flux with respect to both quantity and quality. There were only a few scholars who specialized in the field. Published works were largely descriptive and historical, and hardly any analysis was attempted.

During the post-war reconstruction period, the development of comparative education was given much stimulation. Whilst the post-war educational reform was carried out under the dominant influences of American education and modelled on American theories and practices, its further development required a comparative viewpoint on the educational theories and practices throughout in the world. Academic contacts and exchanges, which were reopened after Japan's re-entry to the international community in 1952, stimulated the study of education in an international perspective. Thus during the 1950s and 1960s much progress was made in the development of comparative education. The establishment of professorships in comparative education at the major universities during this period and the foundation of the Japan Comparative Education Society (JCES) in 1964 highlighted this progress.[16] Thus in 1970, when WCCES was formed, JCES was one of the founding members.

*   *   *

In contrast to the situation in independent nations, modernization in those under colonial rule was either neglected or delayed for many years, and indigenous educational reform got under way only after the achievement of autonomy or complete independence in the latter half of the twentieth century. Under colonial rule interest in foreign education, if any, was limited to that of the colonizing country. Thus in the British colonies, for example, the model for modernization of education was always the British system.[17] In India it was only after achieving complete independence that interest in foreign education was extended to countries other than the United Kingdom. The Education Commission of 1964-66, which was appointed by the Government of India and played an important role in developing education for the new India, was composed of members from many nations: one each from Japan, France, the UK, the USA and the USSR, in addition to the eleven Indian members. In contrast to this the Indian Education Commission of 1882-83, which was appointed by the colonial government of India, consisted of seven Indians and 14 Englishmen, and the Indian University Commission of 1902 was composed, at first, of only Englishmen.[18] Such broadened international interest was reflected in the literature. During the 1950s and 1960s a number of books on foreign educational systems were published, as was the first Indian book entitled *Comparative education.*[19] By the 1970s, interest had grown and resulted in the publication of further books on comparative education and in the founding of the Comparative Education Society of India (CESI) in 1979.

A somewhat similar situation can be observed in Korea.[20] Efforts to modernize education by the Koreans at the turn of the century were interrupted by the annexation of Korea by Japan in 1910. During the following 30 years under the Japanese rule, the school system was completely Japanized and there was little opportunity for the Koreans to set up their own system, either in a traditional pattern or in a non-Japanese foreign pattern. After World War II, the nation achieved independence but became divided. In the north, the People's Democratic Republic of Korea has developed a school system based on the Soviet model, whilst in the south, the Republic of Korea has reconstructed a school system modelled on the American pattern. As for interest in comparative education, little is known about the north, whereas in the south contact with American educators has stimulated a comparative perspective among Korean educators. Thus in the 1960s a number of books on comparative education, as well as on foreign educational systems, were published. The first Korean book entitled *Comparative education* appeared in 1961.[21] The number of scholars interested in the field increased during this period, and in 1968 they formed the Korean Comparative Education Society (KCES), which was one of the founding societies of WCCES.

In China the attempt to modernize the national system of education began during the 1870s, which marked the beginning of a search for a model suited to their needs.[22] Around the turn of the century the Japanese system aroused interest, and the school system of 1903 was modelled on the Japanese. After 1912, however, interest turned toward American education. In 1919-21 and 1921-22, John Dewey and Paul Monroe respectively ho visited China at the invitation of Chinese enthusiasts for the 'new' education. They left a considerable mark on Chinese education. As to literature on foreign education, a journal, *World education* began publication as early as 1901, and books entitled *Comparative education* were published in the late 1920s and 1930s.[23] For some time after the establishment of the People's Republic in 1949, interest in foreign education was focused solely on Soviet education, which was taken as a model for educational practices and ideology. In the early 1950s and 1960s much study and translation was done of the theory and practice of education in USSR in both universities and research institutes and the results published in such journals as *Educational translation series* and *Foreign educational development*. Little interest was shown in Western education during this period. In the following years, during the so-called Cultural Revolution, even such limited interest was prohibited, and it was only after the downfall of the Gang of Four and the end of internal conflict in 1976 that a new era opened for studying foreign education.[24] The creation of the Chinese Comparative Education Society in 1979 and its entry into the WCCES in 1984 symbolize new developments in this field in China.

Present status

Major research and training centres of comparative education
In Japan, universities play a central role in promoting research and training in comparative education. At present the five national universities of Kyushu, Hiroshima, Kyoto, Tokyo and Tsukuba each have in their faculties of education a unit (*koza*) of comparative education, consisting of a professor, an associate professor and an instructor. The unit is responsible for both teaching and research. Teaching is given both at undergraduate and graduate levels. Undergraduate students take courses in comparative education as electives or as major subjects for the BA degree, and graduate students can specialize in this field for the degrees of Master of Educational Studies and Doctor of Educational Studies. For both of these higher degrees, presentation of a thesis or dissertation is required. For those seeking a master's degree, two years of course work are required. The content of the required courses in comparative education varies, but they usually cover the methodology of comparative education, area studies and comparative studies of educational problems. Usually proficiency in two foreign languages is required. For the doctorate, an additional three years of study under professorial supervision is required.

In addition to the universities mentioned above, a number of other national, public and private universities offer programmes relating to comparative education. A survey conducted by JCES in 1981 revealed that 25 national universities, one public university and 22 private universities offered lectures and/or seminars in comparative education at the undergraduate level, while nine national universities (Hokkaido, Ibaragi, Tokyo, Tokyo Gakugei, Tokyo Foreign Studies, Kyoto, Kobe, Hiroshima and Kyushu), one public university (Osaka City), and four private universities (International Christian, Aoyama Gakuin, Tamagawa and Konan Women's) offered graduate programmes in the field.[25] In addition, there are other universities in which lectures in comparative education are given under different titles and students produce theses or dissertations in it.

In these universities, research is conducted by the staff members individually or jointly. In the latter case, graduate students, research fellows and visiting researchers from other universities often participate in research projects, Kyushu is the only university which has a specialized Research Institute for Comparative Education and Culture attached to the Faculty of Education. It conducts research with its own research staff (equivalent to two 'chairs') and in close co-operation with other faculty members. Hiroshima has a Research Institute for Higher Education, which also conducts comparative and international studies on higher education. In addition, the National Institute for Educational Research has a well-staffed division specializing in comparative education and the study of Asian education (equivalent to four 'chairs') and other divisions in which comparative studies are also carried out. These research institutes have no students, but can receive research members from universities under their supervision, and their staff members offer lectures or seminars in universities. Funds for research activities in universities and research institutes are provided in the form of grants-in-aid for scientific research by the Ministry of Education, in addition to the institutions' own regular budget. There are also private foundations which support research projects.[26]

In other Asian countries, research and training in comparative education are also undertaken in universities and research institutes. In India, for example, it is reported that most university departments of education undertake research and train students in comparative education as a part of their academic activities. The Central Institute of Education in New Delhi conducts international and comparative studies of education.[27] In Korea, several universities (Seoul, Ewha Women's, Hanyan, Yongsei, Seikinkan, Reinan and others) offer courses in comparative education, and the Central Institute of Educational Research also conducts research relating to this field. Ewha Women's University has an East-West Education Research Institute which undertakes research in comparative education and educational anthropology.[28] In China, research in comparative education is undertaken in comparative education divisions or institutes in the Central Institute of Educational Sciences and a number of universities (Beijing Normal, East China Normal, South China Normal, North-east China Normal, Shanxi Normal, Fujiang Normal, Honan Normal, Harbin Normal, Hangzhou, Hebei and Tongji). Centres for the study of higher education at several universities (Beijing, Qinghhua, Xianmen, Wuhan and Beijing Normal) and other major universities also conduct comparative studies. Since 1979, seven universities (including Beijing Normal, East China Normal and Hebei) have been offering programmes in comparative education at the master's degree level.[29]

Major research projects and publications

In Japan, the number of research publications in comparative education is enormous. A survey conducted by a committee of the Japan Comparative Education Society in 1979 revealed that during the 1970s alone 518 papers were published by its members.[30] In the following section these publications will be treated statistically for the purpose of analyzing trends in comparative research in Japan. In this section an attempt is made to present an outline of major research projects and their subjects in order to give the reader a more concrete picture. To present all of the major research projects and their themes would be out of question and so, some kind of selection is unavoidable. The criteria used here are; first, research projects sponsored by JCES, second, co-operative or joint research projects on a fairly large scale, and, third, those undertaken in the research centres mentioned in the section above. For other projects, reference should be made to the bibliography, in which an attempt has been made to cover as many of the published works of the publications derived from such projects as possible.

In Japan, research in comparative education has been undertaken in different 'modes': co-operative research done by members of JCES under its auspices, co-operative research by groups of researchers working at the same or different institutions, and work by individual researchers in universities and research institutes or centres. Such co-operative and individual research projects may have been undertaken with or without research grants from the Ministry of Education or other agencies.

Although JCES has no resources of its own, it sponsors research projects and supports applications for research grants for them. Each project is undertaken by a group of researchers, who are members of the Society and belong to different universities and research institutes. In the past fifteen years the Society has sponsored a number of such projects and these have been reported at the Society's annual meetings and published in the Society's Bulletins and/or separate books or monographs. The topics, representatives, and periods of research are as follows:

Secondary education reform, Shigeo Masui, 1971-1973); educational research systems, Taneo Harada, (1974-1976); teacher education, Shigeo Masui and Masatoshi Ohno, (1977-1980); moral education, Masunori Hiratsuka, (1978-1980); international exchanges in education, Shigeo Masui, (1981-1983); structural reform of higher education, Tetsuya Kobayashi, (1985-1986).

In addition, JCES has organized a number of short-term projects, which are of an exploratory nature and have been undertaken by small groups of researchers. The results have been reported in the annual meetings of the Society and published in its Bulletins. Some of these exploratory projects have been followed up in some of the large-scale projects mentioned above. Their subjects are: methodology of comparative education (1974-75); education for international understanding (1977-1978); religious education in public schools (1978-1979); tradition and innovation in education (1978-1979); selection systems of university entrants (1979-1980); the future of higher education (1985-1986); internationalization and education (19185-1986); curriculum standards (1985-1986).

Other major co-operative research projects are listed below by university or research institution. The topics, representatives and dates for activities undertaken are as follows:

Kyushu University Research Institute for Comparative Education and Culture

Education towards national identity in developing countries, Bunkichi Iwahashi, 1980-1982.

Changing processes in educational policies in South-east Asia, Yoshio Gondo, 1983-1985.

Tokyo University

Cultural polarity and structural changes in education, Iwao Matsuzaki, 1982-1983.

Structural changes in vocational education within the school system, Iwao Matsuzaki, 1984.

Hiroshima University

Cleaning in schools abroad, Yutaka Okihara and Akira Ninomiya, 1975-1976.

Corporal punishment in schools abroad, Okihara & Ninomiya, 1977-1978.

School violence abroad, Okihara & Ninomiya, 1981-1982.

Sex education and anti-drug education, Okihara & Ninomiya, 1985-1986.

Hiroshima University Research Institute for Higher Education

Internationalization of higher education, Kazuyuki Kitamura, 1978-1980.

Kyoto University

Japanese overseas and returning children, Tetsuya Kobayashi, 1976-1982.

Ethnic education and multi-cultural education, Kobayashi, 1980-1982.

International consensus in education, Kobayashi, 1983-1984.

Changes in students and structures in higher education, Kobayashi & Takekazu Ehara.

Tsukuba University

Educational legal case studies abroad, Miyao Mno & Toshiaki Kuwabara, 1983-1984.

National Institute for Educational Research

Educational exchanges in Asia, Hiroshi Abe, 1975-1977.

Moral education in Japan and abroad, Masunori Hiratsuka & Masatoshi Ohno, 1978-1980.

Education exchanges and co-operation, Shigeo Masui, 1981-1983.

Selection for higher education, Taneo Harada, 1983-1984.

Mass higher education and the student aid system, Takehiko Tezuka, 1983-1984.

In other Asian countries, as in Japan, research in comparative education is undertaken through individual or co-operative efforts in universities and research institutes. As in the case of Japan, mention will be made mainly of those research activities centred around national comparative education societies in the respective countries.

The Korean Comparative Education Society has held, since its founding in 1968, a number of annual meetings usually on those specific themes which represent the most pressing concerns of Korean comparative educators. The list below may indicate where their interests lie. The Society also organized the pre-congress Conference of WCCES in Seoul in July, 1980, with 'Educational and National Development with special reference to Developing Countries' as its main theme.[31]

Nature and trends of comparative education (1968)

Long-term comprehensive educational planning (1970)

Trends of educational reforms in the world (1971)

Ideal human images in the East and West (1972)

Reflections on and prospects for Korean education (1974)

Perspectives for higher education reform (1975)

Development of public education and its problems (1976)

Korean education after independence (1984)

Methodology of comparative education (1985)

The Comparative Education Society in India has also held, since its establishment in 1979, four annual conferences, the themes of which are as follows; [32]

Education and the new international order (1981)

Education, development, equality and social change (1983)

Education of the disadvantaged in India (1984)

Asian education in a world perspective (1985).

The Chinese Society of Comparative Education has organized, since its founding in 1979, biennial national conferences, each of which was divided into sub-committees. The topics are given below. Between biennial conferences, the Chinese Society organizes local seminars and workshops, the themes of which in 1982 were: evaluation of the educational thought of the Soviet educationists Kaïrov and Zanckov; studies of college entrance examinations; the theory and practice of combining education with production labour; and curriculum development in comparative education.[31] The topics at the national conferences were:

Higher education, general education, and the development of comparative education as a discipline (1979),

The educational system, educational reform, and compulsory education (1981),

Higher education, universalization of primary education, structural reform of secondary education, and the development of comparative education as an academic discipline, and its teaching in teacher training institutions (1983).

Directions of research and methodological trends

In previous sections, mention was made of the establishment of 'chairs' of comparative education at major universities and research institutes, the founding of the Japanese Comparative Education Society, and the publication of numerous papers and books in this field. These may be taken as signs that comparative education in Japan has established itself firmly as a branch of academic studies of education. On the other hand, such indications, above all the quantitative increase of researchers and their publications, have led to serious questions as to the rationale of comparative education: the nature, purpose, scope and methodology etc. of the field. One of the functions of JCES is to provide common ground for discussion of the different views and ideas held by its members. In 1974, JCES held its tenth annual conference on the theme 'The Present Status and Perspective of Comparative Education in Japan', for the purpose of re-examining methodological questions in the Japanese context. The papers presented there were subsequently published in the first issue of the *JCES bulletin*.[33] Though many interesting points were raised at the conference, one cannot help being struck by the gap existing between methodological works and the empirical research, the former having been developed under the influences of methodological discussions in the USA and Europe, but having little connection with actual comparative research in Japan. No new theories regarding such research, moreover, appear to have emerged. Since then, no major attempt has been made by the JCES to stimulate collective thinking on the methodology of comparative education, and few papers have been written by individual researchers on the topic.[34] The difficulties in discussing methodology at this stage lie in the fact that so much research with varied scope, objectives and method has been conducted in the name of comparative education. It is no longer sufficient simply to reinterpret the theories established by the pioneers, Kandel, Schneider, Hans etc., or those advocated in the neighbouring disciplines; any discussion must take into account the methods applied, implicitly or explicitly, in actual comparative studies. It will require more effort and time before we find our own Kandel, whose first effort should be to take stock of the existing works in comparative education.

JCES has carried out bibliographical surveys of the comparative studies of education undertaken by its members twice in 1967 and 1979. Since these surveys were based on the reports made by the members themselves, they may serve as a reliable indicator of how Japanese comparative educators conceive various aspects of comparative education, and, above all, its scope. In the 1979 survey, 2,266 papers and books are classified into five categories; methodology of comparative education, comparative studies on educational thought, educational and cultural exchanges (international education), comparative studies, and area studies. The last two are further classified into eleven sub-categories for geographical areas, and twelve sub-categories for educational fields. The classification was reached by the survey committee after having received reports from Society members. From the survey, several observations can be made concerning the special characteristics of Japanese comparative education, although these observations refer only to the quantity of research.[35]

First, area studies make up a great part of comparative education, and of these many concentrate on such countries as Japan, USA, UK, Germany (both East and West), France and the USSR, whereas relatively little attention is paid to such countries or regions as Korea (and these are mostly historical or relate to South Korea), India and South Asia, China, Latin America, and North Europe; there is less interest in South and Central Europe, the Near and Middle East, Oceania, Canada, Africa and Eastern Europe. Second, studies of educational thought in other countries occupy an important place in comparative education. Third, international education has become increasingly popular. Fourth, interest is concentrated on secondary education, higher education and educational administration, although attention is also given to problems in other fields. Fifth, methodological studies are of less interest to Japanese comparative educators, so far as can be observed by the number of publications.

One can of course question these observations. As stated above, the are based purely on the quantity of publications and show only the general direction of interest in comparative education. In this survey no attempt was made by the survey committee to define comparative education in advance, but individual JCES members were left to decide for themselves which of their works fell within the realm of comparative education. Thus, inclusion in the list of some works, such as those appearing in the category of studies of educational thought, may look absurd to someone who might have a different definition. Nevertheless, the survey is informative in showing how the Japanese conceive comparative education.[36]

The survey, however, does not tell which methods the Japanese comparative educationists employ in their studies. The author once tried to answer this question by analyzing 88 articles appearing in six issues of the

JCES bulletins in the same way as Robert Koehl did for articles in three international journals of comparative education.[37] The observations can be summarized as follows: First, less interest in methodology is observed. Out of 88 articles, there are only 11 dealing with theories and methods of comparative education (nine of these 11 appeared in the first issue of the *Bulletin* mentioned earlier in this section). It presents a striking contrast to *Comparative education review*, whose issues contain 110 theoretical papers out of 287 in all. Second, comparative education in Japan seems now to have reached the stage of genuine comparative studies, emerging from the stage of *Auslandspädagogik*, or studies of foreign education. Of the remaining 77 articles, 31 deal with two or more national cases in comparative perspective and 46 deal with single national cases. Among the latter, however, 30 articles are written as part of co-operative comparative studies, and the remainder include studies of those national problems caused by international or intercultural contacts and exchanges. Third, the methods applied in these studies are largely historical, and the research relies heavily on literature studies (74 out of 88 articles). Most of them are descriptive or use historical causality as an analytical tool. On the other hand, 14 studies apply sociological survey methods and analysis for empirical research, although even in such cases correlational analysis is seldom used. Fourth, more comparative studies have been carried out on problems within schools, such as those relating to curriculum, instruction, administration, etc. Fewer studies have been done on questions of the school-society relationship, although questions such as politics and education, the employment of college graduates, and university autonomy, have been treated. Fifth, few attempts have been made to use correlational analysis between social factors and education, thus making the works largely historical and descriptive. Sixth, over half of the papers (46) deal with developed nations, while 11 deal with developing nations and 21 with both.

These observations, based on other selected works appearing in the *JCES bulletins*, naturally show a different picture from those based on the non-selective materials of the JCES survey. For example, the claim that the status of comparative studies that they are emerging from *Auslandspädagogik* may be wishful thinking, considering the seemingly disproportionate number of area studies publications presented in the JCES survey. Otherwise, however, the observations in both surveys present a fair picture of the content and methodological aspects of comparative education in Japan.

It is perhaps noteworthy that, despite the vigour of comparative studies in Japan, these have had no *direct* impact upon policymaking.

Future prospects

So much for the present status of comparative education in Japan - what of its future prospects? It may be possible from the above observations to deduce the problems which remain to be addressed by Japanese comparative educators. First, methodological studies of comparative education must be further encouraged. In its initial stage of development, comparative education in Japan was much concerned with introducing the scholarly works of Western comparative scholars, precursors in the field, and there was a time during the 1950s when Japanese comparativists were preoccupied with translating and interpreting the theories from abroad. Although in the following decades such efforts continued in parallel with attempts to establish the theoretical frameworks relevant to the Japanese situation, more recently these methodological attempts have been somewhat obscured by the general trend toward emphasizing empirical research that addresses contemporary educational problems. There can be no question of the importance of empirical research, but in seeking a well-balanced development of comparative education, the relative neglect of methodological studies cannot be overlooked, since such empirical research must be based on a sound methodological basis. On the other hand, the methodological studies must take actual empirical investigations into consideration, as stated earlier, examining their methodological bases critically, whilst paying careful attention to methodological discussions in comparative education and in other comparative disciplines elsewhere.

Second, Japanese comparative education may continue to develop comparative studies of 'in-school matters', emphasis on which is one of its special characteristics. Since it is claimed that comparative education is one branch of studies within the discipline of education, and that its function is to render services to educationists, above all teachers, who concern themselves with the theories and practices of education, problems in schooling such as teaching and learning processes, educational achievement, pupil-teacher relations, school discipline, etc., must be taken as the prime concern for comparative research. In order to make such a contribution at a higher level, however, comparative education may need to move from its present static approach to a dynamic one, by introducing such techniques as correlative or longitudinal analysis, while re-enforcing the traditional historical approaches with more rigorous methodological reflections.

Third, following upon the above argument, it is suggested that comparative studies should pay more attention to the relationship between education and other social institutions. Such educational problems occurring within the school will be dealt with in a new dimension if they are examined in a wider social context. More studies must be done of problems such as those relating education to politics, economics and social issues, and on such emerging multi-disciplinary problems as development, ethnic, and multi-cultural education.

Fourth, more studies need to be done on educational problems in developing countries. If, as has been claimed, the purpose of comparative education is to build an educational picture of the world, it is insufficient for comparative educators to be engaged in studies covering only highly industrialized nations. Again, it may not be enough to study these problems in developing countries *per se*, but to examine them in a global context, in particular in relation to developed nations.

Finally, comparative education in Japan will continue to be concerned with the major national and international issues in education. Opinions are divided among comparative educators in Japan as to whether comparative education, or rather comparative educators, should or should not be involved with actual policymaking in educational reform and innovation. It is clear, however, for those refraining from involvement in policymaking, that educational issues of national and international importance can be studied objectively as part of their scientific tasks, while it is equally clear for those advocating involvement that their studies will be put into practice usefully only if they are pursued on a sound scientific foundation.

These observations and prospects for comparative education in Japan may or may not be applicable to other Asian countries, which differ in academic traditions, the educational environment, political ideologies, economic development, etc. Naturally, such differences lead to national variations in the methods and prospects for comparative education in the region. However, comparative educationists in Asia, as elsewhere in the world, will describe, explain and, if they so wish, change the national and international problems of education in their academic endeavours.

To quote a passage from a leading Indian comparative educationist, 'these comparative studies of the relation of education to national and social development are as legitimate as comparative education as they are useful in foreseeing the new international order and the relation of education to it.'[38] Whereas he sees the earlier understanding of comparative education as a tool for educational policy as disappearing,[39] his Chinese colleague states candidly that 'comparative studies mainly serve educational authorities in planning and policymaking that are aimed at improving and modernizing the Chinese educational system. Research projects focus on issues related to major educational reforms under way or to be made in the near future'.[40] Whether these contrasting opinions reflect different political orientations, different degrees of national urgency, or academic maturity, is a question that remains to be answered.

Means of communication

The Japanese Comparative Education Society issues an annual publication in Japanese called the *Nihon hikaku kyouiku gakkai kiyou* [Bulletin of the Japan Comparative Education Society], which contains articles, essays and reports. It has a table of contents in English, and English abstracts of the articles are published separately for each issue. JCES also issues a Japanese newsletter for its members twice a year. In Japan, all universities or their faculties and research institutes have bulletins published annually, containing articles, including those in comparative education, contributed by faculty members and, in some cases, by graduate students as well. There are a few bulletins specializing in comparative education; *Research bulletins* (in Japanese, with English abstracts) by Kyushu University Research Institute of Comparative Education and Culture, *Studies on educational organization* (in Japanese with English abstracts) by Tsukuba University, and *History of education and comparative education* (in Japanese) by Hokkaido University. Papers and articles in comparative education also appear in the bulletins and journals of the following related academic educational societies: the Japanese Society for the Study of Education, History of Education Society, the Japan Society of Educational Sociology, the Japan Educational Administration Society, the French Education Society, and the Intercultural Education Society, Japan.

The Korean Comparative Education Society at one time published its bulletin, which is now discontinued. Korean universities also publish bulletins which contain articles on comparative education. The East-West Education Research Institute of Ewha Women's University publishes a semi-annual English journal *East-West education*, containing articles on comparative education contributed by both Korean and foreign scholars.

The Comparative Education Society of India issues a bi-annual newsletter, *CESI newsletter*. Universities and research institutes in India publish their bulletins. There is however no bulletin or journal specializing in comparative education.

The organ of the Chinese Society of Comparative Education is the bi-monthly *Waiguo jiaoyu* (Foreign education), edited jointly by the Society and the Comparative Education Division of the Central Institute of Educational Sciences. Other journals specializing in comparative education are: *Waiguo jiaoyu dongtai* (New development in foreign education) published by Beijing Normal University, *Waiguo jiaoyuziliao* (Foreign education documents and materials) by East China Normal University, *Waiguo jiaoyu yanjiu* (Foreign education studies) by North-east China Normal University, *Shijie jiaoyu wenzhai* (World education abstracts) by South China Normal University, *Waiguo jiaoyu wenzhai* (Foreign education abstracts) by Fujian Normal University, and *Waiguo zhong xiaoxue jiaoy* (Secondary and primary education abroad) by Shanghai Teachers College. Educational newspaper such as *Zhongguo jiaoyu bao* (Chinese education news) and journals as *Educational research*, edited by the Central Institute of Educational Sciences, also contain articles on comparative education.

Notes

1. During the 1960s, the late Prof. George Z. F. Bereday noted in his book *Comparative method in education*, New York; Holt, Rinehart & Winston, 1964, the existence of comparative educators in universities and research institutes in the Philippines, Singapore, Malaysia, Thailand and Hong Kong, in addition to those in Japan, India and China. Today, such countries as Indonesia, Sri Lanka and Iran should be added to the list.

2. Reischauer, E. O., & Fairbank, J. K., *A history of East Asian civilization, vol. 1: East Asia: the great tradition*, Boston; Houghton Mifflin, 1960. Kobayashi, T., 'Present situation of the study of comparative education', in Organizing Committee of International Conference on Educational Research, *Present status of educational research in Japan*, Tokyo; Bureau of the International Conference on Educational Research, 1961, p.7-17. Kobayashi, T., *Nihon niokeru hikaku-kyouikugaku no hatten* [Development of comparative education in Japan], Kyoto University Department of Comparative Education. *Hikaku-kyouikugaku Shi* [Historiographic study of comparative education], Kyoto, Japan, 1979. Ishii, H., 'Nihon niokeru hikaku-kyouikugaku' [Comparative education in Japan], in Okihara, Y., ed., *Hikaku-kyouikugaku* [Comparative education], Tokyo, Yushindo, 1981, p.57-75.

3. Nimmanheminda, S., 'An historical note on the national educational plans', in Thailand Ministry of Education, *Education in Thailand: a century of experience*, Bangkok, 1969, p.91. Wyatt, David K., *The politics of reform in Thailand: education in the reign of King Chulalongkorn*, New Haven; Yale University Press, 1969.

4. Ogata, H., *Seiyou kyouiku inyu no hoto* [Means for importing occidental education], Tokyo; Kodansha, 1961.

5. Kiyooka, E., *The autobiography of Fukuzawa Yukichi, with preface to the collected works of Fukuzawa*, Tokyo; The Hokuseido, 1981.

6. Japan Ministry of Education, *Riji koutei* [Commissioner's report], Kyoto; Rinsenshobo, reproduced 1974.
7. Pattison, M., 'Report on the state of elementary education in Germany', in England and Wales Education Commission, *Report of the assistant commissioners appointed to inquire into the state of popular education in continental Europe and on educational charities in England and Wales*, London; HMSO, 1861, p.161-266, vol. IV
8. Japan. Ministry of Education Research Section, *Kyoiku-seido no chosa* [Research on educational systems], Tokyo, 1931-42, 16 v.
9. The Imperial University of Tokyo (Japan). Kyouiku-shicho kenkyuukai, *Kyouiku-shicho* [Trend in education], Tokyo; Meguroshoten, 1927-48, 46 v.
10. Nakajima, H., *Doku-futsu-ei-bei kokumin-kyouiku no hikaku-kenkyu* [Comparative study of national education - Germany, France, Britain and the USA], Tokyo; Kyouiku-shicho kenkyukai, 1916.
11. The Imperial University of Tokyo (Japan), Department of Education, *Chuto-kyouiku no hikaku-kenkyu* [Comparative study of secondary education], Tokyo, 1921.
12. Abe, S., 'Hikaku-kyouikugaku' [Comparative education], in *Dobunkan kyouikugaku jisho* [Dobunkan encyclopedia of education], Tokyo; Dobunkan, 1918, vol. 3.
13. Abe, S., *Obei gakkou-kyouiku hattatsushi* [History of school education in Europe and the USA], Tokyo; Meguro-shoten, 1983, p.5.
14. Higuchi, C., *Hikaku kyoiku* [Comparative education], Tokyo; Hobunkan, 1928, p.2
15. Higuchi, C., *Hiaku kyouiku seidoron* [On comparative educational system], Tokyo; Seibido, 1936, p.4.
16. Books (in Japanese) published in the 1950s and 1960s include: Masuda, K., *Comparative study of educational systems in Japan and Abroad*, Nagoya; Reimeishobo, 1950; Ando, T., *Foundations of comparative education*, Tokyo; Iwasaki-shoten, 1965; Oshiba, M., *Comparative education*, Tokyo; Fukumura-shuppan, 1966; Mori, T., *Comparative educational systems*, Tokyo; Fukumura-shuppan, 1968; Suzuki, C., ed., *Comparative education*, Tokyo; Kokudosha, 1968; Hirratsuka, M., ed., *Educational policy in the world*, Tokyo; Kyourits-shuppan, 1968; Ikeda, S., *Study of comparative education*, Tokyo; Fukumura-shuppan, 1969.
17. Nurullah, S.; Maik, J. P., *A history of education in India (during the British period)*, Bombay; MacMillan, 1951.
18. Biswas, A.; Aggarwal, J. C., *Comparative education*, New Delhi, Arya Book Depot, 1972, p. 106.
19. Mukherjee, L., *Comparative education*, Allahabad, India, Kitab Mahal, 1959.
20. Lim, Han Young, et al, *Bikyo kyoyuk* [Comparative education], Seoul, Heundai Kyoyuk Chang Sa, 1961.
21. Han, Ki Un, *History of Korean education*, Seoul, 1963 (in Korean). Han, Ki Un, Hankuk bikyokyoyuk e kwajae wa choenmang [Problems and prospects for Korean

comparative education]. *Sadae nonchong*, Seoul; Seoul University, No.17, June 1978, p. 1-30.

22. Abe, H., ed., *Nichu kyouiku-bunka kouryu to masatsu* [Exchange and conflict in education and culture between Japan and China], Tokyo; Daiichishobo, 1983. Abe, H., ed. *Beichu kyuouiku koryu no kiseki* [US - China educational exchange], Tokyo; Kazankai, 1985.

23. Jing, Shi-bo; Zhou, Nan-zhao, 'Comparative education in China', *Comparative education review* (Chicago, IL), vol.29, 2, May 1985, p. 240-250.

24. Committee on Development of Research and Study in Comparative Education (Japan), 'A survey concerning lectures on comparative education courses in Japan - interim report', November 1981, in Japanese.

25. For an English reference to the present state of comparative education in Japan, see Tsuchimochi, G. H., 'Comparative education in Japan: a note', *Comparative education review*, Vol. 26, no. 3, October 1982, p. 435-441.

26. 'Informations summary on CESI' prepared by Dr. Gulistan J. Karawalla, Secretary of CESI for WCCES in September 1985.

27. Information on comparative education in Korea given by Prof. Pak Chun-hee, formerly Chairman of KCES.

28. Jing, Shi-bo; Zhou, Nan-zhao, *op.cit.* 'A brief account of the Chinese Society of Comparative Education', prepared by Huang Shiqi for WCCES in July 1984.

29. JCES, *Kaiin no kenkyu-ronbu bunken ichiran* [Bibliography on comparative education published by JCES members], no. 2, June 1980, p. 139.

30. KCES, *Outline of the society*, 1985, (in Korean).

31. See Note 26.

32. Jing, Shi-bo; Zhou, Nan-zhao, *op.cit.*, p. 249-250.

33. The present status and perspective of comparative education in Japan: methodological problems in comparative education, *Bulletin of JCES*, No. 1, March 1975, p. 10-48 (in Japanese).

34. Okihara, Y., ed., *Comparative education*, Tokyo; Yushindo, 1981 (in Japanese), includes several papers on methodology.

35. Kobayashi, T., Trends in comparative education, in Okihara, *Ibid.*, p. 158-176 (in Japanese)

36. It is interesting to note that Korean comparative educationists also attach importance to comparative study of educational thought. Han, Ki Un, *op.cit.*, p. 20-24.

37. Koehl, R., The comparative study of education: prescription and practice, *Comparative education review* (Chicago, IL), Vol. 21, nos. 2/3, June/October 1977, p. 177-194.

38. Shukla, S., Comparative education - new directions, *Bulletin of the Indian Institute of education* (New Delhi), Vol.II, 1981, p. 2.
39. *Ibid.* p. 11.
40. Jing, Shi-bo; Zhou, Nan-zhao, *op.cit.*, p. 243.

Bibliography

This select bibliography includes mainly books and monographs published during the 1970s and 1980s in three countries: Japan, Korea and India. For the latter only English publications are covered. No translation works are included.

Japan

Abe, H., ed., (1973), *Nichu kyouiku-bunka koryu to masatsu* [Exchange and conflict in education and culture between Japan and China]. Tokyo; Daiichi-shobo.

Abe, H., ed., (1985), *Beichu kyouiku-koryu no kiseki* [US-China educational exchange]. Tokyo; Reizankai.

Amano, M., (1978), *Gendai doitsu no kyouiku* [Education in contemporary Germany]. Tokyo; Gakuji-shuppan.

Ebihara, H., ed., (1983), *Shiryo gendai sekai no kyoiku kaikadu* [Educational reform in the contemporary world]. Tokyo; Sanseido.

Gondo, Y., ed., (1981), Hatten tojokoku ni okeru nashonaru aidentiti eno kyoiku ni kansuru hikaku-kenkyu [Comparative study on education for national identity in the developing countries], *Research bulletin*, Kyushu University Research Institute for Comparative Education and Culture, 32, March.

Harada, T., ed., (1985), *Oubei shuyoukoku no shoto-chuto-kyouiku no genjou ni okeru mondaiten to kaikaku-doko* [Problems and reforms in primary and secondary education in Europe and the USA].

Harada, T., ed., (1985), *Shogaikoku no shoto-chutou-kyouiku no seido to genjou* [Primary and secondary education in other countries].

Harada, T.; Arai, T., eds., (1981), *Gendai sekai kyoikushi* [Contemporary history of education in the world]. Tokyo; Gyosei.

Hiratsuka, M., et al, eds., (1972, revised ed. 1980, 2 vols), *Sekai kyouiku jiten* [Encyclopaedia of world education]. Tokyo; Gyosei.

Hiratsuka, M., ed., (1973), Daigaku no kanri un-ei ni kansuru hikaku-kenkyu [Comparative study on the administration and management of universities]. *Bulletin* (Tokyo, National Institute for Educational Research), 83, March.

Hironaka, K., ed., (1985), Sengo ajia-shokuku no kyoiku-seisaku no henyo to sono shakaiteki bunkateki kiban ni kansuru sougouteki hikaku-kenkyu [Transformation process of educational policy and its socio-cultural foundation in post-war Asian countries]. *Research bulletin*, Kyushu University Research Institute for Comparative Education and Culture, 36, March.

Hiroshima University (Japan), Research Institute for Higher Education, (1980), Nihon no daigaku ni okeru gaikokujin kyouin [National survey of opinion among foreign teachers at Japanese universities and colleges]. *Notes on higher education*, 43, January.

Hiroshima University (Japan), Research Institute for Higher Education, (1982), Nihon no daigakuin kyouiku ni kansuru ryugakusei no iken-chousa [Survey of opinion among foreign students concerning Japanese graduate education]. *Notes on higher education*, 52, February.

Ino, M., ed., (1974), Tounan-ajia ni okeru kyoiku-bunka no sougouteki hikaku-kenkyu [Comprehensive comparative study on education and culture in Southeast Asia]. *Research bulletin*, Kyushu University Research Institute for Comparative Education and Culture, 25, October.

Ino, M., ed., (1976), Kokusairikai no kyoiku to nashonarizumu no ruikei [Education for international understanding and patterns of nationalism]. *Research bulletin*, Kyushu University Research Institute for Comparative Education and Culture, 27, December.

Institute for Higher Education (Japan), (1981), Daigaku nyuugaku seisaku ni kansuru hikakui kenkyu [Comparative study of policies on university admissions]. *Bulletin*, 1, March.

Ishizuki, M., (1974), *Kokusaika eno kyouiku* [Education toward internationalization]. Kyoto, Japan; Mineruba-shobo.

Ito, H.; Mano, M., eds., (1975), *Kyoiku-seido no kadai* [Problems of educational system]. Tokyo; Diichi-houki.

Iwahashi, B., ed., (19??), *Kokusaika-jidai ni okeru ningen-keisei* [Human development in an internationalizing age]. Tokyo; Gyousei.

Iwahashi, B., ed., (1978), Tounan oyobi minami-ajia ni okeru ningenkeisei no sougouteki hikaku-kenkyu [Comprehensive comparative stidy on human development in Southeast and South Asia]. *Research bulletin*, Kyushu University Research Institute for Comparative Education and Culture, 29, October.

Kaneko, T., (1984), *Henkakuki no amerika kyouiku - daigaku-hen* [American education in a changing age - higher education]. Tokyo; Yushindo.

Kaneko, T., (1985), *Henkakuki no amerika kyouiku - gakkou-hen* [American education in a changing age - school education]. Tokyo; Yushindo.

Kobayashi, T.; Ebuchi, K., eds., (1984), *Tabunka kyouiku no hikaku-kenkyu* [Comparative study of multi-cultural education]. Fukuoka-shi, Japan; Kyushu Daigaku Shuppankai.

Kobayashi, T., ed., (1978), *Zaigai kikoku shijo no tekiou ni kansuru chouse houkoku* [Report on the study of adjustment problems if overseas and returning children]. Kyoto University, Faculty of Education.

Kobayashi, T., ed., (1979), *Hikaku kyoikugakushi kenkyu no kisoteki bunkengakuteki kenkyu* [Historiographic study of comparative education]. Kyoto, Japan, Kyoto University, Faculty of Education.

Kono, M.; Shinbori, M., eds., (1979), *Kyoiku kakushin no sekaiteki doukou* [The trends of educational reform and innovation in the world]. Tokyo; Gakken.

Masui, S., ed., *Kyouiku no kokusai-kouryu oyobi enjo ni kansuru sougouteki hikaku-kenkyu* [Comparative study on educational exchange and assistance]. Tokyo, National Institute for Educational Research.

Matuzaki, I., ed., (1985), *Gakkpu-seido niokeru shokugyou-kyoiku no kouzouteki henyou nikansuru hikaku-kenkyu* [Comparative study on the structural transformation of vocational education in school].

Mano, M., ed., (1977), *Gendai kyoiku-seido* [Contemporary educational systems]. Tokyo; Daiichi-houki.

Mori, T., et al, eds., (1978), *Kyoiku no kokusaika to kyoiku-gyosei* [Internationalization of education and educational administration]. Tokyo; Kyodo-shuppansha.

Nakayama, S., ed., (1979), *Chutogo kyouiku-sisutema no kinou to kouzou ni kansuru hikaki-kenkyu* [A comparative study in the function and structure of postsecondary educational systems]. Tokyo; Koutoukyouiku sogokenkyukai.

National Institute for Educational Research (Japan), (1979), *Daigakuin no kenkyu* [Study on graduate education].

National Institute for Educational Research (Japan), (1982), Doutoku kyoiku kenkyukai, eds., *Doutoku kyoiku no genjo to doukou - sekai to nihon* [Present status and trends of moral education in Japan and the world]. Tokyo; Gyousei.

National Institute for Educational Research (Japan), Japan Comparative Education Society, Joint Research Committee on Teacher Education, eds., (1980), *Kyoshi kyoiku no genjou to hikaku: shogaikoku to nihon* [Present status of teacher education in Japan and other countries]. Tokyo; Daiichi-hoki.

Nihon Kokusai Koryu Centre (Japan), (1979), *Shougai kyoiku no genjo to jittai kara* [Present status of life-long education]. Tokyo; Sougou kenkyu Kaihatu Kiko.

Okihara, Y., ed., (1978), *Gakkou-souji* [Comparative study on school cleaning]. Tokyo; Gakuji-shuppan.

Okihara, Y., ed., (1980), *Taibatsu* [Comparative study on corporal punishment]. Tokyo; Daiichi-hoki.

Okihara, Y., ed., (1983), *Konai-boryoku* [Comparative study on school violence]. Tokyo; Shogakkan.

Okihara, Y., ed., (1981), *Sekai no gakko* [Schooling in the world]. Tokyo; Yushindo.

Okihara, Y., ed., (1981), *Hikaku-kyouikugaku* [Comparative education]. Tokyo; Yushindo.

Okuda, S.;Nagaoka, J., ed., (1980), *Shogaikoku no gakko* [Schooling in various countries]. Tokyo; Gyosei.

Shibanuma, H., ed., (1976), *Shogaikoku no kyoiku no genjou to kadai* [Present status and problems of education in various countries]. Tokyo; Gyosei.

Takagi, H., ed., (1985), *Eibei niokeru shokugyou junbi kyouiku* [Education for vocation and career in Britain and the USA]. Kyoto, Japan, Kyoto University, Faculty of Education.

Tezuka, T., ed., *Shogaku-seisaku no tenkan* [Changes in student aid systems]. Tokyo, National Institute for Educational Research.

Umakoshi, T., (1981), *Gendai kankoku-kyouiku kenkyu* [Study of contemporary education in Korea]. Tokyo; Korai-shorin.

Korea

Chung, Du Yong, (1971), Asia chiyek e kyoyuk balden ka hukuk kyoyuk balden e bikyo [Comparison of educational development in Korea with the Asian region]. *Sege munwha wa kyoyuk*, (Hankuku kyoyukhakhoe, Bikyo kyuyok yunkuhoe), 39-54.

Han, Ki Un, (1971), Ilbonkyoyuk e munhwachek kicho [Cultural foundations of Japanese education]. *Kyoyukhak yunku*, (Hankuk kyoyukhtak hoe), IX-1, 18-36.

Han, Ki Un, (1977), *Hankuk kyoyuk chulhak e kucho* [Structure of Korean philosophy of education]. Seoul; Ulrumuhasa.

Han, Ki Un, (1978), Hankun bikyokyoyuk e kwsjae wa choenmang [Problems and prospects for Korean comparative education]. *Sadae nonchong*. Seoul University, 17, June, 1-30.

Kim, Dong Kyu, (1981), Nanbokukan no kyoikuhatten katei ni okeru ishituka genshono hikaku kenkyu [Comparative study of divergent phenomena in the process of educational development in South and North Korea]. Thesis - Waseda University, Tokyo.

Kim, Jong Chul, (1970, revised edition 1975), *Saege an-uiei hna'guk kyoyuk* [Korean education in the world]. Seoul; Baeyong-sa.

Li, Kyu Han, (1971), *Seudok ka seweden e kyoyuk kaehek e dae ha bikyoienku* [Comparative study of educational reform in West Germany and Sweden]. Seoul; Ridae chulpanbu.

Li, Kyu Han, (1980), *Seongjin'guk ui kyoyuk chedo* [Educational systems of the developed nations]. Seoul; Baeyongsa.

Li, Tae Kn, (1972), Asia chiyek yukkaekuk e chodung kyoyuk e mokeo bunsek [Analysis of objectives of elementary education in 6 Asian countries]. *Nonmun chip* (Seoul kyoyuk daehak), 5, 133-146.

Lim, Han Young, (1976), *Kyoyuk sasang e bikyoyenku* [Comparative study of educational thought]. Seoul; Baeyoungsa.

Mun, Hyung Man, (1970), *Hng'gunk kyoyuk-ui pigyo kyoyuksa-chok i'hae* [Korean education in comparative historical perspective]. Seoul; Hyongsol chulpan-sa.

Pak, Jun Hi, (1975), *Hankukin e kyoyuk kwan* [Korean views on education]. Seoul; Silhanksa.

Yu, In Jongm (1974), *Saege kyoyuk-ui kaehyok dong'hyang* [Trends of educational reform in the world]. Seoul; Ikumensa.

India

Agarwal, J. C., (1971), *An introduction to world education* (2nd ed), New Delhi; Arya Book Depot.

Biswas, A., Aggarwal, J. C, (1972), *Comparative education*, New Delhi; Arya Book Depot.

Chaube, S. P., (1974), *Comparative education* (4th ed), Agra; India, Ram Prasad.

Dobu, G., (1975), *Education in USA*, Calcutta; India, Vijay Prakashan.

Eakin, T. C., (1972), *Students and politics: a comparative study*, Bombay; India, Popular Prakashan.

Ghosh, S. C., ed., (1976), *Educational strategies in developing countries*, ; Sterling Publishers.

Gulati, R.; Gulati, K., (1972), *Comparative education: India; USSR, England and USA*, Chandigarh; India, Mohindra Capital Publishers.

Kim, Y., et al, (1980 *The role of the university in national development: four Asian case studies*, New Delhi; Vikas.

Mukherjee, K. C., (1972), *A comparative study of some educational problems*, Bombay; India, Lalvani.

Mukherjee, L., (1975), *Comparative education*, (3rd ed. revised), Bombay; India, Allied.

Naik, J. P.; Aggarwal, J. C., (1971), *UNESCO's contribution towards world education*, New Delhi, Arya Book Depot.

Narasimha Rao, K., (1974), *Higher education in India and abroad*, Guntur; India, the author.

Narasimhamurthy, P. A., (1973), *The rise of modern nationalism in Japan: a historical study of the role of education in the making of modern Japan*, New Delhi; Ashajanak Publications.

Rai, B. C., (1973), *Comparative education*, Lucknow; India, Prakashan Kendra.

Roy, B. K., (1973), *US infiltration of Indian education*, New Delhi; Perspective Publications.

Saxena, S., (1971), *Education as an academic study: a survey of India, UK and USA*, Bombay; India, Asia Publishing House.

Sharma, S. R., (1979), *American influence on Indian education*, New Delhi; Raaj Prakashan.

Shukla, S., (1981), Comparative education - new directions. Presidential address, First conference of the Comparative Education Society of India at Indian Institute of Education, Pune, October 16-18. *Bulletin of the Indian Institute of Education*, 2, 1981, 1-15.

Sodhi, T. S., (1983), *A textbook of comparative education*, (3rd rev. ed.), New Delhi; Vikas Publishing House.

Suri, M. S., (1979), *American influences on higher education in India: a study of post-independence era*, New Delhi; Sterling.

Trivedi, R. S., et al, eds., (1971), *International education*, Vallabh Vidyanagar; India, Sardar Petel University.

Australia, New Zealand and the Pacific[1]

Robin Burns

In order to understand the role of comparative education in the societies under consideration, it is necessary, in terms of the very logic and methodology of comparative education itself, to have some macro perspective of the societies and the place of education in them, and a micro perspective of the operation of schools, at least in broad outline.

The macro perspectives provide a framework within which comparative education can be located and elaborated within the four countries under consideration, Australia, New Zealand, Papua New Guinea and Fiji. Two factors provide a rationale for considering these societies side-by-side. The first is their geographical location in the South Pacific (but remembering Australia's vast coastline facing the Indian Ocean and Papua New Guinea's border with South-east Asia), and their experience of colonialism, albeit at different stages of global imperialism and leading in turn to Australian and New Zealand colonial mandates in the region after their own independence. In size, terrain, demography, ethnic composition and socio-cultural and economic factors, the differences are large, ranging from the giant in the area, Australia, with 15 million people of whom one in four was born outside Australia and an indigenous minority, the Aborigines, now numbering 145,000, to New Zealand with 3.3 million of whom eight per cent are Maoris and eight per cent are from other Pacific islands, Papua New Guinea with 3.2 million divided into over 700 different tribal groupings (there are two *lingua franca* besides English) and Fiji with 650,000 of whom 49.8 per cent are of Indian origin brought in as labour under colonialism and 44.2 per cent indigenous Fijians. All four countries depend largely on export earnings from primary produce; Australia is the most industrialized and Australia and New Zealand are highly urbanized societies. The United Kingdom has been the dominant educational influence on Australia and New Zealand, and to some extent on Fiji though New Zealand has also had a very strong influence, while Australia established the educational system in Papua New Guinea.

Micro perspectives: significance for comparative education

Generalizations are unwise in and between countries as diverse as the four under consideration. Of most relevance for the purpose of this chapter, is that in each country, the socialization patterns of the indigenous societies were largely ignored and replaced by the educational practices of the colonizers. Further, in each case missionaries, not necessarily of the same nationality as the colonial administrators, were the first educators and their influences are still found in the large private school sectors.

Of particular pertinence to considering the development and growth of comparative education in the area is the fact that, even today, the higher educational institutions preparing the teachers for and researchers into the national education systems, are often non-nationals: if those with overseas higher degrees are included, the proportions of staff with some or all of their education abroad are higher even in Australia and to a lesser extent New Zealand, than in comparable European and North American institutions. Superficially, this paves the way for a 'natural' place, in educational planning, in the education of teachers and in educational research, for comparative education. On the other hand, however, this gives rise to what has been labelled 'partial colonialism',[2] and has three major implications for the explicit study and use of comparative education:

(i) The influence may simply consist of the unacknowledged and unexamined transfer of assumptions and concepts from one situation to the other, for the purpose of influencing the local situation, deliberately or through oversight and unreflected practice;

(ii) This leads in turn to a 'backlash', at certain stages or in particular areas, so that there is a deliberate and conscious attempt either to 'borrow' or eradicate foreign influences;

(iii) At the micro level in particular, there is some indication that 'system level' studies have become the focus for 'foreigners', leaving the 'locals' to undertake detailed 'ethnographies'. This can be partially borne out, for example, through examination of the research and teaching commitments of foreign and local staff.

These three factors have further implications for the nature of comparative education in the area. On the one hand, the percentages of researchers and teach educators born or qualified overseas have enhanced, at least superficially, the international flow of ideas about education. It has led especially in Papua New Guinea and Fiji to the study of foreign influences on the education systems. On the other hand, there has as a result been some 'nationalism' which, coupled with a poor flow between Academe and high-level educational bureaucracies, especially for non-nationals, has led to over-concern by nationals with local and localization issues, almost deliberately resisting the ideas and practices of other systems. In particular, this means, at least in Australia, that comparativists sit uneasily in between, but giving less attention than some would consider methodologically desirable to the day-to-day nature and reality of classrooms, focusing rather on the 'education and society' interface.

Origins of comparative education

A preliminary question to be raised is: when is an educator a *comparative* educator? This is particularly relevant in the region under consideration, since there never has been more than a handful of academics and teacher educators whose sole task is to research and teach comparative education but a number who, at some stage, do one or the other or both. As a result, it is predominantly those trained outside Australia, almost all in the UK and North America, who would claim to be primarily comparativists. To some extent, this reflects ongoing issues regarding the state and status of comparative education itself, especially the question of whether or not it is equivalent to a 'discipline' in its own right, or a particular methodology or content used in an interdisciplinary context within educational studies. Since there is only one academic unit in the region specifically labelled 'Comparative and International Studies in Education', it is the content-based definition and in part, self-definition of individuals, which must be used.

The sources for the development of comparative education in the region are fivefold:

1. Specific individuals, trained overseas, who were able to apply that training to the development of comparative education courses and research on appointment back in the region.

2. Specific individuals whose expertise in a particular aspect of education led them to international advisory or problem-solving roles in intergovernmental, regional or international agencies, for other governments or in their own government's aid to education projects. A sub-

group of these are teachers with overseas, especially developing country, experience, who subsequently moved into tertiary education and maintained their interest in the education systems of other countries.

3. Individuals or groups who, through contacts overseas, became involved in cross-national research, rarely specifically related to comparative education methodologically or feeding into comparative education publications or courses.

4. Individuals simply attracted to the study of education systems other than their own, or transplanted from one system to another who began to research or teach comparatively.

5. On the 'international' edge of a 'comparative and international education formula', individuals with a vision more commensurate with that line traceable back to Comenius and more currently espoused by UNESCO, of the need for education to be seen in an international perspective, and to contribute towards 'international understanding'.

All five strands have played their role in the region, the first and last being most directly traceable as the origins of comparative education in Australia, the second in New Zealand, and the third and fourth in Papua New Guinea and the Pacific. And if the nature of the society in which educators work is another source for the introduction of the field of comparative education, two further strands should also be mentioned:

6. The multi-ethnic nature of all the societies in question, which both creates a 'data base' for those interested in the origins of and contemporary needs for the education of the inhabitants, as well as a 'problem situation' which may in part at least be 'solved' by comparison with other multi-ethnic societies.

7. The emergent nature of all the societies and the fact that, while coming at different stages, all have transplanted formal educational systems and have attempted to adapt these to 'national needs'. This factor is a two-edged sword: on the one hand, it provides at home a source for one type of comparative study, the transfer and change of educational ideas; on the other, it has led at various stages to an inward-lookingness, especially within the educational systems rather than the teacher educators and educational researchers, in attempts to create 'authentic' national systems of education. Interestingly, two of the countries under consideration, Papua New Guinea and Fiji, are still undergoing this

process in relationship to the influence of the other countries under consideration, and all (least in Papua New Guinea) have been heavily influenced by the UK.

The first designated course in Australia was established at the University of Sydney in 1945, by Ivan Turner, himself a graduate of both the UK and the USA and especially influenced by the latter through his doctoral studies with I. L. Kandel. Comparative became one of three strands in the study of education at the third year level in the Faculty of Arts. Through Turner, and through three others: Victor Couch, Trevor Miller and Phillip E. Jones, students and colleagues of Turner's who undertook post-graduate studies in comparative education abroad, it was established in the University of Sydney and at Sydney Teachers' College. As students became staff at other institutions, it spread further afield,[3] especially to the University of New England and then to the newer universities of Macquarie, Monash and La Trobe.

In New Zealand, the close association with neighbouring Pacific Islanders and the education of large numbers in New Zealand provided a more 'natural' base for comparative education, especially of the policy and problem-solving variety. To the extent that New Zealand educators have probably more accumulated experience of education in other countries and for other cultures, as well as the need to 'accommodate' different ethnic groups in New Zealand education, there is a broader base for comparative teaching and research. That it is a more implicit than explicit form of comparative education may be a reflection of changing roles of prominent New Zealand educators, such as C. E. Beeby and R. S. Adams, whose contributions cover academic education, leadership in the Department of Education and the New Zealand Council for Educational Research (NZCER) and international positions, more than their Australian counterparts who are more locked into one slot in education.

Elsewhere in the region, comparative education is barely known as such in formal courses, although it is an option in post-basic courses and comparative research is undertaken. Individual staff, predominantly from the UK, Australia and New Zealand, have been the 'carriers', and its full 'birth' has yet to be witnessed. Individuals have been active in comparative education organizations, including the European, World, British and North American Societies, and have brought this experience to the founding and continuation of the Australian and New Zealand Society.

Training and research centres

There are no specialized training and research centres in comparative education in the region, and only one specifically named Comparative Centre within a School of Education. Nor is it a compulsory part of any course at any level in any of the university schools, faculties or departments of education or teacher training institutes. However, there are no institutions in which it is not possible to study or undertake research in comparative education, if comparative education is broadly defined and includes international, multicultural and development education. However, with the exception of national research organizations (the Australian and New Zealand Councils for Educational Research, ACER and NZCER respectively) and the research function within national or state government departments of education, education itself is located in multi-purpose and multi-level universities and colleges. For all these, the pre-service education of teachers combines a 'general' and a 'teacher training' component, focusing on the theory and practice of education, curriculum, pedagogy and supervised practical experience. At best, a few lectures or an 'elective' may be undertaken in comparative education. Those who return to undertake higher degree work can, in those institutions offering a course, undertake studies in comparative education. Courses such as 'education and development' or national or regional case studies are more common. Approximately half the master's degree students and all doctoral degree students proceed by full thesis alone. They must normally take courses offered at a lower level if they have not previously done so.

The opportunity to undertake any full-time research in education is rare. In universities and colleges, staff teach for about 30 weeks of the year, and compete within their faculty, university and nation for research grants. Fellowships for full-time research are rare, usually of a maximum two years' duration, and none are designated for comparative research. The undertaking of research in comparative education within higher educational institutions is therefore unplanned, depends on the interests (and increasingly on the declining funding opportunities) of staff and graduate students, and competes with growing demands for research and training in those fields of education designated nationally important', especially in curriculum, equal opportunity, and organizational and administrative areas. Papua and New Guinea and Fiji may in some sense be seen to be in a better position than Australia and New Zealand insofar as donor countries and agencies include staff development in their development assistance programs, enabling researchers to obtain training and experience abroad at least in comparative *settings*. Non-governmental funding of educational research is almost non-existent. The ACER, NZCER and departmental research sections do some in-house research and, especially in the departments, commission research. In Australia and New Zealand in particular, comparative education has entered only as an exchange of programs, materials development projects, and regional research-oriented seminars especially addressed to educational planning.

The Comparative Centre at La Trobe University began with the foundation of the School of Education there in 1969. It grew to 10 staff by 1975, and was not able to replace one member who left in 1984. Staff teach at all levels in the School's program, and some elective Comparative courses are taught at all levels. Student numbers in these courses have steadily declined at the lower levels, and continue at around 40 at the graduate levels, largely due to an increasing number of overseas students. Of the present staff, four have graduate qualifications in comparative education from overseas and one completed a doctorate within the Centre. The staff were recruited on a threefold basis: to represent a spread of disciplinary backgrounds (e.g. psychology, sociology, history, social anthropology), to include some with specific comparative educational qualifications, and to develop a particular 'area focus' on Asia. This focus is represented in the individual research and teaching of some members and in activities such as an exchange agreement with the People's Republic of China. Members are active in a range of professional associations, nationally and internationally. There has been no joint research. Publications sponsored by the Centre have been a China documents series, materials for teaching Asian studies in schools, and four monographs. This profile does not differ significantly from units in other institutions with concentrations of three or more comparativists. A National Directory of Education Research and Researchers in Australia, based on a self-report survey, lists only 16 individual projects under the subject 'comparative education'.[4] The situation is similar in the other three countries.

Major research projects and publications

The foregoing section, while not focusing specifically on comparative educational research, is a necessary background for understanding the 'research environment' within which comparative educators can operate. Two further factors operate: the officially defined national needs of the countries in question and their relationship to education, and the position of the countries within the broader region which includes Southern Asia and the Pacific (both the 'basin' and the 'rim').

For all four countries, educational expansion has been a major issue. While Australia and New Zealand have universal compulsory education, the percentages continuing beyond the minimum school leaving-age continue to be low in developed country terms, and with the economic recession of the 1980s, focus on youth unemployment and training has come to be a major political preoccupation, coupled with concern at comparatively low figures for national industrial and technological 'research and development' capacity and investment. The countries present a different picture regarding agricultural research and development, Australia having the additional distinction of sharing the problems of tropical agriculture with many developing countries, and claiming some leadership role in this field as a result.[5] In Papua New Guinea and Fiji there is the sheer size of the problem of meeting educational expectations, from a low base of qualified national teachers, when the pay and conditions in teaching make it relatively non-competitive with other sectors of the economy. There is also the problem (shared with Australia and New Zealand) of isolated and heterogeneous communities, and additionally, that of providing education compatible with the needs for qualified persons at various levels, oriented to their national and local rather than developed country employment expectations: these have dominated educational thinking and action in the period under consideration. Therefore, major nationally funded research in education is largely oriented to national problem-solving, with neither the inclination nor the capacity to undertake this in either a comparative or an international perspective. Curriculum development and structural arrangements for the delivery of educational services at all levels have been major research concerns. Little money is available from non-government channels, and research undertaken outside these channels has scant possibility of feeding into national educational projects and plans.

The second factor, regional location, provides a different perspective and one which contributes to the placing of Australia and New Zealand in a different and structured position from Papua New Guinea and Fiji. There are a number of regional and bilateral research and development programs in education, through such institutions as SEAMEO, ACEIP, especially the APEID program, and the OECD's CEID. While the UNESCO Bangkok Regional Office for Education in Asia and the Pacific is the coordinating agency for a number of these programs, other regional links are also relevant, not least the Commonwealth, especially through its Commonwealth Cooperation in Education Scheme, and also the South Pacific Commission and the South Pacific Aid Program. These institutions tend to structure further the links between the countries under consideration into 'donor' and 'recipient' categories, or 'self-help' groups overseen or sponsored by outside agents, including Australia and New Zealand, for whom the impact on their own educational systems is largely irrelevant, though programs of educational assistance provide some outlet for their researchers and 'experts'.

These factors must be taken into account, together with the fact that in all four countries, self-definition of individual educational researchers as comparativists is largely irrelevant in their recruitment to officially sponsored educational research, while research which is explicitly comparative rarely appears on official or sponsored research agenda, and participation in cross-national research or advice can be claimed as the qualification to become a comparative educationist. Thus the only large-scale and explicitly comparative educational research projects, with both Australia and New Zealand as participating nations, are within the framework of the International Association for the Evaluation of Educational Achievement (IEA) The Councils for Educational Research play a major part in this ongoing research, which fits in with the earlier dominance of measurement in the work of both; as the immediate past director of ACER stated, the Association 'has made an important contribution to the development of a more empirical approach to the comparative study of educational systems'.[6] In addition to international contacts provided within the IEA structure and program, two main outcomes of the IEA participation for Australia can be traced. The first is in the field of science curriculum, although since it is a State matter, the impact of a national project is restricted, and the major national project, the Australian Science Education Project, was commenced before the IEA research. The second is through the provision of a data bank which is available to researchers. This provides both a bank of national and international material for research into fields such as the effects of gender and social class on school achievement, a data bank of test items across the curriculum and school levels which is available for the compilation of more task-specific instruments. This is more of a research than a practical tool, since general achievement tests are rarely used as formal assessment of pupils in schools. With a greater emphasis in New Zealand on pupil assessment and on the effects of culture on achievement, IEA participation has assisted such research there.

In all four countries, major educational research projects in the last decade have focused on the delivery of educational services, curriculum and youth. In Australia and New Zealand multicultural and multiracial education has also been investigated, while non-formal and vocational education has received comparable attention in Papua New Guinea and Fiji, with the education of women and girls and 'other disadvantaged groups' a more recent field.

Multicultural education has become a concern of comparativists, partly because of the interests and needs of students and partly because of the availability of the research field at a time of shrinking funds. Thus, the urgent needs of schools, teachers and ethnic communities provide the motivation for research, which has a practical outlet through teaching. And it is often through former students that research makes an impact on policy and practice. There is some consideration of multicultural issues in the pre-service training of teachers, and up to half the graduate students working with comparativists are researching multicultural issues. While other educators are involved in this field, it is one to which comparative education is making a contribution. It has also affected the types of courses offered by comparativists, and the directions of some research. One might perhaps name no more than six individuals in both countries who are explicitly associated with the policy processes, as comparative researchers, but in their contribution to some 'critical mass' of informed educators and research, their impact is more far-reaching.

National differences are evident in proposed 'solutions' to problems arising from an ethnically diverse population. The focus in Aboriginal education in Australia has some parallels with black educational trends in the US, aboriginal children having been defined as 'disadvantaged'. More radical recent trends include aboriginal language and culture programs, separate schools (the first urban aboriginal college has now opened in Melbourne, for example), and new approaches to teacher selection and education by and in the aboriginal community through training college extension programs, though 'compensatory education' is still the orthodoxy in major areas of aboriginal education. Maori education, on the other hand, received special attention very early on and there is a resurgence of Maori Studies programs for all teachers and for all schools, though the emphasis on improved esteem for Maoris leads to some differences in approaches to the two situations and some separate educational institutions. 'Biculturalism and bilingualism is a prerequisite in the eyes of many Maori people to upward mobility'.[7] The cause of Maori education has been furthered by the different colonial and racial histories of Australia and New Zealand and the emergence much earlier in New Zealand of Maori leaders, senior administrators and educators.

The education of immigrant children has also taken different paths, in keeping with the different origins of these immigrants. In Australia, the large percentage of non-English-speaking background migrants has focused attention on the provision of services, educational and welfare, with a heavy emphasis on language, both the teaching of English as a Second Language (ESL) and more recently, the teaching of community languages.[8] Two sources of immigrants dominate New Zealand: those from the UK and those from other Pacific Islands. The educational problems of the latter have been close to those of the Maori.

Since there is a weak relationship between research and policy-making in both countries, it is through the graduate students who have attained policy positions that an influence from comparative education is made on multiculturalism. Again, a state-by-state analysis of such influence would be necessary to trace the effects accurately in Australia. Researchers are called on from time-to-time, especially in the field of language, to sit on government advisory bodies or participate in special conferences and meetings. The major impact at the national level has been on the introduction of community languages and the supplementary and special funding made available from the Commonwealth as well as at the state level, for programs in schools with a high migrant population.

In New Zealand, senior educational officials with a comparative background have had a higher profile in Maori education. In both countries, 'solutions' have a distinctively local 'flavour' with Maori Studies perhaps providing under-recognized international examples (though to some extent influenced by some earlier approaches in the USA'. In Australia, the dual focus on languages and on the multicultural society and curriculum is similarly under-recognized, partly because the approaches to the education of Third World immigrant children and the children of guest workers in Europe have different political connotations from the education of Southern European and refugee, especially Indo-Chinese refugee, children in Australia where they represent a much bigger proportion of the population than in Europe. Recent statements of national educational aims in Australia incorporate multiculturalism as a core concept and value.[10] Comparativists have contributed, not so much through comparative studies of multi-ethnic societies (although the USA, Canada, the UK, Sweden and Malaysia are cited in courses) but through participating in research and teacher education with multiculturalism as a central concern.

Beyond these project areas, the picture is one of a diversity of projects, largely undertaken by individuals according to interests, experience and availability, if any, of funds. Often the opportunity to undertake subsequent research is dependent on a contract teaching or advisory position overseas, which establishes contacts and information for subsequent research. The following major areas can be identified:

1. Single-country studies of one or more aspects of education, e.g. primary curriculum development in Tonga; education and work in China.
2. Comparative studies of an aspect of education in two or more countries, e.g. population education in Sri Lanka, Singapore and Indonesia; the formation and legitimation of development education in Australia, Europe and North America; the role of school inspectorates in Nigeria and the UK; decentralization of power in educational decision-making in the UK, the US and Australia.
3. The study of the impact of development assistance to education, e.g. developmental literacy as a dependency mechanism; the Overseas Development Council and educational development; overseas student policy.
4. Single country or issue studies, firmly based in a theoretical framework which provides for the location of such case studies, e.g. education and the reproduction of sexual inequality in Bali; curriculum innovation and the secondary social science curriculum project in Papua New Guinea.
5. Intra-national comparisons in the fields of curriculum, control of education, educational decision-making, teacher education, multicultural education. This last field is a recognized grouping of comparativists and non-comparativists in Australia and New Zealand, and covers curriculum, teacher education, critical studies of policy and comparison with approaches in other polyethnic societies.
6. Studies of the international dimensions in education, for example peace education, based on ideas developed cross-nationally and including studies of local adaptations of those ideas.
7. Studies of a more theoretical nature using examples to highlight issues or challenge theory. These include theoretical articles on the nature of comparative education, its use in educational planning and its relationship to cognate disciplines, especially sociology and history.

This list is not exhaustive, but covers the major areas and also indicates that, within the resource limits and priorities in each country, comparable though largely small-scale research in comparative and international education is being done in this region as elsewhere. The fact that the Australian and New Zealand Comparative and International Education Society (ANZCIES) has deliberately chosen its annual conference themes to balance significant national educational issues (multiculturalism, the education of women and girls, quality and equality in education) with international ones (crises in education, the economics of education, ones related to the teaching of comparative education and its relationship to schooling), attracting between twelve and thirty papers, equally divided between 'one-theme' and 'general' (mostly case study) ones, indicates this generality.

Methods and issues

As with research projects, the methods chosen for investigation reflect international diversity and controversy. While writing about comparative education world-wide, Keith Simkin's insightful and incisive survey is applicable to work in the region. He notes that:

> 'When one looks at the relationship between comparative education and macro-sociological theory, the diversity in comparative education has not been as important as the debt it has owed to structural-functional theory.'[11]

The period under consideration saw two main focuses in comparative education: 'like-country' studies and comparisons, and studies of developing countries. The 'orthodoxy' of modernization theory, used by researchers rather than providing an explicit theoretical base for comparative and case studies of developing countries, was extended to form the main base for studies of developing countries, augmented, as Simkin points out, by human capital theories taken from economics.[12] There has been a growing and oppositional theoretical base, in critical, Marxist and neo-Marxist theories originating in economic history and political economy, and best exemplified in comparative education in dependency theory.[13] Despite the many problems with both sets of theories, especially their failure 'to provide a genuinely *macro*-theoretical basis for comparative educational research',[14] both have informed comparative research in the region. The low level of participation by academic comparative educationists in national and even cross-national applied research in all four countries has perhaps assisted in the avoidance of facing some of the problems of the theories as a basis for educational planning, and has exacerbated the gap between 'methodological prescription' and actual research[15] because, lacking a direct application, the researchers have not often had to undertake large scale, change-oriented research.

An area which overlaps with the work of some comparativists is that of development education, defined in the North American rather than the European sense. Development educators have worked in Papua New Guinea and Fiji, including ones from Australia and New Zealand. Both Papua New Guinea and Fiji are committed to a 'modernization' approach to national development. The Eight Point Plan which formed the basic framework for post-colonial development in Papua New Guinea stressed self-sufficiency and rural development, but this has rested uneasily alongside modernization of the monetary sector, increasing the export sector and encouraging import-substitution. The pursuit of the latter has led to a gradual movement away from ideas of self-reliance and rural development. This is perhaps not surprising, given the role that expatriates still play in education and in other areas of national life, building on the modernization perspective on which the colony was brought to independence in 1975.

Until the 1960s, education was largely in mission hands, and the first secondary schools were established in the late 1940s. There are now four residential national schools extending to grade 12 and 97 provincial ones for grades 7-10 with some selection for the national high schools at the end of grade eight. Three Commissions, two Australian-based but stimulated by the UN Trusteeship Council, and one from the World Bank, were important in the establishment in 1970 of a national education system under which most mission schools were incorporated. In 1966, the University of Papua New Guinea was opened. Shortly after, came the Institute of Higher Technology, now Technical University, at Lae. In 1975 the Goroka Teachers College became a campus of the University of Papua New Guinea, and through successive rationalizations, there are now eight primary teacher training colleges as well as a diversity of vocational institutions. It should be remembered, however, that only 67 per cent males and 46 per cent of females, ever begin school, only 10 per cent of the age group complete grade 10, and between 3.5 and 4.5 per cent receive other forms of training (0.5 per cent go on to university).

Australian influence has been very strong, but is declining, with a shift to Melanesian and 'modernization' influences in the last decade or so. Earlier, an input from other Pacific islands was evident through the use of 'pastors' and some teachers in the mission schools. International volunteers now make up almost half the educational personnel at secondary and post-secondary levels.

Development educators - if most expatriate educators could be so defined - have thus played a critical role in Papua New Guinea. This is threefold. First, it can be assumed that, at least unconsciously, every expatriate educator is a carrier of a particular educational and developmental perspective and, since all but the top political and administrative heads are still frequently expatriates, international practitioner and theoretical perspectives are brought to the task of educational development. There has been a conscious effort since independence to diversify the sources for such ideas by preferring non-Australian expatriates to head major projects and international missions and for research and university appointments. Second, there have been conferences, especially in 1972 and 1974,[16] which have exposed Papua New Guinea to major and contradictory inputs, from the views of Phillip Foster to those of Ivan Illich and Paulo Freire, all of which seemed to have greater impact on the expatriates than on the locals. Third, while localization of personnel and curricula has been a consistent theme for some time, the independence thrust of giving Papua New Guineans 'a basic academic education which was useful in the modern cash economy'[17] has now led to an over-supply of qualified school leavers without commensurate expansion in employment opportunities. And while expatriates were advocating localization of the curriculum before independence, solution of the 'dual economy' problem and the provision of dual educational institutions has been, here as elsewhere, politically difficult. The list of educational problems of developing countries generally is evident in Papua New Guinea. The contribution of development educators, despite the problem of high turnovers (not just of expatriates), is in the field of innovation especially through the Secondary School Community Extension Project (SSCEP) which is still on a pilot basis.[18] International experience is brought to bear on the local situation, and international funding as well. Development educators are also involved in the implementation of the major World Bank education project which is currently focusing on staff development.

The situation in Fiji is somewhat similar, complicated by the dual Fijian and Fiji-Indian education systems.

Education was initially in mission hands and a number of schools are still in the private sector today. The situation is complicated further by the existence of separate Indian schools, and 48 per cent of primary schools are still single race. While the government has come close to meeting its target of free primary education for all Fijians, 55 per cent of secondary enrollments are Indians and only 38 per cent Fijians, and there is a greater sex imbalance in enrollments among the Indians. There are now 104 secondary schools, four teacher training colleges (only two government run), a university (a joint venture with 10 other Pacific nations, centred in Suva, Fiji but with a number of campus sites), which was established in 1968 and which, like the University of Papua New Guinea, has an on-site, matriculation-equivalent preliminary year.

With the conclusion in 1974 of a 50-year agreement with New Zealand to supply teachers, the New Zealand influence has declined somewhat, although the continuation of the extensive private school sector has perpetuated a UK influence in particular. The government is still attempting to introduce a more local emphasis, and to upgrade teacher qualifications, and volunteer teachers from the UK, US and New Zealand have rapidly declined in number.

Most of the expatriate personnel for independent Fiji is still provided by the UK and New Zealand within a framework of the Commonwealth assistance program. The multi-ethnic population and its dual schooling system has led to less overt attention to localization issues, and the ready supply of trained expatriates has relieved pressure on - or held up the development of - local training programs.[19] Fijian education is influenced by international development education orthodoxies, filtered through local political problems and expediencies. Fiji is perhaps the largest island nation to be considered by the international education and assistance community as a small state, attempting to decrease reliance on a plantation economy, with tourism as a major (if unreliable) substitute, and drawing educational advice and programs from development education frameworks. Planning, technical and vocational education, here as elsewhere, remain persistent problems and as such, draw on the international orthodoxies for solutions in the interests of Fijian modernization (less influenced by notions of self-reliance than in Papua New Guinea).

In both, there is some tension between international advice (including that of individual expatriates) and local pride and initiative. However, as developing nations dependent not only on fluctuating international commodity markets but on large infrastructural grants especially from their former colonizers, the capacity to 'resist' such influences is largely at the level of inaction, that is, polite acceptance but slow adoption. This includes some rejection of the concept of localization of educational content. As Barrington has recently noted, 'the transfer of educational ideas with at least some links, in terms of underlying rationale, to earlier notions of education for adaption may still have some attraction for policy makers. They, also apparently produce some of the same doubts amongst the recipients of such policies as they have always done'.[20]

While people from both Australia and New Zealand have undertaken government and agency consultancies on development education (in Asia and to a lesser extent Africa as well), they are not very visible on the permanent staff of agencies such as UNESCO or the World Bank's educational sector, although C. E. Beeby and R. S. Adams of New Zealand are internationally well-known in such agencies.

If, as Simkin maintains, comparative education has increasingly faced the general paradigm debates in cognate social sciences, it would be expected that these would be reflected in the methodologies employed and the methodological discussions. However, the place where such discussion is most evident is in the teaching of comparative education. Individual researchers seem more allied to the discussion as it applies in their 'base discipline', or are even atheoretical and 'taxonomic' in their research. The main methodological trends, especially the co-existence of quantitative and increasingly sophisticated analytical studies and more 'hermeneutic' approaches increasingly applying ethnomethodology, are evident, though the former is less evident than the latter. This may be explained by the wide range of base disciplines and the separation, especially in Australia, of comparative educational research and the comparative sociological study of education. It is probably truer here than in other parts of the world, that comparativists come from backgrounds in curriculum rather than sociology, philosophy or psychology, and unless they undertake higher degree work at one of the prestigious UK or USA comparative education centres, give low priority to methodological considerations. This may represent a productive 'tacking between perspectives' with the possibility of new developments; it does not provide for easy justification of the subject as an intellectual endeavour, e.g. Doug White's criticisms of the epistemological and cognitive bases for the act of comparison.[21] It may also contribute to the lack of studies that are explicitly comparative, and it has been debate about the role of comparison, rather than how it is undertaken, that has tended to dominate methodological discussions.

It is perhaps in higher degree dissertations that one would expect to find the greatest attention to methodologies, given that this is the most significant opportunity for many comparativists in the region to undertake a large and sustained comparative research project. Theses rarely get published intact: I can locate none from recent years in which methodology is considered extensively. Although not defining himself as a comparativist, White has written two theses on the nature of comparative education and has published on it, as well as participating in the foundation conference of the Australian and New Zealand Comparative and International Education Society which was on this theme.[22] Burns, Crossley, McLeod and Sheehan have discussed issues of method either in their theses, in articles, or both.[23] The use of case study, participant observation and ethnomethodology have been raised in these, as well as broader issues concerning the 'units' of comparison issue, bringing comparative perspectives to bear on studies of classroom or school level processes, the use of systems approaches from other disciplines and the relevance of anthropological macro-methodology and structural theory. The usefulness of comparison in the study of gender has been raised by Yates.[24] Theoretical debates, especially on the theoretical assumptions of development education, have been considered by Collins, Gillespie, Jones, Simkin and Toh,[25] and Welch has contributed especially to the analysis of the interface between sociology and comparative education.[26] The applications of comparative education to issues such as gender (especially Yates),[27] international education (Cleverley and Jones)[28] and development and peace education (Burns, and Toh)[29] have also been undertaken. Such debates most frequently take place in the framework of conferences and, lacking our own comparative journal, are subordinate to substantive issues in articles by comparativists in other arenas. In fact, it is interesting that a recent 'state-of-the-art' survey of comparative education in English-speaking countries contains no specific reference either to Australian or New Zealand researchers or their work.[30]

The teaching of comparative education

Since it is nowhere a compulsory component of formal education courses, and confining this survey in the main to work within education, it is difficult to piece together an adequate representation of the dissemination of comparative education. The areas outlined in the section on research provide a simple framework for this. All seven types of project can be found in the courses offered in Australia and New Zealand, all elective and all represented at the post-basic teacher education levels. Given, further, the fact that only one professor of education is currently appointed to a position as professor *of* comparative education, in the only distinctly named unit, it is not surprising that comparative education has a low profile. Further, in Papua New Guinea and Fiji, the problems of educational development towards more autonomous national systems, while sometimes undertaken collaboratively within the region, provide a counter-pressure which makes comparative study not aligned to careful planning seem a luxury. The shifting origins of expatriate staff, who often stay only briefly and often with insufficient time to ground themselves in local realities, or who are over-committed to basic teacher preparation and curriculum development, also act against the widespread teaching of comparative education.

In Australia and New Zealand, the number of courses dealing with traditional comparative education topics, especially the comparison of major systems of education, has declined. In their place may be found a range of options on the study of developing countries. Two main approaches are discernible: studies of educational development and planning, and critical studies of educational transfer within a dependency theory framework. There are few specific courses on methodology; where they appear, the most commonly used textbooks are those of Brian Holmes. Dependency theory courses frequently use the writings of Carnoy, Altbach, Kelly and Arnove, so that there is a specific UK and a specific US influence currently dominant. With the declining state of foreign language learning, non-translated writers in other languages are rarely used, nor is major reference made to European as distinct from British comparative education, and the Latin American writers, including Freire and Illich, are studied in translation.

For the past 20 years at least, there has been criticism of the failure of educators in Australia and New Zealand to be more internationalist. This has been redressed to some extent in the past decade by concern, including concern in the teaching of education, for the 'fourth world', defined to include both indigenous ethnic minorities and migrants as well as refugees. Even here, however, there are few institutions where the study of society as a multicultural phenomenon, and the educational implications of this, is compulsory and while probably half of the comparative educators are engaged in teaching and research in this area, it is rarely defined as comparative education in course titles. It has sat uneasily with 'area studies' approaches, at all educational levels, which further divides scarce resources from seeking common cause not only for resource but epistemological advantage.

One area of educational endeavour in both Australia and New Zealand which is separable from comparative education - but not always separated - is the preparation of educational personnel for service overseas and of overseas educational personnel. There was a specialized institution for the training of officers for the colonial service in Papua New Guinea. It included educators on its staff, although it was mainly concerned with general administrative training. Now the International Training Institute, its main function is to provide short courses for middle-level managers in various fields from the Third World, again including educators on its staff, some of whom are undertaking higher degree work in comparative education. Some comparativists have been involved in the in-house training of overseas volunteers. Selected teacher training institutions have had special programs operated by the Commonwealth for training teachers for aboriginal schools in the Northern Territory and other schemes exist in states with high concentrations of aboriginal children. Comparativists, including those with prior experience overseas, have often been key figures in these programs, though the reverse is also true, that people with experience overseas have 'drifted in' to comparative education. In New Zealand, the training of teachers, including Maori teachers, for Maori children has been widespread if at times tokenistic. Further, the long scheme of co-operation with Fiji for the supply of teachers has provided a supply of experienced educators with an interest at least in development education, although the long dominance of the New Zealand upper secondary examinations meant that teachers found little need to adapt to local conditions and Fiji resisted switching to the Cambridge Syndicate examinations as a result of this co-operation. There is also a Pacific Foundation, and in 1971 a Maori Education Foundation was established.[31] Other than teachers, little specific briefing is given to those serving overseas - the numbers are small, and the recruits usually experienced in their field if not in development practice specifically.

Both countries place assistance to education visibly on development assistance programs, and this takes three main forms: the training of overseas students including particular school teacher, tertiary teacher and educational ministry personnel; the fielding of experts, and participation in regional exchanges, programs and projects. Both Universities and Colleges of Advanced Education or Teacher Education have been involved in such activities, often relying on staff with prior experience from other such projects, and varying between tailor-made courses and the placement of overseas students in existing courses with or without additional support and orientation to the specific needs of their home countries. A large variety of bilateral and regional projects exists, including institution-to-institution agreements, and the whole field is currently designated an *export* growth area, especially in Australia. Where segregated courses are established, the spill-over into programs for the broadening of educational understanding of local students is at best haphazard. Further, such developments may well represent a return of comparativists to the more 'orthodox' tradition as they see such projects as an opportunity to gain access to resources for their own research and as the more radical comparativists turn their attention to critiques of the approach, leading to potential for more overt disagreement in what has so far been debate contained largely within scholarly rather than resource contexts.

Papua New Guinea, and particularly Fiji, has been subject to outside influence and it is therefore hardly surprising that the study of the orthodox tradition in comparative education has little place in their courses. More surprising, perhaps, is the under-representation of the radical tradition, though given the expatriate status of senior academics and the overwhelmingly instrumental nature of most education courses, this becomes more explicable.

In all four countries, it is through individual work that a thorough presentation of trends must be discerned, especially given that all doctoral degrees and the majority of masters degrees have no taught component, but rely solely on individual research.

Publications

There is a national general journal of education or of educational research in each country, but none has a policy of specifically including comparative material. There is no comparative education journal in the region with the possible exception of the *South Pacific journal of teacher education*. Papers are published in international journals and this is sought both for the exchange of ideas and for promotion. There are many professional education associations and journals in the region, some exclusively academic, some that include teachers and departmental officials, and comparativists on average belong to several of these, as well as discipline or area associations.

If educational research budgets in the region are tight, publication ones are even more so. Researchers suffer additionally from having few local independent publishers of academic material.

The Australian and New Zealand Comparative and International Education Society (there are as yet no branches, or separate societies, in the Pacific though members of ANZCIES include expatriates currently employed in the Pacific) has a newsletter which is struggles to bring out three times a year. It contains primarily news of members' conference attendance, research, courses and book reviews. The most regular vehicle for contact and exchange is the annual Society conference and its publication of *Proceedings* of each conference. There has been no major book on comparative education written by regional members for some years.

Overview

Comparative educators may sometimes appear to spend as much time in self-criticism as in research, and this is reflected in writings about the field in Australia and New Zealand. Here, it is part of a larger critique of the role of educational research in general. This is reflected in two major publications, the journals of the Australian Association for Research in Education (AARE) and the Sociological Association of Australia and New Zealand (SAANZ). The issue is related to the debate in both Associations about research paradigms, the former focusing on critical evaluation and positivist/ethnomethodological controversies, and the latter on the value of the 'new' sociology of education. Both reflect trends elsewhere. Attempts to make educational research more 'useful', (though the 'clients' are differently perceived by proponents of different paradigms), have not been met with a rush of research commissions and contracts. As a marginal group, despite the strong participation of some, comparativists can be seen as the 'periphery of the periphery' in the debate and, by implication, in education in the region.

Curriculum, participation in education, educational administration and evaluation are major issues in education in the region. These are all international concerns. However, policy makers appear to give little credence to outside experience in approaching the issues, so that the contribution of comparativists is coincidental rather than deliberately sought. And as the political definition of educational problem-solving as an instrumental and pragmatic activity hardens, so that 'theory' becomes a slur, there are profound problems for educators in general, not least the resulting range of 'acceptable' and 'relevant' courses to which students of education seeking recognition or promotion are attracted.

The problems are acute for comparativists. Never 'central' to the study and practice of education in the region, they are in danger of further marginalization. This process is hastened by the lack of formal legitimation of their role. Often trained outside the system with fewer senior academic educators in the subject and no specific national or regional journal, they seek legitimation by continued international contacts and publication in which, because there are few of them, they remain marginal.

Over ten years ago, Cleverley and Jones wrote that there were 'three principal areas in which the international aspects of Australian education have come to the fore: the impact of immigration; the broadening of the cultural base of the curriculum, and education as a focus of foreign aid'.[32] This is partly true for New Zealand, Papua New Guinea and Fiji, too, especially translating the first into the issue of national identity. Have comparativists, in addressing these issues, been by-passed by more pragmatic concerns? The three continue, and have given rise to activities, projects, exchanges and the like, but their significance outside limited, and often academic circles, is declining. This is not unique to the region, but comparativists need to seek actively to pursue and to renew their tasks in dialogue not only with other comparativists but with educators from other fields.

Notes

1. My thanks to Dr. Keith Simkin, Centre for Comparative and International Studies in Education, La Trobe University, for discussions of the issues raised in this section; to members of the Australian and New Zealand Comparative and International Education Society as colleagues and disputants in the field; to Susan Drew, for typing the manuscript rapidly and efficiently, and to Roger Douglas for supporting the task which was undertaken at short notice and under considerable pressure.
2. Thomas, R. Murray; Postlethwaite, T. Neville. Colonization and schooling in Oceania. In Thomas, R. Murray; Postlethwaite, T. Neville (eds), (1984), *Schooling in the Pacific Islands*, 1-28, Oxford, Pergamon Press, 338 pp.
3. Thanks to Victor Couch and Kelvin Grose for background information.
4. Commonwealth Department of Education, (1980), *Directory of education research and researchers in Australia*, 2nd ed., Canberra, Australian Government Publishing Service, 409 pp.
5. Australian Steering Committee on Preparations for the United Nations Conference on Science and Technology for Development, Department of Foreign Affairs, Canberra, (1978), *Australian national paper for the United Nations conference on science and technology for development, 1979*, Canberra, Australian Government Publishing Service, 183 pp.
6. Keeves, J. P. A background paper on the IEA Science Project. Melbourne, Australian Council for Educational Research, n.d., 10 pp.
7. Royal, T. K. What do Maoris in New Zealand want from education? Wellington, Education Department, n.d. (mimeo), 1-12, 3.
8. See e.g. Moore, H., (1978), Language teaching: where do we get our ideas from? *Babel* (Melbourne), vol.14, no.1, 17-23; Australian Department of Education, (1976), *Report of the committee on the teaching of migrant languages in schools*. Canberra, Australian Government Publishing Service; Australia [Schools Commission], (1979), *Education for a multicultural society: report of the committee on multicultural education*. Canberra, Australian Government Publishing Service; Australian Ethnic Affairs Council, Committee on Multicultural Education, (1981), *Perspectives on multicultural education*. Canberra, Australian Government Publishing Service; Falk, B.; Harris, J. (eds.), (1983), *Unity and diversity. Multicultural education in Australia*.

Victoria, Australian College of Education; Francis, R., (1981), *Teach to the difference*. St. Lucia, University of Queensland Press; Rado, M., (1984), *Teaching in the multilingual classroom*. Canberra, Curriculum Development Centre; Smolicz, J., (1979), *Culture and education in a plural society*. Canberra, Curriculum Development Centre.

9. Barrington, John M., (1983), The transfer of educational ideas: notions of adaptation, *Compare* (Oxfordshire), vol.13, no.1, 61-68.
10. Curriculum Development Centre, (1980), *Core curriculum for Australian schools*. Canberra, Curriculum Development Centre.
11. Simkin, Keith, (1981), Comparative and sociological perspectives on Third World development and education. *International review of education* (Hamburg), vol.27, no.4, 427-447, 428.
12. *Ibid.*, 429.
13. *Ibid.*, 435.
14. *Ibid.*, 436.
15. *Ibid.*, 439.
16. Brammall, J.; May, R. J. (eds.), (1975), *Education in Melanesia*. Canberra, Australian National University, and May, R. J. (ed.), (1973), *Priorities in Melanesian development*. Canberra, Australian National University.
17. Papua New Guinea, Department of Education, (1985), *Growth of education since independence 1975-1985*. Port Moresby, Government Printing Office, 45.
18. Cummings, R., (1982), A review of research on SSCEP: 1978-1981. Educational Research Unit *Report* (Port Moresby, University of Papua New Guinea), no.41, 4-59.
19. Hopkin, A. G., (1979), Co-operation or colonialism? Paper presented at the annual conference of the Development Studies Association, University of Reading, UK, September (mimeo), 21 pp.
20. Barrington, *op.cit.*, 67.
21. White, Doug, (1978), Comparisons as cognitive process, and the conceptual framework of the comparativist. *Comparative education* (Oxford), vol.14, no.2, 93-108.
22. *Ibid.* See also White, D. C., (1981), The foundations and standpoint of comparative education. Bundoora, La Trobe University unpublished Ph. D. dissertation, 332 pp; and White, D. The methodology of comparative education and its clarification as a basis for its contribution to the theory and practice of education. In Sheehan, B. (ed.), (1983), *Comparative and international studies and the theory and practice of education*. La Trobe University, ACIES, 101-107.
23. Burns, R. J., (1979), The formation and legitimation of development education with particular reference to Australia and Sweden. Bundoora, La Trobe University unpublished Ph. D. dissertation, 675 pp, ch.2; Crossley, M. W., (1983), Strategies for

curriculum change with special reference to the Secondary Schools Community Extension Project in Papua New Guinea. Bundoora, La Trobe University unpublished Ph. D. dissertation, 482 pp, ch.3. Crossley, M.; Burns, R. J. Case study in comparative and international education: an approach to bridging the theory-practice gap. In Sheehan, B. A. (ed.), (1983), *Comparative and international studies and the theory and practice of education*. Bundoora, ACIES, 1-18; Crossley, M.; Vulliamy, G., (1984), Case study research methods and comparative education. *Comparative education* (Oxford), vol.20, no.2; McLeod, J. N., (1984), Non-western implications for the nature and function of drama in education. Bundoora, La Trobe University unpublished Ph. D. dissertation, 454 pp., chs. 2 and 3; Sheehan, B. A., Intergovernmental relations and educational policy in four federations: USA, Canada, West Germany and Australia. In Welch, A. R. (ed.), (1981), *The politics of educational change*. Armidale, NSW, ACIES, 56-67; Sheehan, B. A. Comparative education: phoenix or dodo? In Sheehan, (ed.)., *op.cit.*, 161-178. See also Gauci, E. Applying empirical methods in comparative education: an example. In Sheehan, (ed.)., *op.cit.*, 108-124.

24. Yates, L. Comparison and the limits of comparison in working towards non-sexist education. In Burns, R. J.; Sheehan, B. (eds.), (1984), *Women and education*. Bundoora, ANZCIES, 27-38.

25. Collins, C. Models and reasons. In Bessant, B.; Price, R. F. (eds.), (1977), *Problems and prospects for comparative and international studies in education in Australia*. Bundoora, ACIES, 1-18; Gillespie, R. R.; Collins, C. B. Productive work and education: Tanzania as case study. In Maddock, J.; Hindson, C. (eds.), (1985), *Quality and equality in education*. Bedford Park, ANZCIES, 250-268; Jones, P. Diversity and unity in the educational thought of UNESCO - developmental literacy as a dependency mechanism. In Francis, R. J. C. (ed.), (1976), *Unity and diversity in education*. Armidale, NSW, ACIES, 161-186; Simkin, K. Theories of educational change and Australian comparative education. In Welch (ed.). *op.cit.*, 21-34.

26. Welch, A. R., (1980), Ideology, sociology and education: some developments and relationships. *Australian and New Zealand journal of sociology* (Melbourne), vol.16, no.2, 71-80; Welch A. R., (1985), The functionalist tradition and comparative education. *Comparative education* (Oxford), vol.21, no. 1, 5-19.

27. Yates, *op.cit.*

28. Cleverley, J.; Jones, P., (1976), Australia and international education: some critical issues, *Australian education review* (Melbourne), no.7, 5-45. See also Jones, P., (1986), *Australia's international relations in education*. Melbourne, Australian Council for Educational Research.

29. e.g. Aspeslagh, R.; Burns, R., (1983), Concepts of peace education: a view of Western experience. *International review of education* (Hamburg), vol.29, no.3, 311-330; Burns, R., (1982), Development education and peace education: from conflict to

co-operation. *UNICEF development education paper*, no.20, 1-10; Burns, R., (1984), Can educational change precede research and development? Reflections on a comparison between peace education and development education. In Australian Association for Research in Education. *Collected papers*, National Conference, Perth, November, 79-86; Burns, R., (1985), Peace education: is it responding sufficiently to children's fear of the future? *Australian journal of early childhood* (Canberra), vol.10, no.4, 16-23; Toh, Swee-Hin, (1981), Social peace and Third World development. In United Nations Association of Australia/Australian Independent School. *Peace education conference papers*, Sydney; Toh, Swee-Hin, (1983), Peace or conflict: regional and international perspectives with particular reference to Asia. *Asia teachers bulletin* (Sydney), vol.11, no.4, 54-63; Toh, Swee-Hin, (1984), No peace without development: solidarity with the Third World in Australian classrooms. In Independent Teachers Federation of Australia. *National peace education conference proceedings*. Brisbane.

30. Kelly, G. P.; Altbach, P., (1986), Comparative education: challenge and response. *Comparative education review* (Chicago), vol.30, no.1, 80-107, 90.

31. Royal, *op.cit.*

32. Cleverley and Jones, *op.cit.*, 39.

Bibliography

Adams, R. S., (1983), Research into educational innovation: a possible case of educational transfer. *Compare* (Oxfordshire), vol.13, no.1, 69-80.

Aspeslagh, Robert; Burns, Robin, (1983), Concepts of peace education: a view of Western experience. *International review of education* (Hamburg), vol.29, no.3, 311-330.

Australia [Schools Commission], (1979), *Education for a multicultural society: report of the committee on multicultural education*. Canberra, Australian Government Publishing Service.

Australian and New Zealand journal of sociology (Melbourne), vol.10, no.1, 1974 and vol.16, no.2, 1980.

Australian Department of Education, (1976), *Report of the committee on the teaching of migrant languages in schools*. Canberra, Australian Government Publishing Service.

Australian Ethnic Affairs Council, Committee on Multicultural Education, (1981), *Perspectives on multicultural education*. Canberra, Australian Government Publishing Service.

Bacchus, M. K., (1984), A review and analysis of educational 'needs' at the secondary level in Papua New Guinea. *Education Research Unit report* (Port Moresby), no.48, 1-142.

Ball, D. G. Maori education. In Mitchell, F. W. (ed.), (1971), *Looking ahead in New Zealand education*. Wellington, A. H. and A. W. Reed.

Barrington, John M., (1983), The transfer of educational ideas: notions of adaptation. *Compare* vol.13, no.1, 61-8.

Bates, Richard J., (1979), What can the new sociology of education do for teachers? Paper presented to the Annual Conference of the Sociological Association of Australia and New Zealand, Canberra, July (mimeo).

Baumgart, Neil; Lindsay, Alan, (1982), Funding educational research: paying the piper and calling the tune. *South Pacific association of teacher educators newsletter*, vol.5, no.3, 5-8.

Bessant, B., A critical look at the functions of Australian universities since 1939 (1978), *Centre for comparative and international studies in education monograph* (La Trobe University, Melbourne), no.1, 1-47.

Bessant, B.; Price, R. F.; (eds.), (1977), *Problems and prospects for comparative and international studies in education in Australia*. Papers presented at the Fifth Annual Conference of the Australian Comparative and International Education Society. La Trobe University, Melbourne, November.

Bray, Douglas H.; Hill, Clement, (1974), *Polynesian and Pakeha in New Zealand education*. vol. II. Auckland, Heinemann.

Brewer, W. B., (1980), *Education for international understanding, peace and the attainment of human rights. An overview of the Australian situation.* Hobart, Department of Education, October.

Brown, Marilyn (ed.), (1984), Department of Education Faculty of Education, University of Papua New Guinea, Annual Report, 1983 and 1984. Waigani. Burns, Robin, (1983), Development education in other Western nations. *Canadian and international education* (Toronto), vol.12, no.3, 33-51.

Burns, Robin; Sheehan, Barry (eds.), (1984), *Women and education*. Bundoora, ANZCIES.

Cleverley, John; Jones, Phillip, (1976), Australian and international education: some critical issues. *Australian education review* (Melbourne), no. 7, 5-45.

Cleverley, John; Wescombe, Christabel, (1979), *Papua New Guinea. Guide to sources in education*. Sydney, Sydney University Press.

Coffey, C. G. (ed.), (1977), *Teacher education for international understanding*. Canberra, Curriculum Development Centre.

Crittenden, Brian, (1983), Education theory: seeking its own voice. *Australian journal of education* (Melbourne), vol.27, no.3, 224-8.

Crossley, Anne (comp.), (1985), Bibliography of education in Papua New Guinea 1981-1982. *Papua New Guinea journal of education* (Port Moresby), vol.21, no.1.

Crossley, Michael, (1984), Strategies for curriculum change and the question of international transfer. *Journal of curriculum studies*, vol.16, no.1, 75-88.

Crossley, M.; Vulliamy, G., (1984), Case study research methods and comparative education. *Comparative education* (Oxford), vol.20, no.2.

D'Cruz, J. V.; Sheehan, P. J. (eds.), (1978), *The renewal of Australian schools*, 2nd ed., Hawthorn, Victoria, Australian Council for Educational Research.

Department of Education, (1985), *Growth of education since independence 1975-1985*. Port Moresby, Government Printing Office.

Director and Staff, Australian Council for Educational Research, (1973), *Education news* (Canberra), vol.14, ns. 5 and 6, 4-11.

Duke, Chris (comp.), (1971), *Teaching about Asia in Australian schools*. Canberra, Centre for Continuing Education, Australian National University.

Education Research Unit, University of Papua New Guinea, *Annual report* series.

Education Research Unit, University of Papua New Guinea, *Research report* series.

Francis, R. J. C. (ed.), (1976), *Unity and diversity in education*. Armadale, NSW, ACIES.

Hindson, Colin, (1982), Teacher education and education plans in Fiji, 1970-1980. *The South Pacific journal of teacher education* (Sydney), vol.10, no.2, 32-40.

Holdaway, E. A., (1976), The organization of educational research in Australia. *Education news* (Canberra), vol.15, no.10, 14-17.

Holmes, Brian, (1981), *Comparative education: some considerations of method*. London, George Allen and Unwin.

Hopkin, A. G., (1979), Cooperation or colonialism? A preliminary consideration of the scheme of co-operation between New Zealand and Fiji, 1924-1975. Paper presented at the Development Studies Association Conference, Reading University, September (mimeo).

Howie-Willis, Ian, (1980), A thousand graduates. Conflict in university *Development in Papua New Guinea, 1961-1976*. Canberra, Australian National University Pacific Research monograph no.3.

Irving, J. C., New Zealand's role in the development of education in the South Pacific. International Education Division, Department of Education, New Zealand, n.d. (mimeo).

Jones, Phillip, E., (1971), *Comparative education: purpose and method*, St. Lucia, University of Queensland Press.

Keeves, John P.; McKenzie, Phillip A., (1985), Interdisciplinary research in education in Australia. *Australian educational researcher* (Melbourne), vol.12, no.2, 31-43.

Kemmis, Stephen, (1984), Educational research as research for education. *Australian educational researcher* (Melbourne), vol.11, no.1, 28-37.

McLaren, Ian A., (1974), *Education in a small democracy: New Zealand*. London and Boston, Routledge and Kegan Paul.

Mitchell, F. W. (ed.), (1971), *Looking ahead in New Zealand education*. Wellington, A. H. & A. W. Reed.

Musgrave, Peter W., (1983), Rigour, relevance and respectability. *Australian journal of education* (Melbourne), vol.27, no.3, 229-233.

Osborne, Charles (ed.), (1970), *Australia, New Zealand and the South Pacific. A handbook.* London, Anthony Blond.

Pacific Circle Consortium, (1980), Pacific Circle Project, *Pacific Circle news* (Canberra), 1-45.

Pettman, Jan, (1981), Adaptation in Education in Papua New Guinea. *The South Pacific journal of teacher education* (Sydney), vol.9, no.1, 55-60.

Sheehan, Barry A. (ed.), (1983), *Comparative and international studies and the theory and practice of education.* Bundoora, ACIES.

Simkin, Keith, (1981), Comparative and sociological perspectives on third world development and education. *International review of education* (Hamburg), vol.27, no.4, 427-447.

Sociological Association of Australia and New Zealand, (1980), *Australian and New Zealand sociology 1971-78: an introduction.* Kelvin Grove, Queensland, SAANZ.

Teasdale, G. R., (1982), Australian educational aid relationships with South Pacific countries. Paper presented to the South Pacific Association of Teacher Educators Conference, Melbourne, July (mimeo).

Thomas, E. B. (ed.), (1976), *Papua New Guinea education.* Melbourne, Oxford University Press.

Thomas, R. Murray; Postlethwaite, T. Neville (eds.), (1984), *Schooling in the Pacific Islands.* Oxford, Pergamon.

Tioti, T.; Williams, Mary (co-ordinators), (1984), *Towards a strategy for higher education in Papua New Guinea.* Boroko, Commission for Higher Education.

Toh, Swee-Hin, (1983), The International Council for Education Development. *Journal of contemporary Asia*, vol.13, no.4, 409-431.

Trethewey, A. R., (1976), *Introducing comparative education.* London, Pergamon,.

Vulliamy, G.; Bray, M., (1985), Planning secondary education in Papua New Guinea: a comment on Bacchus. *Compare* (Oxfordshire), vol.15, no.1, 95-103.

Watson, John E., (1967), *Horizons of unknown power. some issues of Maori schooling.* Wellington, New Zealand Council for Educational Research.

Welch, A. R., (1980), Ideology, sociology and education: some developments and relationships. *Australian and New Zealand journal of sociology (Melbourne)*, vol.16, no. 2, 71-80.

Welch, A. R., (ed.), (1981), *The politics of educational change.* Armidale, NSW, ACIES.

Welch, A. R., (1985), The functionalist tradition and comparative education. *Comparative education* (Oxford), vol.21, no. 1, 5-19.

White, D. C., (1978), Comparisons as cognitive process, and the conceptual framework of the comparativist. *Comparative education* (Oxford), vol.14, no.2, 93-108.

Yates, Lyn, (1984), Comparison and the limits of comparison in working toward non-sexist education. In Burns and Sheehan (eds.), *op.cit.*, 27-38.

Africa

Alin Babs Fafunwa

This chapter on Africa south of the Sahara focuses principally on *Africans'* contribution to comparative and international education, with particular reference to institutions, personnel and publications. This qualification is vital, particularly at a time when the 'African scene' is dominated by European and American scholars who have better library facilities as well as government and foundation support for funding. If the African contribution is modest in terms of international publications, and numerous articles and much research conducted in this field have not been fully recognized or appreciated by non-African scholars, this is due largely to:

(a) the local nature of the journals produced by many African research centres and organizations;

(b) the shortage of foreign exchange needed for buying of international journals and selling of local African journals abroad; and

(c) the ethnocentricism of many European and American scholars.

The rapidly changing nature of African politics, economics and education make Africa a fertile ground for comparative studies by well-funded European and American scholars most of whom carry out their research work in Africa without the collaboration of their African colleagues; and more importantly, without sending a copy of their research findings to the host country, its national or university library. Three principal reasons responsible for this state of affairs are:

(a) ignorance of existing works done by African scholars;

(b) non-availability of such materials or references outside Africa; and

(c) sheer indifference on the part of most foreign scholars.

We must add that this criticism is not limited to the field of comparative and international education alone but applies to most areas of educational research and its publications.

The author is indebted to a number of African scholars who assisted in the collection of useful data for this paper: Mrs. Iyabo Abe of the University of Lagos, Professor O. C. Nwana of the University of Nigeria; Dr. F. X. Gichuru and Mr. H. Rwantabagu both of Kenyatta University, Kenya; Dr. N. K. Pecku of the University of Cape Coast, Ghana; Mr. R. Bernanajara of the Institut de Linguistique Appliquée, Madagascar, Professor N. D. Atkinson of the University of Zimbabwe; Professor I. O. Makinde of the University of Ife, Nigeria; Dr. O. Audsen of the University of Ildrin, Nigeria, Dr. P. J. Ntukidem of the University of Calabar, Nigeria and Dr. Theresa C. Sengova of the University of Sierra Leone. I am especially grateful to Dr. Seth J. Spaulding and Mr. Yuri Alferov, both of the International Bureau of Education, who assisted in no small way in gathering hard-to-get data from some African countries.

Historical

The history of comparative studies of education in Africa spans three historical periods:

(a) Pre-colonial;

(b) Colonial; and

(c) Post-independence.

Pre-colonial

African traders, travellers and pilgrims played a major role in comparative studies. There was an exchange of ideas and institutions, particularly in the economic, political, social and cultural fields. The borrowing of ideas and institutions was very important. Peoples and kingdoms borrowed generously from one another; citizens of one country travelled to and settled in another country, either establishing their own distinctive cultural enclave or merging with the people in the host countries. Hence, Nigerians are to be found today, for example, in Ghana, Senegal, Sudan, and their settlements go back to the last century and earlier. Likewise, Ghanaian, Liberian and Sierra Leonian enclaves are to be found in Nigeria, Senegal and Mali.

But for the travels and records of early Arab and African Islamic scholars between the sixth and the sixteenth centuries, little would have been known of early African civilizations.

The slave trade which ravaged Africa for over 300 years and deprived the continent of millions of its able-bodied men, women and children almost destroyed African civilization and identity, and set back African development by well over 300 years. It curtailed African travels and adventure into other lands within and outside Africa. The end of the slave trade by Europeans and African kings ushered in the colonial era in most parts of Africa. The colonialists, principally British, French, Spanish and Portuguese, controlled all internal and external activities - local and international trade, travel - thus restricting further the spirit of inquiry, adventure and travels.

Colonial

The introduction of a Western-cum-Christian type of education which dislodged the indigenous system and competed with the Koranic school system in certain parts of Africa resulted in a three-pronged system of education on the continent. Thus, children in some countries attended three 'schools' in one day:

1. indigenous education, which is mostly non-formal;

2. the Koranic school; and

3. the Western school.

Each 'school' represents a given religious school of thought; the Western school was Christian-based, the Koranic school was oriented towards Islam, whilst the indigenous system had its own set of religious beliefs.

Both the indigenous and the Koranic system of education are alive and well today, even though many scholars and educational authorities tend to ignore them. There are at present over 100,000 such schools (ranging from 10 to 500 pupils per school) in West Africa.

The vast exploration of Africa in the early nineteenth century and the evangelistic and trading activities that followed led to the eventual establishment of colonial rule over large portions of the continent. Among the principal 'winners' in the scramble were Britain and France. Thus, most countries in Africa, except Liberia and Ethiopia, were at different periods in their history under British or French colonial rule. Although Liberia was never a colony, its history as a nation is usually traced to the activities of the 'American Society for Colonizing the Free People of Color of the United States of America'. Similarly Ethiopia, though never colonized, also had some experience of incursions through the Italian occupation of 1935-41. Cameroon represents a country with a dual colonial experience, while Egypt stands as an exemplar of a country which had a diluted experience or multiple foreign interventions, having been occupied at different points in history by the French, the Ottoman Empire and the British.

Thus, either by way of occupation, direct colonial rule, or through massive migration (as was the case of Liberia), all the countries shared a common history of foreign intervention.

Foreign missions with an interest in Africa pioneered and dominated the educational sector for many years. This pioneering work in education should be judged in the context of the missions' early recognition of the supreme importance of education in the successful prosecution of their evangelistic tasks. In the later years of colonization, when colonial governments began to show interest in education, the general goal of education did not seem to have changed. There was merely a shift in emphasis from a purely religious education to a greater emphasis on the furtherance of colonial interests in Africa. All countries shared this common characteristic in the development of their educational systems.

There were also conscious and obvious attempts, first by the foreign missions and later by the colonial governments, to educate the African away from his culture. This feature was more pronounced in the French colonies where education meant 'frenchifying' the African. (This is not to minimize Britain's activities to this end). For example, indigenous schools, usually referred to as the bush schools, were converted into 'catechetical' schools (as in Kenya, for instance) and the first village elementary schools. The highly sophisticated indigenous PORO school system in Liberia and Sierra Leone was almost completely eradicated.

Furthermore, there was a lack of co-ordination, particularly in the early years of colonization when the missions, to the near-exclusion of the governments, dominated the provision of education to the people. Indeed, each mission or voluntary agency concentrated on its respective area of operation without much regard for developments outside it.

The missionary dominance of educational objectives limited the curriculum of the mission schools to the essentials of the Christian life. In addition to religion, reading, writing and arithmetic were made the pillars of every school curriculum. Such narrowness remained relatively unchanged even after increased government involvement in education. Religious education dominated the curriculum, while the entire school system became bookish and examination-oriented. This development was common to both British and French colonies, where schools were used basically for preparing the African for the semi-skilled job market. In fact, the extent and amount of education the colonial administrators were willing to give the Africans were the barest minimum necessary for such auxiliary positions as clerks, interpreters, preachers, and pupil-teachers.

Over this issue of the volume and quantity of education the British and French and other colonial powers showed considerable differences. Britain, under the policy of 'imperial trusteeship' which, according to Allison Smith, meant a 'limited liability and a reluctance to undertake large-scale projects because of the risks involved', pursued an educational policy which guaranteed a steady flow of African manpower. Britain, unlike France, recognized that the colonized countries might eventually revert to self-rule. Consequently, facilities were expanded to provide secondary and higher education much earlier than in the French colonies.

Britain's recognition of a possible return to self-rule, a possibility not acknowledged by France, accounted largely for the differences in their colonial education policies. For example, while Britain embarked on a policy of partnership soon after the Second World War, France intensified its policy of assimilation and association, intended to ensure continued and perpetual consolidation of French colonial influence and authority in Africa. In fact, the French saw their colonies as overseas units of Metropolitan France. Therefore, rather than develop an educational system which upheld African values, culture and ideals, determined efforts were made to make colonial education a close replica of the educational system of France. As far back as 1924 all mission schools in the French colonies were required to conform to a state model - that of the schools in France.

In terms of quality, structure, curriculum, examinations and certificates, the colonial schools were almost exactly like their counterparts in France. The curricula were decided by officials in the Ministry of Colonies in Paris. The African school child had to recite French poems, sing French hymns and learn French literature, geography and history. He had to contend with French teachers, particularly at the secondary schools (*lycées*) and, of course, grapple with a foreign language as the medium of instruction. By the time the child qualified for the *baccalauréat* he was, in the words of Mumford and Orde-Brown, 'French in all but the colour of his skin'. According to an on-the-spot assessment of the quality of French colonial schools, with the Bamako schools at Mali as reference, Mumford and Orde-Brown wrote:

The general impression gained from a visit to the Bamako School was that the institutions were in standing and equipment equal to the best that Europe can produce. Using the term in its biological sense, these schools are the 'growing points' of French civilization in Africa.[4] In general, French colonial education was essentially a means of producing a nucleus of native aristocracy who would eventually propagate French ideals and uphold French ways of life.

Britain, for its part, showed some concern for the adaptation of education to the African situation. The policy statement issued by the British government in 1925 as a result of the Phelps-Stokes Commission on African Education noted: 'Education should be adapted to the mentality, aptitudes, occupations and traditions of the various peoples, conserving as far as possible all sound and healthy elements in the fabric of their social life...'.[5] Consequently Britain suggested vocational education. But this preference was not backed up in practice, since there was no corresponding growth in industry, agriculture and commerce to guarantee recipients of vocational education a place on the job market. Hence, for example, the insistence on the primacy of industrial and manual education in Sierra Leone as far back as 1926 failed to change the people's preference for classics and literary academic work.

While Britain made efforts, though somewhat superficial, to adapt colonial education to African situations, France's colonial duty in the field of education was, according to Governor Roume, to produce native trained staff who must be auxiliaries in every field and assume the status of a carefully chosen elite. The other task of education, Governor Roume added, was to bring the masses through schools nearer to France and to transform the 'native' system of living. Thus, in place of British partnership and adaptation, the French stood for association and assimilation; and the French colonial schools system consequently remained wholly French.

Another feature of British colonial education was the principle of racial segregation that was perpetuated in Kenya and Tanzania. There was also the 'indirect rule' system in northern Nigeria, with its consequence of an imbalance of educational development between the northern and southern areas of that country.

In Kenya and Tanzania different schools were established for the different racial groups: Europeans, Asian, Arabs and Africans. One of the effects of this segregation was the lack of uniformity in standards and in facilities amongst the African schools. This became in the later years of colonization a target for attack by educated Africans in those countries. Another effect of this development was the growth of community involvement in education in the British colonies.

Apparently in recognition of the need to promote local participation in education, Britain decentralized the control of education. The Advisory Committee on Education in the Colonies, instituted in 1923, gradually shed its controlling powers, first to territorial departments of education, and later to regional and local bodies.

While higher education in the British colonies was largely the development of academic intellectualism, some measure of professionalization and vocational education was introduced by the French. Mali, as an example of the French system, had separate specialized institutions to cater for the different professions and vocational trades. In Nigeria, for example, trade centres were opened at the secondary level while at the higher education level the Yaba Higher College offered specialization in medicine, agriculture, engineering, surveying and teacher training.

In all the countries all educational institutions, including primary schools, were fee-paying under the colonial system. Furthermore, primary education expanded disproportionately to secondary education, while higher education was pathetically inadequate. Although primary education was expanded, illiteracy was widespread. Primary schools were few and scattered; pupils had to walk long distances to school.

Post-independence

Between 1956 and 1964 35 African countries out of a total of 50 regained their independence from their erstwhile colonial masters. With independence all the new African nations without exception saw education as the key to their social and economic development and cultural revival. In the words of Ahmadou Touré of Mali:

> 'Independence in 1960 ushered in a general revival of nationalist feeling among the generality of the people. From time to time, attempts were made to develop a truly Malian system of thinking and living. Everyone was urged to shake off the yoke of colonization and think and behave Malian. To this end, a general reform of education was embarked upon between 1960 and 1962, the product of which was a Malian school system distinct in character and purpose from the colonial school system. In the past colonial era education was seen as a sure weapon of nation building, development and modernization'.[6]

As with Mali, major educational reforms took place in several other African countries Togo, (1959, 1967, 1971), Senegal (1971), Tanzania (1969), Benin (1973), Somalia (1969), Nigeria (1969, 1973, 1976), Cameroon (1967, 1973), Ghana (1961, 1974), Kenya (1967, 1973), Lesotho (1977), Liberia (1970).[7]

All 50 independent African countries have experienced phenomenal growth in educational development since their attainment of self-determination. Practically all have accepted a minimum of six-year primary education as a fundamental human right for every African child. Consequently enormous expansion has taken place in terms of school buildings, facilities and equipment, as well as of pupils and teachers.

During the first decade of independence (1960s and 1970s) enrollments doubled or even trebled in some countries, and teachers (qualified and unqualified) were recruited both locally and abroad. Some countries earmarked between 30 per cent and 40 per cent of their recurrent budgets for education. All African countries without exception believed that education would help transform their economies and improve the lot of their people. Large and elaborate buildings, sophisticated equipment, foreign aid, etc. were generously provided during this early period. Indeed, many countries achieved in five to ten years what the erstwhile colonial governments had failed to accomplish in one hundred years of colonial rule.

But by the next decade of independence (in the 1970s and early 1980s) the governments and the people of many African countries began to realize that education was not bringing quick economic and social changes. Instead, the educational enterprise was claiming more funds and becoming too expensive for poor countries to finance.

The growth of comparative studies in education since independence

As already mentioned, the early African kingdoms had a long history of inter-cultural contacts and exchanges through trade and travels. Even the slave trade had its own redeeming feature - many ex-slaves returned to Africa with Western ideas and concepts and these influenced African education in no small measure during the early stages of Western education. They brought with them a touch of Christianity and a smattering of Western education and culture. Thus in their own way they influenced the development of comparative education in Africa.

During the colonial era students sent to Britain or France by their parents, guardians or missionaries returned with glowing reports of advances in the metropolitan country with particular reference to education, politics, trade, religion and culture. However, comparative education as a serious field study is a post-independence phenomenon. Political independence, between 1956 and 1966 ushered in the establishment of higher educational institutions, *écoles supérieures*, universities, advanced teacher training colleges, etc. With the establishment of these higher educational institutions in English-speaking Africa and their equivalents in francophone Africa, the teaching of comparative education started in earnest. No teacher education programme was considered viable without a course or an historical foundations of education course.[8] Initially comparative studies as a course were limited to the study of the educational systems of Britain for anglophones and of France for francophones.

At first, the emphasis in comparative education courses in the ex-colonies was based on the principle of convergence and divergence or on 'comparing and contrasting' two or more systems of education. Practically all the earlier graduate teachers and professors, whether African or European, were educated abroad - principally in Britain and France, with only a handful from USA and Canada. Towards the end of the 1960s and early 1970s pressure was mounting for reform of education and the need to make education meet the needs of the new nations. This pressure was also accentuated by the new nations' membership of the United Nations and its specialized agencies, including UNESCO, IBE, IIEP, ILO, WHO, and UNICEF. As African delegates met other delegates from several countries and exchanged information and documents on the educational systems of advanced and other developing countries, their desire to re-examine their own system became more intense. The international exposure of African educators, administrators and planners was also increased by their attendance at (British) Commonwealth Education Conferences between 1960 and 1968 (and thereafter); the Afro-Anglo-American Teacher Education Programme for Africa (AAA) founded in 1960 (and which later became Association for Teacher Education in 1969), whose membership included all English-speaking Africa (Liberia, Ethiopia included); the Organization of African Unity (OAU), founded in 1961; and the Association of African Universities (AAU) founded in 1971. Both the latter embrace all universities in Africa except those in South Africa.

Several countries undertook educational reforms between 1960 and 1973, and it was no coincidence that the period of reform occurred when the countries were exposed to the various organizations mentioned above.

Such reform in education has tended to be more far-reaching in anglophone than in francophone Africa for two major reasons:

1. Anglophones have more contacts with other countries and organizations outside the British sphere of influence as compared with the francophones.
2. A more important influence is the assimilation theory of 'frenchifying' the African colonies and the British theory of non-assimilation. Consequently, the anglophones' rejection fostered early nationalism and the search for new associations outside the British sphere of influence.

Table I

Selected countries	1979/80	1980/81	1981/82	1982/83	1983/84	% change 79/80 to 83/84
		Number of students				
Botswana	116	123	196	195	236	+103%
Ghana	712	566	533	457	381	-46%
Kenya	1095	978	885	725	913	-17%
Malawi	281	293	286	397	298	+6%
Mauritius	754	570	433	284	273	-64%
Nigeria	5174	5165	5126	4515	3941	-24%
Sierra Leone	294	250	215	187	174	-41%
Tanzania	638	738	656	481	389	-39%
Uganda	218	232	209	178	180	-17%
Zambia	814	769	653	669	694	-15%
Zimbabwe	2205	1680	901	592	431	-80%

Source: Extract from *Statistics of overseas students in the United Kingdom 1983/84*, British Council.

Large numbers of African students also attend American universities. Thus out of some 340,000 students studying in the USA in 1983-84 no less than 20,000 came from Nigeria.

Today, the former British colonies have greater contact with the USA, Canada, Western Germany and others than the former French colonies have with those countries.

As a result of these contacts most of the 1960s and 1970s comparative educators in English Africa have been products of British, American, Canadian and German universities, whereas almost all the graduates of francophone Africa studied in Paris. Table I above shows the numbers of students from African Commonwealth countries attending British institutions of higher and further education between 1979-80 and 1983-84.

The source just quoted goes on to state:

'France is, after the United States, the world's largest receiver of overseas students. The total number of foreign students enrolled in higher education in France is estimated at 128,000, a figure over double that of student numbers in Britain. The largest percentage of foreign students in France is from Africa, mainly from Francophone countries.'

In 1984, there were some 60,000 students of African origin in France, representing about half of the total foreign student enrollment. However, French overseas student figures may be artificially inflated due to French citizenship regulations (many foreign students are long-term residents or were actually born there).

Personnel and institutions

Most anglophone comparative educators were also products of colleges and faculties of education at home and abroad, specializing in the arts, science, administration or curriculum development. Teaching and research in the field take place predominantly in a faculty, department or an institute or college of education. All universities with faculty and institutes of education in anglophone Africa (21 in all in 1975) offer courses in comparative education. Of the 23 universities in Nigeria today, 20 offer comparative education courses at the undergraduate level and ten offer postgraduate degree courses in the field. By the 1970s anglophone scholars started to extend their comparative studies to francophone Africa.[9]

Some of the leading institutions where postgraduate courses are offered and research is conducted for higher degree purposes include:

Anglophone

1. University of Ibadan, Nigeria
2. University of Ife, Nigeria
3. University of Nigeria, Nigeria
4. University of Benin, Nigeria
5. University of Lagos, Nigeria
6. University of Calabar, Nigeria
7. Ahmadu Bello University, Nigeria
8. University of Cape Coast, Ghana
9. University of Sierra Leone, Sierra Leone
10. Addis Ababa University, Ethiopia
11. University of Nairobi, Kenya (before 1972)
12. Makerer University, Uganda

Table II

University/Institution	No. of CE staff	Year of comm.	No. of C.Ed. courses	Remarks
1. Univ. of Nigeria, Nigeria	3	since 1961	1 undergrad course - 3 grad courses	
2. Univ. of Calabar, Nigeria	2	1981	1 undergrad course - 1 grad course	
3. Univ. of Ife, Nigeria	3 full time	1968	1 undergrad course grad. courses. Degrees of M.Ed., MA and PhD in comp. educ	Dept of Educ foundation offers M.Ed in comp. education
4. Univ. of Lagos	2	1970	1 undergrad course, 5 graduate courses	
5. Kenyatta Univ., Kenya	5 full time & part time	1972	1 undergrad course	Dept of Educ foundation offers M.Ed degree in comp. education
6. Cape Coast Univ., Ghana	4		1 undergrad course	
7. Univ. of Zimbabwe	1		2 years MA course in CE	
8. Univ. of Sierra Leone			1 undergrad course	
9. Institute of Linguistics, Madagascar	1		?	

13. Kenyatta University, Kenya
14. University of Khartoum, Sudan
15. University of Liberia

Francophone
16. University of Abidjan, Ivory Coast
17. University of Dakar, Senegal
18. University of Lomé, Benin Republic

Returns from a questionnaire sent to several African universities by the International Bureau of Education yielded responses from nine universities in six countries. Table II shows the break-down of the responses.

Courses offered in comparative education

Courses in comparative education for both undergraduate and graduate levels are usually offered by the department of education or the department of educational foundations or the department of educational administration and planning. The University of Ife (Nigeria) may be cited as typical, since its Faculty of Education in Nigeria is representative of many faculties of education where comparative education has been developed as a discipline up to M.Ed., MA and Ph.D. levels. The responsibility for teaching comparative education is assigned to the department of Educational Foundations and Counselling which is headed by a professor, three senior lecturers, four lecturers and four part-time staff drawn from other departments and named 'associate staff'. However, of the eight full-time staff, three are full-time comparative education lecturers, while others assist as the need arises.[10]

Description of courses

Undergraduates in education at Ife may choose the introductory comparative education course in the fourth year as one. The course is for one semester. Some *postgraduate* course descriptions are given below:

EFC. 627: Nigerian Education in World Perspective
　　The organization, financing, and purpose of the Nigerian educational system. The historical factors which developed the system and its rule in the society. Current issues and their historical development, comparison of the Nigerian system to those in selected other African countries, Asia, Europe and North America. Examination of current global issues in education.

EAP 619: Comparative Educational Administration
A comparative study of current administration of education in Nigeria and other selected countries and districts in West Africa, East Africa, the United States, the United Kingdom, Continental, Europe, Latin America, USSR, the East and others. Emphasis is on a comparative analysis of the problems and challenges of school-community relations, goals of education, management of resources, organization for effective management and others.

There will also be a passing reference to a comparative study of administration in various types of formal organization in education, business, government, health, religion, and other fields of activity in the Nigerian society.

DCE 611: Comparative Studies in Adult Education (3 units)
Philosophical approach to comparative education, scientific method and comparative education. The contribution of comparative education to comparative studies of adult education. Analytical models for comparative studies in life long education. Selected case studies.

EAP 641: Comparative Studies in Higher Education Systems
An analysis of higher educational systems in selected countries on such bases as organizational structures, administration, financing, curricula, relationship with national economics and problems. An application of selected international strategies (on a trial basis) to problems of higher education administration in Nigeria.

Centres and organizations

Besides universities and colleges of education which offer comparative education courses and seminars, other institutes and organizations are engaged in similar work. For example in Nigeria, the Nigeria Educational Research Council (NERC) established in 1964, the Comparative Education Study and Adaptation Centre (CESAC) and the International Centre for Educational Evaluation (ICEE) represent major centres in educational research. The NERC is a Federal Government unit designed to promote and co-ordinate educational research programmes and disseminate their findings throughout the country. It also promotes curriculum and textbook development for primary and teacher education courses. It was under the auspices of the NERC that the first national curriculum conference for Nigeria was held in 1969 and its recommendations gave birth to a new national policy on education that is a radical departure from the colonial-cum-British system. The new system, commonly styled the 6-3-3-4 system, emphasizes diversification of the curriculum and pre-vocational courses. In 1985 the NERC organized a national conference on 'Current Trends in Nigerian Education Research' on Nigerian educational structure, education policy, finance, *comparative education*, curriculum development, mother-tongue, early childhood, science, mathematics, social studies, special education, adult and community education, guidance and counselling, and tests and measurements.

At that conference C. E. Okonkwo presented a paper on 'Research in Comparative Education in Nigeria'. His references on articles and papers published on the subject numbered over 150 authored by Nigerian and other West African scholars.[11] Most of the papers cited appeared in the *West African journal of education*, based at the University of Ibadan, Nigeria. It is the oldest educational journal in Africa south of the Sahara. (The journal which is jointly sponsored by Nigeria, Ghana, Sierra Leone and Gambia (anglophone West Africa) celebrated its 25th anniversary in 1982.) *The Comparative Education Study and Adaptation Centres* (CESAC) was established in 1964 as a result of the report of a USAID financed 'Technical Education Abroad' team that visited a number of European countries in 1963. It is government supported and located at the University of Lagos. Its main interest lies in secondary education with particular reference to curriculum and textbook development in science, mathematics and technical subjects. It also holds seminars and workshops. In 1984 it organized the first 'International Conference on Comparative Education in Nigeria', which featured embassy representatives from Liberia, Togo, Guinea, China, USA, UK and USSR. It was at this 1984 International Conference that the new Nigerian Association for Comparative Education (NACE) was formally launched.

The International Centre for Educational Evaluation (ICEE), located at the University of Ibadan Institute of Education and established in 1972, is another research centre dealing with international education. The function of the Centre is threefold:

(a) training African evaluators from Nigeria and other countries;

(b) research, with emphasis on evaluation techniques and instruments; and

(c) contractual evaluation of specific educational projects from Nigeria and other parts of Africa.

The ICEE *training* programmes are of two kinds.

The Centre offers three regular programmes that provide for research training and evaluation skills at fairly high levels of sophistication:

1. M.Ed. (12 months); 2. M.Phil. (2 academic sessions); 3. Ph.D. (3 academic sessions)

Between 1972-1973 and 1979-1980 124 students (including three from India) passed through the training course.

Sponsorship

They have been sponsored by several agencies programmes. Science Education Programme for Africa (SEPA); African Mathematics Programme (AMP); Carnegie Foundation; Ford Foundation; The German Foundation for International Development (DSE) (on behalf of the African Curriculum Organization (ACO)); the Anglophone West African Research Consortium (AWARERC), with funds from the Ford Foundation; Commonwealth fund for Technical Co-operation (CFTC); the German Academic Exchange Programme(DAAD).

In addition, several students came on private sponsorship by their parents, or by employers. Makerer University, Kampala, have also sponsored two, and Nigerian Ministries of Education several students.

The centre organized an international training workshop for examiners of the Royal Society of Health, West Africa, in August 1979. It was attended by over 70 participants from three West African English speaking countries.

Individual members of staff of the ICEE have also participated in training programmes in other countries e.g.

1. Asian Regional Training Course in Educational Evaluation, Bangkok, Thailand Oct./Nov. 1978 (4 weeks)

2. Training programmes in

    (i) the Seychelles, (ii) Papua, New Guinea, and (iii) Cairo

3. In Monrovia Liberia on behalf of AWARERC.

Research in the Centre had a modest start with emphasis on individual research by staff and students. Some of the results have been published in journals. Over fifty research papers were published between 1974 and 1984. Examples of those related to comparative studies are:

1. J. K. Adu: A comparison of the academic achievement of project and non-project pupils of the Ife six year (Yoruba medium) primary education project - A Longitudinal Evaluation survey (M.Ed. Thesis).

2. A. Akinjagunla: A comparative Study of Project/non-project pupils of the Ife Six year Primary project in their emotional and social adjustment to Secondary Schools (M.Ed Thesis).

Recently however, the ICEE has steadily moved into bigger institutional research, largely through its membership of two international bodies: the International Association for Evaluation of Educational Achievement (IEA); and the International Association for Educational Assessment (IAEA).

Current researches for these bodies is: Second Mathematics Survey; classroom environment study; item banking project, (all IEA studies); trial and test administration by satellite (IAEA). Other projects in the area of mastery learning and teacher effectiveness are also being pursued.

As regards evaluation, five major projects have been completed:

1. the Namuramba Project in Uganda;

2. the Bendel State Primary Science Project in Nigeria;

3. the Teaching of Modern Mathematics in Mauritius;

4. the Ife six-year primary project in University of Ife, Nigeria;

5. the Trial of the UNESCO Nutrition curriculum.

Two other major evaluation projects are currently in progress.[12]

A significant step forward in dissemination efforts was taken in 1979 with the publication of the first number of the ICEE newsletter *Evaluation in Africa*. This has been favourably received in many quarters.

Several requests for evaluation have been made on which action was expected to start:

1. Development of basic tests in science and mathematics. This request was made by UNESCO.

2. Development of selection tests for nursing school candidates (from Nigerian Nursing Council).

3. Evaluation of curriculum materials developed by the Comparative Education Studies and Adaptation Centre (CESAC).

4. Evaluation of the training programme for teachers of health sciences.

The Network of Educational Innovation for Development in Africa (NEIDA) is an inter-African network for information and exchange in the field of educational innovation for development located in Dakar, Senegal. NEIDA is an arm of UNESCO established at the request of the Conference of Ministers of Education of African member states of West Africa (francophone and anglophone). A similar unit, the Regional Office for Education in Africa, BREDA is located in Nairobi, Kenya, East Africa. These two UNESCO centres provide platforms for African states to exchange ideas and information that are relevant to the educational needs of Africa. They also promote and encourage inter-regional collaboration in educational innovation and research.

Other international and inter-regional organizations that further comparative studies and international education directly or indirectly include:

(a) the Science Education Programme for Africa (SEPA) located in Accra, Ghana and established in 1971.

(b) the African Social Studies Programme (ASSP), based in Nairobi, Kenya.

(c) the Association for Teacher Education in Africa (ATEA), founded in 1970 as an off-shoot of the Afro-Anglo-American Programme for Teacher Education, founded in 1960. The ATEA was based at the University of Lagos and later moved to Fourah Bay College, Freetown, Sierra Leone.

The membership of ATEA comprises all faculties, departments and institutes of education in English-speaking Africa, numbering over 20 from 12 countries. Its aims and objectives are:

(a) to strengthen teacher education programmes in Africa through regular annual conferences of directors of institutes of education, ministries of education and international organizations interested in African teacher education programmes;

(b) to exchange staff and assist in developing staff for its members; and

(c) to conduct research and promote exchange of information among participating members.[13]

Nigeria alone has over twenty education societies, covering subject matter areas (science, mathematics, languages, physics, chemistry, history, etc.) and professional organizations such as the Nigerian Education Administration and Planning Society and the Educational Studies Association of Nigeria.

The Nigerian Academy of Education was founded in February 1985. Similar organizations flourish in some other African countries. Most of these organizations publish their own journals in their own areas of specialization. However, they carry articles on comparative education studies from time to time.

Other international organizations with African membership include the African Curriculum Organization (ACO) based in Ibadan, Nigeria; the International Council on education for Teaching (ICET) based in Washington DC; the Association of African Universities (AAU) based in Accra,

Ghana; the International Congress of African Studies (ICAS) based in Ibadan; the Commonwealth Education Conference based in London; and the French-Speaking Comparative Education Association (Association francophone d'education comparée) (AFEC), based in France.

The largest gathering of African and Black scholars ever assembled in one place was the 1977 Second World Black and African Festival of Arts and Culture (FESTAC '77) which took place in Lagos in February, 1977. The theme of the COLLOQUIUM was 'Black civilization and education'. More than 200 scholarly papers were presented at the three-week Colloquium attended by people from African countries, and people of African descent from the West Indies, North America and Western Europe.

The dialogue offered a unique opportunity for comparative African studies in the arts, philosophy, literature, languages, history, education, government, communication, science and technology.

A new Pan-African Organization known as the 'Council for the Promotion of Research in Education Development (COPREDA) was established in Dakar, Senegal in June 1985. The theme of the inaugural meeting was, 'Whither education research in Africa?' COPREDA plans to hold a continental congress on 'Education and Development in Africa' in 1987.

The major goals of education and comparative studies

The major role of education in the developing countries is to make education relevant to the needs and aspirations of the people. Consequently major emphasis is placed on curriculum reform, educational planning, financing of education, alternative systems of education including the re-examination of the indigenous African educational systems, mother-tongue education, non-formal education, vocational and technical education, education and employment, literacy, women's education. The guiding principle underlying the study of comparative education in Africa is therefore to enable students and planners to acquaint themselves with how other countries have planned and operated their educational systems to meet the needs and aspirations of their peoples, with particular reference to socio-economic and political developments. Consequently, comparative studies in most African countries are not carried out for their own sake, but with a view to reforming African education, and interest is thus directed to understanding the forces which shape educational development in other countries.

Attendance at inter-African and international conferences, workshops and seminars by African countries has yielded dividends in many ways. The account of the work of the International Centre for Educational Evaluation already given is a good example of how African countries have influenced one another.

The bi-annual conferences of the Association for Teacher Education in Africa held in different parts of Africa are another example. This anglophone association (including Liberia and Ethiopia) has exchanged staff, jointly prepared books of reading on Foundations of African Education and conducted a global survey on 'Supply of secondary level teachers in English-speaking Africa' in collaboration with the Overseas Liaison Committee of the American Council on Education. The Association of African Universities exchanges external examiners for degree examinations, although this is limited to anglophone members of the association. In 1986 it set up a clearing house at the Anambra State University, Owerri on international and regional studies and publications.

The anglo- and francophone members cooperate in an internship programme whereby anglophone students in French spend a term at a francophone country and *vice-versa*, particularly among West African countries (Nigeria, Ghana, Sierra Leone and Benin, Togo, Ivory Coast and Senegal).

The University of Ife Six Year (Yoruba Medium) Project in Nigeria has played host to scholars from Mali and the Ivory Coast who were developing mother-tongue programmes in their respective countries. Members of the project have also served as consultants in Liberia, Togo, Benin, Lesotho, and Ivory Coast.

The (Primary) Science Education Programme for Africa (SEPA), which had its origin in Nigeria, now embraces fourteen African countries. SEPA is an organization of fourteen African countries designed to promote the teaching of primary science in African primary schools.

Most of the consultants who have visited African countries to promote, train and help develop the elementary science units and programmes are drawn largely from Nigeria (70 per cent), Sierra Leone, Ghana, Lesotho, Kenya and the United States.

Research trends and priorities

Major research trends and priorities are in the area of educational reform, education innovation, adult and mass education, educational and employment, evaluation of the fitness of the educational system and educational financing. There has not been any major shift from these directions in the past twenty-five years as 'the crisis in education' has almost become a permanent feature in developing countries and this state of affairs may continue until an alternative system is found.

Many anglophone universities have widened their educational horizon by moving away from US and UK comparative studies to studies of French African countries and other developing areas, as well as those relating to other European, Asian and American countries.

The francophone institutions are also looking beyond France for new ideas and factors which shape educational development, e.g., federal system of government, religious factors, political ideologies, social, economic, racial factors, etc.

In the past few years francophone and anglophone universities have been promoting exchange of staff and scholars and both groups have visited the sites of innovative projects in each other's country.

Methods of research

An examination of the available journals, papers, articles and books produced by African comparative educators in the last twenty years shows that four major research methods are employed in the following order:

1. Internal comparison, which is commonly used by undergraduates and graduates for dissertations, etc.;
2. Historical and descriptive, often coupled with comparative statistics and surveys;
3. Cross-national/cross-cultural comparison; and
4. Theoretical and methodological.

In a continent where accurate data and access to information are hard to come by, the descriptive approach is a valuable instrument. For instance, curriculum development, which is one of the major pre-occupations in Africa, is an on-going activity. This calls for formative evaluation, demanding direct observation and content analysis of text materials, etc. An accurate description of two or more educational systems is useful and worthwhile to gain an insight into those systems and our own. Whilst descriptive and historical methods predominate, there is a growing interest in cross-cultural and cross-national studies. There is also an increase in theoretical and methodological papers; however, the descriptive method and the theoretical-cum-analytical approach are not mutually exclusive. It is therefore unlikely that African scholars will abandon one for the other. Indeed when theoretical and analytical methods are used the average administrator, the teacher or the ministry of education official still requires an accurate descriptive summary of the research if it is going to be of practical use.

Major research projects and publications

Major research projects in Africa in the past fifteen to twenty years have concerned educational reform, with particular reference to curriculum development at the primary, secondary and tertiary levels. Some of the well known projects include Ivory Coast's TV and radio education; the Togo, Mali and Benin Republics' reforms in education; education by radio in Kenya; Nigeria's National Curriculum Conference of 1969 which led to the introduction of the new national policy on education in 1979; Tanzania's education for self-reliance scheme; Ethiopia's Youth service programme for undergraduates; Nigeria's one-year Youth service programme for graduates and Ghana's Young Pioneer's scheme.

The now famous Ife University Six-Year Primary Education Project (SYPP) in Yoruba medium is the longest longitudinal study and evaluation on education in Africa. It is certainly also the only one of its kind on the use of mother-tongue as medium of education from Primary I to VI that has a comprehensive evaluation instrument. The project, which is now in its sixteenth year was launched in January 1970, with Yoruba as medium of instruction and English as a second language.

The experiment is predicated on the hypotheses that:

(a) the child will benefit culturally, socially, linguistically and cognitively through the use of his mother-tongue as the medium of instruction throughout the six years of primary school;

(b) that his command of English will be improved considerably if he is taught English as an entirely separate subject by a specially trained teacher throughout the six years.

The main objective of the project is to develop a coherent primary education for the child and make him an intelligent citizen of his country.

The Ife project has generated considerable interest in some African and non-African countries, e.g. Mali, Togo, Ivory Coast and Burkina Faso and some USA and Canadian universities. UNESCO has from time to time invited some of the Ife project members to serve as consultants on the use of mother-tongue to a number of African countries in the last ten years.

The project has also generated a considerable number of research papers, publications and theses in Nigeria, particularly at the University of Ife and University of Ibadan. Two Malian scholars have also conducted part of their Ph. D research at Ife. Some of the dissertations dealt with comparative studies and evaluation.

Research topics and publications in local and international journals by African comparative educators cover a wide range; curriculum development, teacher education and development, mother-tongue education, education and social dynamics, policy and practice in education, school and agriculture, Koranic education, traditional African education, technical and vocational education, politics and education, primary, secondary and tertiary education, moral education, pre-school, non-formal education, 'drop-outs' and 'drop-ins', and trends and issues.

Table III shows the field of interest and current research in some African universities faculties and departments of education:

Journals and publications

In addition to the journals published by the various educational associations, the various faculties and institutes of education publish their own. Nigeria possesses many such journals, but the most widely circulated educational journal in Anglophone Africa is the *West African journal of education*, which is over 25 years old. The Nigerian Educational Research Council also produces *Education and development*.

A few African scholars' works appear occasionally in *Prospects*, the *International review of education*, and *Comparative education review*, but many African scholars in the field of comparative education are less known and less quoted by western scholars.

Book publications

The only known book on comparative education written by Africans (anglophone and francophone combined) is *African education: a comparative survey* in which twelve African authors contributed a chapter on their own country.

The study revealed that all the countries studied have experienced phenomenal growth in education, as compared with their respective colonial periods. All over Africa education has been liberated from the structures of service to the few to freedom of educational opportunity for the many. Increased primary school enrollment has been one of the direct results of a significant development in post-independence Africa.

Kenya introduced partially free primary education in 1971 when a presidential decree abolished tuition fees in some parts of the country considered educationally backward, and in 1974 this was extended to all

Table III

University	Field of Interest	Current research theme
University of Ife Nigeria	Comparative teacher education, secondary education and psychology	Towards an improved teacher structure in Nigeria. A comparative perspective of the American, Indian and Ghanaian systems
Kenyatta University Kenya	African Francophone and Anglophone educ systems	(a) Television education in Ivory Coast; (b) basic educ in the Ujamaa villages of Tanzania
University of Zimbabwe	Education in southern Africa	Multi-cultural education in southern Africa
University of Nigeria	Comparative and international education - Third World nations	Problems of education in Asia, Latin America and Africa
University of Calabar Nigeria	International comparative education	Comparative analysis of elementary school teachers' attitude toward visual art education: Nigeria and United States of America
University of Cape Coast Ghana	Comparative education: school systems, adult education, teacher education	Teacher education in selected African countries - a comparative study
Institut de Linguistique Appliquée Madagascar	Lange et culture dans le cadre de l'enseignement des langues problems	L'enseignement des langues à Madagascar

parts of Kenya. Similarly, primary education became free everywhere in Nigeria in 1976.

The introduction of universal primary education and the resultant increase in primary school enrollment has had a tremendous impact on secondary education. Firstly, more secondary schools have had to be opened and the existing ones expanded to offer more places to the increasing number of primary school leavers aspiring to secondary education. Secondly, the boarding system for secondary education received less emphasis in preference to the day system. In places like Tanzania, for example, the boarding system was abolished. Given the explosive bottleneck in access to secondary education all over Africa and the acute accommodation problem in the universities, we predict an entirely day system operating not only for the secondary schools but also for the universities.

Another mark of progress in African education is in the area of increased facilities for higher education. Before independence most African countries had no universities of their own instead there were, as in British East Africa, territorial universities serving a number of countries. Today every African country has at least one university. For example, Ghana has three universities, Kenya and Liberia two universities each, Sierra Leone has one (and an affiliate institution of university status), and Nigeria has as many as twenty-five. Indeed Africa has recorded phenomenal progress in the provision of more education for more people. But what seems lacking in most African countries is sufficient concern for the quality and relevance of the education provided.

It should be emphasized that with the expansion of education facilities at all levels and the corresponding financial commitment, education in relation to their people's needs and aspirations. The traditional western system which Africa has tended to cling to almost religiously should be jettisoned to intensify the search for newer and more relevant systems, because not only the volume of education but also its very nature demands change to meet the challenge of a rapidly expanding economy and population, and the attendant rising expectations of youth and adults alike.

All African countries have placed undue emphasis on formal education and look down on non-formal and informal systems of learning; even the age-long African traditional apprenticeship system of learning by doing (on-the-job-training) has been largely ignored by the formal system because it is a humble activity as compared with 'school' learning. This has resulted in the 'certificate syndrome', the demand for diplomas, certificates and degrees of all types.

Furthermore, even the modest efforts made by some African countries to accelerate the tempo of development and raise the level of national income is continually hampered by lack of adequate numbers and quality of technical, scientific, professional and managerial personnel for implementing development programmes, in a number of professional and technical occupations Africans are poorly represented, so that their countries rely heavily on external source of recruitment in order to carry out even the most modest activities in some important sectors of their educational and economic life.

Comparative education societies in Africa

The only known comparative education society in Africa south of the Sahara was founded in August, 1984 in Nigeria and sponsored by the only known government-established comparative Education Unit in Africa - Comparative Education Studies and Adaptation Centre (CESAC) located at the University of Lagos. The new society is styled the Nigerian Association for Comparative Education (NACE). Its main aims and objectives are similar to other societies in other countries and it plans to launch the first issue of its journal, entitled the *Journal of Nigerian Association for Comparative Education* in August, 1986.

Future prospects

Comparative and international education as a discipline in Africa is of recent development even though comparative activities date back many centuries. While their contemporaries in Europe and America were exploring new academic fields in the last twenty-five years, most African scholars were pre-occupied with curriculum development, writing of basic primary and secondary education text books for the children of their respective countries.

A number of other constraints militate against the rapid development of this field of study in Africa. Restricted financial resources hamper scholarships. The governments of most developing countries in Africa have not given enough attention to research in education and the private sector has also shown little interest. Consequently many African scholars have limited contact with their international colleagues. Over eight percent of works, articles and journals produced in Africa by African scholars have never crossed the Atlantic. Moreover, foreign exchange is another deterrent to African scholars from the purchase of foreign journals. On the other hand Western scholars, like the anthropologists of old, are having a field day in

Africa because of its rapidly changing circumstances. While their African colleagues are wrestling with the change, their more leisurely colleagues from the West, armed with funds, come on the scene to conduct research. Unfortunately many of such researchers hardly contact their counterparts in the host country or inquire about previous work done in the same or related area before commencing their work. Worse still, the host country scholars have to visit western libraries in Europe or America if they wish to have access to the study done on their country or consult their journal. An examination of articles published in western journals by western scholars on African education reveals unpardonable ethnocentrism. African scholars have published books and articles on their educational systems from primary to tertiary level over the decades and such materials are in their respective country's libraries and universities. Some have even been documented in American and British libraries. But these are rarely quoted by Western scholars. The impression needs to be erased that African scholars have not examined their own system and that only Western scholars have studied the African systems.

Comparative and international education studies are gradually gaining momentum in Africa. A large number of studies have been conducted and published in local journals, most of which are to be found in small libraries of colleges of education and in bigger university libraries scattered all over the world. A national Comparative Education Society has been established in one of the African countries. The next few years will witness more, not less growth in this field.

Comparative education studies has been largely hampered in Africa by shortage of personnel, inadequate statistics and shortage of funds. Furthermore greater attention needs to be directed at identifying the various factors that contribute to or militate against the formal and the non-formal systems of education; among these are religious, economic, cultural, historical and political forces both from within and outside the environment where the educational system operates.

The next decade in comparative education and studies will witness considerable improvement in personnel as the universities continue to produce graduates in this field and as more training facilities become available. Comparative studies will become more sophisticated both qualitatively and quantitatively. The latest development as revealed by this study, that is, the launching of a new Comparative Education Society in Nigeria in 1984, the possibility of a Ghanaian counterpart in 1986 and the newly proposed franco-anglophone 'Council for the Promotion of Research in

Education and Development' (COPREDA) based in Dakar, Senegal augurs well for the future of comparative education studies in Africa. These and other comparative education societies of the future will publish journals that are exclusively devoted to the field. With this new development there will be more intra and inter-state, intra and inter-continental collaborative efforts among scholars in the field.

Bibliography

Abeje, H. Y., (1938), New approaches for creating universal learning opportunities. *Convergence* (Toronto, Ont.), vol. XVI, no. 2, 23-29.

Adaralegbe, A., ed., (1972), *A philosophy for Nigerian education*. Report of the Nigerian National Curriculum Conference, September, 1969. Ibadan, Nigeria, Heinemann Educational Books (Nigeria)

Commonwealth Education Conference, 4th, Lagos, 1968. *Report of the fourth commonwealth education conference, February 26-March 9, 1968*. Lagos, Commonwealth Secretariat, n.d.

Adeniyi, B. F., (1983), A comparative study of indigenous and western style of adult education systems in Yorubaland, 1842 - 1945. Ife, Nigeria, University of Ife. [Thesis - M. Phil.]

Adesina, S., (1977), *Planning and educational development in Nigeria*. Lagos, Educational Industries.

Ahmed, M., (1983), Critical educational issues and non-formal education. *Prospects* (Paris, UNESCO), vol. XIII, no. 1, 35-43.

Akinpelu, J. A., (1974), The educative processes in non-literate societies: an essay in the anthropological foundations of education. *West African journal of education* (Ibadan, Nigeria), vol. 18, no. 3, October, 413-422.

Akintola, J. M., (1981), Educational change in Africa. *Education and development* (Lagos), vol. 1, no. 2, 169-181.

Ameme, M., Comparative study of educational systems of Nigeria, 1960-1983. *Journal of research in curriculum* (Lagos), special issue I, 113-132.

Ankrah-Dove, L., (1982), The deployment and training of teachers for remote rural schools in less-developed countries. *International review of education* (The Hague), vol. 28, no. 1, 3-27.

Asiedu-Akrofi, K., (1977), *School organization in modern Africa*. Tema, Ghana, Ghana Publishing Corp.

Asiedu, K., (1979), The development of adult literacy in Ghana since 1944. *Adult education in Nigeria*, no. 4, December, 69-82.

Asiwaju, A. I., (1975), Formal education in western Yorubaland, 1889-1960: a comparison of the French and British colonial systems. *Comparative education review* (Los Angeles, CA), vol. 19, no. 3, October, 434-450.

Association for Teacher Education in Africa. Conference, Kampala, 1974. *Reform in the professional education of teachers in Africa*. Freetown, ATEA.

Association for Teacher Education in Africa. Conference, Addis Ababa, 1972. *Innovation in teacher education*. Freetown, ATEA.

Association for Teacher Education in Africa. Conference, Ife, Nigeria, 1973. *Innovative projects and experiments in education*, edited by A. B. Fafunwa, et al. Freetown, ATEA.

Association for Teacher Education in Africa. Conference, Nairobi, 1975. *Universal education in Africa and its implications for teacher education*. J. B. C. Bigala, ed., Freetown, ATEA.

Avose, O., (1974), Educational development in sub-Saharan Africa: cross-national longitudinal study. Toronto, Ont., University of Toronto. [Thesis]

Bajah, S. T., (1981), Primary science curriculum development in Africa. *European journal of science education* (London), vol. 3, no. 3, 259-269.

Bamgbose, A., (1983), Mother-tongue medium and scholastic attainment in Nigeria. *Prospects* (Paris, UNESCO), vol. XIII, no. 1, 35-43.

Barkatoolah, A., (1982), L'absence d'évaluation remet-elle en cause l'existence d'une réforme? Le cas de I'Ile Maurice. *Éducation comparée* (Svres, France), no. 28, octobre, 7-11.

Barra, Y., (1982), Evaluation de la réforme de l'éducation au Bénin. *Éducation comparée* (Svres, France), no. 28, octobre, 13-16.

Bojuwoye, O., (1984), Counselling the Nigerian client: a matter of cultural values. *International education* (Knoxville, TN), vol. 13, no. 2, 34-43.

Bude, U., (1983), The adaptation concept in British colonial education. *Comparative education* (Abingdon, UK), vol. 19, no. 3, 341-355.

Chabou, M. D., (1982), L'évaluation des réformes de l'enseignement supérieur entre l'emprise politique et les exigences d'une pédagogie à caractre scientifique. *Éducation comparée* (Svres, France), no. 28, octobre, 27-33.

Cowen, R., (1981), *International yearbook of education*, vol. XXXIII - 1981. Paris, UNESCO.

Cowen, R., (1983), *International yearbook of education*, vol. XXXIV - 1982. *Educational structures*. Paris, UNESCO.

Damiba, A., (1981), La recherche en éducation en Haute-Volta. *International review of education* (The Hague), vol. 27, no. 2, 135-139.

Dawoud, M., (1982), Une grille d'évaluation de la compétence du professeur. *Éducation comparée* (Svres, France), no. 28, octobre, 35.

Diambomba, M., (1981), Research and external aid: a view from the recipient side. *Prospects* (Paris, UNESCO), vol. XI, no. 3, 352-359.

Ezeomah, C., (1983), *The education of nomadic people: the Fulani of Northern Nigeria*. Driffield, UK, Nafferton Books.

Ezewu, E. E., (1983), *Sociology of education*. Ikeja, Nigeria, Longman Nigeria; London, Longman.

Educational reforms and innovations in Africa. Paris, UNESCO, 1978. (International Bureau of Education. Experiments and innovations in education, no. 34).

Fafunwa, A. B., (1984), Education in developing countries. Paper delivered at Comparative Education Study and Adaptation Centre Conference on Comparative Education in Nigeria, August.

Fafunwa, A. B., (1974), Education in the mother-tongue: a Nigerian experiment. *Journal of African studies* (Berkeley, CA), vol. 1, no. 3.

Fafunwa, A. B., (1978), School is other people: for African children the village community is one big family of teachers. *UNESCO courier* (Paris, UNESCO), 31st yr, May, 11-15.

Fafunwa, A. B., (1974), Reform in higher education: an international perspective. In Allen, D. W., et al., eds. *Reform, renewal and reward:* proceedings of the International Conference on improving university teaching, October, 35-44.

Fafunwa, A. B.; Aisiku, J. U., eds., (1982), *Education in Africa: a comparative survey*. London, George Allen & Unwin.

Fumo, C. A., (1984), Accelerated training centres for workers in the Peoples' Republic of Mozambique. *Convergence* (Toronto, Ont.), vol. XVII, no. 1, 1-8.

Conference of Ministers of Education of African Member States, (1976), *Final report*. Paris, UNESCO (ED/MD/41).

Galadanci, S. A., (1971), Education of women in Islam with reference to Nigeria. *Nigerian journal of Islam* (Ile-Ife, Nigeria), vol. 1, no. 2, 5-10.

Habte, A.; Heyneman, S., (1983), Education for national development: World Bank activities. *Prospects* (Paris, UNESCO), vol. XIII, no. 4, 471-479.

Habte, A., (1983), Where the Bank is going in the field of education. *Canadian and international education* (Calgary, Alta.), vol. 12, no. 1, 65-74.

Haddad, W. D., (1983), The World Bank's Education Sector policy paper. *Canadian and international education* (Calgary, Alta.), vol. 12, no. 1, 11-27.

Holmes, B., (1980), *International yearbook of education* vol. XXXII - 1980. Paris, UNESCO.

Ikwue, I. O., (1984), Effective educational language planning in Nigeria. *International education journal*, vol. 1, no. 1, 39-60.

Innovations in African education (1976), UNESCO, Paris. (ED.76/MINEDAF/REF.4) [Paper prepared for the Conference of Ministers of Education of African Member States, Lagos, 1976]

Johnson, M. A., (1974), Recent trends in the education system of francophone West Africa. *West African journal of education* (Ibadan, Nigeria), vol. XVIII, no. 2, June, 189-196.

Kanganga, E., (1982), Comrades in development or suspicious aliens? *Times higher education supplement* (London), no. 497, 14 May, 14.

Kassam, Y., (1982), Formal, nonformal and informal modes of learning: a glimpse of the Tanzanian experience. *International review of education* (The Hague), vol. 28, no. 2, 263-267.

Kouyaté, M., (1978), The teacher shortage and peer teaching in Africa. *Prospects* (Paris, UNESCO), vol. VIII, no. 1, 33-46.

Kuhanga, N. A., (1983), The use of higher education institutions for training and research in education. *International journal of educational development* (Oxford, UK), vol. 3, no. 3, 313-323.

Lassa, P., (1983), The quality of learning in Nigerian primary education: a note on curriculum and community needs - an example from mathematics. *International review of education* (The Hague), vol. 29, no. 2, 245-246.

Lulat, Y. G.-M., (1984), International students and study-abroad programs: select bibliography. *Comparative education review* (Chicago, IL), vol. 28, no. 2, May, 300-339.

Lungu, G. F., (1983), Some critical issues in the training of educational administrators for developing countries of Africa. *International journal of educational development* (Oxford, UK), vol. 3, no. 1, 85-96.Macauley, J. I., (1982), The effect of language of instruction on selected instructional processes and outcomes. Ibadan, Nigeria, University of Ibadan. [Thesis]

Maliyamkono, T. L.; Ishumi, A. G. M.; Wells, S. J., (1982), *Higher education and development in Eastern Africa: a report of the Eastern African universities research project on the impact of overseas training on development*. London, Heinemann Educational.

Maliyamkono, T. L., (1980), The school as a force for community change in Tanzania. *International review of education* (The Hague), vol. XXVI, No. 3, 335-347.

Mammo, G., (1982), The national literacy campaign in Ethiopia. *Prospects* (Paris, UNESCO), vol. XII, no. 2, 193-199.

Matiru, B., (1983), Training literacy teachers through distance education. *Bildung und erziehung* (Köln, Germany FR), 36 Jhrg., Heft 3, September, 327-333.

Matogo, B. B. W. K., (1973), The rationalization of education for librarianship in the UK, US, Ghana and E. Africa. London, University College. [Thesis - M. A.]

May-Parker, J. A, (1977), study of attitudes and home background factors associated with wastage among secondary school girls in Sierra Leone. Glasgow, UK, University of Glasgow. [Thesis]

M'Bow, A., (1983), Adult education central to development. *Convergence* (Toronto, Ont.), vol. XVI, no. 1, 27-29.

Mohapeloa, J. M., (1981), The university and the schools in developing countries. *Higher education* (Amsterdam), vol. 10, no. 3, May, 275-295.

Mirie, N. wa., (1980), Literacy for and by the people: Kenya's Kamirithu Project. *Convergence* (Toronto, Ont.), vol. 13, no. 4, 55-60.

Mosha, H. J., (1983), United Republic of Tanzania: folk development colleges. *Prospects* (Paris, UNESCO), vol. XIII, no. 1, 95-103.

Mukherjee, A.; Umar, F., (1978), Attitudes, attitude change, and mathematics achievements: a study in Nigeria. *International review of education* (The Hague), vol. XXIV, no. 4, 518-521.

Mukweso, M.; Papagiannis, G. J.; Milton, S., (1984), Education and occupational attainment from generation to generation: the case of Zaire. *Comparative education review* (Chicago, IL), vol. 28, no. 1, February 1984, 52-68.

Nduka, O. A., (1980), Moral education in the changing traditional societies of sub-Saharan Africa. *International review of education* (The Hague), vol. XXVI, no. 2, 153-170.

Niane, D. T., (1985), Problmes d'éducation et identité nationale en Afrique de l'ouest depuis 1960. Congress of International African Studies, December 16-22, Ibadan, Nigeria.

Njiri, R. Stutts, (1975), Kenya and North America: education comparison of the black population. Amherst, MA, Education Department, University of Massachusetts.

Nkinyangi, J. A., (1982), Access to primary education in Kenya: the contradictions of public policy. *Comparative education review* (Chicago, IL), vol. 26, no. 2, June, 199-217.Nwagwu, N. A., (1978), The politics of universal primary education in Nigeria, 1955-1977. *Compare* (Oxford, UK), vol. 8, no. 2, 149-157.

Nwagwu, N., (1981), The impact of changing conditions of service on the recruitment of teachers in Nigeria. *Comparative education* (Dorchester-on-Thames, UK), vol. 17, no. 1, March, 81-86.

Nwamuo, C., (1981), Nigeria's higher educational philosophy: a review. *International education* (Knoxville, TN), vol. 11, Fall, 37-43.

Nwankwo, J. I., (1980), The gap between planning and implementation in Nigerian education. *Prospects* (Paris, UNESCO), vol. X, no. 2, 221-233.

Nyirenda, J. E., (1982), Distance learning and access to secondary education in Africa. *International education* (Knoxville, TN), vol. 11, Spring, 7-12.

Obanya, P.; Arinze, E., (1983), *The use of cultural heritage in Nigerian education.* Lagos, National Commission for Museum and Monuments.

Obembé, J.-F., (1983), Die 'École du Peuple' und das bildungswesen in der volksrepublik Kongo. *Vergleichende Pädagogik* (Berlin, German DR), 19 Jahrg., Heft 4, 424-427.

Ocaya-Lakidi, D., (1980), Towards an African philosophy of education. *Prospects* (Paris, UNESCO), vol. X, no. 1, 13-25.

Ogunsanya, M., (1983), The student factor in the achievement of school organizational goals. *International journal of educational development* (Oxford, UK), vol. 3, no. 3, 253-261.

Ojerinde, A., (1978), The use of mother-tongue: Yoruba as a medium of instruction in Nigerian schools. New York, Cornell University. [Thesis]

Okelo, A. Wright, (1976), A comparative study of the recommended art educational curriculum of Kenya and California in terms of achieving the perceived goals of Kenyans and Afro-Americans. Berkeley, CA, University of California. [Thesis]

Omo-Fadaka, J., (1982), Education and endogenous development in Africa. *Prospects* (Paris, UNESCO), vol. XII, no. 2, 261-268.

Omolewa, M., (1984), The first year of Nigeria's mass literacy campaign and new prospects for the future. *Convergence* (Toronto, Ont.), vol. XVII, no. 1, 55-62.

Oomen-Myin, M. A., (1983), The involvement of rural women in village development in Tanzania. *Convergence* (Toronto, Ont.), vol. XVI, no. 2, 59-69.

Ouane, A., (1982), Rural newspapers and radio for post-literacy in Mali. *Prospects* (Paris, UNESCO), vol. XII, no. 2, 243-253.

Owie, I. W., (1982), A comparative study of alienation: American vs. foreign students. *International education* (Knoxville, TN), vol. 11, Spring, 35-38.

Oyeneye, O. Y., (1982), Preschool education in Nigeria. *International journal of early childhood* (Dublin), vol. 14, no. 1, 28-32.

Rukare, E. H., (1975), *African institutes of education* Kampala, Makerere University Printery.

Rwelengera, J., (1975), Problems of transition from primary Swahili Medium teaching to form 1 English medium teaching in Dodoma and Mpwapwa-Dar-es-Salaam. Dar-es-Salaam, University of Dar-es-Salaam Department of Education.

Shiundu, J.; Sukwianob, (1982), *Some thoughts on on the job training of educational researchers in Kenya and Papua New Guinea* Nairobi, Kenyatta University College. (BER, O.P., No. 3046).

Sifuna, D. N., (1983), Kenya: twenty years of multilateral aid. *Prospects* (Paris, UNESCO), vol. XIII, no. 4, 481-492.

Sifuna, D. N., (1976), *Vocational education in schools: a historical survey of Kenya and Tanzania.* Nairobi, Kenya Literature Bureau.

Thobani, M., (1984), Charging user fees for social services: education in Malawi. *Comparative education review* (Chicago, IL), vol. 28, no. 3, August, 402-423.

Uche, U., (1981), Culture and education in Nigerian society. *Alvan school of education journal* (Owerri, Nigeria), vol. 1, no. 2, 57-63.

Uchendu, V. C., ed., (1979), *Education and politics in tropical Africa*. New York, Conch Magazine.

Urevbu, A. O., (1984), English language and the mother-tongue dilemma in Nigeria: a critical assessment of the new national policy on education. *International journal of educational development* (Oxford, UK), vol. 4, no. 1, 23-30.

Urevbu, A. O., (1984), Vocational education in Nigeria: a preliminary appraisal. *International journal of educational development* (Oxford, UK), vol. 4, no. 3, 223-229.

Wagaw, T. G., (1979), *Education in Ethiopia: prospect and retrospect*. Ann Arbor, I, University of Michigan Press.

Wandira, A., (1981), University and community: evolving perceptions of the African university. *Higher education* (Amsterdam), vol. 10, no. 3, May, 253-273.

World Black and African Festival of Arts and Culture, 2nd, Lagos, 1977. Symposium on Black Civilization and Education. [Papers presented:]

    Abbas, A. A. African literature and education. (Col.3/03/SUD.3) Paris, Society of African Culture, 1977.

    Aka, T., et al. Traditional education and modern education. (Col.6/13/IVO.3)

    Fafunwa, A. B. Utilizing an African language for formal education: a Nigerian success story. (Col.6/12/NIG/36)

    Grah, G. The role of women in traditional education in the traditional societies of pre-colonial Ivory Coast. (Col.6/13/IVO.2)

    Jah, G. Traditional system of education in Senegambia. (Col.6/12/Gam.1)

    Kalemba-Vita, K.; Matshoki, I. M.; Mbodi, M. N. Black civilization and education. (Col.6/10/ZAI.1)

    Mbuagbam, T. African methods of education and the problems of modern education. (Col.6/11/Cam.7)

    Moore, B. T. Poeo and Sande schools in Liberia: example of indigenous African education system. (Col.6/1/LIB.1)

    Sawyer, E. S. Traditional education in Sierra Leone: the role of the major secret societies. (Col.6/12/NIG.36)

Yoloye, E. A., (1985), Dependence and interdependence in education: two case-studies from Africa. *Prospects* (Paris, UNESCO), vol. XV, no. 2, 239-250.

Yoloye, E. A., (1983), Personality, education and society: a Yoruba perspective. *International journal of educational development* (Oxford, UK), vol. 3, no. 1, 97-104.

Yoloye, E. A., (1983), *Evaluation for innovation: African primary science programme evaluation report*. Ibadan, Nigeria, Ibadan University Press.

The Arab states

Khemais Benhamida, University of Tunis

Introduction

From the early days of Islam to the present day, Arab scholars and decision-makers have manifested a clear interest in education, and sought to know the new theoretical and practical developments in that field, both in the Arab region itself and elsewhere. The purpose was to update their educational practices and improve the quality of educational results. Thus the idea of comparing aspects of education in the Arab region and in other areas goes as far back in Arab history as Arab interest in education itself.

In the following essay the terms comparative education and comparative studies in education refer particularly to studies of educational issues in two or more countries or regions, or in a country other than that of the author himself. After a brief outline of this historical development of education in the Arab region, we shall describe the state of the art in comparative education since the early 1970s.

Historical background

In order to understand the state and status of comparative education in the Arab region today, as a practice and as a field of theoretical investigation, we need to look at the factors that influenced the development of education in general, and of comparative education in particular. In the Arab countries, this development took place against a religious, linguistic, and cultural background that was characterized by a high degree of similarity and homogeneity. In the Arab region, which stretches from the Atlantic Ocean to the Arab Gulf, the overwhelming majority of the people practice the same faith, speak the same language and share similar customs and traditions.

This homogeneous cultural background exists largely because of the Islamic religion, which spread there during the seventh century and whose concern with education is manifest in the first verse of the Qu'ran (Koran) which ordered the Holy Prophet Muhammad to 'Read in the name of thy Lord'. (Chapter 96, verse 1). The Holy Prophet himself enjoined Moslems to 'seek knowledge even unto China'. In the early decades of Islam, the mosques became centres of learning attended by students from various parts of the Islamic world, a tradition that showed their interest in acquiring views and practices other than those prevailing in their immediate environment.

Scholars and rulers in later periods continued to devote attention to learning and education in the Arab region, and to pay special heed to those of foreign countries. Thus, during the Abbasid Caliphate around the 8th and 9th centuries, major foreign works - mainly Greek, Persian, and Hindi - in the various fields of knowledge were translated into Arabic and served to enrich the quality of the educational programs that were taught in the educational institutions at the time. Special mention should be made of the founding of Bayt al-Hikmah (House of Wisdom) under the Abbasid caliph al-Ma'mun (813-833) as a centre of knowledge. There, full-time scholars were recruited to translate scientific works into Arabic, thus opening Arab-Islamic culture to the influences of the outside world. In the centuries that followed, similar institutions were created in various parts of the Arab region, mainly in Cairo, Egypt, and in Kairouan, Tunisia.

Such foreign works, and others produced by Arab scholars in philosophy, religion, literature and science undoubtedly found their way into the curricula that were taught in the formal educational institutions created during the eleventh century, such as al-madrasah al-Nizamiyah (1065) in Baghdad, Iraq, and al-madrasah al-Nuriyah in Damascus, Syria, both of which served as examples for similar schools in other parts of the Arab region. Such schools served as scientific and cultural centres of learning and were attended by students from various parts of the Arab-Islamic world (al-Malla, 53-59).

Such scholars as Ibn Jubayr, Ibn Battutah and Ibn Khaldun who lived in the twelfth, thirteenth and fourteenth centuries respectively, and travelled far and wide across the Arab region, did not fail to notice the state, conditions, and institutions of learning in the places they visited. Their accounts represent, without any doubt, the first comparative education documents in the Arab region. Ibn-Khaldun, for instance, devotes a chapter of his al-Muqaddima to comparative approaches to the teaching of children in

Islamic countries, namely the Maghreb countries, Andalusia, and al-Mashriq (al-Muqaddima, vol. 2, p.700-703).

Contacts with foreign cultures and educational innovations within the Arab region itself were severely curtailed during the four hundred years of Ottoman occupation, from the early sixteenth century to the end of World War I. The *madrasahs* that had flourished in the previous periods, thanks to generous donations and the system of 'waqr' or 'Habous' which provided permanent support for them, declined gradually and diminished in number.

It was not until the latter part of the nineteenth century that authorities in the Ottoman Empire began to establish a secular, public education system along European lines, for the purpose of meeting the needs of their administration and those of the military bureaucracy. Thus military academies were instituted to build a strong army for the empire, and the teaching of foreign languages was encouraged in order to have access to western knowledge. Such reforms inevitably had their effect on Arab countries throughout the empire.

Indeed, individual rulers such as Muhammad Ali in Egypt (he ruled from 1805 to 1848), and Khayr ad-Din al-Tunisi in Tunisia (in power from 1873 to 1877), both of whom were *mamluks*, understood the necessity to introduce serious changes - i.e., modernization - in the bureaucracy of the army and in education, in order to maintain their prestige and power in their respective domain (cf. Halpern, p.69).

Muhammad Ali established a centralized system of education and military training academies and organized study missions abroad as early as 1809, for the purpose of training the personnel to staff his institutions. By the mid-nineteenth century Egypt had its schools of agriculture, engineering, medicine, administration, etc. Muhammad Ali was assisted by, among other figures, Rifaa Rafi at-Tahtawi (1801-1873) who directed the royal school of administration, and the history of geography school in 1834, the school of languages in 1835, and the department of translation from 1863 to 1873. At-Tahtawi, much like Muhammad Ali, attempted to integrate the products of the liberal revolution in Europe into the Renaissance of Egypt (cf. Abdel Malek, p.47).

Khayr ad-Din at-Tunisi was no less ambitious as chief minister under Muhammad as-Sadiq Bey. He wrote on education in France with full details about the three educational levels, and on the academies and libraries in other European Countries (cf. his Aqwam al-masalik, p.193-203). He also founded Sadiqi College, in Tunis, in 1876, with a curriculum that comprised religious education, foreign languages (Turkish, French, Italian), mathematics, sociology and natural sciences. This secondary school was the prototype of the Franco-Arab school that was to become, after independence, the backbone of the national education system in Tunisia (Brown, p.146). And to acquire knowledge at the source, he, like Muhammad Ali before him, sent students to study in France.

The possibilities and inevitability of comparison in the field of education initiated by these two reformers increased, especially during the latter part of the nineteenth century, as a consequence of the spread of missionary schools in the region. These schools, which were mainly Catholic and Protestant, were sponsored by Christian churches in France, Great Britain and the United States of America.

Other, secular, schools were also founded as early as the 1830s by several European countries throughout the Ottoman Empire. One of these schools, *l'école laïque française*, opened its doors in major Arab cities in Algeria, Egypt, Lebanon, Morocco, Syria and Tunisia.

The existence of these three education systems side by side in various parts of the Arab region (the Ottoman public system, the national private system, and the missionary religious system) made borrowings in curriculum, methods and philosophies possible, if not inevitable, while at the same time giving rise to a growing resistance on the part of nationalist leaders in some of the Arab countries, particularly where the non-native system threatened the values of the local population, as was the case in Egypt and Algeria (see al-Gunaydi, 1965, p.131-36, and 1982, p.40-43).

At the same time, however, it began to be argued in some of the Arab countries that changes should be made in the Arab education systems along the lines characteristic of the French and British systems.

In Egypt, for example, Sheik Muhammad Abduh, who was in 1895 a member of the Board of Directors of al-Azhar University, called for reform in education and linked it with reform in religion. His ideas had wide currency in Arab countries among reform-minded leaders. He visited Tunisia - among other Arab countries - and lectured on the theme of educational reform. Among his followers was Sheikh Abd al-Aziz at-Taalibi - Zaydi (p.55).

In Tunisia, also, Western-trained intellectuals known as 'The Young Tunisians' advocated the modernization of their society and considered themselves the intermediaries between the latter and the French authorities. Significantly enough, they expressed themselves in French and issued a weekly newspaper entitled *Le Tunisien*, which appeared in French from 1907 to 1912 (for its last five years it also had an Arabic edition). The reform advocated in education, in this case, was influenced on the one hand by the intellectual awakening taking place in Egypt and spreading across the Arab region, and on the other by the quality of the educational ideas and practices prevailing in European countries.

With the defeat of the Ottomans in World War I began a period of direct colonization of the Arab countries, mainly by France and the United Kingdom, both of which gradually increased their control over education in the region. This control took the form of imposing French and English as the languages of instruction at all levels, of creating a division between traditional schools for the masses and modern schools attended mostly by children of well-off families and European children in the Arab countries. Demand for reforms was difficult to voice during this post war period, because of the severe control exercised by the European authorities on newspapers and printing in general. In most Arab countries, education, especially the preparation and training of civil servants, was made to serve the purpose of the foreign authorities.

The attainment of independence by some Arab countries (Egypt in 1923, Iraq in 1932, and Syria in 1944) gave a new start to education in the Arab region, in which Egypt played a leading role. it represented for other Arab States an example to follow, particularly by giving the Arabic language and culture their rightful place in the curriculum. In Egypt and Syria, the private foreign schools (English, French, Italian, American, etc.) which were, at the time, attended by both Arab and foreign children and which taught foreign languages and curricula, were soon placed under government control, and made to direct their efforts to achieving the same aims as assigned to national schools (Halpern, p.126 and Said, M. A., p.8). At the same time, the higher educational institutions of these countries began to attract more and more students from other Arab countries, who wanted to start or complete their higher education. This was made easier by the adoption in both countries of measures to co-ordinate cultural relations with the other Arab countries. The idea of cultural agreements between Arab States goes back, in fact, to the period immediately following the first World War as one of the ways of strengthening the Arab *nahda* (awakening). The first project for the establishment of such relations between Egypt and Iraq was mooted in 1943. (al-Husari, 1948, p.22-24).

However, this project was not implemented, as the idea of a more comprehensive one came into being: that of creating a League of Arab States, and the conclusion within that League of a general cultural agreement involving all Arab States. This was, in fact, adopted in 1945 by the Council of the League. Thus the general framework for the development of Arab education, and therefore for comparative education, in the Arab region was defined.

At this time, in Tunisia (as in Morocco) the traditional institutions of az-Zaytunah and al-Qarawiyin were experiencing changes in their curricula. From 1945 to 1950, under the leadership of Sheikh Muhammad Tahar ben Ashur, new scientific disciplines were added to the religious curriculum at az-Zaytunah. These were mathematics, natural sciences, history, geography and philosophy. Furthermore, teachers of these disciplines were recruited from the public instruction directorate and from among graduates of the Khalduniya school who had passed their Arabic baccalaureate examination (which was created in 1947 and was the equivalent of the French diploma with the same name). These graduates usually joined institutions of higher learning in Egypt, Syria and Iraq to complete their education. (Zaydi, p.71) The changes brought into the az-Zaytunah curriculum by Sheikh ben Ashur were similar to those introduced at an earlier date in the curriculum of al-Azhar by Sheikh Muhammad Abduh.

Comparative studies

The truly comparative work in education in the 1940s and 1950s was carried out by Sati al-Husari (1882-1968), the well-known Syrian educator and prominent figure in Arab intellectual thought. As a result of the various educational and political posts he held in his own country, Syria, and in Iraq, and of the various tasks he was assigned to fulfill, al-Husari wrote extensively on education in various Arab countries and of its role as the major instrument in the forging of Arab unity. He also wrote for the League of Arab States an important work in six volumes entitled *Hawiiyyat at-taqafa al-arabiyya* [*The annals of Arab culture*]. This yearbook, published from 1950 to 1963, described and analyzed the education systems in Arab countries over a period of fifteen years (1947-1962). In the first issue the author focused his study on five Arab countries only: Egypt, Iraq, Jordan, Lebanon and Syria. The sixth and last volume, published in 1963, covered all the Arab States.

One sure indication of al-Husari's comparative approach was his insistence that the Arab countries should not rely on *one* particular country in their educational borrowings, but on as many countries as possible. He also advised that educational commissions should comprise people who had studied or observed different education systems, and that students should be sent on educational missions to different countries, so that attempts to improve education in the Arab states would be as enlightened and informed as possible, adopting and adapting only the best in the foreign system to the situation prevailing in the Arab countries.

By the early 1960s, when all the Arab states were independent, a major development began to take place in one Arab country after another. This was educational planning, resulting from the belief prevailing among educationists that education was the panacea to the social and economic problems faced by Third World countries. Educational planning often called for advice from and participation by experts from advanced countries, usually the former colonial powers.

Another development was the increasing role played by international organizations in planning education in the Arab countries. As early as 1958, UNESCO had called for the conduct of an educational survey in the region for the purpose of determining the major issues faced by the Arab states in that field, and laid the bases for convening a conference of Arab ministers of education. The Conference was held in 1960, in Beirut, Lebanon. The foundations for comparative work in education at the level of the Arab region were thus established.

Shortly afterwards, in 1964, the Arab states signed a charter of Arab Cultural Unity stipulating the creation of a specialized organization called the Arab League Educational, Cultural and Scientific Organization (ALECSO). The charter was adopted by the Council of the League the same year. ALECSO held its first Conference in Cairo, Egypt, in July 1970. Article 1 of the Constitution of ALECSO defines the objective of the Organization as being 'the attainment of unity of thought among the Arab countries through education, culture and science, and through the raising of cultural standards in these countries so that they may pursue world progress and participate positively in it'. To achieve this purpose, ALECSO endeavours to:

- co-ordinate efforts of member states in the field of education, culture and science.
- promote education and culture.
- encourage scientific research in the Arab countries.
- propose the conclusion of educational, cultural and scientific conventions and agreements between Arab countries, and
- ensure international co-operation in the educational, cultural and scientific fields.

From 1964 to the present day, Conferences of Arab Ministers of Education have been held periodically in various Arab capital cities. Two such Conferences (the first held in Sanaa, Yemen, 1972 and the second in Khartoum, Sudan, in 1978) took important steps for the implementation of educational promotion in the Arab countries. Indeed, the 1972 Conference adopted a decision concerning the establishment of a strategy for the development of education in the Arab countries. The decision was implemented and led to the publication, in 1979, of *istratigiyyat tatwir at-tarbiya al-arabiyya*, the fundamental reference work defining ALECSO's projects in the educational field. The following summary highlights the importance of the *istratigiyya*. Chapter seven (pages 245-312) discusses the components of the strategy and their possible alternatives. The components are:

- Towards an Arab social philosophy for education, with a discussion of the future profile of the Arab person and Arab society.
- Towards an educated Arab society.
- Towards diversifying the educational structure and guaranteeing its flexibility and comprehensiveness.
- A scientific methodology for the development of education.
- Towards developing the functions and methods of forming and training teachers who are the pioneers and defenders of authenticity and innovation.
- Towards developing educational research to foster efficiency and innovation in education.
- Towards planning and modernizing educational administration.
- The financing of education.
- Towards the development of educational legislation. Towards interaction and complementarity between education and comprehensive development.
- Towards the nationalization of Arab work for the purpose of education and comprehensive development.
- Towards the development of international co-operation and effective participation in it, and orienting it in the proper directions.

Each of these components contains an explanation and discussion of the major issues related to it, and ends with recommendations to decision makers, organizations, institutes and groups in the Arab countries.

The Khartoum Conference (1978) adopted a decision calling for the creation within ALECSO of an educational research unit to investigate educational problems in the Arab countries. This unit soon developed into a fully-fledged Department of Educational Research in 1982. Already in

1980, it had convened a Conference of Arab Experts in Educational Research in Rabat, Morocco (March 1980), and defined a programme for its activities.

Efforts to promote education at the subregional level soon manifested themselves in the Gulf region. The Ministers of education and instruction in the Gulf States convened their first conference in Riyadh in 1975 and adopted a decision to create an Arab Bureau of Education for the Gulf States (ABEGS). The Bureau started work in 1979. Meanwhile, the Arab Ministers of education and instruction in the Gulf region adopted another decision for the founding of a regional educational research centre, known as the Gulf Arab States Educational Research Center (GASERC) which came into being in May 1977. Cooperation between UNESCO and the Arab member states had already borne fruit. As early as 1961, for example, a Regional Center for Educational Planning in the Arab Region (RCEPAR) was created in Beirut, Lebanon, and in 1973, UNEDBAS, in Amman, launched an Educational Innovation Programme for Development in the Arab States (EIPDAS) with headquarters originally in Cairo but now located in Kuwait.

By 1980, a whole network of organizations grouping policy-makers, teachers, researchers, educationists, etc. throughout the Arab region had come into existence and begun to work, and produce results. The concerns of these organizations are comparative by definition, as they relate to education and educational issues in over twenty Arab countries.

Research and training centres

Comparative work in education in the Arab countries is conducted in ministries of education, some faculties of education, the different centres of the Departments of Education and Educational Research in ALECSO, and the various other Arab unions and organizations that are concerned with culture, science and research such as the Arab Bureau of Education for the Gulf States, the Federation of Arab Teachers, the Arab Federation for Technical Education, the Association of Arab Universities, and the Union of Arab Historians, with which ALECSO maintains co-operative relationships.

Faculties of education

The documents made available to ALECSO's Department of Educational Research by faculties of education and research centres in the Arab countries reveal that by 1984, the number of faculties of education had reached 37, only three of which had a comparative education department. They were located at Ain-Shams University and Zagazig University, in Egypt, and at the University of Damascus, in Syria. The remaining faculties of education either do not conduct comparative education research at all, or do so as part of the research they carry out in other education departments, such as the department of educational foundations (as at the Universities of Assiut and Tanta, in Egypt), or the department of educational administration and planning (as at the University of al-Azhar), or the department of Islamic education and curriculum (as at King Abdulaziz University, at Medina, Saudi Arabia).

The education sector of ALECSO

Among the most important Centres for comparative studies in education in the Arab World today are the Department of Education, and the Department of Educational Research in ALECSO, judging by the large number of studies they have carried out involving various aspects of education in the Arab countries. Research is performed either by Arab education scholars who are commissioned by ALECSO, or by education experts working in ALECSO itself.

Affiliated to the Education Sector in ALECSO, are a number of Centres located in various capital cities in the Arab countries. These centres, which carry out research in their own areas of specialization, are as follows:

The Arab Literacy and Adult Education Organization (ARLO), Baghdad.

The Arab States Educational Technology Centre, Kuwait.

The Literacy Leadership Training Centre in the Gulf States, Bahrain.

The Literacy Leadership Training Centre in North Africa, Tripoli, Libya.

The Arab Centre for Higher Education Research, Damascus, Syria.

The Arabization Co-ordination Bureau, Rabat, Morocco.

The Arab Bureau of Education for the Gulf States, the Educational Research Centre, and the Council on Higher Education which are affiliated to it, carry out comparative studies in education. They deal with education in the seven member states: The United Arab Emirates, Bahrain, Kuwait, Saudi Arabia, Iraq, Oman and Qatar.

The other Arab organizations and federations do conduct comparative studies, but most often do so in co-operation with ALECSO. Thus the Arab Federation for Technical Education co-operated with ALECSO in the preparation of the study entitled *Technical education in the Arab world*, in 1985 (see Abd al-Wahhab).

Research projects and publications

The research projects in comparative education can be divided into two major categories: those undertaken in the faculties of education by *undergraduate and graduate students* and by the staff teaching in those faculties, and those carried out by ALECSO or other Arab regional organizations such as the Arab Bureau of Education for the Gulf States. Some of these projects are mentioned in the bibliography annexed to this paper.

Research projects in the faculties of education

Most of the comparative studies in education carried out in faculties of education in the Arab countries are the result of research conducted by individual teachers of education, and published in the education journals issued by their own faculties or by other faculties of education, or delivered to the Ministries of education that commissioned them.

As can be seen from the entries listed in the bibliography, the topics dealt with in these studies cover a wide range of issues such as *foundations* of education, curriculum, educational psychology, teachers and teaching, school and educational administration, evaluation and testing, economics of education, education of women. A number of these studies focus on the education system of a given country, usually the country in which the author has studied and obtained his degree, or which he may simply have visited.

The Educational Innovation Programme for Development in the Arab States (EIPDAS), which was established within the UNESCO Regional Office for Education in the Arab States in 1973, started to implement its projects in 1978, after the Abu Dhabi Conference in 1977. EIPDAS projects include the following Conferences:

- The modernization of educational administration in the context of development and innovation of education in the Arab World (Kuwait, May 1981).
- Innovation in secondary education and training of technicians in Arab countries (Kuwait, October 1982).
- Information and documentation for the purpose of educational innovation in the Arab States (Rabat, November 1982).

The few books available on comparative education (Fahmi, 1981; Lutfi, 1965; Mursi, 1977 and 1981; Simaan, 1980) share similar characteristics: they are didactic in nature, in that they present the field of comparative education in an introductory chapter, and then focus attention on the various components of the education system in other countries, particularly the United

States of America or Great Britain, the USSR and various Arab countries. The authors survey the history of education in the countries concerned, then focus on the major issues related to the system at all the educational levels.

Studies in comparative education also result from research carried out by students for a degree. In this case, the author deals with an educational quest in two countries, his own and the one in which he is studying. A wide range of educational issues in most of the Arab countries have been dealt with in this way.

Research projects of the education sector in ALECSO

The education sector in ALECSO and its branches, the Department of Education, the Department of Educational Research, the Arab Literacy and Adult Education Organization (ARLO, Baghdad since 1970), the Arab States Educational Technology Centre (Kuwait 1975), the Literacy Leadership Training Centres, for the Gulf States (Bahrain) and for North Africa (Tripoli, 1977), and the Arab Centre for Higher Education Research (Damascus, 1982), and the Arabization Coordination Bureau (Rabat, Morocco) have designated the following priority areas for their research projects: basic education; secondary education; higher education; adult literacy; development of internal and external efficiency in education; Arabization and the use of literary Arabic; development of education for science and technology; development of the teaching profession; educational administration; financing of education.

Over the period 1970-1985 more than 560 research projects have been carried out in the ALECSO education sector alone. (ALECSO, *Report*, 1987, p.43-69). While it is not possible to list them all here, the following major projects give an idea of the range and scope of the comparative research carried out by ALECSO in the area of education. The Encyclopedia of Arab-Islamic educational thought; projects for the development of science and mathematics teaching; the reinforcement of comprehensive literacy campaigns in a number of Arab countries; education in the Arab world today, with the focus on the aims of education, curriculum, teacher training, educational administration, and examinations; the Arabization of public and higher education; the education of Palestinian children in and outside the occupied territories.

In the Arab Bureau of Education for the Gulf States, also, several important research projects of a comparative nature are programmed. Those for the period 1979-1981 included: translation of some recent works in educational planning and their distribution in member states; preparation of a study on the education and protection of the handicapped in member states. Research projects for 1982-1983 include: a comparative study of school administration in Arab Gulf states, and a study of the relationship between education and employment opportunities in the Gulf area, with specific reference to secondary and higher education.

In the Council on Higher Education, which is an advisory body within the Bureau, the following research projects have been programmed for the 1982-1983 period: universities in the Arab Gulf states today and their various facilities; requirements and names of university degrees in the Arab Gulf states and the grounds for equivalency between them; rights, duties and responsibilities of the university staff member.

The projects of the Gulf Arab States Educational Research Centre consist of studies that aim at unifying the objectives of education, and the general foundations of the programmes of education in the region. In this respect, it should be noted that the work of the Centre has followed three stages: collection of data concerning the state of education in the member states; definition of common grounds for the conduct of education in various disciplines and at each of the educational levels; production of material for the implementation of what was achieved in the second stage.

Particular research projects of the Centre deal with: The functions and uses of the computer and their effects on the development of secondary education programmes in member states; the feasibility of creating a centre for educational evaluation and measurement in member states.

Directions and trends in contemporary research

Whilst increasing attention is being paid in the Arab countries to the production of general bibliographies on education, specific indexes concerning particular aspects of the field, such as comparative studies in education, have yet to be produced. It thus remains difficult to draw conclusions about the scope, qualities, strengths and weaknesses of the field of comparative education.

On the basis of information available at ALECSO about the comparative studies in education produced in the Arab world, the following remarks can be made:

> Comparative education, in general, appears to be the poor relation in the educational field, in the same way as education itself is the poor relation among the academic disciplines taught in Arab universities. In some of those universities which have, in the past, been influenced by French higher education institutions, education is considered as less important

and valuable than other disciplines, and is often taken to mean simply educational psychology and teaching methods. This means that the status of education itself (whether it is a discipline or not), let alone that of comparative education, is still the object of debate in academic circles. In fact, the placing of comparative education courses in departments that deal with other aspects of education, can be considered as a sign of doubt concerning the legitimacy of comparative education as an autonomous and specific field of knowledge.

Comparative studies in education are mostly empirical and descriptive in nature. They aim essentially at providing information. (This is not to be belittled in a situation where reliable information is often scarce and difficult to obtain. Moreover, because it is often difficult to collect information in his own country, a researcher can only be pleased to find data about other countries.) In this respect it should be pointed out that translation continues to be one of the main sources of access to information about foreign educational concerns, and of making it available to the Arab reader.

The studies conducted in faculties of education have a narrower comparative scope than those conducted in regional centres, as they usually focus on two countries. Consequently, the grounds for the generalization of their results are not always sound. These studies, however, have covered most aspects of the educational enterprise, with a marked emphasis on the curriculum, administration and teaching. Out of 167 studies taken from documents available at the Department of Educational Research in ALECSO, and covering the last 15 years, 49 deal with the levels of education with emphasis on the secondary level, 33 deal with the curriculum, 30 with educational and school administration, 25 with teachers and teaching, seven with students, and five with women and education (see ALECSO, *Dalil kulliyyat at-tarbiya*, 1984). This means that the studies are essentially concerned with the school itself, and that little attention is paid to the social environment in which the school operates, or to the politics of education and how it affects the quality of educational outcomes. The approach used in some of the studies, mainly those involving foreign (United States, French, British, etc.) systems is utilization. The authors often seek to use the components of the foreign systems in order to improve their counterparts in the Arab countries.

The studies conducted by ALECSO's educational departments and their branches are area studies, in that a large number of countries are involved. While they do not enter into a debate over theoretical issues, these studies use statistical analyses and other scientific research instruments. Since they are often recommended by the General Conference of the Organization, they are usually relevant to policy decisions. Most studies contain recommendations defining the future orientations to be followed in developing or reforming a particular aspect of the educational aspect under study. This, in fact, is a characteristic they share with the comparative studies conducted in the academic institutions.

The teaching of the discipline

The teaching of comparative education takes place at the undergraduate and graduate levels in various departments of faculties of education in the Arab countries.

The faculties of education operating in the Arab world today were created after independence with the specific task of preparing and training teachers to staff the newly established elementary and secondary schools. Of the 37 faculties of education operating in 1984, 12 were established before 1970, 19 during the 1970's, and six during the first years of this decade (ALECSO, *Dalil kulliyyat at-tarbiya, 1984*).

Furthermore, comparative education courses are offered essentially in faculties of education in Egypt and the Syrian Arab Republic. This is due to historical reasons, as the two countries have been independent since 1923 and 1944 and have, therefore, had enough time to develop their education systems. Egypt had nine of the 37 faculties of education existing in the Arab countries in 1984. On the other hand, and as a consequence of the scarcity of comparative education departments and courses, the degrees involving comparison are few at the Master's level and fewer still at the Ph.D level.

Thus, comparative education in the Arab faculties of education today constitutes a peripheral concern, limited to a few institutions and involving only a small number of educationists. Only in Egypt do we find a comparative education society. It became a member of the World Council of Comparative Education Societies in 1984.

Specialized journals

While there is, to our knowledge, no journal concerned exclusively with comparative education in the Arab countries that would be the counterpart to the well-established European and American journals in the field, it is safe to say that most of the periodicals published by various educational Departments and Centres in ALECSO and other Arab organizations contain comparative studies in education. Below is a list of the periodicals that include comparative studies in the Arab region and which appear regularly:

al-Magalla al-arabiyya li-al-buhut at-tarbawiyya/Arab journal of educational research (Tunis, Educational Research Unit, ALECSO), 1981 - 2/yr.

al-Magalla al-arabiyya li-at-tarbiya/Arab journal of education (Tunis, Education Department, ALECSO), 1981 - 2/yr.

al-Magalla al-arabiyya li-buhut at-talim al-ali/Arab journal of higher education research (Damascus, Arab Centre for Higher Education Research), 1984 - 2/yr.

Talim al-gamalhir/Education of the masses (Baghdad, ARLO), 1974 - 3/yr.

at-Tarbiya al-mustamirra [Continuing education] (Bahrain, Adult Education Leaders Training Center)

al-Muwagaha as-samila [Total confrontation] (Tripoli, Libyan Arab Jamahiriya, Adult Education Leaders Training Center)

Magallat ittihad al-gamiat al-arabiyya [Journal of the Association of Arab Universities] (Amman, the Association)

al-Muallimun al-arab [The Arab teachers] (Baghdad, Federation of Arab Teachers) 4/yr.

Risalat al-halig al-arabi [Journal of the Arab Gulf] (Riyadh, Arab Bureau of Education for the Gulf States), 1981 - 4/yr.

Bibliography

Abbas, A., (1984), Dawr al-gami fi magal talim al-kibar: dirasa muqarana bayna misr wa-inkiltira [The role of the university in adult education: a comparative study of Egypt and England] Asyut, Egypt, Kulliyyat at-tarbiya, Gamiat Asyut. [Thesis - MA]

al-Abd, H., (1978), Dirasa hadariyya muqarana li-simat sahsiyya at-talib al-gamii al-misri wa-at-talib al-gamii al-amriki [A comparative cultural study of the personal traits of Egyptian and American university students] *Magallat kulliyyat at-tarbiya* (al-Qahira), no. 1, March, 19-28.

Abd ad-Daim, A., (1974), *at-Tarbiya fi al-bilad al-arabiyya: hadiruha wa-muskilatuha wa-mustaqbaluha* [Education in the Arab countries: its present conditions, its problems and its future] Bayrut, Dar al-ilm li-al-malayin.

Abd ad-Daim, F.; Rasid, K. R., (1979), *al-Madrasa as-sabiyya fi yuguslafiya* [The popular school in Yugoslavia] Bagdad, Wazarat at-tarbiya.

Abd al-Gaffar, A. R., (1976), Tatawwur qawanin at-talim fi firansa mundu al-harb al-alamiyya at-taniyya hatta al-an wa-imkaniyyat al-ifada minhu fi islah at-talimi fi misr [The evolution of educational legislation in France from World War II to the present and the possibility of benefitting from it in reforming education in Egypt] al-Qahira, Kulliyyat at-tarbiya, Gamiat Ayn Sams. [Thesis - MA]

Abd al-Lah, A., (1983), Tagribat at-talim al-asasi fi gumhuriyyat misr al-arabiyya wa-tanzaniya: dirasa muqarana [The experience of basic education in Egypt and Tanzania: a comparative study] Asyut, Egypt, Kulliyyat at-tarbiya, Gamiat Asyut. [Thesis - MA]

Abd al-Muttalib, A. M., (1979), Dirasa muqarana li-tarbiyat al-muawwaqin badaniyyan fi gumhuriyyat misr al-arabiyya maa al-isara sifa hassa ila kull min al-wilayat al-muttahida al-amrikiyya wa-ingiltira [A comparative study of the education of the physically handicapped in Egypt with special reference to the USA and England] Asyut, Egypt, Kulliyyat at-tarbiya, Gamiat Asyut. [Thesis - MA]

Abd al-Muti, Y., (1978), *Rihla ila al-madrasa as-samila* [A journey to the comprehensive school] al-Kuwayt, Dar al-buhut al-ilmiyya.

Abd al-Wahhab, H. M. S., (1985), *at-Talim at-tiqni fi al-watan al-arabi: al-waqi wa-al-ittigahat* [Technical education in the Arab world: state and trends] Tunis, ALECSO; Bagdad, al-Ittihad al-arabi li-at-talim at-tiqni.

Abdel Malek, A., (1975), *La pensée politique arabe contemporaine*. Paris, Seuil.

Abid, W., (1980), *Trends of academic research in education in Arab universities* Doha, Faculty of Education, University of Qatar.

Abu al-Azam, M. A., et al., (1986), *Tatwir manahig talim al-kitaba wa-al-imla fi marahil at-talim al-amm fi al-watan al-arabi* [The development of writing and spelling curricula at the general education levels in the Arab world] Tunis, ALECSO.

Abu Hilal, A., et al., (1984), *Taysir talim al-badw fi al-watan al-arabi* [Facilitating the education of Bedouin in the Arab world] Tunis, ALECSO.

al-Afandi, M. H.; as-Safii, I. M.; Salama, A., (1978), Hadir kulliyyat at-tarbiya fi al-alam al-arabi [Present-day faculties of education in the Arab world] ar-Riyad, Kulliyyat at-tarbiya, Gamiat al-Malik Saud.

Aguba, M. I., (1977), *Adwa ala at-tarbiya al-ginsiyya fi ad-duwal an-namiya* [Some light on sex education in developing countries] al-Hartum, Wazarat at-tarbiya.

Ahmad, N. S., (1975), *Hawla at-talim al-amm wa-nuzumuhu: dirasa muqarana* [On general education and its structures: a comparative study] al-Qahira, al-Maktaba al-anglu al-misriyya.

Ahmad, S. M., et al., (1986), *Huttat tarbiyat at-tifl al-arabi fi sanawatihi al-ula ala daw' istratigiyyat at-tarbiya al-arabiyya* [A plan for the early education of Arab children in the light of the Arab educational strategy] Tunis, ALECSO.

Akkila, M. A. K., (1975), Educational development in the Arab countries: some criteria for educational planning. Lawrence, KS, School of Education, University of Kansas. [Thesis]

ALECSO, (1984), *Dalil kulliyyat at-tarbiya fi al-watan al-arabi* [A guide to faculties of education in the Arab world] Tunis.

ALECSO, (1984), *al-Israf at-tarbawi fi al-watan al-arabi: waqiuhu wa-subul tatwirihi* [Educational supervision in the Arab world: its state and ways of developing it] Tunis.

ALECSO, (1979), *Istratigiyyat tatwir at-tarbiya al-arabiyya: taqrir lagnat wad istratigiyya li-tatwir at-tarbiya fi al-bilad al-arabiyya.* [The strategy of Arab educational development: report of the Committee for the Setting Up of a Strategy for the Development of Education in Arab Countries] n.p.

ALECSO, (1986), *Riyad al-atfal fi al-watan al-arabi: al-waqi wa-at-tumuh* [Kindergartens in the Arab world: state and aspirations] Tunis.

ALECSO, (1983), *at-Talim al-ali wa-at-tanmiya fi al-watan al-arabi* [Higher education and development in the Arab world] Tunis.

ALECSO, (1987), *Taqrir al-munazzama ila al-maglis al-iqtisadi wa-al-igtimai li-gamiat ad-duwal al-arabiyya* [ALECSO report to the Social and Economic Council of the League of Arab States] Tunis.

ALECSO, (1984), *at-Tarbiya al-amaliyya wa-wasa'iluha fi maahid idad al-muallimin* [Practical education and its methods in teacher training institutes] Tunis.

ALECSO, (1986), *Tawhid as-sullam at-talimi fi al-bilad al-arabiyya ala daw istratigiyyat tatwir at-tarbiya al-arabiyya* [Towards a unification of the educational ladder in the Arab countries in the light of the strategy for the development of Arab education] Tunis.

al-Amin, M. A., (1978), Dirasa muqarana li-al-ahdaf al-amma ar-rahina li-at-tarbiya fi al-buldan al-arabiyya [A comparative study of present general objectives of education in the Arab countries] Bayrut, al-Gamia al-amrikiyya. [Thesis - MA]

al-Ani, T. A.; Hisawi, G. S., (1986), *at-Talim al-mihni fi al-watan al-arabi* [Vocational education in the Arab world] Tunis, Idarat at-tarbiya, ALECSO.

Arab Unity Studies Center, (1979), *Dawr at-talim fi al-wahda al-arabiyya* [The role of education in Arab unity] Bayrut.

Asur, A. K., (1982), al-Madrasa as-samila al-ingiliziyya ka-namudag li-tanzim at-talim at-tanawi fi al-bilad al-arabiyya [The English comprehensive school as a model for organizing secondary education in the Arab countries] *Magallat at-tarbiya* (al-Qahira), vol. 1, 62-86.

Ata al-Lah, M., (1974), *Dirasa muqarana fi at-tarbiya wa-nuzum at-talim* [A comparative study on education and education systems] al-Qahira, al-Maktaba al-anglu al-misriyya.

al-Azuz, A., et al., (1983), *Dirasat zahirat uzuf as-sabab al-arabi an mihnat at-tadris* [A study of the phenomenon of the aversion of Arab youth to the teaching profession] Tunis, ALECSO.

Baayad, A. H., (1982), *Dirasa muqarana li-waqi al-qiyada at-tarbawiyya wa-al-idariyya fi magal at-tarbiya wa-at-talim fi kull min al-gumhuriyya al-arabiyya al-yamaniyya wa-gumhuriyyat misr al-arabiyya wa-al-wilayat al-muttahida al-amrikiyya* [A comparative study on the state of educational and administrative guidance in the field of education and instruction in the Yemen Arab Republic, Egypt and the USA] al-Qahira, Kulliyyat at-tarbiya, Gamiat Ayn Sams. [Thesis]

al-Bakir, K., (1978), at-Talim al-gamii wa-ad-dirasat al-islamiyya fi al-watan al-arabi [University education and Islamic studies in the Arab world] *Magallat ittihad al-gamiat al-arabiyya* (Amman), no. 14, September, 3-15.

Bassur, M., (1982), *Ittigahat fi at-tarbiya al-arabiyya ala daw taqrir Istratigiyyat tatwir at-tarbiya al-arabiyya'* [Trends in Arab education in the light of the report 'Strategy of the development of Arab education'] Tunis, Wahdat al-buhut at-tarbawiyya, ALECSO.

el-Bouhy, F. S. S., (1980), Secondary school teachers perceptions of pre-service teacher education: a comparative study in the USA and Egypt. Pittsburgh, PA, School of Education, University of Pittsburgh. [Thesis]

Brown, L. C., Tunisia. in: Coleman, J. S., ed., (1965), *Education and political development.* Princeton, NJ, Princeton University Press, 144-168.

Bunni, G. H., (1978), *at-Talim al-ibtida'i fi al-iraq wa-bad al-aqtar al-arabiyya: dirasa muqarana* [Primary education in Iraq and some Arab countries: a comparative study] Bagdad, Wazarat at-tarbiya.

Dama, M. I.; Mursi, M. M., (1982), *al-Kitab al-madrasi wa-madà mula'amatihi li-amaliyyatay at-taallum wa-at-talim fi al-marhala al-ibtida'iyya* [The school textbook and the extent of its suitability for the learning and teaching processes at the primary level] Tunis, Wahdat al-buhut at-tarbawiyya, ALECSO.

Debeauvais, M. Education in former French Africa,. in: Coleman, J. S., ed., (1965), *Education and political development.* Princeton, NJ, Princeton University Press, 75-91.

Eckstein, M. A.; Noah, H. J., (1985), Dependency theory in comparative education: the new simplicitude. *Prospects* (Paris, UNESCO), vol. XV, no. 2, 213-225.

ad-Duwayri, A. A., (1982), Dirasa muqarana li-dawr at-talim at-tanawi al-amm fi at-tanmiya al-iqtisadiyya wa-al-igtimaiyya fi al-urdunn wa-misr wa-al-mamlaka al-muttahida wa-al-ittihad as-sufiyati [A comparative study of the role of general secondary education in economic and social development in Jordan, Egypt, the UK and the Soviet Union] al-Qahira, Kulliyyat at-tarbiya, Gamiat Ayn Sams. [Thesis]

Fahmi, M. S., (1981), *al-Manhag fi at-tarbiya al-muqarana* [The curriculum in comparative education] al-Qahira, al-Maktaba al-anglu al-misriyya.

Farid, Z. M., (1980), *Talim al-mar'a al-arabiyya fi at-turat wa fi al-mugtamaat al-arabiyya al-muasira* [The education of the Arab woman in the past and in modern Arab societies] al-Qahira, al-Maktaba al-anglu al-misriyya.

al-Fawahiri, M. S. M., (1982), Dirasa muqarana li-al-ittigahat al-muttabaa fi idarat at-talim al-gamii fi kull min inkiltira wa-gumhuriyyat misr al-arabiyya [A comparative study of trends followed in the administration of university education in England and Egypt] az-Zaqaziq, Egypt, Kulliyyat at-tarbiya, Gamiat az-Zaqaziq. [Thesis - MA]

al-Gadidi, H., (1981), *Dirasat muzum wa-asalib al-idara at-tarbawiyya fi al-bilad al-arabiyya* [A study on the systems and methods of educational administration in the Arab countries] Masqat, Wazarat at-tarbiya wa-at-talim wa-su'un as-sabab.

al-Gammali, M. F., (1984), *Nahwa tawhid al-bina at-tarbawi fi al-alam al-islami* [Towards a unified structure of education in the Islamic world] Tunis, Société tunisiènne de diffusion.

Gandur, M. M. Y., (1976), Dirasa muqarana li-mustawà al-qalaq inda al-murahiqin al-filastiniyyin wa-al-murahiqin as-suriyyin [A comparative study of the level of anxiety among Palestinian and Syrian youth] Tanta, Egypt, Kulliyyat at-tarbiya, Gamiat Tanta. [Thesis - MA]

Ghubrial, T. K. H., (1979), Teachers' perceptions of selected societal fundamentals of curriculum in American schools and Egyptian schools: a comparative study. Pittsburgh, PA, School of Education, University of Pittsburgh. [Thesis]

Gulf Arab States Educational Research Center, (1981), *Asalib taqwim talabat at-tanawiyya al-amma wa-alaqatuha bi-usus al-qabul fi mu'assassat at-talim al-ali bi-duwal al-halig* [Methods of evaluating general secondary school students and their relationship to the bases of admission to higher education institutions in the Gulf States] al-Kuwayt.

Gulf Arab States Educational Research Center, (1981), *ad-Dirasa al-mashiyya al-muqarana li-manahig at-tarbiya as-sihhiyya bi-al-marhala al-ibtida'iyya fi ad-duwal al-ada' wa-masru al-manahig al-muwahhada li-madat al-ulum* [Comparative survey of health education programmes at the primary level in Member States and the Unified Science Curriculum Project] al-Kuwayt.

Gulf Arab States Educational Research Center, (1985), *Dirasa hawla at-talim ad-dati wa-tatwir al-manahig wa-asalib at-tadris fi duwal al-halig al-arabi* [A study on self-instruction and the development of curricula and teaching methods in the Arab Gulf States] al-Kuwayt.

Gulf Arab States Educational Research Center, (1984), *Dirasa li-tatwir tadris at-tarbiya al-islamiyya fi duwal al-halig al-arabiyya* [A study of the development of the teaching of Islamic education in the Arab Gulf States] al-Kuwayt.

Gulf Arab States Educational Research Center, (1981), *Dirasa muqarana li-waqi asalib at-taqwim wa-al-imtihanat bi-duwal al-halig al-arabi* [A comparative study of the state of evaluation methods and examinations in the Arab Gulf States] al-Kuwayt.

Gulf Arab States Educational Research Center, (1983), *Dirasa muqarana li-manahig al-ulum fi al-marhalatayn al-ibtida'iyya wa-al-mutawassita (al-idadiyya) bi-duwal al-halig al-arabi: ittigahat at-tawhid* [A comparative study of science curricula at the primary and intermediary (preparatory) levels in the Arab Gulf States: unification trends] al-Kuwayt.

Gulf Arab States Educational Research Center, (1984), *Dirasat tatwir al-baramig al-amaliyya fi manahig at-talim al-amm bi-duwal al-halig al-arabi* [A study of the development of practical programmes in the general education curricula of the Arab Gulf States] al-Kuwayt.

Gulf Arab States Educational Research Center, (1981), *al-Ittigahat al-hadita fi at-talim at-tanawi fi ad-duwal al-halig al-arabi* [Recent trends in secondary education in the Arab Gulf States] al-Kuwayt.

Gulf Arab States Educational Research Center, (1985), *Ittigahat talabat at-talim at-tanawi al-amm nahwa al-tahassusat ad-dirasiyya bi-at-talim al-ali wa-alaqatuha bi-magalat al-amal fi duwal al-halig al-arabi* [Trends of general secondary school pupils towards study areas of specialization in higher education and their relationship to fields of work in the Arab Gulf States] al-Kuwayt.

Gulf Arab States Educational Research Center, (1985), *Ittigahat wa-magalat al-baht at-tarbawi bi-duwal al-halig al-arabi wa-bad ad-duwal al-arabiyya: dirasa maydaniyya* [Trends and areas of educational research in Arab Gulf States and some Arab countries: a field study] al-Kuwayt.

Gulf Arab States Educational Research Center, (1981), *Taqwim al-baramig at-tarbawiyya fi al-watan al-arabi* [Evaluation of educational programmes in the Arab world] al-Kuwayt.

Gulf Arab States Educational Research Center, *at-Tawgih at-tarbawi wa-al-mihni li-talabat al-marhala al-mutawassita nahwa at-talim at-tanawi al-amm wa-al-mihni bi-duwal al-halig al-arabi: dirasa maydaniyya* [Educational and vocational guidance for students of the intermediary level to general secondary and vocational education in the Arab Gulf States: a field study]

Gulf Arab States Educational Research Center, (1983), *Waqi at-tarbiya as-sihhiyya fi al-marhala at-tanawiyya bi-duwal al-halig* [The state of health education at secondary level in the Gulf States] al-Kuwayt.

Gulf Arab States Educational Research Center, (1982), *Waqi at-tarbiya as-sihhiyya fi manahig al-marhala al-mutawassita bi-duwal al-halig* [The state of health education in the intermediary level curricula in the Gulf States] al-Kuwayt.

al-Gunaydi, A., (1965), *al-Fikr wa-at-taqafa al-muasira fi samal ifriqiya* [Contemporary thought and culture in North africa] al-Qahira, ad-Dar al-qawmiyya li-at-tibaa wa-an-nasr.

al-Gunaydi, A., (1982), *at-Tarbiya wa-bina' al-agyal fi daw' al-islam* [Education and the building of generations in the light of Islam] Bayrut, Dar al-kitab al-lubnari.

Hafiz, H. M., (1982), *Dirasa muqarana li-madà ta'attur at-talim at-tanawi bi-al-tiqnulugiyya at-talimiyya fi gunhuriyyat misr al-arabiyya wa-bad al-bilad al-agnabiyya* [A comparative study of the degree of influence of educational technology on secondary education in Egypt and some foreign countries] al-Qahira, Kulliyyat at-tarbiya, Gamiat Ayn Sams. [Thesis - MA] al-Hagg Isa, M., (1980), al-Waqi al-hali li-manahig al-ulum fi duwal al-halig al-arabi [The present state of science curricula in the Arab Gulf States] al-Kuwayt, Kulliyyat at-tarbiya, Gamiat al-kuwayt.

Halpern, M., (1963), *The politics of social change in the Middle East and North Africa*. Princeton, NJ, Princeton University Press.

Hammud, H., (1982), *Muskilat al-mar'a al-arabiyya fi at-talim wa-al-amal* [The problems of the Arab woman in education and work] Tunis, Wahdat al-buhut at-tarbawiyya, ALECSO.

al-Hassan, A., (1980), *al-Hutat ad-dirasiyya fi bad ad-duwal: ad-duwal al-arabiyya hattà am 1980. Ard wa-dirasa muqarana* [Curriculum plans in some countries: Arab countries up to 1980. A presentation and comparative study] al-Manama, Muraqabat at-tawtiq wa-al-malumat wa-al-buhut at-tarbawiyya, Idarat at-tahtit at-tarbawi, Wazarat at-tarbiya wa-at-talim.

Hassan, F. G. A., (1982), Dirasa muqarana li-muskilat tanmiyat at-tarbiya fi gumhuriyyat misr al-arabiyya wa-bad ad-duwal an-namiya [A comparative study of the problems of educational development in Egypt and some developing countries] Asyut, Egypt, Kulliyyat at-tarbiya, Gamiat Asyut. [Thesis]

Hug, A., (1984), *Harakat al-muallimin bayna al-aqtar al-arabiyya* [The teachers' movement in Arab countries] Tunis, ALECSO.

al-Husari, S., (1948), al-Alaqat at-taqafiyya fi al-bilad al-arabiyya [Cultural relations in the Arab countries] *Sahifat at-tarbiya*, vol. 1, no. 1, July.

al-Husari, S. *Hawliyyat at-taqafa al-arabiyya* [The annals of Arab culture] (al-Qahira, Gamiat ad-duwal al-arabiyya), no. 1-6, 1950-1963.

al-Husayn, M. M., et al., (1981), *Muskilat at-talim fi ar-rif al-arabi* [The problems of education in Arab rural areas] Tunis, ALECSO.

Ibrahim, I. H., (1981), al-Anmat al-idariyya fi aghizat at-tarbiya al-amaliyya fi misr wa-inkiltira wa-yuguslafiya: dirasa muqarana [Administrative patterns in work education organizations in Egypt, England and Yugoslavia: a comparative study] al-Qahira, Kulliyyat at-tarbiya, Gamiat Ayn Sams. [Thesis - MA]

Ibn-Haldun, A., (1984), *al-Muqaddima* [The introduction] Tunis, ad-Dar at-tunisiyya li-an-nasr.

Ibn Hamida, H., (1986), *Idad muallim al-mutafawwiqin aqliyyan fi al-bilad al-arabiyya* [The preparation of the teacher of the mentally gifted in the Arab countries] Tunis, Idarat al-buhut at-tarbawiyya, ALECSO.

Ibn Hamida, H., (1985), *Muskilat talim as-sabab fi al-watan al-arabi* [Problems of youth education in the Arab world] Tunis, Idarat al-buhut at-tarbawiyya, ALECSO.

Ismail, M. A., (1976), *A cross cultural study of moral judgements: the relationship between American and Saudi Arabian university students on the defining issues test*. Stillwater, OK, Oklahoma State University. [Thesis - Ed. D.]

Iwad, M. A. M., (1985), Bad muskilat at-talim at-tanawi as-sinai fi gumhuriyyat misr al-arabiyya wa-inkiltira: dirasa muqarana [Some problems of secondary industrial education in Egypt and England: a comparative study] Asyut, Egypt, Kulliyyat at-tarbiya, Gamiat Asyut. [Thesis]

Jarragh, A. J. A., (1980), The characteristics of National Science Foundation-sponsored science programs in American secondary schools and implications for science education in Kuwaiti secondary schools. Denton, TX, North Texas State University. [Thesis]

Karam, G. A., (1977), *Riyad al-atfal fi al-iraq wa-bad al-aqtar al-arabiyya: dirasa muqarana* [Kindergartens in Iraq and other Arab countries] Bagdad, Wazarat at-tarbiya.

Kerr, M. H. Egypt. *In*: Coleman, J. S., ed., (1965), *Education and political development*. Princeton, NJ, Princeton University Press, 169-194.

Khayr ad-Din at-Tunisi (1972), *Aqwan al-masalik fi marifat ahwal al-mamalik* [The most appropriate ways of knowing the power of states], ed. by M. Chenoufi. Tunis, Société tunisienne de diffusion.

Koraiem, M. A., (1978), A comparison of philosophical orientations between prospective teachers in the United States and Egypt. Ames, IA, School of Education, Iowa State University. [Thesis]

Kuwait. Wazarat at-tarbiya, (1984), *Dirasa muqarana li-al-hutat ad-dirasiyya fi dawlat al-kuwayt wa-bad ad-duwal al-arabiyya fi marahili at-talim al-amm* [A comparative study of educational programmes in Kuwait and other Arab countries at the general education levels] al-Kuwayt, Markaz buhut al-manahig.

Kuwait. Wazarat at-tarbiya, (1981), *Dirasa muqarana li-muqarrarat ar-riyadiyyat fi dawlat al-kuwayt wa-muqarrarat ar-riyadiyyat fi bad ad-duwal al-agnabiyya* [A comparative study of mathematics curricula in Kuwait and mathematics curricula in some foreign countries] al-Kuwayt, Markaz buhut al-manahig.

Lutfi, M. K. *Dirasat fi nuzum at-talim* [Studies in education systems] al-Faggala, Egypt, Maktabat misr, n.d.

Lutfi, M. K., (1986), *Muallim at-tarbiya al-islamiyya wa-al-luga al-arabiyya: tasawwur muqtarah li-tadribihi wa-tanmiyat maharatihi* [The teacher of Islamic education and the Arabic language: a proposed concept for his training and for developing his skills] Tunis, ALECSO.

al-Malaq, M. b . A., (1984), Manahig ar-riyadiyyat fi al-yaban: dirasa tahliliyya wa-muqarana maa al-manahig as-saudiyya [Mathematics curricula in Japan: an analytical comparative study with Saudi Arabian curricula] ar-Riyad, Markaz al-buhut at-tarbawiyya, Gamiat al-Malik Saud.

al-Malla, A. A., (1979), *Atar al-ulama' al-muslimin fi al-hadara al-urubbiyya* [The influence of Moslem scholars on European civilization] Dimasq, Dar al-fikr.

al-Mamuri, M.; Abid, A.; al-Gazali, S., (1983), *Ta'tir talim al-lugat al-agnabiyya fi taallim al-luga al-arabiyya* [The influence of foreign language teaching on the study of Arabic] Tunis, Idarat al-buhut at-tarbawiyya, ALECSO.

al-Manai, L. A., (1981), *Dirasa tahliliyya fi al-infaq alà at-talim fi al-bahrayn li-al-am ad-dirasi 1980-81 wa-muqaranatuhu bi-takalif at-talim fi duwal al-halig al-arabi* [An analytical study of educational expenditures in Bahrain for the academic year 1980-81 as compared with educational costs in the Arab Gulf States] al-Manama, Muraqabat at-tawtiq wa-al-malumat wa-al-buhut at-tarbawiyya, Idarat at-tahtit at-tarbawi, Wazarat at-tarbiya wa-at-talim.

Mari, S. K., (1971), *Creativity of American and Arab rural youth: a cross-cultural study* Madison, WI, School of Education, University of Wisconsin. [Thesis]

al-Masqati, A., (1978), *at-Talim at-tanawi as-sinai fi duwal al-halig al-arabi* [Secondary industrial education in the Arab Gulf States] al-Manama, Muraqabat at tawtiq wa-al-buhut, Idarat at-tahtit at-tarbawi, Wazarat at-tarbiya wa-at-talim.

al-Masqati, A., (1977), *at-Talim at-tanawi fi duwal al-halig al-arabi minam 1970-1975* [Secondary education in the Arab Gulf States from 1970-1975] al-Manama, Muraqabat at-tawtiq wa-al-buhut, Idarat at-tahtit at-tarbawi, Wazarat at-tarbiya wa-at-talim.

Massialas, B. G.; Jarrar, S. A., (1983), *Education in the Arab world.* New York, Praeger.

Mihriz, Z. M., (1981), *at-Talim al-asasi: amtila min tatbiqat mabadi' wa-usus at-talim al-asasi fi bad ad-duwal al-arabiyya hattà am 1979* [Basic education: examples of the applications of the principles and fundamentals of basic education in some Arab countries until 1979] al-Manama, Muraqabat at-tawtiq wa-al-malumat wa-al-buhut at-tarbawiyya, Idarat at-tahtit at-tarbawi, Wazarat at-tarbiya wa-at-talim.

Mihriz, Z. M., (1980), *at-Talim al-asasi: dirasa muqarana fi bad ad-duwal al-agnabiyya* [Basic education: a comparative study in some foreign countries] al-Manama, Muraqabat at-tawtiq wa-al-malumat wa-al-buhut at-tarbawiyya, Idarat at-tahtit at-tarbawi, Wazarat at-tarbiya wa-at-talim.

Mugawir, M. S. A., (1983), *Namadig min al-ihtibarat al-mawduiyya fi al-luga al-arabiyya bi-al-marhala al-ibtida'iyya* [Models of objective examinations in the Arabic language for the primary level] Tunis, Idarat al-buhut at-tarbawiyya, ALECSO.

Muhammad Ali, A. K., (1978), *Dawr al-munazzama al-arabiyya li-at-tarbiya wa-at-taqafa wa-al-ulum fi tatwir bad gawanib at-talim fi gumhuriyyat misr al-arabiyya wa-al-iraq wa-al-urdunn* [The role of ALECSO in the development of some aspects of education in Egypt, Iraq and Jordan] Asyut, Egypt, Kulliyyat at-tarbiya, Gamiat Asyut. [Thesis - MA]

Mursi, M. M., (1981), *al-Margi fi at-tarbiya al-muqarana* [The reference in comparative education] al-Qahira, Alam al-kutub.

Mursi, M. M.; Simaan, W. I., (1977), *al-Madhal fi at-tarbiya al-muqarana* [An introduction to comparative education] al-Qahira, al-Maktaba al-anglu al-misriyya.

Mursi, M. S., (1979), at-Tarbiya wa-at-tabia al-insaniyya fi al-fikr al-islami wa-bad al-falsafat al-garbiyya [Education and human nature in Islamic thought and some Western philosophies] Asyut, Egypt, Kulliyyat at-tarbiya, Gamiat Asyut. [Thesis]

Mursi, M. S., (1976), Tarbiyat al-mar'a al-misriyya bayna al-fikr al-islami wa-al-fikr al-garbi min al-qarn at-tasi asar [Education and the Egyptian woman between Islamic thought and nineteenth century Western thought] Asyut, Egypt, Kulliyyat at-tarbiya, Gamiat Asyut. [Thesis - MA]

Mutawà, I. I., (1980), Waqi al-gamiat al-arabiyya: nazra tahliliyya naqida [The state of Arab universities: an analytical and critical point of view] *Magallat kulliyyat at-tarbiya*, no. 5, May, 109-129.

an-Nasif, H., (1980), Dirasa muqarana li-ahdaf at-tarbiya ma qabla al-madrasa fi kull min al-kuwayt wa-al-mamlaka al-muttahida [A comparative study of the aims of preschool education in Kuwait and the UK] Reading, UK, School of Education, University of Reading. [Thesis]

Osman, A. M. M., (1981), Comparative education and sociological thought in the Arab region, with special reference to the work of ALECSO. *International review of education* (The Hague), vol. XXVII, no. 4, 483-495.

al-Qadafi, R. M., et al., (1982), *at-Talim at-tanawi fi al-bilad al-arabiyya* [Secondary education in the Arab countries] Tunis, Idarat al-buhut at-tarbawiyya, ALECSO.

al-Qasir, I. A., (1979), Dirasa muqarana li-nizam at-talim fi maahid idad muallimi al-marhala al-ilzamiyya fi suriya wa-al-urdunn [A comparative study of the education system in training colleges for compulsory level teachers in Syria and Jordan] Amman, Kulliyyat at-tarbiya, Gamiat al-urdunn.

al-Qusayri, A. M. A., (1982), Dirasa muqarana li-al-munazzamat al-mihniyya li-al-muallimin fi kull min gumhuriyyat misr al-arabiyya wa-al-wilayat al-muttahida al-amrikiyya wa-dawruha fi tatwir al-makana al-iqtisadiyya wa-al-igtimaiyya li-al-muallim [A comparative study of the professional teachers' organizations in Egypt and the USA and their role in the development of the economic and social status of the teacher] Asyut, Egypt, Kulliyyat at-tarbiya, Gamiat Asyut. [Thesis - MA]

ar-Ragihi, M.; Ammar, A., (1981), *Tarbiyat al-muawwaqin aqliyyan fi al-bilad al-arabiyya* [The education of the mentally handicapped in the Arab countries] Tunis, ALECSO.

ar-Rasid, M. A., (1978), *Dawr kulliyyat at-tarbiya fi tatwir at-talim al-ali fi al-alam al-arabi* [The role of the faculties of education in the development of higher education in the Arab world] ar-Riyhad, Kulliyyat at-tarbiya, Gamiat al-Malik Saud.

Roussen, F., (1984), *Aspects and future plans of educating visually handicapped children in Jordan and the Middle East*. Amman, Faculty of Education, University of Jordan.

Said, T. M., (1979), Tanzim wa-idarat at-talim: dirasa muqarana fi al-gumhuriyya al-iraqiyya wa-gumhuriyyat rumaniya al-istirakiyya [The organization and administration of education: a comparative study of Iraq and Romania] *Magallat al-buhut at-tarbawiyya wa-an-nafsiyya*, vol. 1, no. 1, December, 93-153.

Said, M. A., (1986), *al-Ahdaf at-tarbawiyya fi gumhuriyyat misr al arabiyya* [The aims of education in Egypt] Tunis, ALECSO.

as-Salgi, N. R., (1976), *at-Talim as-sinai wa-az-zirai fi al-iraq wa-bad al-aqtar al-arabiyya* [Industrial and agricultural education in Iraq and some Arab countries] Bagdad, al-Mudiriyya al-amma li-at-tahtit at-tarbawi, Wazarat at-tarbiya.

as-Salih, F. S., (1980), *Ahdaf at-talim fi bad ad-duwal: dirasa muqarana* [Educational aims in some countries: a comparative study] al-Manama, Muraqabat at-tawtiq wa-al-malumat wa-al-buhut at-tarbawiyya, Idarat at-tahtit at-tarbawi, Wazarat at-tarbiya wa-at-talim.

Samut, U.; al-Hatib, A., (1981), *Taqwim muhawalat tawhid al-manahig wa-tatwiriha fi al-alam al-arabi* [Evaluation of the attempts at standardizing and developing curricula in the Arab world] Tunis, Wahdat al-buhut at-tarbawiyya, ALECSO.

as-Sattawi, A.; al-Ahmar, M. A., (1983), *Waqi at-tarbiya ma qabla al-madrasiyya fi al-watan al-arabi* [The state of preschool education in the Arab world] Tunis, Idarat at-tarbiya, ALECSO.

al-Shami, I. A., (1977), Tradition and technology in the development of education of Saudi Arabia and Egypt. Ann Arbor, MI, School of Education, University of Michigan. [Thesis]

Shrida, F. S., (1981), A comparative study of physical education programs' influences on youth physical fitness levels in public schools in Iraq and the United States. Nashville, TN, George Peabody College for Teachers. [Thesis]

Simaan, W. I., (1980), *Dirasat fi at-tarbiya al-muqarana* [Studies in comparative education] al-Qahira, al-Maktaba al-anglu al-misriyya.

Soubeih, N. A. A., (1980), University studies in adult education in the Arab countries: a comparative study. Qatar, Faculty of Education, University of Qatar.

Subayh, N. A. A., (1981), *Dirasat fi at-tarbiya al-muqarana* [Studies in comparative education] al-Qahira, Dar at-taqafa li-at-tibaa wa-an-nasr.

Sulayman, A., (1979), *al-Ittigahat at-tarbawiyya al-muasira: dirasa fi at-tarbiya al-muqarana* [Contemporary educational trends: a study in comparative education] al-Qahira, al-Maktaba al-anglu al-misriyya.

Sulayman, A., (1979), *Dinamikiyyat at-tarbiya fi al-mugtamaat: madhal tahlili muqaran* [The dynamics of education in societies: an analytical comparative introduction] al-Qahira, al-Maktaba al-anglu al-misriyya.

Sulayman, A. A., (1978), *Istratigiyyat al-idara fi at-talim: dirasa tahliliyya muqarana* [Administration strategy in education: an analytical comparative study] al-Qahira, al-Maktaba al-anglu al-misriyya.

at-Tahhan, M. H., (1982), Tarbiyat al-mutafawwiqin aqliyyan fi al-bilad al-arabiyya [The education of the intellectually gifted in the Arab countries] Tunis, Wahdat al-buhut al-arabiyya, ALECSO.

Wahid, N. A., (1980), at-Talim fi al-iraq wa-rumaniya: dirasa muqarana [Education in Iraq and Romania: a comparative study] al-Basra, Iraq, Kulliyyat at-tarbiya, Gamiat al-Basra. [Thesis]

Wasif, A. W., (1981), Ibn Haldun: ittigah fi at-tarbiya al-muqarana [Ibn Khaldun: an approach to comparative education] Paper read at the International and Comparative Education Conference, London, November.

Zaydi, A., (1986), *Tarih an-nizam at-tarbawi li-as-suba al-asriyya az-zaytuniyya* (1951-1965) [A history of the education system of the modern branch of az-Zaytunah (1951-1965)] Tunis, Centre de recherches en bibliothéconomie et sciences de l'information.

PART III

The national and international impact of comparative education infrastructures

Robert Cowen

Introduction

As comparative educationists, we do not know very much about ourselves.[1] What are the social structures of our professional lives and how do they act upon us? Is there one comparative education world-wide, or are there different national views of what comparative education is? What is the interplay of comparative education at the national and the international levels through the infrastructures of comparative education: the centres of comparative and international educational studies, the international, regional and national professional societies of comparative educationists, and the specialized journals associated with comparative education?

Such questions are normally of interest to sociologists of knowledge, rather than to practitioners within a field, at work on the puzzle-solving of routine research. However, comparative education is currently in an unstable condition. On the one hand it is expanding, on a world basis, as a set of professional and academic activities: on the other, some of its earliest ideological certainties have disintegrated. This is a good time to explore more fully some of the working structures which help to define our identity.

Comparative education as a field of study is without a major classic literature and without founding fathers of the stature of those in sociology (or economics, or political science); it is without the massive accumulation of research work which characterizes history; it is without the secure institutional university and research base of some of the natural sciences;

and it is without the recognized utility of engineering or computer studies. Among educational studies, there are world-wide only a few specialist centres for comparative education. As a field of study, comparative education is neither discipline based, nor immediately useful in schools.

Comparative education is interstitial. In its forms of understanding, it falls between the proto-theoretic and the directly useful; between the nation-specific and the completely relativistic; between hard policy science and *Verstehen*. In its institutions, it is partly of the university research world; partly of the world of the international educational agency, the think-tank, and the development agency; partly an idealistic element in the training of young teachers; and occasionally part of the policy advice structures of governments.

This lack of clarity over what is the epistemological core and institutional centre of comparative education means that the networks of connection between the bits and pieces of comparative education take on extra importance. Changes in networks (of new centres, journals and societies) are one measure of what comparative education is, and one indication of the definition, demand, and supply of comparative education on a world basis.

At the moment it seems that the growth of comparative education is at its strongest away from the historically important metropolitan centres for the study of comparative education: western and eastern Europe, and northern America. Comparative education is changing: non-metropolitan university centres are being developed, more professional Societies are being created in more parts of the world, and more specialist professional interaction is taking place.

If we are to strengthen these processes, do we know whether the university is the best, or even the minimally necessary, base for the creation of comparative education as a specialist professional identity? Do journals need a university home, or are they better located within a national professional Society? Are the best international and comparative Societies essentially national institutions? What is the point and purpose of the supranational professional Societies? What is the international interplay of 'comparative education(s)'?[2] And what are the educational politics of our self-construction?

It is probable that we do not know, except by piecemeal personal experience, the answer to many of these questions. But the questions and answers are of both practical and theoretical importance. They are of practical importance because building some of the infra-structures of comparative education, mainly a 1960s process in North America and Europe, is a 1980s process in many other countries. The theoretical importance rests in the question of how fields of study are constructed, sustained, and redefined through networks in an international context. The more self-conscious we are about the theoretical implications of the practical processes, the less likely we are to construct unintentional hegemonies of knowledge. Or, faced with an intended knowledge hegemony, we are in a better position to know what to do about it.

Understanding such processes is of great importance to comparativists. We have already combined an ideology of internationalism with ethnocentric praxis.

Ideology and integration

Comparative education as an academic field of study has often prided itself on its commitment to the reduction of ethnocentricism through knowing and teaching about other nations.[3] Its professional networks, including the World Council of Comparative Education Societies, are international. The language based professional societies (such as the francophone, and Dutch speaking societies) and the Comparative Education Society in Europe are, purposefully supranational. Comparative education is proudly international. The international orientation of the personnel in the field, the few specialist scholars who claim to be 'comparative educationists' and the frequency of their interaction, permit the implicit, occasionally explicit, assumption that national boundaries, though they are central to much of our substantive research work, are marginal in our sense of professional identity.[4]

This international orientation is expressed in many of the institutions through which our professional energies flow. For example, most of the specialist journal editors seek authors outside the national boundaries of the country in which the journal is located. This is true even when the journal is heavily associated with one national comparative education society, as in the case of *Comparative education review* and *Compare*; and even more true when the journal is non-national, like the *International review of education*.[5] Similarly, major university centres of comparative education will attract scholars and students from all over the world. Such departments, in order to remain major centres for the study of comparative education, seek international salience for their publications or research output. Major centres have a national base but, in some important respect, an international clientèle and reference group.

Thus both the liberal stance of one of our major traditions, and the way some of our institutions work, stress our unity as an international community. This professional ideology - comforting, even pleasant - tends to obscure the question of when, how and why comparative education becomes 'comparative educations'.

Practice and diversity

This chapter will argue that comparative education is not, in a number of important ways, international any longer. The small networks and the epistemological assumptions that made it so, temporarily, are breaking up. Different comparative educations are emerging in different places.

One set of variations is institutional, embedded in the relations between the university and research institute bases of comparative education, the structures and networks of publication, and links with governments. The institutional base for the production of comparative education knowledge is centrifugal, nationally specific in its administrative-political linkages, and tends to contradict the professional ideology that comparativists make a special international community. Only some institutions are international in their clients, patronage and academic production. More typically, there emerge national and quite local definitions of who works in comparative education, through what kind of institutional arrangements, and for what purposes.

Other important variations emerge from different assumptions about what should be the academic contents which are accepted as comparative education, and the methodological principles which define how good work may be created. For example, quite sharp differences have been identified between 'socialist' and 'capitalist' assumptions in this area. Equally, several disciplinary areas now do comparative work but do not always take or want for themselves the title 'comparative education'. One obvious example is the work of several sociologists and historians.[6] There is also the academic work on development and education. Historically this field, often practical in orientation, also contains works which are deliberately comparative[7] and there have been very marked national differences in whether a clear distinction has been drawn between development education and comparative education.[8]

The remainder of the chapter will explore some of these institutional and epistemological tensions. In the first line of educational politics, illustrating how parts of the infrastructure of comparative education create - in local ways - the conditions for doing comparative education. Is it the case, everywhere, that the university must establish and legitimate an academic field or study called comparative education; do journals and professional societies and links with governments, follow this first step? Or have there been very different links within the infrastructures of comparative education, and does this suggest how comparative education might be extended and strengthened as an area of enquiry in places where it is only recently developing? The second part of the chapter will concentrate on a different aspect of educational politics: looking at the social construction of comparative education knowledge, and some of the national and international forces which influence its definition. The last part of the chapter will return to the question of the balance between the international and the national in comparative education.

The institutional base

The immediate, perhaps obvious assumption - that it is the university which is the basic institution around which journals and professional societies are created and stabilized - is too unsubtle and may be ethnocentric. It is doubtful if the assumption applies to all countries and it certainly overlooks the importance of the mix of universities, research institutes, and government action in developing and defining the networks of comparative education.

For example, in China, since 1976, university activity in comparative education and the Chinese Comparative Education Society have been created, a journal has been founded, and the Ministry itself has established a department of comparative education. Though there was an earlier involvement in China in comparative study, after Liberation this international interest diminished.[9] What was mainly studied was Soviet education. During the Cultural Revolution 'the few institutions studying foreign education were disbanded or at least forced to stop operating'.[10]

Following 'the downfall of the Gang of Four' in 1976, there was a rebalancing of political and educational policy towards more international involvement. In consequence, about a dozen universities have departments or centres for the study of comparative education; by 1979 the Chinese Comparative Education Society was established in Shanghai - and now has over 300 members - and by 1979 seven universities had begun to take graduate students (mainly at the masters level) in comparative education.[11] The Central Institute of Educational Sciences, which is a national education research institute affiliated to the Education Ministry, has a comparative education division, and indeed publishes comparative material in its journal

Educational research.[12] The comparative education division of the Central Institute of Educational Sciences also publishes and edits the bimonthly specialist comparative journal *Foreign education* - jointly with the Chinese Comparative Education Society.[13]

Clearly the policy to establish and develop comparative education has been a matter of government decision. Thus, in the Chinese case, what is visible is a strong working relationship between the government, the universities and the publication structures following China's new openness about, and political stance toward international influence. The university has not been central to these processes, at least in the early stages of activity.

Another variant on the non-primacy of the university in the creation of comparative education, its societies and its journals, may be noted. In several countries, which include the Democratic Republic of Germany, Poland[14] and the USSR, the tradition of the research institute has been strong. This tradition has been compounded by the creation of the network of Academies of Pedagogical Sciences which have undertaken so much of the important comparative research activity. For example, in the 1960s the Academy of Pedagogical Sciences of the USSR created a department of comparative education within one of its units concerned with 'general problems of education'.[15] Similarly, in the German Democratic Republic, the Academy of Pedagogical Sciences organizes large-scale research, including research in comparative education.[16] Within the Academy (formerly the Central German Institute of Education, Berlin) two departments concentrate on comparative education research: the Department of Comparative Education, which deals in comparative international research; and the Department of West German Education which researches educational developments in the Federal Republic of Germany.[17] There is, in addition to this central core of research, a broader research and teaching base composed of universities and institutes such as Karl Marx University, Leipzig; Humboldt University, Berlin; and *Hochschulen* in Potsdam and Erfurt.

However, the strength of comparative education is not drawn from its role in teacher training; nor even from the fact that it is a 'regular subject of instruction only in post-graduate training'.[18] The balance of the institutional base of comparative education in the German Democratic Republic, and the bias toward advanced research, is reflected in one of the main outlets for comparative material, the journal *Vergleichende pädagogik*, which, though it contains articles from a variety of sources (including foreign authors), is clearly not dependent on the writings of specialist teachers of comparative education.

Here again it is not merely the elements present within the infrastructure but also the relation between the elements, which defines the pattern of educational politics. A strong government interest in international comparisons of educational policy, the Academies of Pedagogical Science and specialist research units, and publication structures stand in close relation to each other. It has been this research activity, with a strong applied motif, rather than the teaching and research activities of the universities, which has been central to the infrastructures of comparative education, and which has dominated their relation.

Within Western Europe as a whole, and in particular countries within Western Europe, the educational policies are different; the relation of the elements of the infrastructure of comparative education is much looser. A university base does exist. Many European academics, in countries ranging from Norway to Spain and Italy, manage to do some comparative education; although only rarely is teaching a sequence of comparative courses their main professional responsibility. Consequently, the Comparative Education Society in Europe is buttressed partly from a university base - but not, in any major way, by a university base of specialist comparative education departments.[19] Rather it mobilizes a number of scholars inside Europe (and outside it) in biennial meetings. It manages to publish conference proceedings as well as a newsletter, which may not, however, be considered a journal.

It has no clear relationship with any government, though typically some subsidy to the costs of Conferences has come from a national or regional government source (normally from the country which is hosting the biennial conference). To this Society (CESE), scholars belong as individuals, a situation repeated in the range of national or language-based comparative education societies based in western Europe.

Of course the parlous condition of the various comparative education societies within western Europe is not merely a consequence of the difficulties of organizing and articulating the infrastructures of comparative education. It is also an expression of the political location of university-linked comparative education in several of the countries of Western Europe: almost all governments have been indifferent to the opportunity to anticipate domestic educational reform by the use of continuous comparative qualitative assessment and analysis.[20]

One of the latest recruits to be struggling to create a comparative education infrastructure under similar incohate conditions, and within patterns of educational politics which are becoming similar to those described for the Western European infrastructures is Brazil, which established a national Comparative Education Society in 1983. The Society has no widespread university base; has only intermittent links with government; and is without an organized publications structure.

In Brazil, as in China, there had been an earlier tradition of comparative education, associated particularly in the early post-war period with the names of Anisio Teixeira and Lourenco Filho.[21] However, this early tradition weakened, and when choices were being made of the subjects which would be a mandatory part of graduate studies in education, comparative education was not one of these subjects.[22]

Nevertheless, a small number of scholars were strongly committed to comparative education. There were two groups, one centring mainly on Brazilia and including among its members Eurides Brito da Silva, Clelia Capanema and Jacira Camara; and another group centring around universities in Niteroi and Rio, including Roberto Ballalai, Mabel de Oliveira and Fatima Ferreira Pinto. Through an initiative by Professor Eurides Brito da Silva, the Secretary of State of the Federal District of Education, a discussion was held between these two groups and other invited persons, such as Marcos Manuel Formiga and Claudio de Moura Castro, which laid the foundations for the Society.[23] From this initial discussion came the first business and academic meeting of the Society (also in Brasilia) in September 1983 and, indirectly, the fact that the Brazilian Society hosted the meeting of the World Congress of Comparative Education Societies in 1987.

In Brazil, the university teaching of comparative education was not a pre-requisite for the establishment of a Society of Comparative Education, nor were all the founders specialists in comparative education itself.[24] Networks of a certain sort and personal commitment were sufficient - though it is noticeable that the main movers in the creation of the Society had undergone some of their training overseas in the USA and France. At the moment in Brazil there is no comparative education journal. Traditionally it has been the National Institute for Educational Research (INEP) which has published comparative material, though comparative material may also be found in the journal *Educacao e sociedade*.[25]

Thus, in many parts of Europe, in China and Brazil, university people have had some influence in the creation of comparative education societies and comparative education journals, but the university has not necessarily been the decisive agency. The role of governments, the existence of research institutes, the networks of those returning from overseas graduate education have also been important, even decisive. Shifts in perception - of international politics, in assumptions about where, geographically, interesting reform in education might be taking place, and whether domestic educational reform is needed - have been influential. in such situations the universities may become, subsequently, a source of specialist scholars but they have not been, in the educational politics of several places, the prime movers in creating and sustaining comparative education infrastructures.

In contrast, in Australia, Britain, Canada and the United States, specialists and sometimes specialist departments within the university have been important in the creation and definition of the societies and journals of comparative education. Even within this group of countries, however, it is possible to see responsiveness to local conditions producing variations in how things were created and subsequently held together.

In Britain, for example, university specialists were important in the development of the field of study, but it has been the colleges of teacher education which have provided the broad base of membership necessary to sustain the British Comparative and International Education Society and its journal.[26] By the 1960s a number of university centres had been established where the academic study of comparative education had been institutionalized; there were teachers, courses, degrees and textbooks. In the 1960s these centres were, primarily, London, the University of Reading and the University of Oxford.[27] Of these, London was undoubtedly the most important, because of the number of its staff, the number of their publications, and the visibility accorded to London by the *(World) yearbook of education*. These university centres (and particular individuals) were important in the creation of the British Society in 1966, but it was the depth of membership in the teachers colleges which was important in defining the Society. The teachers colleges were crucial to the identity of the Society - indeed much of the early work to sustain the Society and its journal came out of Didsbury College of Education, and later Chester College. The Society was in some ways caught between two masters: its creation followed a conference held at Reading in 1965 on *The place of comparative education in the training of teachers*;[28] and it took as its titles, the Comparative Education Society of Europe (British Section). Thus, on the one hand it was linked with the teaching of comparative education, rather than the advancement of research;[29] and, on the other hand, it was linked with those who had recently (1962-63) played a major role in the creation of the Comparative Education Society in Europe and who clearly saw the British Society as an integral, but subordinate, part of a more important body.[30]

With some difficulty the British Society managed to create a journal, which grew out of a newsletter edited initially by people working in the college sector of higher education. By 1971 the newsletter had become the journal *Compare*. The journal, it has been suggested, was very narrow in its content and its readership.[31] It took another half decade to break away from its origins as a vade-mecum for college teachers of comparative education, though this it did with increasing speed from the late 1970s, especially under Peter Ragatt's editorship.

However, while these changes were underway with the journal, the institutional base of comparative education was itself changing. From the mid-1970s, the colleges of education in which there had been some teaching of comparative education began to collapse with the national contraction in teacher training. This made even clearer the importance of the university sector within which comparative education was still of interest to scholars in universities like Bristol, Cambridge, Durham, Glasgow, Hull, Leeds, Manchester, Reading and the Open University - even though the reputation of a particular university in comparative education was frequently linked with the efforts of one individual.[32]

Fortunately, at this time of contraction, the British Society was able to act as an important outlet - through national conferences, through regional meetings, and by providing writing opportunities - for the talents of those working in comparative education in universities. The result has been a double one. First, London no longer dominates the national scene, as it did in the mid-1960s. Second, in its own right, the British Comparative and International Society has become an important network and an avenue of opportunity. From the Society comes a series of publications, notably through links with the publishers Croom Helm. Individuals can now edit Conference Proceedings, as books, for the Society. In times of university, career and publishing contraction, the Society has become attractive as an arena within which to make a mark. This represents a reversal of the 1960s situation, when working in a university was impressive to the British Comparative Society. Now work in the Society may be useful in impressing the university.

The more general version of this principle is to be seen in the increasing importance of publishers in sustaining the networks and activities of comparative educationists. Obviously publishers in many countries have always played a role in the development of comparative education but now in the British context, their role in holding the networks together is crucial. The most obvious example here is the journal *Comparative education* edited by E. J. King. Without an institutional base, it has survived to become a major comparative journal not only in Britain but world-wide. *Compare* and *Comparative education*, are in the absence of major new British textbooks in comparative education, important in giving a sense of identity and professional community to those interested in comparative education within Britain.[33]

The Canadians have faced a similar problem and found a similar solution. They created a journal *Canadian and international education*, which has survived extremely well (alongside the powerful American *Comparative education review* despite a relatively thin university base and despite being only briefly subsidized. The *Canadian and international education* journal, together with the annual meetings of the Canadian Learned Societies (within which the Comparative and International Society has traditionally held its meetings) has helped the Canadian specialists within universities to stay in touch with each other. The university base has been important; but it is heavily dependent on graduate study in a few major centres, such as the Ontario Institute for the Study of Education, the Universities of Calgary, Edmonton, Montreal, McGill, Ottawa and Toronto.[34] In the networking of the Canadian scholars the Society (founded in 1967) and the Journal (1972) have been vital, not least because the Canadian networks extend into the (American) Comparative and International Education Society, in which several Canadians have been Officers, including Presidential Officers. In Australia, too, the tyranny of distance, a similarly scattered set of places where comparative education is taught and studied, and a similar intermittent relation with state and federal governments, are the basic conditions which face the scholars in the field. Historically, the Centre for Comparative and International Education at La Trobe has been the biggest specialist centre for comparative scholars, but there is a network held together by the Australian and New Zealand Comparative and International Education Society, which began life in 1973.[35] The Society does not at the moment run a journal, though it has published annual Conference Proceedings since 1980.

The earliest model of the creation of a Society and a Journal from a university base was that of the USA.[36] However - and this is of importance for scholars in other countries - the network was created on a very narrow institutional base which included Teachers College, Columbia, New York, the University of Chicago, Kent State University and New York University. The journal and the Society helped to create the field of study inside the university, with some intermittent interest from the Federal Government and other research funding agencies interested in education in particular parts of the world.

In the initial phase of coming together, it was not an established group of university (comparative) departments which combined to create the networks.[37] Rather it was the networks - particularly of those who had had foreign educational experience either as individuals or as servants of the American government in educational reconstruction overseas - which helped to combine and focus a series of scattered efforts in comparative education.[38] In addition, there was much international visiting, especially by Gerald Read and William Brickman;[39] and there was clearly consolidation of overseas networks by American and expatriate scholars.[40] Nor was it merely the networks which was important. From early days an effort was made to involve those within educational policy making, and find support from the Foundations.[41]

In time, the university base widened and fed back on these pioneering efforts to produce the largest comparative education society in the world. Later, Teachers College, Columbia, ceased to exert such a major influence over the national field of study. Still later, the journal of the Society moved to other universities as newer strong centres of specialist study, such as Wisconsin and the State University of New York at Buffalo, emerged. In these later formations, the university core of specialist scholars has probably[42] dominated the publication outlets, the funded research patterns and effective purposes of the Society and the Journal, which gradually growing toward its present condition of excellence, has become under Altbach's editorship definitive of the mainstream US field of study.

However, the main point is not here the example of success in itself, but the particular American patterns of the educational politics which underpinned and framed the formation of the comparative education infrastructures. In the earlier period in the USA, the infrastructural relationships of comparative education were not linear - with the university determining the rest - but symbiotic: each of the parts - individual biographies and personal networks, university departments, the Journal and the Society - contributed, with some help from the Foundations and interest by government agencies, to the growth of the other.

In this section of the chapter a sketch has been offered of the institutional infrastructure of a number of comparative educations. Each is a product of educational politics. These educational politics define the wide variations in the relations of scholarly networks, governments, professional societies, university centres, the specialist journals, publishing and teaching activities, in producing comparative educations.

This is not to forget, amid the complexities of the educational politics, that what are being created are *dedicated* networks and infrastructures: most of the social actors and agencies which constitute the infrastructures are concerned with the definition, creation and reorganization, and transmission of 'comparative education' as a field of knowledge. It is now useful to look directly at some aspects of the social creation of that knowledge, as a second step in analyzing the national and international infrastructures of comparative education.

Comparative education knowledge

The obvious place to look for definitions of comparative education is in the writings of comparative educationists. The boundaries and contents of a field of knowledge are decided by the academics who work within it.

While academics do write books, articles, conference papers and so on, both the institutions inside which they work, and the broader social and political world to which they respond, affect what they perceive as problems to be resolved. Thus their academic definitions of their field of study should be noted, but should also be understood as reflecting some of the institutional, social and political contexts of their work. This social contextualization of comparative education leads to different comparative educations in different parts of the world - and, it will be suggested, the ideology of internationalism which disguises the ethnocentric praxis of comparative education is itself the product of a particular moment in the history of comparative education.

There are several possible illustrations of the social contextualization of comparative education. Here three will be pursued. First, the struggle to control the meta-principles of the field. Second, the social framing of reconstruction and reform in the post-war world, and the internationalist perspective. Third, development as a theme for comparative education.

Meta-principles and categories of attention

Unlike a piece of substantive research work, a methodology of research asserts meta-principles: about the appropriate categories in which to organize knowledge, and about the value assumptions around which knowledge is created. A methodology defines how new knowledge may be gained, or be rejected as not having the status of knowledge. Methodologies clarify the principles for defining who and what is inside a field of study;

and who is outside that field. Wide acceptance of any one methodological position has a tendency to encourage only some styles of research, to legitimate only some forms of explanation and understanding, and to restrict the topics which can be investigated.[43]

Several textbooks of the 1960s initiated an English and American debate about the methodology of comparative education. Around the texts, commentaries emerged and were themselves published as books.[44] The texts asserted metaprinciples about the kinds of knowledge which should be sought, and defined the analytical categories through which the world should be construed comparatively. These debates, of course, were not merely an assertion of meta-principles; they were an assertion of meta-principles in a social world. They had much to do with clarifying why, given the internal sociology of the universities of the USA and Britain at that time, comparative education should be accepted as a university study as a science.[45] The debate, then, was probably necessary, became complicated, and has been rehearsed frequently enough in the literature. However, amid the intricacies of the debate within the Anglo-Saxon perspective,[46] the broader social contextualization of the debate and its ethnocentrisms can, but should not be, overlooked.

The meta-principles - categories of analysis, value assumptions, and what will be taken as knowledge - of comparative education in the socialist countries are sharply different. 'In our comparative studies of education, historical and dialectical materialism functions as a guideline, which provides a scientific methodological basis' is the Chinese version[47] of the general principle that in the German Democratic Republic 'our approach to problems of comparative education as a science is certainly different in some important ways from the various conceptions to be found among comparatists (sic) in capitalist countries... The differences between bourgeois and Marxist comparatists are still more marked in their views on the nature of human society, the driving force in its development and the general laws underlying it than in the field of methods of research and logic of science.'[48] A similar clarity of position has been identified within the USSR: 'pedagogical phenomena can be analyzed objectively only from the standpoint of Marxist-Leninist philosophy, which is the methodological basis of Marxist comparative pedagogy'.[49]

Not only are the meta-principles clear; they are also explicitly judged to be in conflict with the meta-principles of identified writers on comparative education from the United States, the Federal Republic of Germany, France and Great Britain, who are seen as having more commonalities than differences. Indeed, the conflict between the two sets of meta-principles is judged to demonstrate a law of development: 'the dialectical law of development through the struggle of opposites is most vividly manifested in the fierce struggle between socialist and bourgeois ideologies in comparative pedagogy in the modern world'.[50] However, whether a comparative education is being constructed in a socialist country or in a capitalist country is not the only important form of social contextualization.

There are also major socio-economic and historical forces which affect the creation of comparative educations. In particular, there are very specific spatial lines of attraction which, as a consequence of history and politics, affect the categories of attention, and thus the knowledge content, of a comparative education. Note the mutual fascination of the Federal Republic of Germany and the German Democratic Republic with each others' educational systems. Note the traditional concern of Japanese comparative education with questions of morality and the moral order, and more recently with the United States. Note also the balances of area studies in the United States and the United Kingdom: in the USA, the early post-war concern with the USSR; the continuing interest in Latin America and Africa; and now, China and Japan; in the United Kingdom, in addition to the countries of north-west Europe, interest in (English-speaking) Africa remained strong after 1945 and interest in the USSR was stimulated. Conversely, in the United Kingdom and in contrast with France, the comparative education community has been little interested in China, Francophone Africa south of the Sahara, Latin America, the Maghreb, or South East Asia.[59] In other words, much substantive research work carried out in comparative education is given its categories of attention, and even its categories of analysis, by social influences rather than by methodologies from within the field itself. What is studied is affected by politics, including international politics. What is usually studied is publicly visible problems of domestic educational policy.[52]

In the years after 1945, it was the new strategic problems of the world outside comparative education that defined its major continuities of concern, and academic content. Two main lines of analysis helped to hold the contents of the field together: reconstruction and reform on the one hand and development on the other.

Reconstruction and reform

One of the strategic problems of the post-war world was reconstruction, that is, reconstruction of the social fabric and education systems of several countries including, immediately after 1945, most of the European countries and countries such as China, Japan and Korea, which war and revolution had affected badly. This theme of reconstruction entered immediately into the academic contents of comparative education through the *Yearbook of education* of 1948,[53] 1949,[54] and 1952.[55]

Although the first post-war volumes of the *Yearbook* were concerned specifically with reconstruction, the *Yearbook* was also a considerable signal that the intent and content of post-war comparative education would be reformist. The problems of reconstruction and educational reform were to be the major replacement of the strategic concern for 'forces and factors', so important in the academic definitions of European comparative education emerging between the First and Second World Wars.[56]

The *Yearbook*'s steady concern was with the interaction of major worldwide changes (such as urbanism), which seemed to create the need for educational reform; or with world-wide questions about education, such as the relationship of church and state in education, or teacher training or universities, which were posing reform problems.[57] Thus the range of issues which took an annual treatment in the *Yearbook of education* (edited jointly from Teachers College, Columbia and the Institute of Education, London University) look, in their titles, discontinuous. They are united by the view that it was necessary to understand the world comparatively to act upon it.

It is this reformist view of comparative education - a milder version of the confidence in a positive science and the historical link between practical administration and comparative education - which has accounted for much of the regular recurrence in the specialist literature of certain themes, such as curriculum, teacher education, examinations, the relations between school and work, or the reform of universities.

As with the *Yearbooks*, the reformist view of comparative education gives us our occasionally jerky work agenda. As the world changes, so must the work agenda. The tradition is institutionalized in the Proceedings of Conferences[58] in textbooks[59] and in the contents of journals.[60] It is also part of the stated purposes of one of the journals of the field - *Comparative education*, which is concerned with 'significant trends', and 'analytically comparative aspects of the following themes: educational reform and problems of implementation; education and socio-economic or political development; relationships between education and a working life - or unemployment; post-compulsory and 'young adult education'; part-time, recurrent, or alternating education/training; [61] The list is notably in tune with contemporary changes and reform problems.

The reformist theme has also another significance. It was the insertion of this theme into the post-war debates among comparative educationists, many of whom were consultants to the newly established agencies, and all of whom had been affected by the war, which gives us the *leitmotif* of internationalism. The professional internationalism is itself a product of social context. It is this motif which is visible in the phrasings of the time and visible in the discussions about the creation of the professional societies. The feeling was perhaps assisted in its growth by the relatively small numbers of persons who were involved; they could the more easily feel part of an international professional community.

World War II, and the problems of post-war reconstruction, had made the interconnectedness of events very immediate and very personal. From it could come a set of beliefs about post-war beneficial intervention on the world, in which those doing (international) comparative education could participate. These values, formed out of the centrality of the European cultural experience of many of those then working in comparative education, became a professional commitment and a professional belief system, institutionalized in the stated aims of the new societies, the new journals, and the aims of those international agencies concerned with education.

Even when it was emerging, this professional belief system hid certain biases. There were, for example, spheres of influence in interventionist comparative education, for example, within Africa, within Asia and even within Europe; there was a domination of persons from the English-speaking world and north-west continental Europe among the academic networks; and the main client of comparative education at this time was governments. The gradual emergence of these contradictions, between professional ideology and practice, can be seen in the insertion and treatment of development within the comparativists' agendas.

Development

The problems of development, another major theme of post-1950 comparative education, initially confirmed the ethical, emotional and practical significance of international action and comparative education - which now ceased (in most institutionalizations) to be concerned with Europe, and European educational policy choices.

Although there were considerable differences in the terms in which the early workers viewed the world,[62] there was an increasingly strong shift towards economics and sociology, and a tendency to work within an emerging paradigm of modernization theory.[63] Of course the tendency to utilize the categories and concepts of other social sciences within comparative education, was not monolithic.[64] However, the common assumptions were that intervention and reformism were benign; and benign on an international scale. Thus the professional ideology of the field, including the assumptions of the international agencies, stressed unities of purpose and intent, and the power of planning and scientific approaches to create social improvement. Dissatisfaction with what are now interpreted as some of the structural functional assumptions within this earlier tradition of comparative work has led to a revitalization of American comparative education. The important English language textbooks of comparative education in the mid-1970s were Martin Carnoy's *Education as cultural imperialism*, and Altbach and Kelly's *Education and colonialism*.[65] Whilst dealing with issues of development, they structured their analyses within more radical assumptions than the earlier work on development done in the United States. Put too succinctly, the texts broke with modernization theory.[66]

This had had advantages. It has stimulated a very detailed debate in the literature which is re-examining fundamental assumptions about development and education and comparison.[67] The texts of the mid-1970s were important; they broke the professional consensus on internationalism - both as an ideology and as a set of assumptions about benignly working international agencies.

A different world-view is now being energetically explored in the literature.[68] This view stresses that comparative education, comparative educationists, and the infrastructures of comparative education participate in an exploitative and divisive world. The ethical problem and the professional problem of a major strand in the post-1970 comparative education is to understand the acceptable terms on which to act upon the world - and on whose behalf. This new focus to the question of how, finally, to act as a comparative educationist, breaks the old consensus. Reformist interventionism is less possible; partly because of suspicions that very little foreign interventionism is benign; and partly because of shifts in the balance of economic and political power among the nations of the world.

These new ethical and intellectual concerns have already had an impact on the infrastructure of comparative education. For example, the lines of analysis chosen for several of the national or language based Society meetings before the World Congress of Comparative Education Societies in 1984 in Paris, and for the World Congress itself were those of dependence and interdependence. However, the ideas are also likely to have a political impact on the infrastructures of comparative education, particularly the

World Council and the World Congress of Comparative Education Societies. The World Council and the World Congress are the most visible points where the national and international modalities of comparative education intersect. At this intersection there are some considerable tensions.

The World Council of Comparative Education Societies and its congress originally arose out of internationalist philosophical assumptions, and from some of the same networks which had been so influential in north America and western Europe in the 1950s and 1960s. Much of the original stimulus for the creation of the World Council of Comparative Education Societies in 1970 came from Joseph Katz of Canada. He and others, such as Leo Fernig, formerly of IBE, and Joseph Lauwerys (formerly Professor of Comparative Education at the University of London) later became consultants to the World Council whose Presidents have included Michel Debeauvais from France, Erwin Epstein from the United States, Professor Hiratsuka from Japan and Brian Holmes from England. The sequence of conferences has been: Toronto 1970; Geneva 1973; London 1977; Tokyo 1980 with a formal pre-conference meeting in Seoul; Paris in 1984; Rio de Janeiro, 1987.

The membership of the World Council is (representatives of) Societies of Comparative Education; other members may be added through co-option. During each World Congress there is a formal business meeting - a General Assembly - which elects the President, accepts (or otherwise) the nomination of a Secretary General, and decides on admission of new members to the Council. The technical status of the World Council is that of an International Society (in terms of Swiss law) and it is recognized by UNESCO as a Category C non-governmental organization. In fact, much of the support for the World Council originally came from the IBE in Geneva, with assistance from directors such as Leo Fernig, support for a Newsletter and translation help from Madame Anne Hamori, and an accumulation of experience in terms of organizing the World Congress. The World Council tries to carry out its aims - to encourage the development of comparative education on a world wide basis, to encourage research and to encourage scientific meetings - in the face of a number of problems and difficulties which are obscured by the preceding anodyne description.

There is, of course, great difficulty in financing the World Congresses. In the last decade, help from IBE has had to diminish, and the Bulletin/Newsletter was for a time at risk: the Francophone Association (AFEC) was able to help in this regard. Universities themselves help to some extent - by providing help with typing, mailing and photocopying, telephone and telex communication, and through the provision of lecture halls and seminar rooms - to disguise the real costs of a conference. Some form of government assistance is essential for running a World Congress of Comparative Education Societies and, in fact, the list of supporting institutions is normally quite long. For example, for the Paris Congress support was promised by the University of Paris VIII St Denis, Paris IX Dauphine, the French Ministry of National Education, the French Ministry of Foreign Affairs, the Institut National de Recherche Pédagogique; the International Institute for Educational Planning; and the International Bureau of Education.

Nevertheless it is doubtful if finance is the main concern of the World Council and its Presidents. Rather, it is the problems posed by the worldwide nature of the Congress and Council which is the greatest source of cohesion. The Congress and the Council are where domestic comparative educations and national assumptions meet international aims and aspirations. At this intersection of the national and international, actual and potential fissures become visible, and are, occasionally, widened.

One considerable source of difficulty and division is the location of the Congress. The locales of the Congress have reflected the economic and political realities of a divided world, and have contradicted hopes of holding meetings in what used to be called the Third World. Notably, efforts to place the Congress in Mexico in 1983 failed. Similarly, various discussions aimed at holding the Congress in other countries undergoing the strains of development - such as India - always ran into difficulties. Only with the Rio meeting in 1987 did the World Congress move to a city outside the northern hemisphere and to a country with difficult contemporary economic development problems.

The second centrifugal tension within the World Congress is that each Congress needs a theme to which everyone can contribute. Thus the themes of the congresses have to be broadly phrased and loosely interpreted. In the last decade for example, the themes have been: diversity and unity (Third Congress, London, 1977); education and national development (Fourth Congress, Tokyo, 1980); dependence and interdependence (Fifth Congress, Paris, 1984); and education, crisis and change (Sixth Congress, Rio, 1987). The difficulties of intellectual focus, range and balance are considerable and are well illustrated in a note in the *Bulletin* of the World Council before the Paris Congress: 'The central theme - *Dependence and interdependence* - may give rise to differing interpretations. This would be a handicap for defining a research topic or a topic for a seminar. For an international congress, however, it is desirable to allow a great variety of comparative education specialists to report on their respective research in relation to the theme of the Congress.' Thus the congresses, through a cumbersome planning structure and within the boundaries of trying to produce sub-sections (commissions) run by individuals of several nationalities, have also to be very sensitive to domestic comparative educations: there was an attempt to take into account as far as possible the different interests of members of comparative education societies through the medium of the Programme Committee in which comparative education societies are represented.

Something similar is of course a feature of most conference organization, but it is compounded within comparative education, in its international constituencies, by there being no common work agenda to lend coherence. There are - to borrow a phrase of Robert Nisbet - no 'unit ideas' in comparative education: ideas which are taken by workers in the field as defining a permanent intellectual content and shared analytic categories through which the ever-changing events of the world can be conceptualized, researched, and understood.

Thus each President of the World Congress faces an unenviable task: through an attenuated and occasionally opportunist planning structure, to provide a strategic intellectual agenda from the starting point of a topic chosen for its obvious world-wide relevance and contemporary impact. For that intellectual agenda there are unclear boundaries and varied definitions of what is comparative education and what is not. It says a great deal for the diplomatic skills, intellectual flexibility, commitment, and organization powers of successive Presidents that the congresses are held at all.

The third centrifugal tension in the World Council and World Congress is its patterns of representation. The Council is a collection of societies. Normally, the Chairman or President of the Comparative Societies of the world sit on the Council. Until recently, those societies have been language or nation specific. It is the intention of the World Council, as indicated by Erwin Epstein's message in the Bulletin after the Japan Conference, to broaden that membership: the Council's major thrust for the next three years will be extension of our field by means of the professional organization of comparative educators in nations not yet represented in the Council. The prospect for success is excellent. Indeed, since Epstein's message, the number of formally constituted professional comparative education societies has increased. As a consequence, the World Council contains embryonically most of the problems of representation experienced in more famous international organizations where governments are the units of representation, and it is likely that the politics and educational politics of the World Council will become more visible.

In particular, it is likely that the relative hegemony of the northern hemisphere countries in the Council debates, the commissions at the congress, and definitions of the Conference topic will be disturbed. This will happen to the extent that new members of the Council feel that the activities of the World Council represent special interests. Clearly the idea that the World Council might represent special interests was and is antithetical to the intent and internationalism of such distinguished comparative educationists as Professor Hiratsuka or Professor Debeauvais, or to Consultants such as Leo Fernig. But divisions have occurred in the Council before, notably over membership problems; they are likely to occur again, with an increased probability that formal voting will be used to resolve issues.

In other words, the World Congress itself has mirrored in microcosm some of the economic power, and networks of political influence of the world outside of comparative education. Some of the strains of that external divided world are likely to become more visible in the politics of the Council. Much of this debate will be filtered through questions of locale and the intellectual structure of the Congress, as the normal but considerable problems of finance and organization are compounded by tension between the domestic, national agendas of a variety of comparative educations and internationalist assumptions of the Council's traditions. And this is understandable: the World Council and the World Congress of Comparative Education Societies is that part of our professional infrastructure where the national and the international elements in our professional identity meet most visibly.

Conclusion

These pressures and tensions within comparative education have advantages. They raise crisply what the role of the formal international institutions (e.g. the World Bank, IBE itself) is, and of what now does unite a scattered community of persons interested in understanding education in other countries - the wish to act perhaps, to improve and to reform, but on what terms and through what forms of understanding.

In particular if we are agreed on the need to diffuse and institutionalize comparative education more widely - to 'internationalize' comparative education - there are important gaps in our knowledge.

1. We need to know more about centres of study in 'the peripheries' and how to encourage them, if we are to understand how comparative education is likely to grow and change. We need to know at what point

do countries (including 'developing' countries) develop their 'own' comparative education. In itself the creation of a specialist professional society does not solve the problem, though it may be a useful step. Thus the creation of the Comparative Education Society of India in 1979, of the Nigerian Association of Comparative Education in 1984, or the Brazilian Society, is an important set of events. But do we know what is the critical mass of interested persons; are they nowadays specialists in comparative education, or do they normally share only the experience of having studied education overseas? Are they copying foreign models of professional societies, or has their experience made them alert to the need to resist, or at least understand very thoroughly the nature of foreign educational influence? Clearly, this issue - resistance to excessive external influence - was part of the intention in founding the Canadian comparative education journal and it is a theme in Australian and New Zealand comparative education. More subtly, one aspect of the problem is excellently expressed by calling one of the units of the University of Lagos: the 'Comparative Education Study and Adaptation Centre'. In other words, we may hope that comparative education will institutionalize itself world-wide but we are not too clear about either the practicalities or the purposes which are the most efficient in achieving that goal. Nor are we very clear about the political and epistemological price tags which may come with that diffusion.

2. We need to know more of the precise effects of our metropolitan institutions. We all know of persons who have trained in such centres who are working elsewhere; but our knowledge is not systematic. For example, are several of the strengths of French comparative education and its remarkable linkages overseas due not only to French universities as such, but to the role of the International Centre for Pedagogical Studies at Sèvres[69] and the support of the French government itself to French cultural presence overseas? Were there metropolitan influences and assistance within the socialist world in the creation of comparative education in Vietnam and its strengthening in Cuba? How far have common work agendas been established in comparative education among the socialist countries of Eastern Europe, and the USSR?

3. We need to know something of the mechanisms of insulation which prevent us importing other peoples' comparative educations; thereby confusing an intended solution with a worsening of a problem. Comparative education is itself part of some of the international stratifica-

tions which exist in the creation, and distribution of knowledge, and our relative lack of knowledge of the mechanisms of our international interactions compound the processes. What would permit us to receive international influences on acceptable terms?

4. In these processes, we need to know more about the penetration of our journals and their networks. Who actually reads some of the excellent articles in *Prospects*? In other words, it is one thing to compile a list of specialist journals in comparative education, or a list of journals which publish comparative articles; and another to understand their sources of support, and the extent of their international penetration, and their influence. What knowledge do we have to offer to assist the survival of the *Nigerian journal of comparative education*, announced in January 1986, as the intended journal of the Nigerian Association of Comparative Education? What insulation mechanisms, of political prejudice and language, limits the impact of journals such as *Vergleichende pädagogik*? What audiences within comparative education are served by the (relatively new) *International journal of educational development*, and what networks does the remarkable list of executive editors, editorial board corresponding editors, and editorial consultants signal? What audiences are reached by journals apparently targeted on area specialists, such as *Soviet education*, *Chinese education*, and the *European journal of education*? How far are they read by both comparative educationists and policy makers?

5. Obviously we need far more knowledge than is in print at the moment not only on the international interrelations between the infrastructures of comparative education and the OECD, the OAS, the World Bank, IIEP, and IBE, and UNESCO itself, but further knowledge of the regional interrelationships between these institutions and, in Europe, say, the European Institute of Education and Social Policy; and in Latin America, between the OAS, and the Ministry-level funding and research agencies, and those universities with a comparative presence such as San Luis in Argentina, or the Autonomous University in Mexico, or the Federal University in Rio. Some of these kinds of international, regional and national links which were important in the construction of the IEA project are known, but this general set of questions is only just coming into the literature.[70]

This is a difficult moment for comparative educationists. The recent conventional academic definition of comparative education, as a policy oriented, government-assisting, extension of administrative science, is under attack from within comparative education. Other scholars from other disciplines are writing with skill and judgment and different forms of understanding - the price of entry to the journals is merely the cultural capital to analyze education in other countries. Interventionist comparative action - by agencies, governments, consultants - meanwhile continues. But some of the old confidence has been lost. We have become more nervous interveners, and suspicious domesticators of the foreign - including the foreigner's comparative education.

One way to diminish this suspicion is to continue to try to understand the interrelationships of our domestic and international professional structures. These structures have helped construct our peculiarly relativistic and ambivalent identities as persons who are simultaneously professional foreigners and professional friends. These structures help to explain how we work and who we are.

Notes

I am grateful to Kazim Bacchus, Edward Berman, and Ronald Goodenow for critical comments on an earlier draft of this article.

1. Only a few sketches have been done of the networks of scholars, institutions and publications which make up 'comparative education'. Until the appearance of the present book, the best sustained treatment was: Bereday, G. Z. F., (1964), *Comparative method in education*. New York, Holt, Rinehart and Winston, 171-266.
2. The answers to these questions can at this stage be only illustrative. The cliché about further research being needed is always inelegant and unsatisfying; which does not prevent it being true, sometimes. Ideally this topic will now be explored systematically over a time span of several years. The topic is, after all, our professional selves.
3. Bereday, G. Z. F. *op.cit.*, 4-7.
4. The early history of the (American) Comparative and International Education Society is an example of these principles. See especially Brickman, W. W. Ten years of the Comparative Education Society. *Comparative education review* (Kent, OH), vol. 10, no. 1, 1966, 4-15.
5. It is a normal practice of this journal to seek foreign guest editors, who in conjunction with the very professional in-house editing provided from Hamburg, produce the journal on an internationally mobile basis.
6. See, for example, such texts as Archer, M. S. (1979), *Social origins of educational systems*, London, Sage; and the work of comparative historians such as Ringer, F. F. K., (1979), *Education and society in modern Europe*. Bloomington, IN, Indiana University Press,

and Wilkinson, R., (1964), *The prefects: British leadership and the public school tradition*. London, Oxford University Press.
7. For example, much of the writing of C. A. Anderson and Philip Coombs.
8. For example, the range of work of C. A. Anderson in the Chicago Comparative Education Centre can be compared with the institutional distinction between the Chair of Comparative Education, and the Chair of Education in Developing Countries, in the University of London, where it was not until November 1985 that a unified Department of International and Comparative Education was created.
9. Jing, Shi-Bo; Zhou, Nan-Zhao, (1985), 'Comparative education in China'. *Comparative education review* (Chicago, IL), vol. 29, no. 2, May, 241.
10. *op.cit.*, 242. The author (of this chapter) visited a small specialist institute of comparative education which had a remarkable range of professional journals in Shanghai in 1975, so the ban was not total.
11. *op.cit.*, 244-245.
12. *op.cit.*, 248.
13. *op.cit.*, 247.
14. The German Democratic Republic and the USSR are discussed later in this chapter, but Poland is not. On Polish comparative education, see Zelazkiewicz, M. 'Sociology of education, comparative education and social problems: a Polish comment', (1981), *International review of education* (The Hague), vol. 27, no. 4. Cf. also chapter III of the present book.
15. Source: Professor H.-G. Hoffman, 'Research work and organizations of comparative education of the socialist countries', manuscript submitted to the IBE, 1986. The point about the importance of the research institute should not, of course, be permitted to obscure the fact that comparative education is also taught in some of the major Pedagogical Institutes in the USSR. A similar pattern has been created in Czechoslovakia, Hungary and Romania, and seems to be emerging in Cuba and the Democratic Republic of Vietnam.
16. Kienitz, W. 'On the Marxist approach to comparative education in the German Democratic Republic', (1971), *Comparative education* (Oxford, UK), vol. 7, no. 1, August, 21-31.
17. *op.cit.*, 29.
18. *op.cit.*, 29.
19. For an analysis of the Comparative Education Society in Europe and a brief commentary on the other comparative societies within Europe, see Cowen, R. Comparative education in Europe: a note, (1980), *Comparative education review* (Chicago, IL), vol. 24, no. 1, February, 98-108.
20. Ministers or Secretaries of Education have, however, been known to be impressed by figures (e.g. on the flow of engineering graduates) or to use examples of overseas practice to argue a case, e.g. for centralization of curriculum, or for changes in

vocational training. Where alertness to comparative example has been strong, e.g. in Scandinavia, it has tended to be within a regional, Scandinavian, frame. It will be interesting to see whether other sub-regions within the EEC develop a similar sensitivity.

21. See, for example, Lourenço Filho, M. B., (1961), *Educaçao comparada*, Sao Paulo, Melhoramentos. Foreign texts were also translated and used in teaching, including Nicholas Hans and (as in China) Isaac Kandel.
22. See Senta, T. G. della, (1987), The structuring of educational knowledge in Brazil. In: *Seminar on perspectives on Brazilian education*, First Anglo-Brazilian Conference, London, Institute of Education, London University.
23. The writer of this chapter was present at the meetings which are mentioned in the text.
24. It should also be noted that the research institute tradition in Brazil is strong, and that several research institutes have an interest in comparative study. Cf chapter V of the present book.
25. Given the number of comparative journals, world-wide, the publishing of comparative material in non-specialist journals is the norm; and it is always of importance to identify journals which are sympathetic to comparative material, such as *Perspectivas pedagógicas* in Spain. The (American) Comparative and International Education Society reports, in a Note to IBE, that it has identified '... 125 journals that accept manuscripts treating comparative and international education.'
26. The Society changed its name in 1979; before then it used to be known as the Comparative Education Society of Europe (British Section).
27. The teachers, institutions and courses included N. Hans, J. A. Lauwerys, B. Holmes and E. J. King, based in London, and V. Mallinson at the University of Reading, most of whom published textbooks on comparative education. Other scholars of national reputation such as W. D. Halls, at Oxford, or Nigel Grant, then at Edinburgh, were at that time (and within comparative education) better known for their area texts, on France and the USSR respectively.
28. See Peter Raggatt's very interesting analysis, Scholarship, learned societies and international academic journals: some observations and a case study. *In*: Smawfield, D., ed., (1985), *International academic interchange and co-operation in higher education: proceedings of the 20th Annual Conference of the British Comparative and International Education Society*. Hull, UK, British Comparative and International Education Society, 1985.
29. cf. Raggatt, P. *op.cit.*
30. See, for further details, Cowen, R. Comparative education in Europe: a note. *op.cit.*, 98-99.
31. Raggatt, P. *op.cit.*

32. For example, the major centre for the study of comparative education in Scotland was the University of Edinburgh, until Nigel Grant moved to the University of Glasgow.
33. For comment on journals as avenues of communication see, Sutherland, M.B. Communication and comparative education: the use of international journals,.in: Smawfield, D., ed. *op.cit.*
34. cf. Ray, D. Comparative and international education in Canada 1973, (1974), *Canadian and international education* (Toronto, Ont.), vol. 3, no. 1, June, 1-3.
35. Source: Notes provided for IBE by Robin Burns, President, ANZCIES and the personal experience of the author who worked in the La Trobe Centre 1974-1975.
36. See for example the brief note by Johnson, W. H. E. 'The Comparative Education Society', (1957), *Comparative education review* (Kent, OH), vol. 1, no. 1, June; Brickman, W. W. Ten years of the Comparative Education Society, (1966), *Comparative education review* (Kent, OH), vol. 10, no. 1, February, 4-15; Brickman, W. W. 'CIES: an historical analysis', (1977), *Comparative education review* (Chicago, IL), vol. 21, nos. 2-3, June-October, 396-404.
37. 'Under the guidance of Professor George Z. F. Bereday of Teachers College, Columbia University, who is probably the only full-time professor of comparative education in this country, the *Comparative education review* will...' Brickman, W. W. 'A new journal of comparative education', (1957), *Comparative education review* (Kent, OH), vol. 1, no. 1, June, 1. It is also relevant that the first issue of the new journal contained 'A note on textbooks in comparative education'. *op.cit.*, 3-4.
38. Johnson, W. H. E. *op.cit.*, 16.
39. See Editorial, (1957), *Comparative education review* (Kent, OH), vol. 1, no. 2, October, 7.
40. For example, while the Executive Committee of the Society and the Board of Directors of the Society were mainly Americans, the Editorial Board of the Comparative Education Review after its first couple of years of publication included not only James Bryant Conant, Isaac Kandel and Robert Ulich, but also Nicholas Hans and Joseph A. Lauwerys. See *Comparative education review* (Kent, OH), vol. 3, no. 1, June 1959. For a fuller treatment of the deliberate international stance of the Comparative Education Society and why the term American Comparative Education Society was avoided see, Brickman, W.W. Ten years of the Comparative Education Society. *op.cit.*
41. The Board of Directors of the Society included an official from the US Office of Education (which continued a long tradition of mutual interest). Similarly, the Ford Foundation gave 350,000 dollars in 1957 to create the University of Chicago Comparative Centre. See Editorial, (1957), *Comparative education review* (Kent, OH), vol. 1, no. 2, October, 1.
42. 'perhaps', because the detailed historical account has not yet been constructed.

43. These potential pathologies were, fortunately, avoided because no single methodology was institutionalised in more than one or two centres.
44. For example, Jones, P. E., (1971), *Comparative education: purpose and method*. St. Lucia, Qld, University of Queensland Press; Trethewey, A. R., (1976), *Introducing comparative education*. Rushcutters Bay, NSW, Pergamon Press.
45. Sometimes it seemed that a science of the comparative education would best be created if new scholars were to follow the pattern of life experience or formal academic training of the author(s) in question. On the interrelationship of biography, the internal sociology of universities, and the institutionalisation of comparative education, see Cowen, R. The place of comparative education in the educational sciences. In: Cavicchi-Broquet, I.; Furter, P. eds., (1982), *Les sciences de l'éducation: perspectives et bilans européens*. Actes de la Xe Conférence de l'Association d'éducation comparée pour l'Europe. Genève, Section des Sciences de l'éducation, Faculté de psychologie et des sciences de l'éducation, Université de Genève, 107-126.
46. The phrase, which is a good one, is borrowed from Brian Holmes' The positivist debate in comparative education - an Anglo-Saxon perspective, *Comparative education*, vol. 13, no. 2, 1977.
47. Jing, Shi-Bo; Zhou, Nan-Zhao. *op.cit.*, 247.
48. Kienitz, W. *op.cit.*, 27.
49. Sokolova, M. A.; Kuz'mina, E. N.; Rodionov, M. L., (1978), *Sravnitel'naja pedagogika* Moskva, Prosvescenie, translated in *Soviet education* (White Plains, NY), vol. XXI, nos. 7-8, May-June 1979, 30.
50. *op.cit.*, 31.
51. Accidents of travel, and professional biography produce individual exceptions to the generalization. Published comparative education work can be found by British scholars on south east Asia, China, and Latin America. Nevertheless, the main weight of British publication is on Europe, including the USSR, the United States in which problems similar to those of Britain are identified - while for Africa problems to which Britain made a contribution are analysed.
52. This is not to suggest that methodologies are unimportant. An introduction to methodological scholasticism is part of the professional socialization of most PhD students, and the choice of categories of analysis for substantive research is very important (cf. Marxism and structural functionalism). However, it is to suggest that proposals by specialist academics, about what should be studied and how it should be studied if it is to be comparative education, are likely to be ignored outside of the university if the proposals distract from socially dominant categories of attention.
53. *The yearbook of education, 1948* London, Evans, 1948.
54. *The yearbook of education, 1949* London, Evans, 1949.

55. *The yearbook of education, 1952* London, Evans, 1952.
56. The major historical forces which affected that emerging definition of comparative education (especially in the work of Hans) are familiar, but rarely invoked to explain it. It is of course true in the currently fashionable complaint, that the nation state was taken implicitly as the main unit of analysis in inter-war comparative education. But it should also be stressed that a concern over nationalism, including its pathological fascist forms, and a concern over supra-national belief systems such as socialism, can be understood within the *Zeitgeist* which had followed from the stress on the nation, the principles of self-determination, and nationalism which were embedded within the Versailles treaty and the historical reactions to it. A historically urgent question became explaining the relation of education to the coherence of nations, assessing the significance of tradition, and understanding the power of the State - and these questions of the epoch, which affected other social sciences too, are well reflected in the work of Hans, Schneider and Kandel.

    Their share in the tradition of comparative education has never been sharply and explicitly dismissed i.e. as a consequence of a major professional debate within the literature. Rather, their work, with some commentaries, has merged into our collective professional history; it has been sub-merged as tradition. This gentle discontinuity may perhaps be understood by the fact that the problems in the post-war world, in the world outside comparative education, were changing rapidly. This affected the assumptions about what comparative education was for and the strategic problems it should address.
57. See Cowen, R. The yearbooks of education,. in: McLean, M., ed., (1981), *Joseph A. Lauwerys: a festschrift*. London, University of London Institute of Education Library. (Education Libraries bulletin, supplement 22)
58. For example, the CESE conference themes since the mid-1960s.
59. For a recent textbook, see Nicholas, E. J., (1983), *Issues in education: a comparative analysis*. London, Harper and Row. Among the issues which Nicholas identifies are schools and classrooms, curriculum, administration of education, and equality and education.
60. For analyses of journal content, see *Comparative education review* (Chicago, IL), vol. 21, nos. 2-3, June/October 1977 (The State of the Art).
61. The list is quoted from the standard cover notes printed in each copy of the journal (1985).
62. For example the Department of Tropical Areas in the Institute of Education, London, with Margaret Read, played an important role in emphasizing, through the perspective of anthropology, the importance of traditional modes of education and early child rearing practices. In contrast, the Chicago Centre of Comparative Education used concepts and categories from sociology and economics.
63. Anderson himself has argued that borrowing from academic neighbours accelerated with the result that over the relevant period of time '...the greatest

contribution to comparative education has come from economics. A large proportion of comparativists have always found their most useful models in sociology, while others have made principal use of political science.' Anderson, C.A. Comparative education over a quarter century: maturity and challenges. *Comparative education review* (Chicago, IL), vol. 21, nos. 2-3, June/October 1977, 411.

64. See for example Noah, H. J.; Eckstein, M. A., (1969), *Toward a science of comparative education*. London, Macmillan. For a combination of questions about development with answers in statistical form, see Eckstein, M. A.; Noah, H. J., eds., (1969), *Scientific investigations in comparative education*, London, Macmillan. Compare Halsey, A. H.; Fould, J.; Anderson, C. A., eds., (1965), *Education, economy and society: a reader in the sociology of education*, London, Macmillan. For an interesting assessment of the period, see Kazamias, A. M.; Schwartz, K., (1977), Intellectual and ideological perspectives in comparative education: an interpretation. *Comparative education review* (Chicago, IL), vol. 21, nos 2-3, June/October, 153-176.

65. Carnoy, M. *Education as cultural imperialism*. New York, McKay, 1974; Altbach, P. G.; Kelly, G. P., (1978), *Education and colonialism*, New York, Longman.

66. For an excellent analysis which includes the American literature but goes beyond it, see Simkin, K., (1981), Comparative and sociological perspectives on Third World development and education. *International review of education* (The Hague), vol. 27, no. 4, 427-447.

67. See, for example, Arnove, R. F. Comparative education and world-systems analysis, (1980), *Comparative education review* (Chicago, IL), vol. 24, no. 1, February, 48-62; Epstein, E. H., (1983), Currents left and right: ideology in comparative education. *Comparative education review* (Chicago, IL), vol. 27, no. 1, February, 3-29; and Zachariah, M., (1985), Lumps of clay and growing plants: dominant metaphors of the role of education in the Third World, 1950-1980. *Comparative education review* (Chicago, IL), vol. 29, no. 1, February, 1-21.

68. Probably the 1982 textbook *Comparative education* represents a transitional balancing of traditional and more contemporary concerns. See Altbach, P. G.; Arnove, R. F.; Kelly, P. G., eds., (1982), *Comparative education*. New York, Macmillan. The text combines and balances issues of educational policy, assessments of status and achievement outcomes of schooling, analyses of socialist and nonsocialist educational reforms, with questions of education and development

69. See Auba, J., The International Centre for Pedagogical Studies at Sèvres, and education in the world, (1981), *Compare* (Abingdon, UK), vol. 11, no. 2, 129-133.

70. Apart from the increasing number of American studies, there is for example, the interesting theory of Michel Debeauvais, The role of international organisations in the evolution of applied comparative education, in: Holmes, B., ed., (1980), *Diversity and unity in education: a comparative analysis*. London, George Allen and Unwin, 18-30. See also Carnoy, M. International institutions and educational policy,. in: Comparative Education Society in Europe, 9th General Meeting,

Valencia, Spain, 1979, *Influencias de la investigación educativa internacional en las políticas nacionales de educación*, Valencia, Spain, Instituto de Ciencias de la Educación, Universidad Politécnica,; and Spaulding, S., (1981), The impact of international assistance organizations on the development of education. *Prospects* (Paris, UNESCO), vol. XI, no. 4, 421-433.